WEBSTER'S DICTIONARY

For home, school and office

New computer terms & meanings

Authoritative up-to-date definitions

Easy-to-read format

Syllabled pronunciations

New, Revised & Expanded Edition

Contains valuable tables and guides.

◢⦚⦚Kappa Books, Inc.
Ambler, Pennsylvania 19002

Guide to Dictionary Abbreviations

a.	adjective
abbr.	abbreviation
adv.	adverb
Amer.	American
Anat.	Anatomy
Astron.	Astronomy
Biol.	Biology
Bot.	Botany
cap.	capitalized word
Chem.	Chemistry
Conj.	Conjunction
Eng.	English
Engin.	Engineering
esp.	especially
Geog.	Geography
Geol.	Geology
Gram.	Grammer
Inf.	Infinitive
interj.	interjection
Math.	Mathematics
Med.	Medical
n.	noun
Obs.	Obsolete
Phys.	Physical
pl.	plural
possess.	possessive
p.p.	past participle
prep.	preposition
pron.	pronoun
v.	verb

Measures and Weights

Metric Equivalents of Common U.S. Units

This measurement equals...	this metric measurement.
inch	2.54 centimeters
foot	0.3048 meters
yard	0.9144 meters
mile	1.6093 kilometers
acre	0.4046 hectares
square mile	2.5899 square kilometers
cubic inch	16.39 cubic centimeters
cubic yard	0.7645 cubic meters
quart (dry)	1.101 liters
quart (liquid)	0.9464 liters
gallon (liquid)	3.785 liters
ton	1.0161 metric tons

Metric Measures of Weights

This weight equals...	this weight...	and this weight.
10 milligrams	1 centigram	0.1543 grams
10 centigrams	1 decigram	1.5432 grams
10 decigrams	1 gram	15.432 grams
10 grams	1 decagram	0.3527 ounces
10 decagrams	1 hectogram	3.5274 ounces
10 hectograms	1 kilogram	2.2046 pounds
10 kilograms	1 myriagram	22.046 pounds
100 kilograms	1 quintal	220.46 pounds
1000 kilograms	1 metric ton	2,204.6 pounds

Metric Measures of Length

This length equals...	this length...	and this length.
10 millimeters	1 centimeter	0.3937 inches
10 centimeters	1 decimeter	3.937 inches
10 decimeters	1 meter	39.37 inches
10 meters	1 decameter	393.7 inches
10 decameters	1 hectometer	328.0 feet, 1 inch
10 hectometers	1 kilometer	0.62137 miles
10 kilometers	1 myriameter	6.2137 miles

A

a-ban'don (a-ban'dun) 1. To give up wholly; forsake or renounce utterly. 2. To yield (one's self) unrestrainedly; as, to **abandon** one's self to vice.

a-ban'doned (dund) 1. Forsaken; deserted.

a-bate' (a-bat'), v.t. To reduce in amount, number, degree, intensity, etc.; lessen; moderate. — v.i. To be abated; grow less; decrease.

ab'bey (-i), n.; pl. -BEYS (-iz). 2. The church of a monastery.

ab'di-cate (ab'di-kat), v.t. To give up or relinquish power.

ab-duct (ab-dukt') 1. To take away surreptitiously by force.

ab'hor (ab-hor') v.t. Detest.

a-bide' (a-bid'). v.i. 1. To continue in a place; dwell. 2. To remain stable or fixed in some state; continue.

a-bil'i-ty (a-bil'i-ti) Quality or state of being able; power to perform; capacity; skill; in pl., faculty, talent.

a'ble (a'b'l) 1. Having sufficient power, force, skill, etc.; competent; as, an able workman. 2. Having strong mental powers; talented; clever.

ab-nor'mal (ab-nor-mal) Not according to rule; unnatural; irregular.

a-board' (a-bord') On board.

a-bol'ish (a-bol'ish) To do away with wholly.

a-bor'tion (a-bor'shun) n. A premature birth; miscarriage.

ab-ra'sion (ab-ra'zhun) Act of abrading; also, an abraded place.

a-broad' (a-brod') 1. At large; widely; broadly; as, "the fox foams far abroad." 2. Outdoors; outside a country; in foreign countries.

ab-rupt' (ab-rupt') 1. Sudden; hasty. 2. Having sudden transitions; unconnected; broken.

ab-sent (sent) 1. Being away; not present; lacking. 2. Inattentive; absent-minded.

ab'so-lute (so-lut) 1. Perfect; complete; as, absolute purity. 2. Free from limit, restriction, or qualification.

ab'so-lu'tion (ab'so-lu'shun) Act of absolving.

ab-solve' (ab-solv') To set free, or release, as from obligation or the consequences of guilt. 2. To free from a penalty; pardon.

ab-sorb' (ab-sorb') To swallow up; engulf; suck up; drink or take in; engross; occupy fully.

ab-sorb'ent (sor'bent) Absorbing; as, absorbent earth. — Anything that absorbs.

ab-stain' (stan) To do without or give up voluntarily; refrain; —with from. — -er, n.

ab'sti-nence (ab'sti-nens) Act or practice of abstaining, esp. from indulgence of appetite.

ab'stract (ab'strakt) 1. Considered apart from any object; as, abstract numbers. Hence: Abstruse; difficult; as, an abstract subject. 2. Expressing a quality apart from any particular subject.

ab-surd' (ab-surd) Contrary to reason or propriety; obviously and flatly opposed to truth; nonsensical; ridiculous.

a-bun'dance (a-bun'dans) An overflowing fullness; great plenty; profusion.

a-bun'dant (dant) Overflowing; more than sufficient; plentiful; ample.

ac-cel'er-ate (ak-sel'er-at) 1. To move faster; quicken; — opposed to retard. 2. To quicken the natural progression or process of. 3. To hasten, as the occurrence of an event.

ac-ces'so-ry (-ses'o-ri), n. 1. Something additional and subordinate; adjunct. 2. Law. One who, not being present, contributes to the commission of an offense, or one who aids or shelters the offender to defeat justice.

accident (dent), n. 1. An unforeseen or unexpected event, usually unfortunate; chance; mishap. 2. A nonessential.

ac-claim (a-klam'), v.t. To applaud.

ac-com'mo-da'tion (-da'shun), 1. Lodgings and food.

ac-com'plish (-plish), v.t. 1. To bring to a successful issue; effect; fulfill. 2. Formerly, to equip thoroughly; hence, to render accomplished.

ac-cord'ing-ly, adv. 1. Agreeably; suitably; conformably.

ac-count'a-ble (-koun'ta-b'l), a. 1. Liable to be called to account; answerable. 2. Capable of being accounted for; explicable — - **ness**, n.

ac-crue' (-kroo'), v.i. 1. To increase. 2. To come or be added as increase, esp. as the produce of money lent.

ac-cu'mu-late (-ku'mu-lat), v.t. To heap up; pile up; amass; collect; aggregate. — v.i. To increase; collect.

ac'cu-sa'tion (ak'u-za'shun), n. 1. Act or fact of being accused. 2. That of which one is accused.

a-chieve' (a-chev'), v.t. 1. To carry on to a final close; accomplish; perform. 2. To get by effort; win; attain. — v.i. To effect something; attain a desired end.

ac'id (as'id), a. 1. Sour, sharp, or biting to the taste; tart, also, sour-tempered. 2. Of, pertaining to, or of the nature of, an acid. — n. A sour substance.

ac-knowl'edge (ak-nol'ej), v.t. 1. To own or admit the knowledge of; declare one's belief in; admit as true; confess; as, "I acknowledge my transgressions" (Ps. li.3). 2. To admit the claims or authority of; recognize; as, "In all thy ways acknowledge him" (Prov. iii.6).

ac-quaint' ('a-kwant'), v.t. 1. To furnish or give knowledge (of) by trial or experience; — followed by with. 2. To notify; inform.

ac-quire' (a-kwir'), v.t. To gain, usually by one's own exertion; get as one's own.

ac'tion (ak'shun), n. 1. State of motion; activity.

ac'tive (-tiv), a. 1. Quick in physical movement; agile; nimble.

ac'tor (ak'ter), n. 1. One who acts; a doer. 2. A theatrical performer; a player.

ac'tu-al (-tu-al), a. 1. Existing in act, reality, or fact; real. 2. In action at the time being; now existing; present.

ad-he'sive (-siv), a. 1. Sticky; tenacious; of the nature of adhesion. 2. Apt or tending to adhere; clinging.

ad-ja'cent (-sent), a. Lying near; close, contiguous; neighboring.

ad-journ' (-jurn'), v.t. To put off or defer to another day, or indefinitely; to close or suspend for the day, as a legislative meeting. — v.i. To suspend business for a time, esp. public business, as of legislatures, courts, etc.

ad-just' (-just'), v.t. 1. To settle or arrange; free from differences or discrepancies. 2. To make exact; fit; make correspondent or conformable. 3. To put in order; regulate.

ad-min'is-ter (ad-min'is-ter), v.t. 1. To manage or conduct, as public affairs; direct the execution, application, or conduct of. 2. To dispense; serve out; supply.

ad'o-les'cent (-ent), a. Growing to maturity; in a state of adolescence. — n. A youth.

a-dopt' (a-dopt'), v.t. 1. To take by choice into a relationship, esp. that of a child or an heir. 2. To take or receive as one's own (what is not so naturally).

a-dult' (aa-dult'), a. Having attained full size and strength; matured. — n. An adult person, animal, or plant.

a-dul'ter-y (-i), n. Unfaithfulness of a married person to the marriage bed.

ad-vance' (ad-vans'), v.t. 1. To move forward. 2. To raise to a higher rank; elevate; promote; as, he was advanced to captain.

ad-ven'ture (ad-ven'tur), n. 1. Chance of danger or loss. 2. The encountering of risks; a bold undertaking.

ad-vice' (ad-vis'), n. 1. An opinion recommended or offered to be followed; counsel.

ad'vo-cate (-kat), n. One who pleads the cause of another, as a lawyer or counselor in court; pleader; intercessor. — (-kat), v.t. To plead in favor of; support publicly.

af-fair' (a-far'), n. 1. That which is, or is being, or is to be, done; concern; business. 2. A material object (vaguely designated).

af-fect' (a-fekt'), v.t. 1. To fancy; be fond of. 2. To make a display of liking; adopting, or following after.

af'fi-da'vit (af'i-da'vit), n. A sworn statement in writing, esp. one made before an authorized officer.

af-firm' (-furm'), v.t. & i. 1. To conform, or ratify. 2. To assert positively;

aver.

af-flict' (a-flikt'), v.t. To inflict some great injury or hurt on, causing continued pain or distress.

af-ford' (a-ford'), v.t. 1. To give forth; yield, furnish, or the like, as the natural result, fruit, or issue. 2. To incur, stand, or bear, or manage without serious detriment (as to financial condition, health, reputation, etc.)

a-fraid' (a-frad'), p.a. Impressed with fear or apprehension; in fear; apprehensive.

aft'er (af'ter), adv. & conj. Subsequently in time or place; behind; later than. — prep. 1. Behind in place.

aft'er-noon (-noon), n. the part of the day between noon and evening.

aft'er-thought (-thot/), n. Reflection after an act.

a-gain' (a-gen'), adv. 1. In return; back. 2. Another time; anew. 3. Once repeated; as, as large again.

a-gainst' (a-genst'), prep. 1. From an opposite direction and so as to strike or touch; in contact with. 2. In opposition to; counter to; adverse to.

a-gape' (a-gap'; -gap'), adv. & a. Gaping, as with wonder, expectation, or eager attention.

a'gen-cy (a'jen-si), n. 1. Faculty or state of acting; action; instrumentality. 2. Office or business of an agent.

a'gent (a'jent), a. 1. One that exerts power, or has power to act; one that acts; as, the bee is an agent of fertilization. 2. One who acts for, or in the place of, another by authority from him; deputy.

ag'gran-dize (ag'ran-diz), v.t. To make great or greater; to exalt.

ag'gra-vate (ag'ra-vat), v.t. 1. To make worse, or more severe; intensify. 2. To exasperate; provoke; irritate. Colloq.

a-ghast' (a-gast'), a. & p.p. Terrified.

ag'ile (aj'il), a. Apt or ready to move; lively.

ag'i-tate (aj'i-tat), v.t. 1. To move with a violent, irregular action. 2. To stir up; disturb; perturb.

a-glow (a-glo), adv. & a. Glowing.

ag-nos'ti-cism (-ti-siz'm), n. 1. The doctrine that neither the nature nor the existence of God can be known. 2. Any doctrine which affirms that all knowledge is relative and uncertain.

a-go' (a-go'), a. & adv. Past; gone by.

ag'o-nize (ag'o-niz), v.t. To cause to suffer agony; torture. —v.i. 1. To suffer anguish. 2. To struggle or strive desperately.

ag'o-ny (ag'o-ni), n. 1. Extreme pain of mind or body; anguish. 2. Death struggle.

a-gree' (-gre'), v.i.; A-GREED' (a-gred'); A-GREE'ING. 1. To yield assent or favor; consent; accede. 2. to be in unison, concord, or harmony; concur.

a-gree'a-ble (-a-b'l), a. 1. Pleasing, either to the mind or senses; pleasant; grateful. 2. Willing; ready to agree or consent.

a-gree'ment (-ment), n. State or act of agreeing.

a-ha (a-ha'), interj. An exclamation expressing triumph mixed with derision, or simple surprise.

aid (ad), v.t. To help. — n. 1. Help. 2. One that helps; assistant; a military or naval officer acting as confidential assistant to a superior.

ail'ment (al'ment), n. Indisposition; a bodily disorder or disease.

aim (am), v.i. 1. To point or direct a weapon toward an object with the intent of hitting it. 2. To direct the intention or purpose; try; endeavor. — v.t. To direct or point (as a weapon, a blow, a remark, a proceeding) at, or so as to hit or affect, a particular object. — n. 1. Act of aiming something. 2. Intention; design.

air (ar), n. 1. The invisible, odorless, and tasteless mixture of gases, chiefly nitrogen and oxygen, surrounding the earth; the atmosphere.

air'craft' (ar'kraft), n. A machine capable of floating in, or flying through, the air.

air'ing (ar'ing), n. 1. An exposure to air, as for drying. 2. A walk or a ride in the open air.

air'ship' (ar'ship'), n. A dirigible balloon, as distinguished from the simple balloon or the aeroplane.

aisle (il), n. 1. A passage into which the pews of a church or seats of an assembly room open.

a-jar' (a-jar'), adv. Slightly turned or open.

a-kin' (a-kin'), a. Related.

al'a-bas'ter (al'a-bas'ter), n. A gypsum of fine texture and usually white and translucent; also, a variety of calcite.

a-lac'ri-ty (a-lak'ri-ti), n. A cheerful willingness.

a-larm' (a-larm'), n. 1. A summons to arms. 2. Any sound or signal notifying danger.

al-bi'no (al-bi'no), n. 1. A person born with deficiency of pigment in the skin, hair, and eyes. 2. An animal or plant similarly deficient in pigment.

al'co-hol (al'ko-hol), n. A colorless, volatile, inflammable liquid, which is the intoxicating principle for fermented and distilled liquors.

al'co-hol-ism (al'ko-hol-iz'm), n. A disease due to excessive use of alcohol.

al'cove (al'kov), n. A recessed portion of a room, as for a bed, or a small room opening into a larger one.

a-lert' (a-lurt'), a. 1. Watchful; vigilant. 2. Brisk; nimble. — n. Mil. An alarm; warning signal.

al'ien (al'yen), a. 1. Of another country; foreign; as, an alien race.

a-lign'ment (a-lin'ment), n. Act of aligning; formation in a straight line.

a-like' (a-lik'), a. Having resemblance; similar. — adv. In the same manner, form, or degree; in common; equally.

al'i-mo-ny (al'i-mo-ni), n. Law. An allowance made to a woman out of the property of him who is or was her husband, on legal separation or divorce, or during a suit for it.

a-live' (a-liv'), a. 1. Living. 2. being in a state of action, force, or operation.

all (ol), a. 1. The whole quantity, extent, duration, amount, quality; or degree of; the whole; any whatever; every. 2. Only; alone; nothing but; as, it was all profit and no loss. — adv. Wholly; entirely; quite; very. — n. The whole; totality; hence, everything or every person.

al'le-ga'tion (al'e-ga'shun), n. Positive assertion.

al-le'vi-ate (a-le'vi-at), v.t. To lighten or lessen (physical or mental troubles); mitigate.

al'ley, n. A narrow passage; esp.: 1. A bordered walk as in a park. 2. A narrow way in a city.

al-lit'er-a'tion (a-lit'er-a'shun), n. Repetition of the same letter or sound at the beginning of words succeeding each other immediately, or at short intervals, as in one form of verse.

al-lot' (a-lot'), v.t. 1. To distribute in portions; assign or set apart as a share, lot, or part.

al-lot'ment (-ment), n. Apportionment.

al-low (a-lou'), v.t. 1. To grant; give; to let one have. 2. To own or acknowledge, as a claim; accept as true; concede.

al-low'ance (-ans), n. A limited or stated amount, as of income or food.

all'spice (ol'spis'), n. The berry of the pimento; also, the spice prepared from it.

al-lude' (a-lud'), v.i. To refer indirectly or by suggestion.

al'ma-nac (ol'ma-nak), n. A calendar of days, weeks, and months, to which astronomical data and various statistics are often added.

al'mond (a'mund), n. A small tree of the same genus as the peach; also, its fruit, esp. its nut-like kernel.

al'most (ol'most; emphatic ol'most'), adv. Nearly; for the greatest part.

alms (amz), n. sing. & pl. A gift of charity.

al'oe (al'o), n.; pl. -OES (-oz). 1. In pl. A kind of fragrant resin or wood. 2. Any of a large genus of succulent plants, of the lily family, sereral of which yield a medicinal juice; also, usually in pl., the thickened juice.

a-loof' (a-loof'), adv. At or from a distance; apart; away. — **a-loof'ness**, n.

al'pha-bet (al'fa-bet), n. The letters of a language in their usual order; a set of letters or signs which form the elements of a written language.

al-read'y (ol-red'i), adv. Prior to some specified time; previously.

al'so (ol'so), adv. & conj. In the same manner (as something else);

likewise; in addition; too.

al'tar (ol'ter), n. 1. A raised structure in religious worship.

al'ter (-ter), v.t. To make otherwise; made different without changing into something else; vary; modify. — v.i. To become different; change.

al-ter'nate (al-tur'nat; al'ter-), a. 1. Occurring or succeeding by turns; one after the other; first one and then the other by turns; reciprocal.

al'to-geth'er (ol'too-geth'er), adv. Without exception; wholly; completely.

al'tru-ism (al'troo-iz'm), n. Regard for the interests of others, as a principle of conduct.

a-lu'mi-num (a-lu'mi-num), n. A bluish silver-white malleable metal, noted for lightness and resistance of oxidation.

al'ways (ol'waz; -waz), adv. At all times; ever; continually; invariably; uniformly.

am'a-teur' (am'a-tur'); am'a-tur), n. 1. One attached to or following a particular pursuit, study, or science, but not pursuing it professionally.

a-maze' (a-maz'), v.t. To confound or bewilder, as by fear of wonder; astound.

a-maz'ing (-maz'ing), p.a. Astounding; astonishing.

Am'a-zon (am'a-zon), n. 1. Gr. Myth. One of a race or nation of female warriors. 2. [Often l.c] A tall, strong, masculine woman.

am-big'u-ous (am-big'u-us), a. Doubtful; uncertain, esp. as to meaning; capable of being understood in either of two or more senses.

am-bi'tion (-bish'un), n. Eager or inordinate desire for preferment, honor, superiority, power, or attainment; also, an object of such desire.

a-mend' (a-mend'), v.t. 1. To reform or correct, as conduct; to mend; repair. 2. To improve; better.

a-mend'ment (a-mend'ment), n. A thing done or a change made; correction.

A-mer'i-can (a-mer'i-kan), a. Of or pertaining to America or the United States. — a A native of America; orig., an American aborigine; now, a person of European descent born in America. b A citizen of the Unites States.

a'mi-a-ble (a'mi-a-b'l), a. Having those qualities, as good nature, kind-heartedness, and friendliness, which cause one to be liked.

a-mid' (a-mid'), prep. In the midst of.

a-miss' (a-mis'), adv. Astray; faultily; improperly. — a. Wrong; faulty, as, what is amiss?

am'i-ty (am'i-ti), n. Friendship; friendly relations; friendliness.

am-mo'ni-a (a-mo'ni-a), n. 1. A colorless gas with extremely pungent smell and taste.

am'mu-ni'tion (am'u-nish'un), n. 1. The materials, as powder, shot, balls, bombs, etc., with which firearms are charged. 2. Any stock of missiles.

am'nes-ty (am'nes'ti), n. An act of the sovereign power granting general pardon for a past offense.

a-mong' (a-mung'), prep. 1. In or into the midst of; surrounded by; in connection with. 2. In the number or class of.

am'o-rous (am'o-rus), a. 1. Inclined to love; loving; fond. 2. Affected with love; in love.

a-mount' (a-mount'), n. 1. Sum total of two or more sums or quantities; aggregate.

am-per'age (am-par'aj; am'per-), n. Strength of a current of electricity measured in amperes.

am-pere' (am-par'), n. The practical unit of electrical current; the current produced by one volt acting through a resistance of one ohm.

am-phib'i-ous (-us), a. Able to live both on land and in water, as frogs.

am'phi-the'a-ter (am'fi-the'a-ter), n. 1. An oval or circular building with rising tiers of seats about an arena. 2. Anything resembling an amphitheater in form.

am'pli-fy (-pli-fi), v.t. 1. To render larger, more intense, or the like; — used esp. of telescopes, microscopes, etc. 2. To enlarge (as a statement) by adding particulars, illustrations, etc.

am'u-let (am'u-let), n. Some small object worn as a charm against evil.

a-muse' (a-muz'), v.t. To entertain or

occupy pleasurably; divert; excite to mirth.

a-muse'ment (-ment), n. State of being amused; also, that which amuses.

an-ach'ro-nism (an-ak'ro-niz'm), n. 1. An error in chronology by which events are misplaced in order, esp. one by which an event is placed too early. 2. Anything incongruous because its surroundings are not appropriate in time.

an'a-gram (an'a-gram), n. The change of one word or phrase into another by the transposition of its letters.

a-nal'o-gy (a-nal'o-ji), n. Agreement between things in some circumstances but not in others.

a-nal'y-sis (a-nal'i-sis), n. 1. A resolution of anything into elements; an examination of component parts separately, or in relation to the whole.

an'a-lyze (-a-liz), v.t. To resolve into elements or constituent parts; to separate or discriminate the parts of in relation to the whole and to one another; to subject to analysis.

an'arch-ism (an'ar-kiz'm), n. 1. The theory that all government is evil.

an'ces-tor (an'ses-ter), n. One from whom a person is descended; a progenitor.

an-cho'vy (an-cho'vi; an'cho-), n. Any of various small herring-like fishes of the Mediterranean, used for pickling or making a sauce.

an'cient (an'shent), a. 1. Old; antique; old-fashioned. 2. Belonging to times long past.

and (and), conj. 1. A particle expressing the general relation of connection or addition, and used to conjoin word with word, clause with clause, or sentence with sentence.

a-new' (a-nu'), adv. Over again; in a new form.

an'ec-dote (an'ek-dot), n. A short account of a single incident or fact of an interesting nature, esp. in the life of a well-known person.

a-new' (a-nu'), adv. Over again; in a new form.

an'gel (an'jel), n. 1. A spiritual, celestial being, superior to man in power and intelligence. 2. A person like an angel in goodness or loveliness.

an'ger (an'ger), n. A strong passion or emotion of displeasure or antagonism excited by what is regarded as an injury or insult done by another or by the intent to do such injury. — v.t. To excite to anger; enrage; provoke.

an'gle, n. 1. The enclosed space near the point where two lines meet; corner; nook.

an'gry (an'gri), a. 1. Affected with anger; enraged. 2. Showing, or proceeding from, anger.

an'guish (-gwish), n. Extreme pain of body or mind; agony; torture; torment.

an'i-mos'i-ty (-mos'i-ti), n. Violent hatred leading to active opposition.

an'kle (an'k'l), n. The joint between the foot and the leg; also, the region of this joint.

an'nals (-alz), n. pl. 1. A relation of events in chronological order. 2. Chronicles; history.

an-neal' (a-nel'), v.t. To subject to high heat and then cool; to soften and render less brittle.

an-nex' (a-neks'), v.t. 1. To join (one thing, usually something smaller or subordinate, to anther). 2. To attach as a consequence, condition, etc.

an-ni'hi-late (a-ni'hi-lat), v.t. 1. To reduce to nothing. 2. To destroy the form or essential character of. 3. To destroy the force, etc., of; make void.

an'ni-ver'sa-ry (an'i-vur'sa'ri), a. 1. Returning with the year; annual. 2. Of or pertaining to an anniversary.

an'no-tate (an'o-tat), v.t. To explain or criticize by notes. —v.i. To make notes or comments.

an-nu'i-ty (a-nu't-ti), n. An amount payable yearly; the right to such payments.

an-nul' (a-nul'), v.t. To nullify; abolish; avoid.

a-non (-non'), adv. 1. At once. 2. Soon; in a little while. 3. At another time; again.

a-non'y-mous (a-non'l-mus), a. Nameless; of unknown name; also, of unknown or unavowed authorship.

an-oth'er (a-nuth'er), pron. & a. 1.

One more; an additional one. 2. Not the same; different. 3. Any or some other; any one else; some one else.

an'swer (an'ser), n. 1. A reply to a charge, question, call argument, etc.; defense; also, a correct or adequate reply. 2. A responsive or retaliatory action.

ant (ant), n. Any of certain social insects allied to the bees, wasps, etc.

an-tag'o-nism (an-tag'o-niz'm), n. Opposition of action; mutual opposition of two forces.

an-tag'o-nist (-nist), n. One who contends with another, esp. in combat; adversary; opponent.

an-tag'o-nize (-tag'o-niz), v.t. & i. 1. To contend with; oppose actively.

ant'eat'er (ant'et'er), n. Any of several mammals that feed largely or entirely on ants.

an'te-lope (an'te-lop), n. Any of a group of graceful ruminant animals related to the oxen, sheep, and goats.

an-ten'na (an-ten'a), n.; L. pl. 1. A movable organ of feeling on the head of insects, myriapods, and crustaceans; feeler. 2. Wireless Teleg. A wire or wires supported in the air for directly transmitting or receiving electric waves.

an'thro-pol'o-gy (-pol'o-ji), n. The science of man, esp. in relation to physical character, distribution, culture, etc.

an-tic'i-pate (an-tis'i-pat), v.t. 1. To do, take up, or deal with, before another; preclude or prevent by prior action; forestall. 2. To take up, use, or introduce before the proper or normal time; cause to occur earlier or prematurely.

an'ti-dote (-dot), n. 1. A remedy for poison. 2. Whatever tends to prevent or counteract evil.

an-tique' (an-tek'), a. 1. Old, as respects the present time; antiquated; old-fashioned. — n. Anything very old, esp., a relic or object of ancient art.

an'ti-sep'tic (an'ti-sep'tik), a. 1. Tending to prevent putrefaction, pus formation, etc. 2. Using antiseptics. —n. An antiseptic substance.

ant'ler (ant'ler), n. The entire horn, or any branch of the horn, of an animal of the deer family.

anx'ious (ank'shus), a. 1. Disquieted over a possible or impending ill; concerned or solicitous, esp. as to a future or unknown thing. 2. Accompanied with or causing anxiety; worrying.

an'y (en'i), a. & pron. One indifferently out of a number; one (or, as pl., some) indiscriminately of whatever kind or quantity. — adv. To any extent; in any degree; at all.

an'y-bod-y (-bod-i), n. & pron. Any person.

an'y-how (-hou), adv. & conj. In any way or manner whatever; at any rate; in any event.

an'y-thing (-thing), n. Any object, act, state, event, or fact whatever; a thing of any kind.

an'y-way (-wa), adv. & conj. At all; in any case.

an'y-where (-hwar), adv. In any place.

a-or'ta (a-or'ta), n. The artery which carries the blood from the heart to all the body except the lungs.

a-part' (a-part'), adv. 1. Separately as to space or company; aside. 2. Separately as to purpose, use, character, etc.; independently. 3. Aside; away. 4. In two or more parts; asunder.

a-pol'o-get'ic (a-pol'o-jet'ik), Defending by discourse; of the nature of an apology. — **-i-cal-ly**, adv.

a-pol'o-gize (-jiz), v.i. To make an apology.

a-pol'o-gy (a-pol'o-ji), n. 1. Something said or written by way of defense or justification. 2. An acknowledgement intended as an atonement for an improper or injurious remark or act.

a-pos'tro-phe (a-pos'tro-fe), n. The mark ['] used to indicate the possessive case, the close of a quotation.

ap-pall' (a-pol'), v.t. To overcome, depress, or discourage with fear or horror; dismay.

ap'pa-ra'tus (-ra'tus), n. 1. Things provided as means to an end. 2. A set of implements or utensils for a given work; a complex instrument or appliance; mechanism.

ap-par'el (a-par'el), n. Dress; garb; raiment. — v.t. 1. To equip. 2. To clothe.

ap-par'ent (a-par'ent; a-par'-), a. 1. Open to view, visible. 2. Clear or manifest to the understanding; plain; evident; obvious. 3. Appearing as actual; seeming.

ap'pa-ri'tion (ap'a-rish'un), n. 1. A preternatural or unexpected appearance; ghost; specter; phantom.

ap-pend' (a-pend'), v.t. 1. To attach, as by a string, so as to suspend. 2. To add as accessory; annex.

ap-pen'di-ci'tis (-si'tis), n. Inflammation of the vermiform appendix.

ap-pen'dix (a-pen'diks), n. 1. Matter added to a book but not necessarily essential. 2. Anat. An appendage; esp., the vermiform appendix.

ap'pe-tite (ap'e-tit), n. 1. An inherent or habitual desire or propensity for some personal gratification of body or mind; craving; longing. 2. Desire for, or relish of, food or drink; hunger.

ap-plaud' (a-plod'), v.i. To express approbation loudly, emphatically, or significantly. — v.t. 1. To show approval of by clapping the hands, acclamation, etc.

ap'ple (ap'l), n. 1. The fruit of an apple tree.

ap-pli'ance (a-pli'ans), n. Device.

ap-plied' (a-plid'), p.a. Put to use; — said of various sciences, and distinguished from pure.

ap-ply' (a-pli'), v.t. 1. To place in contact; put or adjust (one thing to another). 2. To use for a particular purpose, or in a particular case; devote. 3. To use as relative or suitable to some person or thing.

ap-point' (a-point'), v.t. 1. To fix firmly; establish. 2. To fix by a decree, order, or mutual agreement; ordain.

ap-point'ment (a-point'ment), n. Designation of a person to hold an office.

ap-prais'al (a-praz'al), n. Act of appraising; also, the value fixed by appraising.

ap'pre-hend' (ap're-hend'), v.t. 1. To arrest. 2. To become conscious or sensible of as existing; to anticipate, esp. with fear.

ap-pren'tice (a-pren'tis), n. One bound to serve another for a certain time in consideration of instruction in an art or trade, and formerly, usually, of maintenance. — v.t. To bind or indenture as an apprentice.

ap-proach' (-a-proch'), v.i. & t. To come or go near; draw nigh; approximate; also, to make advances to. — n.

ap-pro'pri-ate (a-pro'pri-at), a. Belonging peculiarly; suitable; fit; proper. — (-at), v.t. 1. To take to one's self or to claim in exclusion of others. 2. To assign to a specific person or use.

ap-prove' (a-proov'), v.t. 1. To make proof of; demonstrate. 2. To sanction officially; ratify; confirm. 3. To regard as good; commend. — v.i. To pass or judge favorably.

ap-prox'i-mation (-ma'shun), n. 1. An approach to a correct estimate, or conception.

a'pron (a'prun), n. 1. An article of dress worn on the fore part of the body as a covering or to protect the clothes. 2. Something like an apron.

apt (apt), a. Fit or suited; suitable; appropriate. 2. Having a habitual tendency. 3. Ready; quick to learn; expert.

apt'ti-tude (ap'ti-tud), n. 1. Natural or acquired capacity for a particular purpose, or tendency to a particular action or effect. 2. General fitness; adaptation. 3. Readiness in learning; aptness.

aq'ue-duct (ak'we-dukt), n. 1. Any conduit for water, esp. a large one. 2. A structure for conveying a canal over a river or hollow.

ar'bi-trate (-trat), v.t. & i. 1. To hear and decide, or to act, as arbitrator; hence, to decide; determine. 2. To submit to arbitration.

arch'er-y (-i), n. 1. Art or practice of shooting with bow and arrows. 2. Archers collectively.

ar'chi-tect (ar'ki-tekt), n. A person skilled in architecture; one who plans and oversees the construction of buildings, etc.

ar'chi-tec'ture (ar'ki-tek'tur), n. 1. Art or science of building, esp. for the purpose of civil life. 2. Construction, in general; structure.

ar'chives (-kivz), n. pl. 1. A place for keeping public records. 2. Public records; — also in sing.

a're-a (a're-a), n. 1. Any plane surface. 2. The sunken space or court affording access and light to a basement. 3. A particular extent of surface; region.

a-re'na (a-re'na), n. 1. Place of public contest; sphere of action.

ar'gue (-gu), v.i. 1. To offer reasons for or against something; reason. 2. To contend in argument; dispute. — v.t. 1. To debate; discuss; as, to argue a case. 2. To manifest by reasoning; prove. 3. To persuade by reasons.

ar'gu-ment (-gu-ment), n. 1. A reason or reasons offered for or against something; reasoning. 2. Discussion; debate.

a'rise (-riz'), v.i.; 1. To ascend; rise.

ark (ark), n. 1. A chest or coffer. 2. The vessel in which Noah and his family were preserved during the Deluge; hence, any place of refuge.

arm (arm), v.t. 1. To furnish with weapons. 2. To cover with a strengthening or protective covering. — v.i. To provide one's self with arms.

arm, n. 1. A human upper limb, esp. the part between shoulder and wrist. 2. Something suggestive of an arm; a projecting part.

arm'ful (arm'fool), n.; pl. -FULS. As much as the arm, or both arms, can hold.

arm'pit' (arm'pit), n. The hollow, or pit, beneath the junction of the arm and shoulder.

ar'my (ar'mi), n.; pl. -MIES (-miz). 1. An organized body of men armed for war. 2. A large body of persons organized to advance a cause.

a-ro'ma (a-ro'ma), n. the distinctive fragrance of a substance; agreeable odor.

a-rouse' (-rouz'), v.t. & i. To excite to action from a state of rest; stir; rouse.

ar-raign' (a-ran'), v.t. 1. Law. To call or set (a prisoner) at the bar of a court to answer an indictment. 2. To call to account, or accuse, before any tribunal.

ar-range' (ranj'), v.t. 1. To put in proper order; dispose in the manner intended, or best suited for the purpose. 2. To adjust; settle; prepare.

ar-ray' (a-ra'), n. 1. To dispose in order, as troops; marshal; draw up. 2. To deck; dress.

ar-rest' (-rest'), v.t. 1. To stop; check; as, to arrest decay; arrest the current of a river. 2. To take or keep in custody by authority of law. 3. To hold; catch; seize on and fix the attention of; as, the display arrested his attention. — n. Act of arresting. — **ar-rest'er**, n.

ar-riv'al (a-riv'al) n. 1. Act of arriving. 2. The person or thing arriving or that has arrived.

ar-rive' (-riv'), v.i. 1. To come to the end of a journey; reach a destination; come upon the scene. 2. To gain or compass an object or attain a state by effort, study, etc.; — with at.

ar'ro-gant (-gant), a. 1. Making, or disposed to make, exorbitant claims of rank, estimation, or importance; assuming; haughty. 2. Containing, or marked with, arrogance. — **-ly**, adv.

ar'row (ar'o), n. The missile used with a bow, a long, slender shaft with pointed head.

ar'son (ar'sun), n. The malicious burning of a building or other structure, esp. the burning of a dwelling house or outhouse of another.

art (art), n. 1. Skill in performance; knack. 2. Human contrivance or ingenuity, as in adapting natural things to a man's use.

ar'ter-y (ar'ter'i), n.; Anat. One of the tubular branching vessels which distribute the blood from the heart through the body.

ar'ti-choke (ar'ti-chok), n. 1. A certain tall plant of the aster family; also, its edible flower head.

ar'ti-cle (-k'l), n. 1. A clause in a contract, treaty, or the like. 2. A literary composition forming an independent part of a periodical, cyclopedia, etc. 3. Something considered by itself; also, a thing of a particular class or kind; as, an article of diet.

ar-tic'u-late (-lat), a. 1. Jointed; formed with joints. 2. Characterized by division into words and syllables; spoken intelligibly.

ar'ti-fi'cial (ar'ti-fish'al), a. 1. Made or contrived; —opposed to natural. 2. Feigned; fictitious. — **ar'ti-fi'cial-ly**, adv.

a-shamed' (a-shamd'), p.a. Affected by shame.

ash'es (-ez), n. pl. 1. The earthy or mineral parts of combustible substances left after combustion. 2. The remains of the human body when burned, or when "returned to dust" by natural decay. 3. Fine lava thrown out in a volcanic eruption.

a-shore' (a-shor'), adv. To, or toward, the shore; on the shore.

a-side' (a-sid'), adv. 1. On or to one side; out of the way; apart. 2. So as not to be heard by others; privately. — n. Something spoken aside, as an actor's remark which the other players are supposed not to hear.

as'i-nine (as'i-nin), a. Stupid.

ask (ask), v.t. 1. To inquire of; question; as, ask him the way. 2. To request; solicit; as, he asked for a drink. 3. To demand, claim, or expect; as, he asks a high price.

as-par'a-gus (as-par'a-gus), n. 1. Any of a large genus of perennial plants. 2. The tender shoots of one species, used as food.

as'phalt (as'falt), n. 1. A brown to black bitumen used in paving.

as-phyx'i-a (as-fik'si-a), n. Suffocation due to lack of oxygen and excess of carbon dioxide in the blood.

as-pir'ant (as-pir'ant), a. Aspiring. — n. One who aspires.

as-pire' (as-pir'), v.i. 1. To desire with eagerness; seek; long. 2. To rise; tower; soar.

as-say' (a-sa'), n. Analysis, as of an ore, to determine the amount of one or more components.

as-sem'ble (-b'l), v.t. 1. To collect into one place or body; convene; congregate. 2. To fit together the parts of, as a machine. — v.i. To meet together; convene; congregate.

as-sent' (a-sent'), v.i. To admit a thing as true; express agreement; acquiesce; concur. — n. Act of assenting; consent; acquiescence.

as-sert' (a-surt'), v.i. 1. To maintain or defend, as a cause or a claim; vindicate or insist upon a claim or title to. 2. To affirm; state positively.

as-sess' (-ses'), v.t. 1. To fix the rate or amount of. 2. To apportion (a sum to be paid) in the nature of a tax, fine, etc.

as'sets (ets), n.pl. The entire property of a person, corporation, or estate, applicable or subject to the payment of his or its debts.

as-sid'u-ous (a-sid'u-us), a. Constant in application or attention; devoted.

as-sign' (-sin'), v.t. 1. To appoint; allot. 2. To specify; designate; point out authoritatively or exactly.

as-sim'i-late (a-sim'i-lat), v.t. 1. To bring to a likeness or to conformity. 2. To appropriate so as to incorporate into itself; absorb, as nourishment. — v.i. To be or become assimilated.

as-sist' (a-sist'), v.t. To give support to; help; aid; succor. —v.i. To lend aid; help.

as-so'ci-ate (a-so'shi-at), v.t. 1. To join as a friend, companion, partner or accomplice. 2. To join; connect; combine. — v.i. To unite in company or action; keep company; — implying intimacy.

as-sort-ment (-ment), n. 1. Act of assorting; assorted condition. 2. That which is formed by assorting, as a group or class.

as-sume' (a-sum'), v.t. 1. To take or adopt; take to or on one's self, as without authority. 2. To pretend to possess. 3. To take upon one's self (to do); undertake. 4. To take for granted; suppose.

as-sum'ing (a-sum'ing), p.a. Pretentious; presumptuous; arrogent.

as-sure' (a-shoor'), v.t. 1. To insure. 2. To give confidence to; convince; make sure, or certain. 3. To declare solemnly (to a person).

as'ter-isk (-isk), n. A figure of a star [*], used in printing and writing as a reference mark.

a-stern' (a-sturn'), adv. 1. Backward; to the rear. 2. Behind a vessel; in the rear.

as'ter-oid (as'ter-oid), n. A rocky

stellar body.

asth'ma (az'ma; as'ma), n. A disease characterized by difficult breathing, a sense of constriction in the chest, a cough, and expectoration.

a-stig'ma-tism (a-stig'ma-tiz'm), n. A defect of the eye or a lens because of which rays from one point do not focus at a point.

a-stray' (a-stra'), adv. & a. Wandering; straying.

a-stride' (-strid'), adv. With one leg on each side.

as-trin'gent (-jent), n. An astringent medicine or other substance.

as-tron'o-my (as-tron'o-mi), n. The science which treats of the heavenly bodies.

as-tute' (as-tut'), a. Critically discerning; sagacious; shrewd.

a-sun'der (a-sun'der), adv. Apart; into parts.

a'the-ism (a'the-iz'm), n. 1. Disbelief in, or denial of, the existence of God. 2. Godlessness.

ath-let'ic (ath-let'ik), a. 1. Of or pertaining to athletes or athletics. 2. Befitting an athlete; strong; robust.

at'las (at'las), n. 1. Anat. The first vertebra of the neck. 2. A collection of maps in a volume.

at'mos-phere (at'mos-fer), n. 1. The whole mass of air surrounding the earth. 2. Any surrounding or pervading influence. 3. The air in any place.

a-tom'ic (a-tom'ik), a. 1. Of or pertaining to atoms. 2. Very minute; tiny.

at'om-ize (at'um-iz), v.t. To reduce to atoms, or to fine spray.

a-tone (a-ton'), v.i. To make amends for an offense. — v.t. To expiate.

a-tone'ment (a-ton'ment), n. 1. Reconciliation; concord. Archaic. 2. Satisfaction or reparation; expiation; amends; — with for.

a-tro'cious (a-tro'shus), a. Savagely brutal; outrageously cruel or wicked.

at-tach' (a-tach'), v.t. 1. To take by legal authority, esp. under a writ as a means of enforcing a deb. 2. To bind; fasten; tie; connect.

at-tach'ment (a-tach'ment), n. 1. Act of attaching; state of being attached; close adherence or affection; fidelity. 2. That by which one thing is attached to another; connection.

at-tack' (a-tak'), v.t. 1. To fall upon or set upon with force; assault. 2. To assail with unfriendly speech or writing; censure; as, to attack one's reputation. 3. To set to work on, as on a task or problem.

at-tain' (a-tan'), v.t. 1. To reach or come to by motion; arrive at. 2. To achieve; accomplish; gain; compass. — v.i. To come or arrive by motion, growth, or effort; reach.

at-tend' (a-tend'), v.t. 1. To care for; take charge of; as, to attend to a machine. 2. To go with or stay with as a companion, nurse, or servant; serve; accompany; escort.

at-ten'tive (-tiv), a. 1. Heedful; observant. 2. Heedful of the comfort of others; courteous; regardful. — -ly, adv. — -ness, n.

at-test' (-test'), v.t. 1. To bear witness to; authenticate by signing as a witness or officially. 2. To afford proof of; manifest. — n. Witness; attestation.

at-tic (at'ik), n. The room or space of rooms immediately below the roof in a house; a garret.

at-tire' (a-tir'), v.t. To dress; array; esp. to clothe elegantly or splendidly; apparel. — n. Dress; clothes; esp., elegant or splendid clothing.

at'ti-ude (at'i-tud), n. 1. Posture; position assumed or studied to serve a purpose. 2. Position or bearing as indicating action, feeling, or mood.

at-tract' (a-trakt'), v.t. 1. To draw to or toward one's self or itself; esp., to cause to approach, adhere, or combine. 2. To draw by influence of a moral or emotional kind; invite; allure.

at-trib'ute (a-trib'ut), v.t. To ascribe; impute; consider as due or appropriate (to); assign.

au'burn (o'burn), a. Reddish brown.

au-dac'i-ty (-das'i-ti), n. Boldness, impudence.

au'di-ble (o'di-b'l), n. Audible quality, actually heard. — **au'di-bly** (-bli), adv.

au'dit (o'dit), n. An examination; esp., a formal or official examination and authentication of accounts.

au'di-to'ri-um (-to'ri-um), n. The part of a church, theater, or the like assigned to the audience.

aug-ment' (og-ment'), v.t. & i. to increase.

Au'gust (o-gust'), a. The eighth month of the year, having 31 days.

aunt (ant), n. The sister of one's father or mother; also, an uncle's wife.

au'ri-cle (o'ri-k'l), n. 1. The external ear. 2. One of the two chambers of the heart that receive the blood from the veins.

au-ro'ra (o-ro'ra), n. 1. The light of dawn; dawn. 2. The aurora borealis. — **au-ro'ra bo're-a'lis** (bo're-a'lis), an atmospheric phenomenon consisting, usually, of streams of light radiating upward and outward toward the east and west from the north polar region.

aus-pi'cious (os-pish'us), a. 1. Giving promise of success; propitious. 2. Prosperous; fortunate. 3. Favoring.

au-then'tic (o-then-tik), a. 1. Having a genuine original or authoritative source; genuine; real; as, an authentic paper. 2. Of approved authority; true; credible.

au'thor (o'ther), n. 1. The beginner of anything; hence, creator; originator. 2. One who composes or writes something, as a book; a composer; also, an author's writings.

au-thor'i-ty (-ti), n.; pl. -TIES (-tiz). 1. Legal or rightful power; a right to command or to act; dominion; jurisdiction. 2. Government; those exercising power or command; — usually in pl.

au'to-bi-og'ra-phy (-bi-og'ra-fi), n. A biography written by the subject of it; memoirs of one's life written by one's self.

au-toc'ra-cy (o-tok'ra-si), n. 1. Absolute supremacy. 2. Supreme governing power in an individual; authority of an autocrat.

au'to-crat (o'to-krat), n. An absolute sovereign; a monarch ruling by claim of absolute right; despot.

au'to-graph (o'to-graf), n. That written with one's own hand; a person's own signature.

au'top-sy (o'top-si), n.; pl. -SIES (-siz). Med. Dissection of a dead body to learn the cause, seat, or nature of a disease, or the cause of death.

au'tumn (o'tum), n. The season between summer and winter, often called fall.

a-vail' (a-val'), v.i. To be of use; to have strength, force, or efficacy sufficient to accomplish the object in mind. — v.t. To benefit; help. — to avail one's self of, to make use of; take advantage of.

a-vail'a-ble (a-val'a-b'l), a. Usable.

av'a-rice (-ris), n. Excessive or inordinate desire of gain; covetousness; cupidity.

a-venge' (a-venj'), v.t. To take vengeance for; exact satisfaction for.

a-ver'sion (-vur'shun), n. 1. A state of mind in which attention to an object is coupled with dislike of it and desire to turn from it. 2. An object of dislike or repugnance.

a-vert' (a-virt'), v.t. To turn aside or away; ward off or prevent the occurrence or effects of.

a'vi-a-ry (a'vi-a-ri), n. A place, as a house, for keeping birds confined.

a'vi-a'tion (-a-shun), n. Art or science of locomotion by aeroplanes.

a-vid'i-ty (a-vid'i-ti), n. Greediness; eagerness.

a-void' (a-void'), v.t. 1. To make void, as a contract; annul; vacate. 2. To keep away from; shun; abstain from; as, to avoid evil.

a-wait' (a-wat'), v.t. To wait for; stay for; expect. 2. To be in store for; be in waiting for.

a-ware' (a-war'), a. Conscious; informed; cognizant.

a-way' (a-wa'), adv. 1. From a place, hence, aside; from one's possession. 2. From a state of being into extinction or termination; out of existence; as, to sleep the day away.

awe (o), n. Profound reverence; solemn wonder. — v.t. To strike or inspire with awe.

a-while' (a-hwil'), adv. For a while or a short time.

awk'ward (ok'werd), a. 1. Not dexterous; clumsy; ungraceful. 2. Not easily managed or effected; embarrassing; as, an awkward affair.

ax'le (ak's'l), n. 1. The pin or spindle on which a wheel revolves, or which revolves with a wheel. 2. A transverse bar or shaft connecting the opposite wheel of a car.

B

bab'ble (bab'l), v.i. 1. To utter words indistinctly or unintelligibly; utter inarticulate sounds. 2. To chatter; prate. 3. To murmur, as a brook.

ba'by (ba'bi), n. An infant.

bac'ca-lau're-ate (bak'a-lo're-at), n. The degree of bachelor, conferred by universities and colleges.

bach'e-lor (bach'e-lor), n. A man of any age who has not married.

back (bak), n. 1. The hind part of the human body, or, of animals, the upper part, from the neck to the end of the spine. 2. The rear part of a thing.

back'bone (bak'bon'), n. 1. The spine. 2. Firmness; moral principle.

back'log (bak'log'), n. A large log of wood forming the back of a fire on the hearth.

back'ward (-werd), adv. 1. Toward the back or rear. 2. With the back in advance or foremost. 3. On the back, or with the back downward; as, to fall over backward.

ba'con (ba'k'n), n. The back and sides of a pig, salted and smoked.

bac-ter'ri-a (bak-ter'ri-a), n. pl. Microscopic organisms. Some species convert dead organic matter into soluble food for plants; some cause fermentation; and some cause disease.

bad (bad), a. 1. Injurious; hurtful. 2. Offensive; disagreeable; annoying. 3. Inadequate; unfit.

badge (baj), n. 1. A distinctive mark, token, or sign, worn on the person. 2. A mark or token.

badg'er (baj'er), n. A flesh-eating burrowing animal with long claws on the forefeet. — v.t. To tease or annoy persistently; worry.

baf'fle (bak'l), v.t. To perplex; thwart; foil.

bag (bag), n. A sack or pouch.

bag'gage (bag'aj), n. A container for carrying belongings during travel; luggage.

bake (bak), v.t. 1. To prepare, as food, by cooking in a dry heat. 2. To dry or harden (anything) by subjecting to heat. — v.i.

bal'ance (bal'ans), n. An instrument for weighing. — v.i. To counter or apportion equally.

bal'co-ny (bal'ko-ni), n.; pl. -NIES (-niz). A projecting platform inclosed by a parapet or railing.

bald (bold), a. 1. Destitute of the natural or common covering on the head or top, as of hair. 2. Destitute of ornament; bare.

bald eagle, the common eagle of North America; — from the white feathers of the head and neck of bald eagles several years old.

bale (bal), n. 1. Evil; an evil influence. Chiefly Poetic. 2. Pain, calamity; sorrow.

balk (bok), n. A hindrance; disappointment; check.

ball, n. A social assembly for dancing.

bal'lad (bal'ad), n. 1. A simple song of any kind; specifically, a romantic song. 2. A popular kind of short narrative poem.

bal-loon' (ba-loon'), n. A bag or envelope, as of silk, filled with a gas lighter than air, as hydrogen, so as to rise and float in the atmosphere.

bal'lot (bal'ut), n. 1. Any object, esp. a printed ticket, used in secret voting. 2. Act or system of secret voting (or, loosely, open voting), by tickets, or ballots.

bam-boo' (bam-boo'), n. A woody or treelike tropical plant of the grass family.

ban (ban), n. 1. A public proclamation or edict. 2. pl. Notice of a proposed marriage, proclaimed in church. 3. Ecclesiastical interdict, anathema, or excommunication. 4. A curse, bringing evil.

band'age (ban-daj), n. A strip, usually of cloth, used in dressing wounds, etc. — v.t. To bind, dress, or cover with a bandage.

ban'dit (-dit), n. An outlaw; hence; lawless marauder.

bane (ban), n. Any cause of ruin or injury.

bang (bang), v.t. & i. To beat or thump with a resounding blow. —n. 1. A resounding blow; thump; whack. 2. A sudden noise, as from a heavy blow or an explosion. — adv. With a violent blow, clap, or noise; also, all of a sudden. Colloq.

ban'gle (gan'g'l), n. An ornamental circlet, as of glass, gold, or silver.

bank (bank), n. 1. A ridge of earth; anything shaped like a ridge of earth. 2. A shoal, shelf, or shallow in the sea bottom; as, the New-foundland banks. 3. A steep slope, as of a hill.

bank, n. 1. Originally, a money changer's table; now, an office for banking purposes.

bank'rupt (-rupt), a. Being a bankrupt; unable to pay; or discharged from paying, one's debts. — v.t. To make bankrupt.

ban'quet (ban'kewt), n. A feast; a ceremonious feast followed by speeches. — v.t. & i. to feast.

bap'tism (bap'tiz'm), n. 1. Act of baptizing, esp. as a Christian sacrament. 2. Any act or experience by which one is purified, initiated, etc.

bar (bar), n. A slender, rigid piece of wood, metal, etc.

bar-ba'ri-an (bar-ba'ri-an), n. 1. A foreigner, esp. in speech and manners. 2. a A rude, uncivilized person. b A person devoid of culture.

bar'ber (bar'ber), n. One whose occupation it is to shave, trim beards, cut the hair, etc. — v.t. To shave, trim, or dress the beard or hair of.

bare (bar), a. 1. Naked; nude. 2. With head bare. 3. Open to view.

bare'ly, adv. 1. Nakedly. 2. Without concealment or disguise. 3. But just; scarcely; hardly.

bar'gain (bar'gen), n. 1. An agree-ment between parties settling what each shall give and receive in a transaction; agreement. 2. A thing got by bargaining; a purchase, esp. an advantageous purchase. — v.i.

bark, v.i. To utter a short, explosive cry; — of a dog, and hence of certain other animals.

bar'ley (bar'li), n. A hardy bearded cereal grass; also, its seed or grain, used as food and in making malt.

barn (barn), n. 1. A covered building used chiefly for storing grain, hay, etc. A part is often used for stables. 2. Hence: A building in which to keep horses, vehicles, etc.

ba-rom'e-ter (ba-rom'e-ter), n. An instrument for determining the weight or pressure of the atmo-sphere.

bar'rack (bar'ak), n. [Usually in pl.] Mil. A building or group of buildings for lodging soldiers.

bar'rel (-el), n. 1. A round bulging vessel or cask having flat ends or heads. 2. The quantity constituting a full barrel. 3. A drum or cylinder or similarly round part, hollow or solid.

bar'ri-cade' (-i-kad'), n. Any bar or obstruction.

bar'ri-er (bar'i-er), n. A fence or railing to mark the limits of a place.

bar'ter (bar'ter), v. i. & t. To exchange economic commodities.

base (bas), n. The bottom of anything considered as its support; that on which a thing rests for support; foundation. 2. The chief ingredient of anything; viewed as its funda-mental constituent.

base'ment (-ment), n. The floor of a building beneath the ground floor, usually an underground floor.

bash'ful (bash'fool), a. Very or excessively modest; indicating excessive modesty; shy; retiring.

bas'ic (bas'ik), a. Of or pertaining to the base or a base; fundamental.

ba'sis (ba'sis), n. Foundation; base. 2. Chief component. 3. Groundwork.

bas'ket bas'ket), n. 1. A vessel made of osiers, rushes, splints, or other flexible material, inter-woven. 2. The contents of a basket.

bas'tard (bas'tard), n. An illegitimate child. — 1. Illegitimate by birth. 2. Not genuine; spurious.

baste (bast), v.t. To wet (roasting meat, etc.) with melted butter, fat, etc.

bat (bat), n. A stout, solid stick; club; a club with one end thicker or broader than the other, used in baseball, cricket, etc.

bat, n. Any of numerous mammals having the fore limbs modified to form wings.

bath (bath), n. 1. Act of subjecting the

body to water for cleanliness. 2. A quantity or supply of water prepared for bathing.

bat'ter-y (bat'er-i), n. Law. The unlawful beating of another.

bat'tle (-'l), n. 1. A general encounter between armies or ships; engagement. 2. Fighting of armed forces; war.

bat'tle-ship' (-ship'), n. Naval. One of a class of the largest, most heavily armed and armored vessels.

bawl (bol), v.i. & t. 1. To cry out with a loud, full sound; to shout. 2. To cry loudly, as from pain; howl. — n. A loud, prolonged cry; outcry.

bear (bar), v.t. 1. To support and move; carry. 2. To render or give, as testimony. 3. To carry (one's self); behave. 4. To possess or have; wear.

beard (berd), n. 1. The hair on the chin, lips, and adjacent parts of a man. 2. Any of certain appendages likened to a man's beard; as, a goat's beard, the beard of grain. — v.t.

beat (bet), v.t. 1. To strike repeatedly. 2. To punish by blows; thrash. 3. To overcome in a contest, game, etc.; vanquish; surpass. 4. To measure or mark off by strokes.

beau'ti-ful (-ti-fool), a. Having beauty; full of beauty.

be-cause' (-koz), adv. & conj. By or for the cause that; for the reason that; since.

beck'on (bek'n), v.i. & t. To signal, or call, by or as by a motion of the hand, finger, or head.

be-come' (-kum), v.i. To pass from one state to another; come to be. — v.t. To suit or be suitable to; befit; accord with.

be-com'ing (-kum-ing), p.a. Suitable; proper; appropriate or fit.

bed (bed), n. That upon or within which one sleeps or rests.

bed'rid'den (bed'rid'n), a. Confined to the bed by sickness or infirmity; decrepit; worn out.

beef (bef), n. The flesh of a steer or cow used for food.

beer (ber), n. 1. A brewed liquor made with malted grain, commonly barley, and flavored with hops.

be-fore (be-for'), adv. 1. On the fore part; in front. 2. In advance. 3. In time past; previously. 4. Earlier; sooner. — prep.

be-fore'hand (-hand'), adv. In advance, as by way of forethought. — a. Forehanded.

be-friend' (be-frend'), v.t. To act as a friend to.

be-fud'dle (-fud'l), v.t. To becloud and confuse, as with liquor.

beg (beg), v.t. 1. To ask for as a charity; esp. habitually; as, he begs his bread. 2. To supplicate for; beseech; entreat. — v.i.

be-gin' (be-gin'), v.i.; 1. To do the first act or take the first step; start; as, let us begin. 2. To come into existence; commence. — v.t. To set about; commence; as,, they began to get dinner.

be-have' (-hav'), v.t. To carry; conduct;—used reflexively. — v.t. to act; conduct one's self or itself; often, to conduct one's self well or properly.

be-hav'ior (-hav'yer), n. Act or manner of behaving; conduct; bearing; deportment.

be-hind' (-hind'), adv. 1. Back in place or time. 2. Not yet produced or exhibited to view; remaining; still to come. 3. After the set or proper time; late; slow, as a watch. 4. Toward the back; as, to look behind. — prep.

be-hold'er (-der), n. A spectator; looker-on.

be-hoove' (-hoov'), v.t. To be proper for or incumbent on; as, it behooves you to go.

be'ing (be'ing), p. pr. & p. a. of BE. Existing. — n. 1. Existence; life. 2. That which exists.

be-lat'ed (-lat'ed), p.a.aa Overtaken by night; delayed.

belch (belch), v.i. 1. To eject wind or gas spasmodically from the stomach through the mouth.

be-lief' (-lef'), n. 1. A state or habit of mind in which trust is placed in some person or thing; trust; confidence. 2. A persuasion of the truths of religion; faith. 3. Thing believed; doctrine; creed.

be-lieve' (-lev'), v.i. 1. To have faith or confidence. 2. To exercise belief or faith, esp. as to the truths of religion. 3. To think; judge. — v.t. To regard, accept, or hold as true; also, to think; consider.

be-lit'tle (-lit'l), v.t. to make little or less; speak of in a depreciatory way.

bell (bel), n. 1. A hollow, often cup-shaped, metallic vessel, giving forth a ringing sound when struck. 2. A bell rung to tell the hours; also, a stroke of such a bell, esp. on shipboard.

be-low' (-lo), adv. In a lower place, with respect to any object; beneath. — prep. Under, or lower than, in place, rank, value, etc., not so high as.

bench (bench), n. 1. A long seat. 2. The seat where the judges sit in court; judge's seat; hence, office or dignity of judge. 3. The judges collectively, or a judge, sitting in court; also, a court. 4. A long worktable.

ben'e-fi'cial (ben'e-fish'al), a. Conferring benefits; helpful; advantageous. — - ly, adv.

ben'e-fit (ben'e-fit), n. 1. Act of kindness; favor; gift. 2. Whatever promotes prosperity and personal happiness; advantage; profit. — v.t. & i. To give, or to receive, benefit; profit.

be-nev'o-lence (be-nev'o-lens), n. 1. Quality of being benevolent; disposition to do good; charitable-ness. 2. An act of kindness; good done.

bent, n. 1. A leaning or bias; tendency of mind; disposition. 2. Power of endurance; capacity.

be-queath' (be-kweth'), v.t. 1. To give or leave by will. 2. To hand down; transmit.

best (best), a. 1. Having good qualities in the highest degree; most excellent. 2. Most productive of good; most advantageous, serviceable, etc.

be-stow' (-sto'), v.t. 1. To deposit; stow. 2. To give or confer, as in marriage.

be-tray' (be-tra'), v.t. 1. To deliver to the enemy by treachery or fraud. 2. To fail or desert in need. 3. To mislead; lead into error, sin, or danger. 4. To disclose or reveal. —

be-tray'er, n.

bet'ter-ment (-ment), n. A making better; improvement; permanent improvement, as of property.

be-tween' (be-twen'), prep. 1. In the space which separates; betwixt. 2. From one to another of. 3. in common to; in the joint possession of; by the united action of.

be-ware' (-war'), v.i. To be on one's guard; to take care. — v.t. To have a care for.

be-yond' (be-yond'), adv. Farther away; at a distance; yonder. —prep. 1. Of space or time: On or to the farther side of; farther on or away than. 2. Out of the reach or sphere of; greater than; further than.

bi-an'nu-al (bi-an'u-al), a. Semian-nual.

bib'li-og'ra-phy (bib'li-og-ra'fi), n.; pl. -PHIES (-fiz). 1. The history or description of books. 2. A list of books relating to a given subject.

bi'ceps (bi-seps), n. The large muscle of the front of the upper arm.

bi'cy-cle (bi'si-k'l), n. A light vehicle having two wheels one behind the other and propelled by the rider's feet acting on pedals.

bide (bid), v.t. To wait for.

big (big), a. Large in size, bulk, or extent.

big'a-my (-mi), n. Act of marrying one person when already legally married to another.

big'ness, n. Quality or state of being big.

big'ot (big'ut), n. One obstinately and blindly devoted to his own church, party, etc.

bi-lat'er-al (bi-lat'er-al), a. Having two sides.

bill, n. 1. A document containing a petition. 2. A draft of a law presented to a legislature for enactment.

bin (bin), n. A box, frame, crib, or inclosed place, used as a recep-tacle; as, a coal bin.

bind (bind), v.t. 1. To tie or confine with a cord, band, chain, or the like. 2. To confine, restrain, or hold by physical force or influence of any kind. 3. To cover as with a bandage; bandage.

bi-og'ra-phy (bi-og'ra-fi), n.; pl. -

PHIES (-fiz). 1. The written history of a person's life. 2. Biographical writing or composition in general.

bi·ol'o·gy (bi-ol'o-ji), n. Science of life; science which treats of plants and animals.

bird (burd), n. Any of a class of warm-blooded egg-laying animals having the body more or less completely covered with feathers and the fore limbs modified into wings.

bird's'-eye' (burdz-i'), a. Seen from above, as if by a flying bird; hence, general; not minute.

birth'day' (-da'), n. 1. Day of birth, origin, or commencement. 2. The anniversary of one's birth.

birth'mark' (-mark'), n. Some peculiar mark or blemish on the body at birth.

bis'cuit (bis'kit), n.; pl. _CUIT (-kit) or -CUITS (-kits). 1. A kind of unraised bread, baked hard in flat cakes; — usually called cracker in the U.S. 2. A small cake of bread raised and shortened, or made light with soda or baking powder.

bish'op (bish'up), n. A clergyman of the highest order in various Christian churches.

bi'son (bi'sun), n. A large bovine quadruped, with massive shaggy fore quarters and head.

bisque (bisk), n. A kind of rich soup.

bit (bit), n. The biting or cutting edge or part of a tool.

bit'ter (-er), a. 1. Having a peculiar, characteristically disagreeable taste. 2. Painful; distressful. 3. Characterized by severity or cruelty; harsh; caustic.

bit'ters (-erz), n. pl. A liquor, generally spirituous, in which a bitter herb, leaf, or root is steeped.

bit'ter-sweet' (-er-swet'). a. Mingling bitter and sweet.

bi'week'ly (bi'wek'li), a. Occurring or appearing every two weeks; also, semiweekly. — n. A biweekly publication.

blab (blab), v.t. & i. 1. To talk foolishly or idly; chatter; babble. 2. To speak, talk, or tell unnecessarily or thoughtlessly.

black (blak), a. 1. Destitute of light, or incapable of reflecting it. 2. Having very dark skin and, usually, dark hair and eyes. 3. Soiled with dirt; foul. 4. Dismal, gloomy, or forbidding, like darkness. 5. Destitute of moral light or goodness; wicked.

black'guard (blag'ard), n. A person of low character, esp. one who is scurrilous or abusive; a scoundrel. — v.t. To revile or abuse scurrilously. — a. Low; abusive; scurrilous.

black'mail' (-mal'), n. Extortion by threats of public accusation or exposure. — v.t. To exact blackmail from.

blade (blad), n. 1. A leaf of a plant; the flat or expanded portion of a leaf, esp. of grass. 2. The thin cutting part of an instrument. 3. A sword; also, one who bears an edged weapon.

blame (blam), v.t. To censure; find fault with; reproach. — n. 1. Expression of disapproval; censure. 2. Fault; culpability.

blanch (blanch), v.t. To take the color out of; make white; bleach. — v.i. To become white.

blank (blank), a. 1. Free from writing, printing, or marks. 2. Empty; void; fruitless. 3. Lacking variety or interest. 4. Expressionless; vacant. — n.

blast (blast), n. 1. A violent gust of wind. 2. A forcible stream of air or other gas from an orifice. 3. The sound made by a wind instrument. 4. A sudden pernicious effect; blight.

bla'tant (-tant), a. Offensively obtrusive; coarse.

blaze (blaz), n. 1. A glowing flame; a fire. 2. Intense, direct light accompanied with heat. 3. An active display of any quality; outburst. 4. Splendor; effulgence. — v.i.

blaz'er (blaz'er), n. A light jacket, usually bright-colored, for wear at tennis, cricket, or other sport.

bleach (blech), v.t. To make white or whiter; blanch; whiten. —v.i. To grow white or lose color; whiten.

blem'ish (blem'ish), v.t. To injure; mar; sully. — n. Any marks of deformity or injury.

bless (bles), v.t.1. To consecrate or hallow by religious rite or word. 2.

To pray for the happiness of. 3. To make happy, confer prosperity or happiness on. 4. To praise or glorify.

bless'ed (bles'ed), p.a. 1. Hallowed; holy. 2. Favored with blessings; happy. 3. Enjoying spiritual happiness.

blind (blind), a. 1. Sightless. 2. Not having or not using discernment or judgment. 3. Difficult or impossible to see; dim; hidden. 4. Having no opening for light or passage, as a wall; blank. 5. Having but one opening, as an alley. 6. Unintelligible; also, illegible. — v.t.

blind'fold' (blind'fold'), v.t. To cover the eyes of, as with a bandage.

blink (blink), v.i. 1. to look with eyes half shut; see indistinctly. 2. To wink. 3. To look evasively or indifferently.

bliss (blis), n. 1. Gladness; enjoyment. 2. Exalted happiness; heavenly joy.

blis'ter (blis'ter), n. 1. A vesicle of the skin containing watery matter. 2. Any cavity resembling a blister (sense 1). — v.t. & i. to affect or be affected with a blister or blisters.

bliz'zard (bliz'ard), n. A dry, cold, violent storm, with high wind and fine driving snow.

bloat (blot), v.t. 1. To cause to swell up, as with air, water, etc. 2. To puff up; inflate; make vain. — v.i. To puff out; swell.

block (blok), n. 1. A bulky, solid piece of wood, stone, or the like, usually with one or more flat faces. 2. A row of houses or shops, esp. when built in contact so as to form one building.

block-ade' (blok-ad'), n. 1. The shutting up of a place by troops or ships so as to prevent ingress or egress. 2. An obstruction to passage. — v.t. To subject to a blockade.

block'head' (blok-hed'), n. A stupid fellow; dolt.

blonde (blond), a. 1. Of a fair color. 2. Having yellowish brown or light brown hair.

blood (blud), n. 1. The fluid, commonly red in vertebrates, which circulates in the heart, arteries, and veins of animals. 2. Relationship by descent from a common ancestor; kinship; kindred; race.

blood'shot' (-shot'), a. Red and inflamed; suffused with blood; — said of the eye.

bloom'ing, p.a. a 1. Blossoming; flowering. 2. Thriving in health, beauty, and vigor.

blos'som (blos-um), n. 1. the flower of a seed plant; bloom. 2. A blooming period or stage of development. — v.i. To flower; bloom.

blotch (bloch), n. 1. A blot or spot, as of ink. 2. A large pustule, as on the face. — v.t. & i. To cover with blotches; make or cause a blotch.

blotting paper. A spongy paper for absorbing ink from fresh manuscript.

blouse (blouz; blous), n. A loose shirtlike over-garment of various lengths and styles.

blow, n. 1. A forcible stroke with the hand, fist, or some instrument. 2. A sudden or forcible act or effort; assault. 3. A sudden calamity.

bludg'eon (bluj'un), n. A short club with one end weighted, or thick and heavier than the other.

blue (bloo), a. 1. Having the color of the clear sky, or a hue resembling it. 2. Low in spirits; melancholy. 3. Tending to produce low spirits. Colloq. 4. Severe or overstrict in morals; suiting one overstrict in morals. — n.

blue'bird' (-burd'), n. A small song bird, native east of the Rocky Mountains in North America (primarily in the U.S.)

blun'der (blun'der), v.i. 1. to move clumsily; stumble. 2. To make a gross error or mistake.

blunt (blunt), a. 1. Not sensitive; obtuse in feeling or perception. 2. Dull-witted; stupid. 3. Having a thick edge or point, as an instrument; dull. 4. Abrupt in speech or manners. —v.t. & i.

blur (blur), v.t.; BLURRED (blurd); BLUR'RING. 1. To make indistinct and confused. 2. To cause imperfect vision in; dim. —v.i. To become blurred or obscure. — n.

blurt (blurt), v.t. To utter suddenly and indiscreetly; — commonly with out.

blus'ter (blus-ter), v.i. 1. To blow

fitfully and noisily, as the wind; be windy and boisterous, as the weather. 2. To talk with noisy violence; swagger. — n.

board (bord), n. 1. A piece of timber sawed thin, relatively broad, and long.

boat (bot), n. 1. A small open vessel, or watercraft, usually moved by oars or paddles; any vessel for navigating the water. 2. A vehicle or utensil suggestive of a boat. — v.t. To transport or place in a boat. — v.i. To go or row in a boat.

bod'i-ly (-i-li), a. Of or pertaining to the body. — adv. 1. In bodily form; in the body. 2. In respect to the whole body; all at once; completely.

bod'y (bod'i), n. 1. The whole material organism of an animal or plant. 2. The central or main part. 3. A person; a human being.

boil (boil), v.i. 1. To be agitated by the generation and rising of bubbles of vapor; — said of a liquid. 2. To be agitated like boiling water; to seethe. 3. To be excited with passion.

bois'ter-ous (bois'ter-us), a. Tumultuously violent; rough; turbulent; loud; violent; tumultuous.

bold'ness, n. State or quality of being bold.

bol'ster (bol'ster), n. A long pillow or cushion for a bed. — v.t. 1. To support with a bolster or pillow. 2. To support, hold up, or maintain, esp. with difficulty; — often with up.

bom-bard' (-bard'), v.t. To attack with artillery or bombs.

bo'nafi'de (bo'nafi'de). [L.] In or with good faith; without fraud or deceit; as, a bona fide sale.

bo-nan'za (bo-nan'za), n. In mining, a rich ore body; hence, anything that yields a large income. Colloq., U.S.

bon'fire (bon'fir'), n. A large fire built in the open air as an expression of public joy.

bon'net (bon'et), n. 1. A soft woolen cap without brim or visor, worn by men in Scotland. 2. A head covering, worn by women and children out of doors, usually tied on with strings.

bo'nus (bo'nus), n. Something given beyond what is usual or strictly due.

boo (boo), interj. An exclamation used to frighten.

book (book), n. 1. A literary composition of considerable length. 2. A collection of sheets of paper bound together; usually, a printed and bound volume.

book'keep'ing, n. Art or practice of keeping a systematic record of business transactions.

boom'er-ang (boom'er-ang), n. 1. A curved or angular club used, mainly by the natives of Australia, as a missile weapon. It can be hurled so that its flight will bring it back near to the place from which it was thrown.

boor (boor), n. 1. A peasant; esp., an awkward, ill-bred countryman. 2. A rude, ill-bred person.

bor'der (bor'der) n. 1. The outer part or edge; margin. 2. A boundary or frontier. — a. Pertaining to a boundary district or frontier. — v.t.

boss (bos), n. A master workman; superintendent; manager; political dictator. — v.t. To be master over; direct. — v.t. To be master. All Colloq.

bot'a-ny (-ni), n. Science of plants and plant life.

both (both), a. or pron. The one and the other; the two. — conj. & adv. 1. As well; not only; equally; — used with and; as, both the quick and the dead. 2. As well; also; too.

both'er (both'er), v.t. To annoy; worry; perplex. — v.i. To feel care or anxiety. — n. One who or that which bothers; embarrassment; worry.

bot'tle (bot'l), n. 1. A hollow vessel, usually of glass or earthenware, with a narrow neck or mouth and without handles. 2. The contents of a bottle; fig., intoxicating liquor. — v.t. To inclose in or as in a bottle or bottles.

bot'tom (-um), n. 1. The part of anything under and supporting the contents or bulk; under surface; foot; base, foundation. 2. Bed of a body of water. 3. Low alluvial land along a river.

bou'le-vard (boo'le-vard), n. A broad avenue.

bound'a-ry (boun'da-ri), n. That which

indicates or fixes a limit, as of a territory.

boun'ty (-ti), n.; pl. -TIES (-tiz). 1. Liberality in giving. 2. That which is given liberally. 3. A reward; a premium to encourage an industry.

bou-quet' (boo-ka'), n. 1. A bunch of flowers. 2. A perfume; aroma, as of wine.

bow'el (bou'el), n. 1. An intestine; entrail, esp. of man; gut; —usually in pl. 2. pl. the interior of anything, as of the earth. 3. pl. The seat of pity or kindness; tenderness; compassion.

bowl (bol), n. 1. A concave vessel to hold liquids, etc. 2. A part suggestive of a bowl.

box, n. 1. A case or other receptacle usually having a lid or cover. 2. Drive's seat on a carriage. 3. A limited compartment in a public place, as in a theater, or its occupants. — v.t.

boy (boi), n. 1. A male child from birth to about 14 years of age; a youth. 2. A male servant.

boy'cott (boi'kot), v.t. 1. To subject to a boycott. 2. To refrain from the use of; keep aloof from. — n. A combining to withhold business or social relations from a tradesman, etc.

brack'et (-et), n. 1. A projecting supporting piece [], used to set something off from the context. — v.t. To place within brackets; connect by, or furnish with, a bracket or brackets.

brain (bran), n. 1. In vertebrate animals, the large mass of nerve tissue inclosed in the skull or cranium, regarded as the seat of consciousness. 2. Understanding; intellect; — often in the pl. —v.t. To dash out the brains of.

brake, n. Any device for retarding or stopping by friction. — v.t. To apply a brake to.

bran'dy (bran'di), n.; pl. -DIES (-diz). A spirituous liquor distilled from wine or, sometimes, from the fermented juice of peaches, cherries, or applies. — v.t. To flavor or treat with brandy.

brass (bras), n. 1. An alloy of copper and zinc, and, sometimes tin. 2. pl.

Brass utensils, ornaments, musical instruments, etc.

brawl (brol), v.i. 1. To quarrel noisily. 2. To make a loud confused noise. — n. Noisy quarrel.

breach (brech), n. 1. Act of breaking; gap or opening made by breaking; break. 2. A breaking or infraction of a law, obligation, or tie. 3. A breaking up of amicable relations; rupture.

bread (bred), n. 1. A common article of food made from flour or meal.

break'down (-doun), n. 1. A breaking down; failure. 2. A noisy, rapid, shuffling dance.

breast (brest), n. 1. The fore part of the body between the neck and the belly. 2. A mammary gland. 3. Something like the human breast.

breath (breth), n. 1. An exhalation or emanation. 2. Air inhaled and exhaled in respiration; a single respiration. 3. A very slight breeze.

breath'less (breth'les), a. Holding the breath from fear, expectation, or intense interest.

breeze (brez), n. A gentle wind.

brew (broo), v.t. 1. To prepare, as beer, by steeping and fermentation, or infusion and fermentation. 2. To foment; plot. —v.i.

brib'er-y (-i), n.; pl. -ERIES (-z). Act or practice of giving or taking bribes.

brick (brik), n. 1. A building and paving material made from clay molded into blocks and baked in the sun or by fire; also, one of these blocks. 2. Any of various oblong rectangular masses.

brid'al (brid'al), n. A wedding. — a. Of or pertaining to a bride or a wedding; nuptial.

bride (brid), n. A woman newly married, or about to be married.

bridge (brij), n. 1. A structure erected over a depression or an obstacle, as a river, railroad, etc., carrying a passageway.

bri-gade' (bri-gad'), n. 1. Mil. A body of troops consisting of two or more regiments. 2. Any body of persons organized to act or march together.

bright'en (-'n), v.t. & i. to make or grow bright.

bril'liance (bril'yans), n. Brilliancy.

bril'lian-cy (-yan-si), n. Quality or

state of being brilliant; glitter; great brightness.

brim (brim), n. 1. Edge or margin; brink; border. 2. Rim or upper edge of a dish or other vessel. 3. The projecting edge or rim of a hat. — v.t. & i.; BRIMMED (brimd); BRIM'MING. To fill, or be full, to the brim.

bring (bring), v.t. 1. To convey from a more distant to a nearer place. 2. To procure in or as in exchange; fetch; produce.

brit'ish (brit'ish), a. Of or pert. to Great Britain or its inhabitants. — n. 1. Language of the ancient Britons. 2. The people of Great Britain.

brit'tle (brit'l), a. Breaking easily and suddenly, like glass; fragile. — -**ness**, n.

broad (brod), a. 1. Wide; extended in breadth. 2. Spacious, vast. 3. Clear; full. 4. Plain; evident; obvious.

broad'cast (-kast'), n. A casting of seed in all directions. — a. Cast or scattering in all directions; widely diffused. — adv. So as to spread widely.

broad'cloth (-kloth), n. A kind of fine smooth woolen cloth, usually of double width.

broad'en (-'n), v.i. & t. To grow, or to make, broad.

broad'side' (brod'sid'), n. 1. Naut. The side of a ship above the water line, from bow to quarter. 2. A broad surface.

bro-cade' (bro-kad'), n. Silk stuff woven with gold and silver threads, or ornamented with raised flowers, foliage, etc. — **bro-cad'ed** (-kad'ed), p.a.

broil, v.t. 1. To cook by direct exposure to heat over a fire. 2. To subject to great heat. — v.i. To be subjected to heat, as meat over the fire. — n. Act of broiling; also, something broiled.

bro'ken (bro'k'n), p.a. 1. a Violently separated or fractured; sundered. b Subdued; crushed. c Violated, as a vow.

bro'ker (bro'ker), n. A dealer in money, notes, drafts, stocks, etc.

bronze (bronz), n. 1. An alloy chiefly of copper and tin. 2. A statue, bust, or the like, of bronze. 3. Yellowish or reddish brown; bronze color. — v.t. To give the appearance of bronze to.

brooch (broch; brooch), n. An ornamental clasp.

brook (brook), n. A natural stream of water smaller than a river or creek.

broom (broom), n. 1. Any of several European shrubs. 2. An implement for sweeping.

broth (broth), n. Liquid in which flesh (or, sometimes, barley or rice) has been boiled; thin soup.

browse (brouz), n. 1. Tender shoots or twigs, fit for food of cattle; green food. 2. A browsing. — v.t. 1. To eat or nibble off, as tender branches.

bruise (brooz), v.t. 1. To injure, as by a blow, without laceration; contuse. 2. To batter or indent, as with the fists. 3. To break, as in a mortar; crush; triturate. — v.i. To fight with the fists. — n. An injury without laceration, as from a blow with a blunt or heavy instrument; a contusion.

bru-net' (broo-net'), a. Having brown or olive skin and dark hair and eyes. — n. A brunet person.

brush (brush), n. 1. An implement composed of bristles, or the like, set in a back or handle. 2. The bushy tail of some animals, esp. of the fox.

brute (broot), a. 1. Irrational; unthinking. 2. Without life or sensibility; inanimate; soulless. 3. Brutal; savage; coarse; sensual.

bub'ble (bub'l), n. 1. A thin film of liquid inflated with air or gas. 2. A small body of air or gas within a liquid or a transparent solid.

buck'et (-et), n. 1. A vessel for drawing, holding, or carrying something, as water, coal, etc. 2. The quantity a bucket will hold.

buck'le (-l'), n. 1. A certain device for uniting two loose ends, as of a belt or strap.

buck'shot' (-shot'), n. A coarse leaden shot.

buck'wheat' (-hwet'), n. An herb much cultivated for its triangular seeds, which are ground into flour. Also, the seed, or the flour.

bud (bud), n. 1. Bot. An undeveloped shoot or stem consisting of rudimentary foliage or floral leaves.

buf-fet' (boo-fa'; F. bu'fe'),n. 1. A cupboard or set of shelves for displaying silver, china, etc. 2. A counter for refreshments; a restaurant.

bus'y (biz'i), a. 1. Engaged in some business; hard at work. 2. Constantly or actively at work; active.

but (but), prep. & conj. 1. Outside of; without; except; save; that.

butch'er (booch'er), n. 1. One whose business is to slaughter animals, or dress their flesh, for market; a dealer in meat. 2. One who kills in large numbers or brutally. — v.t.

but'ter (but'er), n. 1. The fatty substance got from milk or cream by agitation, as by churning.

but'tock (but'uk), n. The part at the back of the hip; in pl., rump.

buzz (buz), v.i. To make a low, continuous, humming sound, as that made by bees.

C

cab'bage (kab'aj), n. A common vegetable; one of the heads.

cab'in (-in), n. A small house.

cab'i-net (kab'i-net), n. 1. A case, set of drawers, or cupboard. 2. A body of advisers.

ca'ble (ka'b'l), n. 1. A strong rope.

ca-boose' (ka-boos'), n. 1. A car on a train.

cack'le (kak'l), v.i. 1. To make the sharp, broken noise of a hen. 2. To laugh or chatter with a noise like a hen's cackle. —n. Act or noise of cackling; idle talk.

cake (kak), n. 1. A sweetened mixture of flour and other ingredients baked in a loaf or mass.

cal'ci-um (-si-um), n. A soft silver-white metal.

cal'cu-late (-lat), v.t. 1. To compute; estimate. 2. To adjust, adapt, or fit for a purpose. — v.t. To count or rely.

cal'cu-la'tion (-la'shun), n. 1. Act, process, or result of calculating. 2. A forecast.

calf (kaf), n.; pl. CALVES (kavz). The fleshy part of the leg below the knee.

call'ing (kol'ing), n. 1. Act of one that

calls; as; a A crying aloud. b An invitation. 2. Vocation.

cal'lous (kal'us), a. 1. Hardened. 2. Insensible.

calm (kam), n. Freedom from motion or disturbance. — v.t. To make or become calm. — a. 1. Not stormy; serene. 2. Tranquil.

cam'el (kam'el), n. Either of two large animals used in the desert regions of Africa and Asia to carry burdens and ride upon.

ca-mel'li-a (ka-mel'i-a; -mel'ya), n. A greenhouse shrub with red or white roselike flowers.

cam'er-a (per-a), n. A chamber. 2. An apparatus for taking photographs.

cam-paign' (kam-pan'), n. 1. A series of military operations forming a distinct stage in a war. 2. Any similar undertaking. —v.i. To serve in, or go on, a campaign.

cam'pus (kam'pus), n. The grounds of a college or school.

can, n. A vessel of sheet metal of various forms. — v.t.; CANNED (kand); CAN'NING. To put in a can or cans.

Ca-na'di-an (ka-na'di-an). a. Of or pertaining to Canada or her people. — n. A native of Canada.

ca-nal' (ka-nal'), n. An artificial channel filled with water for navigation, irrigation, etc.

ca-na'ry (ka-na'ri), n.; pl. -RIES (-riz). 1. A canary bird. 2. A light yellow color.

can'cel (kan'sel), v.t. 1. To cross and deface; to annul.

can'did (kan'did), a. 1. Fair. 2. Open.

can'died ('did), p.a. 1. Preserved in or with sugar, as fruit. 2. Converted into sugar or candy.

can'dle (kan'd'l), n. A slender rounded body of tallow, wax, or the like, containing a wick, burned to give light.

can'dor (kan'der), n. Frankness.

can'dy (-di), n.; pl. -DIES (-diz). A preparation, usually flavored, made of sugar or molasses boiled down and crystallized.

cane (kan), n. 1. Bot. Any hollow or pithy jointed stem, usually slender and more or less flexible. 2. A walking stick.

ca-nine' (ka-nin'), a. 1. Of or

pertaining to the family consisting of the dogs, wolves, jackals, and foxes. 2. Anat. Pertaining to or designating the pointed tooth next to the incisors, or one of like shape.

can'is-ter (kan'is-ter), n. 1. A small box or case for tea, coffee, etc.

can'ker (kan'ker), n. 1. A corroding or sloughing ulcer. 2. A cankerworm. — v.t. To eat away.

can'on (kan'un), n. 1. A law or rule of church doctrine or discipline. 2. A general rule, law, or truth.

can'on-ize (kan'un-iz), v.t. To declare (a deceased person) a saint.

can'o-py (-o-pi), n.; pl. -PIES (-piz). 1. A covering fixed over a bed, dais, or the like. 2. An over-hanging shelter or shade.

can'ta-loupe (kan'ta-loop), n. A variety of muskmelon having a hard furrowed rind and orange flesh; loosely, any muskmelon.

can-teen' (kan'ten'), n. 1. A sort of shop connected with a military post for supplying extra provisions to the enlisted men. 2. A small vessel or flask used for carrying liquids.

can'vass (-vas), v.t. To go through (a district), or to (persons), in order to solicit orders, votes, etc.

cap (kap), n. 1. A brimless covering for the head. 2. Anything like, or suggestive of, a cap. — v.t.; CAPPED (kapt); CAP'PING. To cover with or as with a cap.

ca'pa-ble (ka'pa-b'l), a. 1. Able to receive. 2. Competent.

ca-pac'i-ty (-pas'i-ti), n.; pl. -TIES (-tiz). 1. Power of receiving or containing. 2. Active mental power.

ca'per (ka'per), v.i. To leap or jump about in a sprightly way. —n. Skip.

cap'i-tal (kap'i-tal), a. 1. Involving, or punishable with, death. 2. Of primary importance. 3. Chief, in a political sense. 4. Of first-rate quality.

cap'i-tal-ist, n. One who has capital.

Cap'i-tol (kap'i-tol), n. The edifice at Washington in which Congress holds its sessions; also [often l.c.], a statehouse.

ca-pit'u-late (ka-pit'u-lat), v.i. Make terms of surrender.

ca-price' (ka-pres'), n. An abrupt change in feeling, opinion, or action

due to a whim or fancy.

cap'tain (-tin), n. A chief or leader.

cap'tion (-shun), n. The heading of a chapter, section, page, or article.

cap'ti-vate (-ti-vat), v.t. To acquire ascendancy over by art or attraction.

cap'tive (kap'tiv), n. A prisoner. — a. Made or held prisoner.

cap'ture (-tur), n. 1. Act of seizing by force or stratagem. 2. Thing captured. — v.t. To seize by force.

carbon dioxide. A heavy colorless and odorless gas.

car'cass (-kas), n.; pl. -CASSES (-ez). A dead body.

card (kard), n. 1. A playing card. 2. pl. A game or games played with cards.

car'di-ac (kar'di-ak), a. Anat. Of, pertaining to, or situated near, the heart.

care'ful (kar'fool), a. Taking care or heed; cautious.

care'less (-les), a. Free from care; inattentive.

ca-ress' (ka-res'), n. An act of endearment. — v.t. To fondle; pet.

car'go (kar'go), n. The freight of a ship or other vessel.

car'nage (-naj), n. Slaughter.

car'nal (-nal), a. Animal; fleshly.

car'ni-val (kar'ni-val), n. Any merrymaking, feasting, etc.

car-niv'o-rous (kar-niv'o-rus), a. Eating flesh.

car'ol (kar-ul), n. A song, usually of joy or mirth. — v.i. To sing, esp. joyfully. — v.t. To praise or celebrate in song.

ca-rouse' (-rouz'), n. A drinking match or bout. — v.i. To drink deeply.

car'pen-ter (-pen-ter), n. An artisan who frames and builds houses, ships, etc.

car'riage (kar'ij), n. 1. Act of carrying. 2. The price or expense of carrying. 3. Manner of carrying one's body or self.

carte' blanche' (kart' blansh'). Unconditional terms of power.

car-toon' (kar-toon'), n. A pictorial caricature. — v.t. To make a cartoon of.

carve (karv), v.t. 1. To cut; sculpture. 2. To cut into pieces or slices, as meat at table. — v.i. To cut up meat, as at table.

cas-cade' (kas-kad'), n. A fall of water over a precipice.

case (kas), n. 1. An instance. 2. Condition.

cash (kash), n. 1. Money. 2. Money or its equivalent paid promptly after purchasing. — v.t. To pay or receive cash for.

cas'ket (kas'ket), n. 1. A small chest or box, as for jewels. 2. A coffin, esp. an expensive one.

cast (kast), v.t.; pref. & p.p. CAST; p.pr. & vb. n. CAST'ING. 1. To throw. 2. To project. 3. To deposit or place.

cas'tle (kas'l), n. 1. A large fortified building or set of buildings; fortress.

cas'trate (kas'trat), v.t. To geld.

cas'u-al (kazh'u-al; kaz'-), a. 1. Happening without design and unexpectedly. 2. Coming without regularity. 3. Having the air of a chance occurrence.

cat'a-ract (-rakt), n. 1. A waterfall. 2. A flood. 3. Med. A disease of the eye, characterized by opacity of the lens.

catch'ing, p.a. 1. That catches. 2. Captivating.

cat'e-chism (kat'e-kiz'm), n. 1. Instruction by question and answer. 2. A book containing a summary of principles, esp. religious, in the form of questions and answers.

ca-the'dral (ka-the'dral), n. Designating, or pert. to, the bishop's church, which is the head church of a diocese. — n. The head church of a diocese; improperly, any large church.

cau'cus (ko'kus), n. A meeting of the members or leaders of a party or faction to decide on policies or candidates to be supported.

cau-sa'tion (-za'shun), n. 1. Act of causing. 2. Causality.

cause (koz), n. 1. That which produces an effect or result. 2. The person or thing that brings about or does something.

cau'ter-ize (ko'ter-iz), v.t. To burn or sear with or as with a cautery or caustic.

cau'tion (shun), n. 1. A warning against evil. 2. Cautiousness. — v.t. To warn.

cau'tious (ko'shus), a. Wary.

cave (kav), n. Cavern; den. — v.t. To hollow out.

cease (ses), v.i. To stop. — v.t. To discontinue.

ce'dar (se'der), n. Any of various trees, chiefly of the pine family, having fragrant, durable wood.

ceil'ing, n. The lining of a room, esp. that overhead.

ce-les'tial (se-les'chal), a. 1. Of or pertaining to the sky. 2. Divine.

cell (sel), n. A small hollow receptacle, as in a honeycomb.

cel'lar (sel'er), n. A room or set of rooms below the surface of the ground.

ce-ment' (se-ment), n. 1. A substance used in a soft state to join bricks in building, cover floors, etc., which afterwards becomes hard like stone. v.t. To unite by, or overlay with, cement.

cent (sent), n. 1. A hundred. 2. The 100th part of the unit in various monetary systems, or a coin of this value.

cen'ter (sen'ter), n. 1. Middle point of a circle or sphere. 2. Middle or central point or part of anything.

cen'tral (-tral), a. Relating to the center.

cen'tu-ry (sen'tu-ri), n.; pl. -RIES (-riz). A period of 100 years.

cer'e-mo'ni-al (ser'e-mo'ni-al), a. Of or pertaining to ceremony; characterized by, or of the nature of, ceremony. — n. 1. A system of rules and ceremonies, as in worship; ritual. 2. A ceremonial usage or formality; a rite. — **cer'e-mo'ni-al-ly** (ser'e-mo'ni-al-i), adv.

cer'e-mo-ny (ser'e-mo-ni), n.l pl. -MONIES (-niz). 1. A formal act or series of acts, often symbolical, prescribed by law, custom, or authority in matters of religion, of state, etc.

cer'tain (sur-tin), a. 1. Fixed. 2. Reliable. 3. Not to be doubted or denied. 4. Sure. 5. One or some specific thing or person not further described.

cer-tif'i-cate (sur-tif'i-kat), n. A certified statement.

ces-sa'tion (se-sa'shun), n. A stop.

chair (char), n. A movable single seat with a back.

chalk (chok), n. 1. Min. A soft limestone composed of certain minute sea shells. 2. Chalklike material; a piece of such material.

cham'ber (cham'ber), n. 1. A room in a house; esp., a bedroom. 2. pl. Rooms for single persons in a lodging house or tenement, or arranged in sets for offices, etc. 3. A hall for deliberative meetings.

cham-pagne' (sham-pan'), n. A white sparkling wine made in the old province of Champagne, France; also, any wine of this type.

cham'pi-on (cham'pi-un), n. 1. Defender. 2. One acknowledged supreme. —v.t. To attend or defend as champion.

chan'de-lier' (shan'de-ler'), n. A branched candlestick, lamp stand, gas fixture, or the like.

change (chanj), v.t. 1. To alter by substituting something for, or by giving up for something else. 2. To give and take reciprocally; exchange. 3. To make different; turn; convert. — v.i.

change'a-ble (chan'ja-b'l), a. 1. Capable of changing. 2. Appearing different in different lights or circumstances.

chan'nel (chan'el), n. 1. The bed of a natural stream. 2. The deeper part of a waterway.

cha'os (ka'os), n. Any confused state of things.

chap'ter (chap'ter), n. 1. A main division of a book, treatise, or the like.

char'ac-ter (kar'ak-ter), n. 1. A distinctive mark. 2. A symbol used in writing or print.

char'coal' (char'kol'), n. Carbon made from vegetable or animal substance; esp., coal made by charring wood in a kiln, retort, etc.

charge (charj), v.t. 1. To load; lade; to task or load (with) mentally. 2. To place a charge, as of powder, electricity, or gas within or upon.

char'i-ta-ble (char'i-ta-b'l), a. 1. Liberal in benefactions. 2. Of or pertaining to charity. 3. Forgiving.

char'i-ty (-ti), n.; pl. -TIES (-tiz). 1. Christian love and benevolence. 2. Liberality in judging men or actions. 3. Good will to the poor. 4. Whatever is given to the needy.

charm (charm), n. 1. The reciting of a magic verse. 2. Amulet. 3. That which fascinates.

charm'ing, pa. Fascinating.

char'ter (char'ter), n. 1. An instrument in writing from the sovereign power of a state or country, granting or guaranteeing rights. 2. A writing from the authorities of an order or society creating a lodge or branch.

chase (chas), v.t. & i. 1. To cause to flee. 2. To hunt. — n. 1. Act of chasing or pursuing; hunting. 2. That which is hunted.

chaste (chast), a. 1. Virtuous; modest. 2. Pure in design and expression.

chat (chat), v.i. CHAT'TED; CHAT'TING. To talk in a light and familiar manner. — n. Light, familiar talk.

chat-ter (-er), v.i. 1. To utter rapid, inarticulate, but speechlike sounds. 2. To jabber. 3. To make a noise by rapid collisions, as the teeth. — v.t. To utter rapidly, idly, or indistinctly. — n. Act or noise of chattering.

cheap (chep), a. 1. Of small cost or price. 2. Of comparatively small value. — adv. Cheaply.

cheat (chet), n. 1. A deception. 2. A swindler. — v.t. & i. 1. To deceive.

cheek (chek), n. 1. The side of the face below the eye and above and to the side of the mouth. 2. Saucy talk.

cheer (cher), n. 1. State of mind or heart. 2. Gayety. 3. That which cheers or gladdens. 4. A shout of joy.

cheer'ful (-fool), a. Having or showing good spirits.

cheer'less (-les), a. Without cheer.

cheese (chez), n. The compressed curd of milk.

chee'tah (che'ta), n. An animal of the cat family.

chem'ist (kem'ist), n. 1. One versed in chemistry. 2. A druggist.

cher'ish (cher'ish), v.t. 1. To hold dear. 2. To harbor in the mind.

cher'ry (cher'i), n.; pl. -RIES (-iz). A common fruit tree, related to the plum; its fruit.

chess (ches), n. A well-known game played on a chessboard with pieces called chessmen.

chest (chest), n. 1. A large box for keeping valuables. 2. The place for the keeping of the money of a public institution; the fund itself. 3. The part of the body inclosed by the ribs and sternum.

chew (choo), v.t. & i. 1. To bite and grind with the teeth; masticate. 2. To meditate or plan. — n. Act of chewing; that which is chewed.

chick (chik), n. 1. A chicken, esp. a young one.

chick'en (-en), n. 1. A cock or hen.

chic'o-ry (chik'o-ri), n. A common perennial plant with bright blue flowers; its root, which is roasted and mixed with coffee.

chief (chef), n. The head or leader of any body; one in authority. — a. 1. Highest in office or rank. 2. Principal or most eminent.

chief'ly (-li), adv. 1. In the first place. 2. Mostly.

child (child), n.; pl. CHILDREN (chil'dren). 1. A baby. 2. A young person of either sex. 3. A son or daughter. 4. Any descendant.

child'hood (-hooD), n. State or time of being a child.

chill (chil), n. 1. A sensation of cold attended with convulsive shaking. 2. A moderate but disagreeable degree of cold. 3. A check to enthusiasm; discouragement. — a.

chime (chim), n. 1. Mechanical arrangement for chiming a bell or set of bells. 2. A set of bells musically attuned. — v.i.

chim'ney (chim'ni), n.; pl. -NEYS (-niz). 1. An upright flue for smoke.

chin (chin), n. The lower extremity of the face.

chi'na (chi'na), n. Porcelain ware, originally made in China. Loosely, crockery.

Chi-nese' (chi-niz'; -nes'), a. Of or pertaining to China. — n. sing. & pl. 1. A native of China. 2. The language of the Chinese.

chip (chip), v.t.; CHIPPED (chipt); CHIP'PING. 1. To cut or hew with an ax, chisel, etc. 2. To break or crack off a bit or bits of, as of a piece of crockery. — v.i. To break or fly off in bits. — n.

chip'munk (chip'munk), n. Any of many small striped rodents of the squirrel family.

chirp (churp), v.i. To make a short, sharp sound, as small birds or crickets. — v.t. To utter by chirping. — n. A short, sharp note, as of some birds.

chis'el (chiz'el), n. A tool with a cutting edge at the end of a blade, used in shaping wood, etc. — v.t. & i. To cut or work with a chisel.

chiv'al-rous (shiv'al-rus), a. Pertaining to chivalry; valiant; also, gallant; courteous; brave and generous.

chlo'rine (klo'rin; -ren), n. A poisonous, greenish yellow gas. An element.

chlo'ro-form (-ro-form), n. A colorless sweetish liquid used to produce unconsciousness. — v.t. To make insensible with chloroform.

choc'o-late (chok'o-lat), n. 1. A preparation of roasted cacao seeds, or a beverage made with it. 2. Dark brown.

choice (chois), n. 1. Act of choosing; option. 2. Best part, the pick.

choir (kwir), n. 1. An organized company of singers. 2. That part of a church appropriated to the singers.

choke (chok), v.t. 1. To suffocate. 2. To check the growth, progress, or action of.

chol'er-a (-a), n. Med. A kind of infectious, and usually fatal, disease, more fully called Asiatic cholera.

chop'stick (-stik'), n. One of two small sticks or slips of wood, ivory, etc. used by the Chinese and some others in taking food.

chore (chor), n. A small or odd job.

cho'rus (ko'rus), n. Music. a A company of singers singing in concert; choir. b The simultaneous song of a number of persons. c A composition to be sung by voices in concert.

Christ (krist), n. 1. The Messiah, whose coming was prophesied by the Jews. 2. Jesus, as fulfilling this expectation.

Chris'tian (kris'chan), n. One who believes in Jesus Christ. — a. 1. Professing, or belonging to, Christianity.

Christ'mas (kris'mas), n. An annual

festival (December 25) in memory of Christ's birth.

chrys-an'the-mum (kris-an'the-mum), n. Any of many species of perennial plants of the aster family. The cultivated species have large double flowers.

chub'by (chub'i), a. Short, plump, and round.

chuck'le (chuk'l), v.i. To laugh in a suppressed manner. — n. Act or sound of chuckling.

church'yard' (-yard'), n. The inclosure about a church often used as a burial place.

churn (churn), n. A vessel in which milk or cream is agitated in making butter. — v.t. 1. To agitate (milk or cream), in a churn. 2. To agitate violently; to make foamy by so doing. — v.i. To perform the operation of churning.

ci'der (si'der), n. The expressed juice of apples, used for drinking, making vinegar, etc.

cin'na-mon (-mun), n. 1. The aromatic bark of any of several trees of the laurel family, much used as a spice.

cir'cu-lar (sur'ku-lar), a. 1. Of or pertaining to a circle. 2. Circuitous.

cir'cu-la'tion (-la'shun), n. 1. Act of circulating. 2. The movement of the blood in the vessels of the body. 3. Circulating coin, notes, or bills.

cir'cu-la-to-ry (sur'ku-la-to'ri), a. Of or pertaining to circulation.

cir-cum'fer-ence (ser-kum'fer-ens), n. The outer boundary, or perimeter, of a circle.

cir'cum-spect (sur'kum-spekt), a. Watchful on every side.

cir'cum-vent' (-vent'), v.t. To gain advantage over by craft.

cir'cus (sur'kus), n. An inclosure for exhibition of feats by horsemen, acrobats, etc. The performers, or the performance.

ci-ta'tion (si-ta'shun), n. 1. A summons to appear before a court of justice. 2. Act of citing a passage, as from a book, or the passage cited.

cite (sit), v.t. 1. To summon before a court. 2. To quote.

cit'i-zen (sit'i-zen), n. 1. An inhabitant of a city or town. 2. A civilian.

cit'y (sit'i), n.; pl. CITIES (-iz). 1. A town, esp. a large or noted town. 2. In the United States, an incorporated municipality, variously governed.

civ'ic (-ik), a. Of or pertaining to a citizen, or a city, or citizenship; civil.

civ'i-li-za'tion (siv'i-li-za'shun), n. Act of civilizing.

claim (klam), v.t. 1. To demand as due. 2. To assert as a fact which ought to be conceded.

clair-voy'ance (klar-voi'ans), n. A power of discerning objects concealed from sight or at a distance, of reading thought, etc.

clam (klam), n. Any of various bivalve mollusks.

clam'my (-i), a. Soft and sticky; coldly damp and adhesive.

clan (klan), n. 1. A social group comprising a number of households the heads of which claim descent from a common ancestor.

clap (klap), v.i.; CLAPPED (klapt) or CLAPT; CLAP'PING. 1. To make a clatter. 2. To clap the hands in applause.

clar'i-fy (klar'i-fi), v.t. & i. To make or become pure and clear.

clar'i-net' (-net'), n. Music. A wind instrument having a bell-mouthed tube with a single reed.

clash (klash), v.i. 1. To make a clash. 2. To collide. — v.t. To strike with a clash. — n. 1. A loud noise resulting from collision. 2. Opposition.

class (klas), n. 1. A group or division of persons or things of the same rank, or having common characteristics. 2. A rank or grade of society.

clas'si-fi-ca'tion (-fi-ka'shun), n. 1. Act of classifying. 2. A systematic arrangement in classes.

clause (kloz), n. 1. A single passage of a discourse or writing; a distinct article in a formal document. 2. In grammar, a simple sentence forming part of a complex or compound sentence.

claw (klo), n. 1. A sharp nail on the finger or toe of an animal, esp. when slender and curved. 2. One of the pincerlike organs forming the end of certain limbs of lobsters, crabs, etc.

clean (klen), a. 1. Free from what

defiles; untarnished; unsoiled. 2. Habitually clean; cleanly. 3. Free from obstructions or imperfections.

clear (kler), a. 1. Free from all that dims, blurs, or obscures. 2. Clean; pure. 3. Distinctly heard, seen, or understood.

clear'ing, n. 1. Act or process of one that clears. 2. A tract of land cleared of wood, as for cultivation.

cleav'er (klev'er), n. One that cleaves, as a butcher's instrument for cutting up carcasses.

clem'en'cy (-en'si), n.; pl. -CIES (-siz). 1. Disposition to forgive and spare; leniency or an act or instance of it. 2. Mildness (of the weather, climate).

cler'i-cal (-i-kal), a. 1. Of or pert. to the clergy. 2. Of or pert. to a clerk or copyist.

cli'ent (kli-ent), n. One who consults a legal adviser or submits his cause to his management; also, one who consults any expert.

cli-en-tele' (kli-en'tel'; -tel'), n. A body of clients; clients collectively; hence, a body of customers.

cli'mate (kli-mat), n. The average condition of a place or locality as to temperature, moisture, etc.

climb (klim), v.i. & t. 1. To ascent or mount, esp. by using the hands and feet; ascend. 2. Bot. To ascend in growth by twining or by tendrils, aerial roots, etc. — n. Act of climbing; a place to be climbed.

clip, v.t. 1. To cut or cut off. 2. To curtail.

clock (klok), n. Any of various devices for measuring and indicating time; a timepiece, not intended to be carried on the person.

clod (klod), n. 1. A lump or mass. 2. The earth.

clois'ter (klois'ter), n. 1. A monastery or nunnery. 2. A covered passage, usually having one side an open arcade or colonnade. —v.t. To confine in a cloister; seclude.

close (klos), a. 1. Shut fast; closed. 2. Narrow; confined. 3. Strictly confined; guarded.

close'fist'ed (klos'fis'ted), a. Stingy.

clos'et (kloz'et), n. 1. A close small room for privacy. 2. A potentate's private chamber for counsel or

devotions. 3. A small room or recess for clothing, etc.

cloth (kloth), n.; pl. CLOTHS (klothz; kloths), except in the sense of garments, when it is CLOTHES (klothz). 1. A pliable fabric for garments. 2. pl. (CLOTHES). 3. The distinctive dress of any profession, esp. of the clergy; hence, with the, the clergy.

clothes (klothz), n. pl. 1. Covering for the body; dress. 2. Bedclothes.

clown (kloun), n. 1. A rustic; ill-bred fellow; boor. 2. The buffoon in a play, circus, etc.

cluck (kluk), v.i. To utter the call of a brooding hen. — n. The call of a hen to her chickens.

clum'sy (klum'zi), a. Without skill or grace; awkward; hence, ill-made or inappropriate.

clus'ter (klus'ter), n. A number of similar things growing or grouped together; bunch. — v.i. & t. To grow or gather in a cluster.

coach (koch), n. 1. A kind of large, close, four-wheeled carriage. 2. Colloq. a One who coaches a student. b An instructor in athletics. 3. A passenger car. — v.t. To prepare (another) for examination, or for a contest, privately.

co'a-li'tion (ko'a-lish'un), n. A union; combination; alliance.

coast (kost), n. The seashore, or land near it. — v.i. 1. To sail along a coast. 2. To slide, as on a sled, or glide, as on a bicycle, down a hill. — v.t. To sail along the coast of.

coat (kot), n. 1. An outer garment fitting the upper part of the body. 2. The natural covering of animals (as fur, hair, etc.). 3. A covering layer of anything. — v.t. To cover with a coat. — coat of arms, the heraldic emblems of a person, taken together.

coax (koks), v.t. 1. To influence by gentle courtesy, flattering, or fondling; wheedle. 2. To obtain, induce, or effect by such acts. — v.i. To coax a person; use coaxing.

cob'bler (-ler), n. 1. A mender of shoes. 2. A clumsy workman; botcher.

co'bra (ko'bra), n. A very venomous snake of the warm parts of Asia, esp. India.

cock, n. 1. The male of the common barnyard fowl or of any of various birds. 2. A weathercock.

cock'roach' (-roch'), n. A well-known nocturnal insect of flattened form.

co'coa (ko'ko), n. 1. = CACAO, 1. 2. Pulverized seeds of the cacao or the beverage from them.

co'co-nut' (-ko-nut'), n. The fruit of the coconut palm.

co-coon' (ko-koon'), n. The silky envelope in which many insects pass the pupa stage.

code (kod), n. 1. A systematic body of law; digest. 2. Any system or collection of principles or rules relating to one subject.

co-erce' (ko-urs'), v.t. To constrain or restrain by force, esp. by authority; force. — v.i. To use coercion.

cof'fee-house' (-hous'), n. A restaurant where coffee and other refreshments are served.

cof'fin (kof'in), n. A chest or case for a corpse.

co'gnac (ko'nyak), n. A superior French brandy.

cog-ni'tion (kog-nish'un), n. Act or fact of knowing; also, knowledge.

co-here' (ko'her'), v.i. To stick together; be united.

co-her'ent (-ent), a. 1. Sticking together. 2. Following logical order, connection, or arrangement; consistent.

co'in-cide' (ko'in-sid'), v.t. 1. To occupy the same place in space or the same period in time. 2. To correspond exactly; agree.

col'an-der (kul'an-der), n. A perforated vessel used as a sieve or strainer.

cold (kold), a. 1. Of a temperature sensibly lower than that of the body; chilly. 2. Deficient in emotion or cordiality. 3. Having the sensation of cold. — n.

cold'ness, n. State of being cold.

col-lab'o-rate (ko-lab'o-rat), v.i. To labor together; work or act jointly. — -ra'tor, n.

col-lapse' (ko-laps'), v.i. 1. To fall or shrink together abruptly. 2. To break down or fail abruptly. — n. An act or instance of collapsing. — **col-laps'i-ble** (-lap'si-b'l), a.

col'lar (kol'ar), n. 1. A band, chain, or the like, worn or placed round the neck for dress, restraint, etc. 2. An encircling strap or band. — v.t. To put a collar on; to seize by the collar.

col-late' (ko-lat'), v.t. To compare critically, as books or writings.

col-lat'er-al (-lat'er-al), a. 1. Subordinate; indirect. 2. Designating an obligation or security attached to another to secure its performance; hence, secured by additional obligation or security. 3. Parallel; concomitant; coordinate.

col-lect' (ko-lekt'), v.t. 1. To gather into one body or place; assemble. 2. To demand and obtain payment of, as a bill.

col-lec'tion (-lek'shun), n. 1. Act or process of collecting. 2. That which is collected; accumulation.

col-lide' (ko-lid'), v.i. To strike or dash against each other; come into collision.

co-logne' (ko-lon'), n. An aromatic toilet water.

co'lon (ko'lon), n.; pl. E. -LONS (-lonz), l. -LA (-la). Anat. That part of the large intestine extending from caecum to rectum.

colo'nel (kur-nel), n. The commanding officer of a regiment.

col'or (kul'er), n. 1. A property of visible objects, distinct from form and from light and shade, depending on the kind of light reflected from their surfaces. 2. A particular variety of the above quality; — strictly, excluding black and white.

col'or-ing, n. 1. Act of applying color, the effect so produced, or that which produces color. 2. Change of appearance, as by color.

colt (kolt), n. 1. The young of the horse. 2. One like a colt, esp. in youth and inexperience.

co'ma (ko'ma), n. A state of deep insensibility, due to disease, injury, or poison.

com'a-tose (kom'a-tos; ko'ma-), a. Relating to or like coma; lethargic.

comb (kom), n. 1. a A toothed instrument for adjusting; cleaning, or confining the hair, or for adornment. b A currycomb.

com'bat (kom'bat), v.i. To contend, as

with an opposing force; fight. — v.t.
To oppose by force, argument, etc.;
resist. — n. A fight; contest.

com'bi-na'tion (kom'bi-na'shun), n. 1.
Act or process of combining; state
of being combined. 2. A union or
aggregate made by combining one
thing with another.

com-bine' (kom'bin'), v.t. & i. To unite
or join.

com-bus'ti-ble (-bus'ti-b'l), a. 1.
Capable of combustion; inflammable. 2. Easily kindled or excited;
fiery. — n. A thing that is combustible.

com-bus'tion (-chun), n. Act or
instance of burning; chemical
combination of a substance with,
usually, oxygen so rapidly as,
generally, to produce heat and light.

come (kum), v.i.; pref. CAME (kam);
p.p. COME (kum), p.pr. & vb. n.
COM'ING (kum'ing). 1. To approach. 2. To arrive at, or appear
on, a scene of action. 3. To
approach or arrive in time,
sequence, or order; also, to
approach in kind or quality.

co-me'di-an (ko-me'di-an), n. 1. An
actor in comedy. 2. A writer of
comedy.

com'et (kom'et), n. A kind of heavenly
body, often having a long nebulous
train, or tail.

com'fort (kum'fert), n. 1. Strengthening aid; solace; consolation. 2.
State or feeling of having relief,
cheer, or consolation. 3. That which
gives or brings comfort. — v.t. To
impart strength and hope to;
console.

com'fort-a-ble (-fer-ta-b'l), a. 1.
Affording comfort. 2. In a state of
comfort.

com'ic (kom'ik), a. 1. Relating to
comedy, as distinct from tragedy. 2.
Causing mirth.

com-mand' (ko-mand'), v.t. 1. To
direct authoritatively. 2. To have at
command; have command over. 3.
To dominate in situation, as by
height. — v.t. To have or exercise
direct authority. — n.

com'man-deer' (-der'), v.t. 1. Mil. To
force into military service. 2. To
seize arbitrarily or forcibly.

com-mand'er (ko-man'der), n. 1. One

who commands; chief or leader.

com-mem'o-rate (-mem'o-rat), v.t. To
call to remembrance.

com-mence' (ko-mens'), v.i. & t. To
originate; begin.

com-mend' (-mend), v.t. 1. To
commit, intrust, or give in charge for
care or preservation. 2. To
recommend as worthy of confidence or regard. — **com-mend'a-
ble** (-men'da-b'l), a. — **com-
mend'a-bly**, adv.

com-men'su-rate (-rat), a. 1. Equal in
measure or extent; also, proportion-
ate. 2. Commensurable. — v.t. & i.
To make, or to be, commensurate.

com'ment (kom'ent, ko-ment'), v.i. To
make comments; — with on or
upon. — (kom'ent), n. 1. An
explanatory, illustrative, or critical
note on a writing book, etc.,
annotation. 2. A remark or criticism.

com'men-ta-ry (kom'en-ta'ri), n.; pl. -
RIES. A series of comments or
memorandums; exposition.

com'men-ta'tor (kom'en-ta'ter), n.
One who writes a commentary;
annotator.

com'merce (kom'ers), n. 1. Business
intercourse; the buying and selling
of commodities, esp. on a large
scale; trade. 2. Personal intercourse.

com-mer'cial (ko-mur-shal), a. Of or
pertaining to commerce.

com-mis'er-ate (ko-miz'er-at), v.t. To
feel or express sorrow or compassion for; condole with.

com-mis'sion-er (-er), n. 1. One
commissioned. 2. An officer in
charge of some department or
bureau of the public service. 3. A
member of a commission, such as
now governs many cities.

com-mit' (ko-mit'), v.t.; -MIT'TED; -
MIT'TING. 1. To give in trust;
consign. 2. To consign (for
preservation); as, to commit to
memory (also, simply, to commit).
3. To imprison.

com-mit'tee (-e), n. 1. A person to
whom some trust or charge is
intrusted. 2. A body of persons
appointed to deal with some matter.

com'mon (kom'un), a. 1. Shared
equally or similarly by two or more
individuals. 2. Of frequent occur-

rence; familiar. 3. a Ordinary. b
Below the ordinary standards.

com'mon-ly, adv. In a manner or
degree that is common; ordinarily.

com'mon-place' (-plas'), n. 1.
Anything common or trite. 2. That
which is commonplace. — a.

com-mo'tion (ko-mo'shun), n.
Disturbed or violent motion; tumult.

com-mune' (ko-mun'), v.i. 1. To
confer; converse intimately. 2. To
receive the Communion.

com-mu'ni-cate (-kat), v.t. 1. To
impart; convey. 2. To have
intercourse; be connected. 2. To
take part in the Communion;
commune. — **com-mu'ni-ca'tor** (-
ka'ter), n.

com-mu'ni-ca'tion (-kaa-shun), n. 1.
Act of communicating. 2. That
which is communicated; message.
3. Means of communicating;
passage.

com-mun'ion (-mun'yun), n. 1. Act of
sharing; community. 2. Intercourse,
esp. intimate, between persons;
fellowship.

com-mu'ni-ty (ko-mu'ni-ti), n.; pl. -
TIES (-tiz). 1. A body of people or
animals living in the same place
under the same conditions. 2. The
body of people living in the same
locality. 3. Society at large. 4. Joint
ownership or participation.

com-mute' (ko-mut'), v.t. To exchange; substitute. — v.i. To pay in
gross, at a reduced rate, instead of
part by part.

com-pact' (kom-pakt'), a. 1. Closely
united or packed; dense, also,
arranged in narrow compass. 2.
Brief; pithy. — v.t.

com-pan'ion (kom-pan'yun), n. One
that accompanies, or is associated
with, another or others; fellow. —
v.t. To accompany.

com-par'a-tive (kom-par'a-tiv), a. 1.
Of or pertaining to comparison. 2.
Proceeding from or by comparison.

com-pare' (kom-par'), v.t. 1. To
represent as similar; liken. 2. To
examine in order to discover
resemblances or differences.

com-par'i-son (-par'i-sun), n. 1. Act of
comparing. 2. A relation between
things which admits of their being
compared.

com-part'ment (-part'ment), n. One of
the parts into which an inclosed
space is divided; a separate
division, as of a structure.

com'pass (kum'pas), n. 1. Boundary.
2. An inclosed space; limits;
bounds; esp., moderate bounds.

com-pas'sion (kom-pash'un), n.
Literally, suffering with another;
sympathy.

com-pas'sion-ate (-un-at), a.
Disposed to pity; sympathizing.

com-pat'i-ble (kom-pat'l-b'l), a.
Capable of existing together in
harmony; congruous. — **com-pat'i-
bly**, adv.

com-pel' (kom-pel'), v.t.; -PELLED' (-
peld'); -PEL'-LING. 1. To drive or
urge irresistibly. 2. To exact;
command.

com'pen-sa'tion (kom'pen-sa'shun),
n. 1. Act or principle of compensat-
ing. 2. That which compensates;
amends.

com-pete' (-pet'), v.i. To contend in
rivalry.

com'pe-tent (-tent), a. 1. Answering
to all requirements; capable. 2.
Legally qualified or capable.

com-pile' (kom-pil'), v.t. To compose
out of existing materials, esp. from
other books or documents.

com-plain' (kom-plan'), v.i. 1. To give
utterance to grief, pain, discontent,
or the like. 2. To make accusation.

com'plai-sance' (kom'pla-zans), n.
Disposition to please; obliging
compliance.

com-plete' (kom-plet'), a. 1. Filled up;
with no part lacking. 2. Perfectly
equipped or skilled. — v.t. To bring
to entirety; finish.

com'plex (kom'pleks), a. 1. Composed of two or more parts; not
simple. 2. Complicated; intricate. —
n. A whole made up of complicated
or interrelated parts.

com-plex'ion (kom-plek-shun), n. 1.
Disposition. 2. Hue of the skin, esp.
of the face. 3. General appearance;
character.

com-pli'ance (kom-pli-ans), n. Act of
complying; yielding.

com'pli-ca'tion (-ka-shun), n. Act of
complicating; state of being
complicated; intricate or confused
relation of parts; complexity.

com'pli-ment (kom'pli-ment), n. 1. An expression of approbation, civility, or admiration. 2. A ceremonious greeting; — usually in pl.

com-ply' (kom-pli), v.i. To yield or acquiesce.

com-pos'ite (kom-poz'it; kom'po-zit), a. 1. Made up of distinct parts or elements; compounded. —n. A composite thing.

com'post (kom'post), n. A fertilizing mixture, esp. one composed of leaf mold, manure, etc.

com-pound' (kom-pound'), v.t. & i. 1. To put or unite together into a whole; mix. 2. To adjust by agreement; compromise, as a dispute, a debt.

com'pre-hend' (-pre-hend'), v.t. 1. To understand. 2. To contain; include.

com'pre-hen'sion (-shun), n. 1. Act of comprehending, containing, or comprising. 2. Power or act of grasping with the intellect; understanding.

com-press' (kom-pres'), v.t. To press or squeeze together; condense.

com'pro-mise (kom'pro-miz), n. 1. A settlement reached by mutual concessions. 2. An endangering; exposure to risk or suspicion.

com'pu-ta'tion (kom'pu-ta'shun), n. 1. Act or process of computing. 2. The amount computed.

com-pute' (kom-put'), v.t. & i. To determine by calculation; reckon.

com'rade (kom'rad; -rad), n. A companion. — **com'rad-ship**, n.

con-ceal' (kon-sel), v.t. To hide or withdraw from observation or sight; withhold knowledge of.

con-cede' (-sed'), v.t. 1. To admit to be true; acknowledge. 2. To grant, as a privilege.

con-ceit' (-set'), n. 1. Conception; personal judgment or opinion. 2. An overweening pride, vanity. 3. A fanciful, odd, or extravagant notion; a witty thought or turn of expression.

con-ceive' (-sev'), v.t. 1. To become pregnant with. 2. To imagine.

con'cen-trate (kon'sen-trat), v.t. & i. 1. To bring to or towards, or to approach, a common center; gather into one body or force. 2. To increase in strength as by reducing bulk; condense.

con'cen-tra'tion (-tra'shun), n. 1. Act of concentrating; state of being concentrated. 2. Specifically, close mental application.

con-cep'tion (kon-sep'shun), n. 1. Act of becoming pregnant. 2. The action or faculty of forming an idea of anything. 3. An image or idea.

con-cern' (-surn'), v.t. 1. To relate or belong to; to affect the interest of. 2. To engage; interest; — usually reflexive or passive. — n.

con'cert (kon'sert), n. 1. Agreement in a design or plan; simultaneous action. 2. A musical entertainment in which several voices or instruments take part.

con-ces'sion (kon-sesh'un), n. 1. Act of conceding or yielding; admission. 2. A thing yielded; acknowledgment.

con-cil'i-ate (kon-sil'i-at), v.t. To reconcile; win over from hostility.

con'clave (kon'klav), n. 1. A set of rooms in which the Roman Catholic cardinals are secluded while choosing a pope. 2. The meeting of cardinals to choose a pope. 3. A private meeting.

con-clude' (kon-klood'), v.t. 1. To bring to an end; close; finish. 2. To come to a conclusion. 3. To bring about as a result; effect. — v.i. To terminate.

con-clu'sion (kno-kloo-zhun), n. 1. The last part of anything; end. 2. Final decision; outcome. 3. The summing up of a discourse.

con-coct' (kon-kokt'), v.t. To prepare, as food, by combining ingredients; to make up, as a story.

con-cord'ance (kon-kor'dans), n. 1. Agreement; harmony; as, concordance of opinion. 2. An alphabetical index of the principal words in a book, citing the passages in which they occur.

con-cur'rent (-ent), a. 1. Running together; existing or happening at the same time. 2. Agreeing; cooperating.

con-demn' (-dem'), v.t. 1. Censure. 2. To pronounce guilty; to sentence; doom.

con-dense' (kon-dens'), v.t. & i. Compress; concentrate.

con'de-scend' (kon'de-send'), v.i. To

stoop or descend; waive the privilege of rank or dignity.

con'di-ment (kon'di-ment), n. A relish; seasoning.

con-di'tion (kon-dish'un), n. 1. Prerequisite. 2. Qualification. 3. Social estate; rank. 4. State of being fit, as for work. — v.t.

con-do'lence (-do'lens), n. Expression of sympathetic sorrow or grief.

con-done' (kon'don'), v.t. To forgive (an offense).

con'duct (kon'dukt), n. 1. Guidance. 2. Management; direction. 3. Behavior.

con-duc'tion (-duk'shun), n. 1. Transmission, as of heat or electricity.

con-fec'tion (-fek'shun), n. 1. A making by combining ingredients. 2. A sweetmeat; preserve.

con-fed'er-a-cy (-fed'er-a-si), n.; pl. -CIES (-siz). 1. Alliance. 2. Confederation.

con-fer' (-fur), v.t.; -FERRED' (-furd'); -FER'RING. 1. To grant; bestow. 2. To compare; — v.i. To converse; deliberate.

con'fer-ence (kon'fer-ens), n. 1. Act of conferring; serious consultation or discussion. 2. A meeting for consultation or discussion.

con-fes'sion (-fesh'un), n. 1. Act of confessing. 2. What one confesses.

con-fide' (kon'fid'), v.i. Trust. — v.t. 1. To tell or impart confidentially. 2. Commit.

con'fi-dence (kon'fi-dens), n. 1. Act of confiding; trust. 2. State of feeling sure. 3. Relation or state of trust or intimacy.

con'fi-den'tial (-den'shal), a. 1. Communicated in confidence; secret. 2. Indicating close intimacy. 3. Enjoying, or treated with, confidence. — **con'fi-den'tial-ly**, adv.

con-fig'u-ra'tion (kon-fig'u-ra'shun), n. Relative disposition of parts; contour.

con-fine' (kon-fin'), v.t. 1. To restrain within limits; restrict.

con-firm' (-furm'), v.t. 1. To establish. 2. To sanction. 3. To administer the rite of confirmation to. 4. To corroborate.

con-flict' (kon'flikt'), v.i. To contend; fight; be contradictory.

con'flict (kon'flikt), n. 1. A strife; fight; esp. a prolonged contest. 2. Opposing action.

con-form' (-form'), v.t. To make like; bring into harmony or agreement, as with law. — v.i. 1. To be in accord or harmony. 2. To be a conformist.

con-front' (kon-frunt'), v.t. 1. To face, esp. hostilely; oppose. 2. To cause to face or meet.

con-fuse' (-fuz'), v.t. 1. To perplex. 2. To throw into disorder. 3. To mistake for another.

con-gen'ial (kon-jen'yal), a. 1. Kindred; sympathetic. 2. Naturally adapted; agreeable.

con-gest' (kon-jest'), v.t. 1. To cause overfullness of the blood vessels of (an organ or part). 2. To make overcrowded. — v.i. To become congested.

con-grat'u-late (-grat'u-lat), v.t. To address with expressions of pleasure at some event happily affecting the person addressed; felicitate.

con-grat'u-la'tion (-la'shun), n. A congratulating; an expression of sympathetic pleasure.

con'gre-gate (kon'gre-gat), v.t. & i. To collect into a crowd, mass, or assemblage; assemble.

con'gre-ga'tion (-ga'shun), n. 1. Act of congregating. 2. An assemblage of separate things. 3. An assembly of persons, esp. for worship.

con'gress (kon'gres), n. 1. A gathering or assembly, as of delegates or representatives. 2. [cap.] The body of senators and representatives of the United States. 3. Any similar national legislative body.

con-gru'i-ty (kon-groo'i-ti), n.; pl. -TIES (-tiz). Quality of being congruous; agreement; correspondence, also, an instance of being congruous.

con'gru-ous (kon'groo-us), a. 1. Suitable; harmonious. 2. Accordant with what is proper, reasonable, or right.

con-jec'ture (-tur), n. A guess. — v.t. Infer. — v.i. To form conjectures.

con'ju-gal (kon'joo-gal), a. Pertaining

to marriage; connubial.

con-junc'tion (kon-junk-shun), n. 1. Act of conjoining; union.

con'jure (kun'jer), v.i. to summon or command a devil, spirit, etc., by invocation or a spell; practice magic; juggle. — v.t.

con-nect' (ko-nekt'), v.t. To join together. —v.i. To join, unite, or cohere.

con-nec'tion (-nek'shun), n. 1. Act of connecting; union, relationship. 2. A continuity or coherence of words or ideas. b Context. c Relation of things mutually involved. 3. That which connects; bond; tie. 4. A person connected with others by some tie.

con-nive' (-niv'), v.i. 1. To feign ignorance. 2. To have a secret understanding (with).

con'nois-seur' (kon'i-sur'; -sur'), n. One competent to act as a critical judge of an art.

con'quer (kon'ker), v.t. 1. Vanquish; overcome. 2. Win. — v.i. To be victorious. — a.

con'science (kon'shens), n. Consciousness of the moral goodness or badness of one's own conduct or motives, together with a feeling of obligation to do or be good.

con'sci-en'tious (-shi-en'shus), a. 1. Influenced by conscience. 2. Done according to conscience.

con'scious (kon'shus), a. 1. Aware or sensible. 2. Self-conscious. 3. Mentally awake. 4. Involving consciousness of something.

con-sec'u-tive (kon-sek'u-tiv), a. Following in regular order; with no interval; successive.

con-sen'sus (kon-sen'sus), n. Agreement in opinion, custom, or function.

con-sent' (-sent'), v.i. 1. To agree together. 2. To give approval.

con'se-quence (kon'se-kwens), n. 1. Result. 2. Importance; value.

con-serv'a-tive (-tiv), a. 1. Preservative. 2. Tending or disposed to maintain existing institutions or views; opposed to change or innovation. — n. A conservative person or thing.

con-sid'er (kon-sid'er), v.t. & i. 1. To think. 2. To heed or regard. 3. To view; look upon.

con-sid'er-a-ble (-a-b'l), a. 1. Worthy of consideration; of importance. 2. Rather large in amount, extent, etc. — -a-bly, adv.

con-sid'er-ate (-at), a. Thoughtful of consequences; careful, esp. of others' rights, feelings, etc.

con-sign' (-sin'), v.t. 1. To give or transfer, formally. 2. To intrust.

con-sist' (kon-sist'), v.i. To be composed or made up (of).

con-sist'en-cy (-ten'si), n.; pl. -ENCIES. 1. Firmness or degree of firmness. 2. Harmony.

con-sole' (-sol'), v.t. To cheer in distress or depression.

con-sol'i-date (kon-sol'i-dat), v.t. & i. To make or become solid; bring or come into close union. — **con-sol'i-da'tor** (-da'ter), n.

con'so-nant (-nant), a. 1. Having agreement; consistent. 2. Harmonizing.

con'sort (kon'sort), n. 1. Spouse.

con-spic'u-ous (-spik'u-us), a. Obvious to the eye or mind; striking; remarkable.

con-spir'a-cy (-spir'a-si), n.; pl. -CIES (-siz). Act of conspiring; combination for an evil purpose.

con-spire' (-spir'), v.t 1. To make an agreement to do something wrong; plot together. 2. Agree. — v.t. To plot.

con-stant (-stant), a. 1. Firm or steadfast; true. 2. Unchanging. — n. That which is unchanging or invariable.

con'stel-la'tion (kno'ste-la'shun), n. Any of various arbitrary groups of fixed stars.

con'sti-pa'tion (-pa'shun), n. A state of the bowels in which evacuations are infrequent and difficult.

con-stit'u-ent (-ent), a. 1. Component. 2. Having power to elect or appoint. — n.

con'sti-tute (kon'sti-tut), v.t. 1. To appoint to the office or function of. 2. To set up.

con-strain' (kon-stran'), v.t. 1. To force. 2. Confine; restrain.

con-straint' (-strant') n. 1. Compulsion. 2. Repression.

con-struct' (-strukt'), v.t. To build; devise.

con-struc'tion (-struk'shun), n. 1. Process or art of constructing; composition; structure. 2. Form or manner of constructing.

con'sul (kon'sul), n. A government official residing in some foreign country to care for the commercial interests of the citizens of his government.

con-sult' (kon-sult'), v.i. To confer. — v.t. 1. To ask the advice or opinion of. 2. To have regard to; consider.

con'sum-mate (kon-sum'at), a. Complete; perfect.

con-sump'tion (kon-sump'shun), n. 1. Act or process of consuming. 2. Progressive wasting of the body, esp. from pulmonary tuberculosis.

con'tact (kon'takt), n. A touching or meeting of bodies.

con-ta'gious (-jus), a. Communicable or spreading by contagion.

con-tain' (-tan'), v.t. 1. To include. 2. To be equivalent to.

con-tam'i-nate (-tam'i-nat), v.t. To soil, stain, or corrupt by contact.

con'tem-plate (kon'tem-plat), v.t. 1. To view or consider with continued attention. 2. To look forward to; purpose. — v.i. To ponder.

con-tem'po-ra-ry (-tem'po-ra'ri), a. 1. Living, occurring, or existing at the same time. 2. Of the same age. — n.; pl. -RIES (-riz). One contemporary with another.

con-tempt' (-tempt'), n. 1. Act of condemning or despising. 2. State of being despised. 3. Law. Willful disobedience to, or open disrespect of, a court of justice.

con-tend' (-tend'), v.i. To strive in opposition or rivalry; also, to strive in debate. — v.t. To maintain; assert.

con-test' (kon-test'), v.t. 1. To contend about or for. 2. To strive earnestly to gain, hold, or maintain. — v.i. To engage in contention.

con'text (kon'tekst), n. The part or parts of a discourse that precede, follow, or are intimately associated with any particular passage or word and determine its meaning.

con'ti-nent (-nent), n. 1. A continuous extent or mass, esp. of land. 2. One of the grand divisions of land on the globe.

con-tin'gent (-jent), a. 1. Possible. 2. Happening from unforeseen causes. 3. Conditional. — n. That which falls to one in a division or apportionment; quota.

con'tour' (kon'toor'), n. The outline of a figure or body.

con'tra-band (-band), n. 1. illegal or prohibited traffic. 2. Contraband or smuggled goods. — a. Prohibited or excluded by law or treaty.

con'tract (kon'trakt), n. An agreement between parties to do or forbear something; covenant.

con'tra-dict' (kon'tra-dikt'), v.t. To assert the contrary of. — v.i. To oppose in words.

con'tra-ry (kon'tra-ri), a. 1. Opposed. 2. Unfavorable.

con'trast (kon'trast), n. 1. Opposition or unlikeness of associated things or qualities.

con-trib'ute (kon-trib'ut), v.t. To give in common with others. —v.i. To lend aid to a common purpose.

con'tro-ver'sy (kon'tro-vur'si), n.; pl. -SIES (-siz). Dispute; debate.

con'va-les'cence (-les'ens), n. Recovery of health after disease.

con-ven'ience (kon-ven'yens), n.; pl. -CES (-sez). 1. State or quality of being convenient. 2. Ease.

con-ven'ient (-yent), a. Suited to or affording ease, comfort, or advantage; saving trouble.

con'vent (kon'vent), n. 1. A community of recluses, as monks, friars, or nuns, devoted to a religious life. 2. A monastery or nunnery.

con-ven'tion (kon-ven'shun), n. 1. Act of convening. 2. A body of persons met for a common purpose. 3. Agreement.

con-verge' (kon-vurj'), v.i. To incline and approach nearer together. — v.t. To cause to converge.

con'ver-sa'tion (-sa'shun), n. Familiar talk or discourse.

con-verse' (kon-vurs'), v.i. To talk.

con-vert' (-vurt'), v.t. 1. To change or turn from one belief or course to another. 2. To produce spiritual conversion in (any one). 3. To transform.

con-vey' (kon-va'), v.t. 1. To carry or transport. 2. To transmit.

con-vict' (kon-vikt'), v.t. To prove or

find guilty.

con-vince' (-vins'), v.t. To persuade by argument.

con-vul'sion (-vul'shun), n. 1. A violent and involuntary contraction or series of contractions of the muscles. 2. Tumult.

cook (kook), n. One who prepares food. —v.t. 1. To prepare food by boiling, roasting, baking, broiling, etc.; prepare or treat (anything) by heat. 2. To prepare; tamper with.

cool (kool), a. 1. Moderately cold. 2. Not retaining or admitting heat. 3. Not ardent or passionate; self-possessed.

co-or'di-nate (-or'di-nat), a. Equal in rank, order, or importance. — n. 1. To make or become coordinate. 2. To adjust.

cope (kop), v.i. To contest hostilely; to contend on equal terms or with some success.

cop'per (kop'er), n. 1. A common metal, reddish, ductile, malleable, and tenacious, an excellent conductor of heat and electricity.

cop'y-right' (-rit'), n. The exclusive right for a term of years to repro-duce, publish, sell, etc., a literary or artistic work. — v.t. To secure a copyright on.

cord (kord), n. 1. A string or small rope.

cor'dial (kor'jal), a. 1. Tending to revive, cheer, or invigorate. 2. Hearty; sincere.

corn (korn), n. 1. A small, hard seed, esp. of a cereal grass, as wheat, rye, etc. 2. Grain; in the U.S. usually Indian corn; maize.

cor'ner (-ner), n. 1. The point or place where two converging lines, dies, or edges meet; angle. 2. A position from which retreat is impossible. 3. A secluded place.

cor'o-ner (kor'o-ner), n. A public officer whose duty it is to inquire, by an inquest, into any death suppos-edly not due to natural causes.

cor-po-ra'tion (-ra'shun), n. Any body consisting of one or more individu-als treated by the law as a unit.

corpse (korps), n. The dead body of a human being.

cor-ral' (ko-ral'), n. An inclosure for confining or capturing animals; also,

one for defense and security. — v.t.; -RALLED'; -RAL'LING. To confine or as in a corral; form into a corral.

cor-rect' (-rekt'), a. 1. Conforming to a just, acknowledged, or conventional standard. 2. Conforming to fact or truth. — v.t.

cor-re-spond' (kor'e-spond'), v.i. 1. to answer in character, function, amount, etc., to suit, agree, or match. 2. To have intercourse, esp. by sending and receiving letters.

cor-rob'o-rate (ko-rob'o-rat), v.t. To confirm.

cor-rode' (ko-rod'), v.t. 1. To diminish gradually by chemical action or the like. 2. To consume.

cor-rupt' (ko-rupt'), a. Changed from a state of uprightness, correctness, truth, etc., to a bad state.

cost (kost), v.i.; pref. & p.p. COST; p.pr. & vb. n. COST'ING. 1. To be of the price of. 2. To require or cause to be borne or suffered.

cos'tume (kos'tum), n. 1. Dress in general, including ornaments and the style of wearing the hair. 2. A dress of a particular period or locality, worn in the drama, etc.

cot (kot), n. A portable or small bed.

cot'tage (kot'aj), n. A small house.

cot'ton (kot'n), n. 1. A soft, white, fibrous substance composed of the hairs clothing the seeds of various plants of the mallow family. 2. The cotton plant or crop.

couch (kouch), n. 1. A structure for repose or sleep. 2. Any place for repose.

cough (kof), v.i. To expel air, or obstructing or irritating matter, from the lungs or air passages in a sudden noisy manner. —v.t.

coun'cil (koun'sil), n. 1. An assembly convened for consultation, advice, or agreement. 2. A body constituted as an advisory or legislative body.

coun'sel (-sel), n. 1. Mutual advising. 2. Advice. 3. One who gives advice.

coun'ter-feit (koun'ter-fit), a. Given or assuming the appearance of something genuine or original. — n. That which is made in imitation of something else with intent to deceive. — v.t.

coun'ter-part' (-part'), n. 1. A copy; facsimile. 2. A person closely resembling another. 3. A thing that serves to complete or complement something else.

coun'try (-tri), n.; pl. -TRIES (-triz). 1. A district. 2. An inhabited region of more or less definite limits, or the people of a region.

cou'ple (kup'l), n. 1. That which links two things together. 2. A pair. 3. A man and woman married or betrothed, or partners at a dance.

cou'pon (koo'pon), n. 1. A certificate of interest due, to be cut from transferable bonds, and presented for payment. 2. A section of a ticket, showing the holder to be entitled to something.

cou'ri-er (koo'ri-er), n. 1. A special, swift messenger.

course, v.t. To pursue.

cour'te-sy (kur'te-si), n.; pl. -SIES (-siz). 1. Politeness. 2. An act of civility or respect. 3. Favor or indulgence, as distinguished from right.

cous'in (kuz'n), n. The son or daughter of one's uncle or aunt.

cov'e-nant (kuv'e-nant), n. An agreement between two or more persons or parties. — v.i. & t. To agree.

cov'er (-er), v.t. 1. To place a covering over. 2. To hide from sight; conceal.

cow (kou), n.;pl. COWS (kouz). The mature female of any bovine animal, or of any other animal the male of which is called a bull.

cow'ard (kou'erd), a. 1. Destitute of courage. — n. A person who lacks courage.

cow'boy (-boi'), n. A cattle herder, esp. one of the mounted herdsmen of the western United States.

cow'er (-er), v.i. To stoop by bending the knees; crouch.

coy (koi), a. Reserved; shy; modest.

co'zy (ko'zi), a. Snug; comfortable.

crack (krak), v.i. 1. To make a sharp, sudden sound in or as in breaking. 2. To break with or without quite separating into parts. 3. To become cracked; — said of the voice.

crack'er (-er), n. 1. One that cracks. 2. A firecracker. 3. A thin hard biscuit.

cra'dle (kra'd'l), n. 1. A bed for a baby, usually on rockers or pivots; place

of origin. 2. Something suggestive of a baby's cradle.

craft (kraft), n. 1. Art or skill. 2. A power; faculty.

cramp (kramp), n. 1. Any of various holding devices. 2. A constraint.

cran'ber-ry (kran'ber-i), n.; pl. -RIES (-iz). The bright red, acid berry of a certain plant of the heath family; also, the plant.

cran'ny (kran'i), n.; pl. -NIES (-iz). A small, narrow opening; crevice.

crash (krash), v.t. & i. To break violently and noisily. — n. 1. A loud, sudden, confused sound. 2. Ruin; failure.

crave (krav), v.t. To long for. — v.i. To desire strongly.

crawl (krol), v.i. To creep.

cray'on (kra'on), n. 1. A stick of chalk, clay, or the like used in drawing.

craze (kraz), v.t. & i. To render or become insane. — n. 1. A mania, or temporary passion or infatuation. 2. Insanity. 3. In pottery, a crack in the glaze or enamel.

creak (krek), v.i. To make a squeaking sound. —v.t. To cause to creak. — n. The sound of creaking.

cream (krem), n. 1. The rich, oily, and yellowish part of milk. 2. A fancy dish, or sweet, made from cream, etc., or so as to resemble cream.

crease (kres), n. A line or mark made by folding any pliable substance. — v.t. To wrinkle. — v.i. To become creased.

cre-ate' (kre-at'), v.t. 1. To cause to exist.

cre-a'tive (-tiv), a. 1. Having the power or quality of creating. 2. Productive.

cre'dence (kre'dens), n. Belief.

cre-den'tial (kre-den'shal), n. 1. That which gives a title to credit or confidence. 2. pl. Testimonials accrediting a person.

cred'i-bil'i-ty (kred'i-bil'i-ti), n. Quality of being credible, or an instance of it.

cred'i-tor(-i-ter), n. One to whom money is due.

creed (kred), n. An authoritative formula, as of the essential articles of Christian faith.

creek (krek), n. 1. A small inlet or bay. 2. A stream of water, smaller than a river.

creep (krep), v.i.; CREPT (krept); CREEP'ING. 1. Crawl.

cre-mate' (kre-mat'), v.t. To burn.

cres'cent (kres'ent), n. 1. The increasing moon, or new moon, or a representation of it.

crest (krest), n. 1. A tuft, comb, or similar process on the head of a bird or animal. 2. The plume, or other decoration, worn on a helmet.

crev'ice (kre-vas'), n. A narrow opening resulting from a split or crack.

crew, n. 1. Any band or force of armed men. 2. A company. 3. Those who man a ship, collectively.

crib (krib), n. 1. A manger or rack for feeding animals. 2. A small bedstead with high sides, for a child.

crick'et, n. A kind of leaping insect.

crim'i-nal (krim'i-nal), a. 1. Involving, or of the nature of, a crime. 2. Relating to crime or its punishment. — n. One who has committed a crime.

cringe (krinj), v.i. To draw one's self together in fear or servility. — n. Servile civility.

crip'ple (krip'l), n. One who creeps, halts, or limps. — v.t. To deprive of the proper use of a limb.

cri'sis (kri'sis), n.; pl. CRISES (-sez). 1. Decisive moment; time of difficulty or danger.

crit'i-cism (-i-siz'm), n. 1. A critical judgment; esp., an unfavorable judgment or opinion; censure. 2. The art of critical judging.

cro-chet' (kro-sha'), n. A kind of knitting done with a single hooked needle. — v.t. & i.; -CHETTED' (-shad'); -CHET'ING (-sha'ing). To knit with a crochet needle or hook.

croc'o-dile (krok'o-dil), n. Any of several large, thick-skinned, long-tailed, aquatic reptiles.

crook'ed (krook'ed), a. 1. Character-ized by a crook, or curve. 2. Not straightforward. 3. False; dishonest.

cro-quet' (kro-ka'), n. A familiar game played with balls, mallets, and arches.

cross'ing, n. 1. A point of intersection. 2. A place where anything, as a street, is crossed.

crouch (krouch), v.i. 1. To bend or stoop low, with bent legs, as an animal waiting for prey, or in fear. 2. To bend servilely.

crowd (kroud), v.i. 1. To urge forward. 2. To collect in numbers. — v.t. 1. To shove or push. 2. To press, force, or thrust, as into a smaller space or time.

crown (kroun), n. 1. A royal head-dress.

cru'cial (kroo'shal), a. Of the nature of, or pertaining to, a supreme trial or final choice.

cru'ci-fix (kroo'si-fiks), n. A represen-tation of Christ on the cross.

cru'ci-fy (-fi), v.t. 1. To put to death by fastening to a cross of execution. 2. Fig., to subdue; mortify.

cru'el (kroo'el), a. 1. Disposed to give pain. 2. Causing or attended by pain, grief, or misery.

cruise (krooz), v.i. To sail about or to and fro, as for pleasure. — n. A sailing to and fro.

crumb (krum), n. 1. A small fragment or piece, as of bread. 2. A little. 3. The soft part of bread. — v.t. & i. To break into crumbs.

crum'ple (-p'l), v.t. & i. to press into wrinkles or folds. — n. A wrinkle, fold, or crease made by crumpling.

crunch (krunch), v.i. & t., To chew noisily. — n. Act or noise of crunching.

crush (krush), v.t. 1. To compress so as to bruise or squeeze out of the natural shape. 2. To reduce to fine particles by pounding or grinding.

crust (krust), n. 1. The hardened surface of bread. 2. The cover or case of a pie. 3. A hard external covering; shell. — v.t. & i. To incrust; become incrusted.

crutch (kruch), n. A staff with a crosspiece at the top, used to support the lame in walking.

cry'ing (kri'ing), p.a. That cries; hence, compelling attention.

crypt (kript), n. A vault wholly or partly under ground.

crys'tal (kris'tal), n. 1. Quartz transparent or nearly so, or a piece of it. 2. A body formed by a substance solidifying so that it has plane surfaces symmetrically arranged. 3. Glass of superior brilliancy. 4. The glass over a watch dial. — a. Clear.

cub (kub), n. The young of the fox, bear, etc.

cube (kub), n. 1. Geom. The regular solid of six equal square faces. 2. Math. The product got by taking a number or quantity three times as a factor. — v.t. To form the cube of.

cuck'oo (kook'oo) n. 1. A European bird that lays its eggs in the nests of other birds for them to hatch. 2. The call of the cuckoo.

cu'cum-ber (ku'kum-ber), n. The fruit of a vine of the same genus as the muskmelon, cultivated as a garden vegetable; also, the vine.

cud'dle (kul'l), v.t. To embrace closely. — v.i. To lie close or snug.

cue (ku), n. 1. A queue. 2. A tapering rod used to impel the balls in billiards, etc.

cuff (kuf), v.t. To strike with or as with the flat of the hand. — n. A blow so made.

cuff, n. An ornamental band covering the wrist.

cu'li-na-ry (ku'li-na-ri), a. Of, pertaining to the kitchen or cookery.

cull (kul), v.t. 1. To select. 2. To subject to culling.

cul'mi-nate (kul'mi-nat), v.i. To reach its highest altitude, point, or degree.

cul'prit ('prit), n. 1. One arraigned for a crime, as in court. 2. One guilty of a crime or a fault.

cult (kult), n. 1. Worship. 2. Devotion to a person, idea, or thing, esp. by a body of admirers.

cul'ti-vate (kul'ti-vat), v.t. 1. To prepare (land) for the raising of crops. 2. To raise, or foster the growth of (a plant), by tillage. 3. To civilize. 4. To devote time and thought to. 5. To seek the society of.

cul'ti-va'tor (kul'ti-va'ter), n. 1. One who cultivates. 2. An implement or machine to loosen the earth and kill weeds between the rows of crops.

cul'ture (-tur), n. 1. Cultivation. 2. Act of improving or developing by education, discipline, etc. 3. The enlightenment and discipline acquired by mental training.

cum'ber (kum'ber), v.t. To hinder or burden.

cum'ber-some (-sum), a. Unwieldy.

cu'mu-late (ku'mu-lat), v.t. To heap together; accumulate.

cu'mu-la-tive (-la-tiv), a. 1. Formed or increasing by additions. 2. Subject to cumulation; that is to be added to something else.

cun'ning (-ing), a. 1. Skillful. 2. Wrought with or exhibiting skill or ingenuity. 3. Crafty, sly, or artful.

cup (kup), n. 1. A small drinking vessel or its containing part. 2. A thing suggestive of a cup. 3. A drinking vessel and its contents; a cupful.

cup'board (kub'erd), n. A closet with shelves for dishes, food, etc.; a small closet.

Cu'pid (ku'pid), n. Roman Myth. The god of love, represented as a naked, winged boy with bow and arrow.

curb (kurb), v.t. 1. To guide and manage, or restrain, as with a curb. 2. To furnish with a curb, as a sidewalk. — n.

cure (kur), n. 1. Spiritual charge. 2. Medical care; method of medical treatment. 3. Act of healing, or state of being healed. 4. Means of removing disease or evil. — v.t.

cu'ri-os'i-ty (-os'i-ti), n.; pl. -TIES (-tiz). 1. Disposition, often a meddling disposition, to inquire into anything. 2. That which is curious, or fitted to excite or reward attention.

cu'ri-ous (ku'ri-us), a. 1. Careful or anxious to learn. 3. Exciting attention or inquiry.

curl (kurl'), v.t. & i. 1. To twist, bend, or form into ringlets, as the hair. 2. To form into a curved shape. — n.

cur'rant (kur'ant), n. 1. A small seedless raisin. 2. The acid berry of a shrub of the gooseberry family; also, the shrub.

cur'ren-cy (-en-si), n.; pl. -CIES (-siz). 1. State of being current; circulation, as of bank notes. 2. A circulating medium of exchange, including coin, government notes, and bank notes.

cur'rent (-ent), a. 1. Now passing, as time, belonging to the present time. 2. Passing from person to person, or from hand to hand; circulating. 3. Commonly acknowledged or accepted. — n.

curse (kurs), v.t.; CURSED (kurst) or CURST: CURS'ING. 1. To call on divine or supernatural power to send injury upon. 2. To use profanely insolent language against. 3. To bring great evil on. — v.i. To utter curses. — n.

curs'ed (kur'sed), p.a. 1. Being under a curse; damned. 2. Deserving a curse.

cur-tail' (kur-tal'), v.t. To shorten.

cur'va-ture (kur'va-tur), n. Act of curving; state of being curved; a bend.

curve (kurv), n. A curving. — v.t. & i. to bend; crook.

cush'ion (koosh'un), n. 1. A soft pillow or pad. 2. Something like a cushion. — v.t.

cus'tard (-tard), n. A sweetened mixture of milk and eggs, baked or boiled.

cus-to'di-al (kus-to'di-al), a. Relating to custody.

cus-to'di-an (-an), n. One who has custody, as of a public building; a keeper.

cus'to-dy (kus'to-di), n. 1. A keeping or guarding. 2. Judicial or penal safe-keeping. 3. State of being guarded.

cus'tom-a-ry (-a-ri), a. Agreeing with, or established by, custom; habitual.

cus'tom-er (-er), n. 1. One who regularly or repeatedly deals in business with a tradesman or business house; a purchaser.

cut (kut), v.t.; pref. & p.p. CUT; p.pr. & vb. n. CUT'TING. 1. To penetrate, divide, or sever with or as with an edged instrument. 2. To reduce. 3. To intersect.

cu'ti-cle (ku'ti-k'l), n. The epidermis.

cut'ler-y (-i), n. Edged instruments collectively.

cy'cle (si'k'l), n. 1. A period of time occupied by one round or course of events. 2. A complete course of operations returning to the original state. 3. An age; long period.

cy'clone (si'klon), n. 1. A violent storm characterized by high winds rotating about a calm center of low atmospheric pressure. 2. A tornado.

cyn'ic (sin'ik), n. One who believes human conduct to be directed

wholly by self-interest or self-indulgence.

cyn'i-cal (-i-kal), a. Of the character of a cynic; given to sneering at virtue and morality.

D

dag'ger (dag'er) n. 1. A short weapon for stabbing. 2. In printing, a mark of reference.

dai'ly (da'li), a. Happening, belonging to, done, or issued, each or every day.

dain'ty (dan'ti), n. Something that arouses favor or pleasure; now esp. a delicacy. — a. 1. Delicious to the taste; toothsome. 2. Of a delicate beauty or charm. 3. Having or showing delicate taste, esp. as to food or material comforts.

dai'ry (da'ri), n.; pl. -RIES (-riz). 1. A place, as a room or building, where milk is kept and made into butter or cheese. 2. The business of producing milk, butter, and cheese.

dam (dam), n. A bank or wall across a watercourse to keep back water.

dam'age (dam'aj), n. 1. Loss or detriment due to injury; hurt; harm. 2. pl. Law. The estimated reparation in money for detriment or injury sustained. — v.t. To harm; impair.

damn (dam), v.t. 1. To adjudge guilty; sentence; doom. Archaic. 2. To doom to eternal punishment.

damp'en (dam'p'n), v.t. 1. To depress or deaden; to damp;, as, to dampen one's ardor. 2. To make damp or moist.

dance (dans), v.i. 1. To perform a regulated and rhythmical series of movements, commonly to music. 2. To move nimbly or merrily. —v.t.

dan'druff (-druf), n. A scurf that forms on the head and comes off in small scales or particles.

dan'ger (dan'jer), n. Exposure or liability to loss, pain, or other evil; risk; also, a case or cause of such exposure or liability; in pl., perils, risks.

dan'gle (dan'g'l), v.i. 1. To hang loosely with a swinging or jerking motion. 2. To be a hanger-on or dependent; to hang about any one.

dap'per (dap'er), a. Little and active; spruce; trim; neat in dress and personal appearance.

dark, n. 1. Absence of light; darkness; dark place; time, or color. 2. State of being secret or obscure, often, underhand secrecy; also, ignorance.

dar'ling (dar'ling), n. One dearly beloved. — a. Dearly beloved; favorite.

dart (dart), n. 1. A short lance or javelin; hence, any sharp-pointed missile weapon, as an arrow. 2. A darting movement. — v.t. To throw with a sudden effort or thrust (as a dart, etc.); cast emit; shoot out. — v.i. To move like a dart; shoot rapidly along.

date, n. 1. That statement affixed to a writing, coin, etc., which specifies the time, and often the place, of making. 2. A given point or period of time.

daugh'ter (do'ter), n. 1. A human female considered with reference to her parents or either of them, or, more remotely, to any ancestor or ancestors; a female descendant; also, a woman of a given country, faith, etc. 2. A daughter-in-law.

dawn (don), v.i. To begin to grow light in the morning. 2. To begin to appear, develop, or give promise. 3. To begin to make a mental impression (on or upon); as, the fact dawned upon him. — n. 1. Daybreak. 2. First appearance; rise.

daze (daz), v.t. To stupefy with excess of light, with a blow, with cold, or with fear, grief, etc.; stun; dazzle. — n. State of being dazed.

dea'con (de'k'n), n. An officer performing varying subordinate functions in Christian churches.

dead, n. 1. One who is dead; usually, collectively (with the), those who are dead. 2. The most quiet or deathlike time. — adv.

dead'lock' (-lok'), n. A complete obstruction of action by the counteraction of persons or events.

dead'ly (-li), a. 1. Causing, or capable of causing, death. 2. Aiming or willing to destroy; implacable. 3. Like or pertaining to death; deathly.

deaf (def), a. 1. Wanting, or deprived of, the sense of hearing, wholly or in part. 2. Unwilling to hear; willfully inattentive.

deaf'-mute', n. A person both deaf and dumb.

deal, v.t. 1. To give in portions or as one's portion; distribute; apportion. 2. To deliver, as blows. —v.i.

dean (den), n. 1. In a cathedral church, or any church having a chapter of canons, the head of the chapter. 2. The chief administrative officer, under the president, of a college or university faculty or department.

death (deth), n. 1. Total cessation of life, as in animals or plants; act or fact of dying. 2. Personified [often cap.]: The destroyer of life. 3. State of being dead. 4. Anything so dreadful as to be like death. 5. Total privation or loss; extinction; annihilation. 6. Cause or occasion of loss of life.

de-bate' (-bat'), v.i. To dispute; hence, to deliberate; consider; to discuss or examine by argument. — v.t. To strive to maintain by reasoning; dispute. — n. Contention; discussion; controversy.

de-bauch' (-boch'), v.t. To lead away from purity, virtue, or excellence; corrupt; seduce.

de-bil'i-ty ('ti), n. Weakened or feeble condition; weakness; feebleness.

deb'it (deb'it), n. Bookkeeping. An entry, in an account, of something owed; also, the left-hand, or debtor, side of an account. — v.t. To charge with, or as, a debt.

debt (det), n. 1. That which is due from one to another; obligation; liability. 2. A sin; trespass.

de-ca'dence (de-ka'dens; dek'a-), n. A falling away; decay; decline.

de-cap'i-tate (-kap'i-tat), v.t. To behead.

de-cay (de-ka'), v.i. 1. To pass gradually from a sound or prosperous state to one of imperfection, adversity, or dissolution; decline; fall. 2. To decrease in numbers, volume, or intensity, or in health or vigor. 3. To rot. — n.

de-cease' (de-ses'), n. Death. — v.i. To die.

de'ceit' (-set'), n. An attempt to

deceive; disposition to deceive; a trick; fraud.

de-ceive' (-sev'), v.t. To lead into error; impose upon; mislead.

De-cem'ber(-sem'ber), n. The 12th and last month of the year, having 31 days.

de'cent (de'sent), a. 1. Suitable in words, behavior, etc.; becoming; fit; modest. 2. Moderate, but competent; hence, respectable; fairly good.

de-cep'tion (-sep'shun), n. 1. Act of deceiving; fact of being deceived. 2. That which deceives or is intended to deceive; fraud.

de-cide' (de-sid'), v.t. & i. To determine; settle; conclude.

de-ci'pher (de-si'fer), v.t. 1. To translate from secret characters, or ciphers, into intelligible terms. 2. To find out the meaning of; make out, as words partly obliterated.

de-ci'sion (-sizh'un), n. 1. Act of deciding; settlement; conclusion. 2. A report of a conclusion; as, a decision of the Supreme Court. 3. Quality of being decided; ready determination.

de-cline' (de-klin'), v.i. 1. To draw toward a close or extinction; fail; diminish; decay. 2. To bend downward; hang down. 3. To refuse; reject with thanks. — v.t.

de'com-pose' (de'kom-poz'), v.t. & i. To separate into the constituent parts; to resolve into original elements or into simpler compounds; rot; decay.

de-coy' (de-koi'), n. 1. A place into which wild fowl, esp. ducks, are enticed. 2. Anything intended to lead into a snare; lure; bait; esp., a fowl, or likeness of one, used to entice birds within gunshot. 3. One employed to lead a person into a position where he may be swindled or the like. — v.t. To lead into danger by artifice; entice.

de-cree' (de'kre'), n. An authoritative order or decision determining what is done, or is to be done; edict; law; ordinance. — v.t. & i. To command authoritatively; appoint by decree; ordain.

ded'i-cate (ded'i-kat), v.t. 1. To set apart and consecrate; devote

solemnly; as, to dedicate a church. 2. To devote, as one's self, to a duty or service. 3. To inscribe by way of compliment, a book.

de-duct' (-dukt'), v.t. To take away in numbering or calculating; subtract.

deep (dep), a. 1. Extending comparatively far below the surface; of great, or a specified, perpendicular dimension (measured downward). 2. Extending far back, or a specified distance, from the front or outer part. 3. Hard to comprehend; profound; mysterious.

de-face' (de-fas'), v.t. To destroy or mar the face or appearance of; disfigure.

de-feat' (-fet'), v.t. 1. To bring to naught; render null and void; frustrate, as hope. 2. To overcome; vanquish; overthrow. — n. Act of defeating or bringing to naught (plans, hopes, etc.); overthrow, as of an army; — opposed to victory.

de-fect' (de-fekt'), n. 1. Want of something necessary to completeness; deficiency. 2. Failing; fault; imperfection.

de-fend' (-fend'), v. 1. To repel danger or harm from; protect; uphold. 2. To oppose or resist, as a claim at law; contest.

de-fend'ant (de-fen'dant), n. One required to make answer in a legal action.

de-fense' (-fens'), n. 1. Act of defending; state of being defended. 2. That which defends or protects; guard. 3. Protecting plea; vindication; justification. 4. Law. The defendant's denial, answer, or plea.

de-fer' (-fur'), v.t. To put off; postpone; withhold. — v.i. To wait; procrastinate.

def'er-en'tial (-en'shal), a. Marked by deference.

de-fi'ance (de-fi'ans), n. 1. Act of defying. 2. Disposition to resist; contempt of opposition.

de-fi'ant (-ant), a. Full of defiance; bold; insolent.

de-fi'cient (-ent), a. Lacking some element of completeness; insufficient; defective; incomplete.

def'i-cit (def'i-sit), n. A falling short, esp. of income; deficiency; as, a deficit of a hundred dollars.

de-file'ment (-ment), n. Act of defiling; state of being defiled; pollution, uncleanness.

de-fine' (-fin'), v.t. 1. To determine the boundaries or limits of; hence, to fix clearly and authoritatively. 2. To fix the meaning of; explain; interpret.

def'i-nate (def'i-nit), a. 1. Having certain or distinct limits; fixed. 2. Having certain limits in meaning; precise, exact. 3. LImiting; determining; as, the definite article, Gram., the article the, used to designate a particular person or thing or class of persons or things.

def'i-ni'tion (-nish'un), n. 1. Act of defining; esp., act of making definite or clear. 2. Distinctness. 3. A description of a thing by its properties; an explanation of the meaning of a word or term.

de-fin'i-tive (de-fin'i-tiv), a. 1. Determinate; positive; final; express. 2. Limiting; determining; as, a definitive word. — n. A word used to define or limit the extent of the signification of a common noun, such as the definite article and some pronouns.

de-form' (-form'), v.t. 1. To distort; disfigure. 2. To deprive of beauty, grace, or perfection.

de-fraud' (-frod'), v.t. To deprive of some right, interest, or property, by deceit; cheat.

de-gen'er-ate (-at), a. Having become worse than one's kind, or one's former state; degraded; low.

de-grade' (de-grad'), v.t. 1. To reduce from a higher to a lower rank or degree; deprive of office, dignity, or position. 2. To reduce in character or reputation; debase; disgrace.

de-gree' (-gre'), n. 1. A step or station in a series; point or stage of advancement or retrogression. 2. Relative quantity, quality, or intensity. 3. Gram. One of the three grades — positive, comparative, superlative — in comparing an adjective or adverb.

de-ject' (de-jekt'), v.t. To cast down the spirits of; dishearten.

de-jec'tion (-jak'shun), n. Lowness of spirits; depression; melancholy.

de-lay' (-la'), v.t. & i. 1. To put off; postpone; defer; linger; tarry. 2. To retard; to stop, detain, or hinder for a time. — n. A putting off or deferring; stop; detention.

de-lec'ta-ble (de-lek'ta-b'l), a. Highly pleasing; delightful.

del'e-gate (del'e-gat), n. One sent and empowered to act for another; deputy; representative. — (-gat), v.t. 1. To send as one's representative; commission; depute. 2. To intrust to another's care or management; commit.

de-lib'er-ate (de-lib'er-at), a. 1. Carefully considered; not sudden or rash; as, a deliberate opinion. 2. Weighing facts and arguments; careful and slow in determining; as, a deliberate speech.

del'i-cate (del'i-kat), a. 1. Character-ized by daintiness, softness, or effeminacy; hence, tender; frail.

de-li'cious (de-lish'us), a. Affording exquisite pleasure; delightful; esp., very pleasing to the taste.

de-light' (-lit'), n. 1. A state of extreme satisfaction; joy. 2. Anything that gives delight; an object of delight. — v.t. To give delight to; please highly. — v.i. To be greatly pleased or rejoiced.

de-lin'e-ate (de-lin'e-at), v.t. 1. To sketch out; portray. 2. To set forth in words; describe.

de-lin'quen-cy (-lin'kwen-si), n. Failure, omission, or violation, of duty; offense.

de-lir'i-ous (de-lir'i-us), a. Having a delirium; raving.

de-lir'i-um (-um), n. 1. A more or less temporary state of mental distur-bance. 2. Strong excitement.

de-liv'er (de-liv'er), v.t. 1. To set at liberty; save. 2. To give or transfer; part with (to); surrender, resign. 3. To disburden (a woman) of young. 4. To give; utter; communicate; impart.

de-lude' (de-lud'), v.t. To lead from truth or into error; impose upon.

de-lu'sion (de-lu'zhun), n. 1. Act of deluding. 2. False belief; miscon-ception.

dem'a-gogue (dem'a-gog), n. An insincere politician or popular orator or leader who stirs up popular prejudice to gain office or influence.

de-mand' (de-mand'), v.t. 1. To ask or

call for with authority or peremptorily; claim as due. 2. To inquire authoritatively or earnestly; question.

de-mean' (de-men'), v.t. To debase, lower, or degrade one's self). Colloquial.

de-ment'ed (-men'ted), p.a. Insane; mad.

de-mer'it (-mer'it), n. Merit; desert; — now only in a bad sense; that which deserves blame; fault.

de-moc'ra-cy (de-mok'ra-si), n. 1. Government by the people, as in a republic.

de-mol'ish (de-mol'ish), v.t. To throw or pull down; to ruin; destroy.

de-mon'stra-tive (de-mon'stra-tiv), a. 1. Making evident; exhibiting clearly. 2. Gram. Serving to point out the thing referred to; as, a demonstrative pronoun or adjective, as this or that. 3. Given to the display of feeling or sentiment. — n. Gram. A word having a demonstrative function.

de-ni'al (de-ni'al), n. 1. Refusal to grant; rejection of a request; an instance of such denying. 2. Refusal to admit the truth, or assertion of the untruth, of a thing stated; contradiction. 3. Refusal to acknowledge; disavowal; disowning.

de-nom'i-na'tor (-na'ter), n. Part of a fraction below the horizontal line. In simple fractions it shows into how many equal parts the unit is divided.

de-note' (de-not'), v.t. 1. To mark out plainly; indicate. 2. To betoken; signify.

de-nounce' (de-nouns'), v.t. To invoke censure on; also, to inform against.

dense (dens), a. 1. Having its parts crowded together; compact; close; thick. 2. Of ignorance, etc. impenetrable; hence, of persons, stupid.

den'si-ty (den'si-ti), n. The ratio of mass to bulk or volume; ratio of the mass of any volume of a substance to the mass of an equal volume or some standard substance.

dent (dent), n. A slight depression as from a blow or pressure; indentation. — v.t. To make a dent on; indent. — v.t. to become indented.

den'tal (den'tal), a. 1. Pertaining to the teeth or to dentistry. 2. Articulated with the tip of the tongue applied to the back of the upper front teeth, or to the gum above; — said of certain consonants, as t, d, n. — n. A dental consonant.

de-ny' (de-ni'), v.t. 1. To declare not to be true; contradict. 2. To disclaim connection with or responsibility for; disown. 3. To reject as a false conception. 4. To refuse to grant or gratify, as a request, or one requesting.

de-part' (de-part'), v.i. 1. To go forth or away; leave. 2. To pass away; die. 3. To turn aside.

de-part'ment (-ment), n. 1. A part or subdivision. 2. A distinct division or course of something, as of action, study, etc.; sphere; province.

de-par'ture (de-par'tur), n. 1. A departing, or going away. 2. A setting out or beginning. 3. Death.

de-pend'ence (-dens), n. 1. State of being influenced and determined by, or of being conditional on, something else. 2. State of depending; subjection; inability to provide for one's self. 3. Reliance; assured confidence or trust. 4. That on which one depends or relies.

de-pend'ent (-dent), a. 1. Hanging down. 2. Relying on something else for support; conditioned; subordinate. — n. 1. That which depends; dependency. 2. One sustained by another, or relying on another for support or favor.

de-pict' (-pikt), v.t. 1. To represent by a picture. 2. To portray in words; describe.

de-plete (de-plet'), v.t. 1. To empty or unload, as the vessels of the body by purgation. 2. To exhaust, as of strength.

de-pop'u-late (-pop'u-lat), v.t. To deprive of inhabitants, wholly or in part.

de-port' (-port'), v.t. To banish; transport; exile.

de'por-ta'tion (de'por-ta'shun), n. Act of deporting; state of being deported; esp., the removal from a country of an alien considered undesirable.

de-pose' (de-poz'), v.t. 1. To remove

C
D

from a throne; deprive of office. 2. To say under oath, esp. by an affidavit. — v.i. To bear witness.

de-pos'it (-poz'it), v.t. 1. To lodge for sake-keeping or as a pledge; intrust; put on deposit in a bank. 2. To lay down; place, to let fall or throw down (as sedimenT). — n.

dep'o-si'tion (dep'o-zish'un; de'po-), n. Testimony under oath, esp. in writing; evidence.

de-pre'ci-ate (de-pre-shi-at), v.t. & i. To lessen in price or estimated value; also, to disparage.

de-press' (de-pres'), v.t. 1. To press down; let fall; lower. 2. To lessen the activity, value, or the like, of; make dull, as trade, etc. 3. To lower the pitch of, as the voice. 4. To sadden.

de-pres'sion (de-presh'un), n. 1. Act of depressing; state of being depressed. 2. That which is depressed or is made by depressing, as a hollow.

dep'u-ty (-ti), n.; pl. -TIES (-tiz). One appointed to act for another; a substitute in office; delegate.

de-rail' (de-ral'), v.t. To cause to run off the rails.

der'e-lict (der'e-likt), a. 1. Abandoned by the natural owner or guardian.

de-ride' (de-rid'), v.t. To laugh at with contempt; mock; taunt.

de-rive' (-riv'), v.t. 1. To receive, as from a source; obtain by descent or transmission; deduce. 2. To trace the origin, descent, or derivation of, as of a word.

de-scend' (de-send'), v.t. 1. To pass or come down from a higher to a lower place, station, scale, etc.; to come or go down. 2. To make an attack or incursion, esp. suddenly or with violence. 3. To come down, as from a source or stock; fall or pass by inheritance. —v.t. To go down upon or along.

de-scribe' (-skrib'), v.t. 1. To represent by words written or spoken; give an account of. 2. To trace or traverse the outline of.

de-scrip'tive (-tiv), a. Serving to describe; characterized by description.

des'ert (dez'ert), n. 1. A deserted region; solitary place. 2. A barren

tract almost destitute of moisture and vegetation.

de-sign' (-zin'), v.t. 1. To intend or purpose. 2. To draw in outline; sketch. 3. a To plan or devise. b To make a design or pattern for. — v.i. To produce a plan for anything.

de-sir'a-ble (-zir'a-b'l), a. Worthy of desire or longing; pleasing; agreeable.

de-sire' (de-zir'), v.t. 1. To long for; covet. 2. To express a wish for; ask. — n.

de-sist' (-zist'), v.i. To cease to act; stop.

desk (desk), n. A table, frame, or case with a slopping or a flat top for the use of writers or readers.

des'o-late (des'o-lat), a. 1. Destitute or deprived of inhabitants; deserted; hence, gloomy. 2. Land waste; in a ruinous or neglected state. 3. Left alone; forsaken. -lat), v.t. 1. To make desolate; ravage. 2. To forsake; leave along.

de-spair' (de-spar'), v.i. To be hopeless; give up hope. — n. 1. Loss of hope; hopelessness. 2. That which is despaired of, or which causes despair.

des'per-ate (des'per-at), a. 1. Beyond or almost beyond hope or cure; causing, despair. 2. Proceeding from, or expressing, despair.

des'pi-cable (des'pi-ka-b'l), a. Fit to be despised; contemptible.

de-spise' (de-spiz'), v.t. To look down upon with disfavor or contempt; scorn.

de-spond'en-cy (-den'si), n. Loss of hope and cessation of effort; discouragement; dejection.

des'ti-na'tion (des'ti-na'shun), n. 1. Act of destining or appointing. 2. The place set for the end of a journey, or to which something is sent.

des'tine (des'tin), v.t. 1. To decree beforehand, as by divine will; predetermine; foreordain. 2. To appoint (to) or design (for a given end, use, or purpose), specif., passive, to be bound (for).

des'ti-ny (-ti-ni), n. 1. That to which any person or thing is destined; lot; doom. 2. The predetermined course of events, often conceived as a resistless power; fate.

des'ti-tute (-tut), a. Bereft or not in possession (of something needed or desired); lacking.

de-stroy' (de'stroi'), v.t. 1. To unbuild; break up the structure and organic existence of; demolish. 2. To kill; slay. 3. to counteract; nullify.

de-tach' (de-tach'), v.t. To part; separate; disunite; disengage.

de-tain' (de-tan'), v.t. To keep back; restrain from proceeding; delay.

de-tect' (-tekt'), v.t. To discover (something obscure); find out; expose.

de-tec'tive (-tiv), n. One whose occupation it is to detect concealed matters, as crimes.

de-ter'gent (-tur'jent), a. Cleansing; purging. — n. A cleansing substance.

de-ter'mi-nate (-nat), a. Having defined limits; fixed, as by a rule; definite; decisive.

de-ter'mine (-min), v.t. 1. To fix the boundaries of; limit; bound. 2. To bring to a conclusion; decide.

de-test' (-test'), v.t. To hate intensely; abhor.

de-test'a-ble (-tes'ta-b'l), a. Worthy of being detested; abominable; odious; hateful; execrable.

de-tract' (de-trakt'), v.t. To withdraw; subtract; as, the defect detracts something from the beauty of the picture. — v.i. To take away a part, or something, esp. from one's credit or reputation.

det'ri-ment (det'ri-ment), n. Injury or damage, or that which causes it; mischief; harm.

de-vel'op (de-vel'op), v.t. 1. To lay open or unfold by degrees or in detail; disclose; reveal. 2. To open up and expand the possibilities of.

de'vi-ate (de'vi-at), v.i. To turn aside, as from a course or method; stray; digress; wander.

de-vice' (de-vis'), n. 1. That which is devised, or formed by design; contrivance; scheme; stratagem. 2. An emblematic design, esp. one used a s heraldic bearing. 3. Will; desire.

dev'il-ish (a. Resembling, or characteristic of, the Devil; diabolical. — adv. Excessively;

extremely. Colloq.

de-vise' (de-viz'), v.t. & i. 1. To form in the mind by new combinations of ideas, etc.; contrive; invent.

de-void' (de-void'), a. Destitute (of); not in possession; entirely without; — with of.

de-volve' (de-volv'), v.i. To pass or be transferred from one person to another, as by succession; to be handed over or down.

de-vote' (de-vot'), v.t. 1. To appropriate or dedicate by a vow; consecrate; also, to doom. 2. To give up wholly; addict; attach; apply.

de-vot'ed (-vot'ed), p.a. 1. Consecrated to a purpose; strongly attached. 2. Dedicated; also, doomed.

de-vo'tion (de-vo'shun), n. 1. State of being devoted; zeal; esp., feelings toward God expressed in worship; devoutness. 2. An act of worship; prayer. 3. Consecration; dedication.

de-vour' (-vour'), v.t. 1. To eat up greedily or ravenously; to prey upon. 2. To seize and destroy, or appropriate greedily or wantonly; consume; waste; annihilate. 3. To take in eagerly by the senses.

de-vout' (-vout'), a. 1. Devoted to religion; pious; religious. 2. Expressing devotion or piety. 3. Warmly devoted; sincere; as, a devout friend.

di'a-be'tes (di'a-be'tez; -tis), n. A disease attended with an excessive discharge of urine.

di'ag-no'sis (-no'sis), n. 1. Art or act of recognizing disease from its symptoms. 2. Scientific determination; critical scrutiny, or judgment based on it.

di'a-gram (di'a-gram), n. 1. A drawing composed of lines, or in outline, as for scientific purposes. 2. Any graphic representation; a scheme, chart, or plan.

di'al (di'al), n. 1. A sundial. 2. The graduated face of a timepiece. 3. A plate or face having a pointer or pointers for indicating something; as, the dial of a speedometer.

di'a-lect (-a-lekt), n. 1. Language; tongue; phraseology. 2. A form of speech marked by local peculiarities; esp. a local form of a language differing from the standard, or literary, form.

di'a-logue (di'a-log), n. A colloquy or conversation between two or more.

di'a-mond (di'a-mund), n. 1. Native crystallized carbon, highly valued as a precious stone when transparent and free from flaws; also, a piece of this material.

di'ar-rhe'a (di'a-re'a), n. A purging or looseness of the bowels.

di'a-ry (di'a-ri), n. A daily record; esp., a book of personal notes or memoranda.

dice (dis), n. Small cubes marked, usually, with spots from one to six, used in gaming; also, gaming with dice.

dic'tion (dik'shun), n. Choice of words for expressions of ideas; mode of verbal expression.

dic'tion-a-ry (-a-ri), n. A book containing the words of a language, or of any system or province of knowledge, usually arranged alphabetically, with their meanings; a lexicon.

di'et (di'et), n. A course of food selected with reference to a particular state of health.

dif'fer (dif'er), v.i. To be or stand apart; be unlike; be of unlike or opposite opinion; disagree.

dif'fer-ent (-ent), a. 1. Of various or contrary nature, form, or quality; unlike; dissimilar. 2. Distinct; separate; other.

dif'fi-cult (dif'i-kult), a. 1. Hard to do or to make; beset with difficulty; also, hard to understand; obscure. 2. Hard to manage or to please; exacting.

dif'fi-dent (-dent), a. Wanting confidence, esp. in one's self; not self-reliant; timid; modest; shrinking, bashful.

dig (dig), v.t. 1. To turn up, or delve in (earth), with a spade, hoe, etc.; pierce, open, or loosen with or as if with a spade. 2. To bring to the surface or get by digging; exhume.

di-gest' (di-jest'; di-), v.t. 1. To distribute methodically; classify. 2. To arrange methodically in the mind; comprehend. 3. To convert (food) in the stomach or intestines into the form in which it is assimi-

lated by the system. — v.i. 1. To digest food. 2. To undergo digestion.

dig'it (dij'it), n. 1. A finger or toe. 2. Math. Any of the ten figures or symbols, 0, 1, 2, 3, 4, 5, 6, 7, 8, 9, by which all numbers may be expressed.

dig'ni-ty (-ti) n. 1. Quality of being worthy or honorable; worth; nobleness. 2. Elevated rank; also, an office, rank, or title of honor. 3. Nobleness of manner, aspect, or style.

di-gress' (di-gres'; di-) v.i. To turn aside; deviate, esp. from the main subject of discourse.

di-lap'i-date (di-lap'i-dat), v.t. To bring (a building) into decay or partial ruin. — v.i. To fall into decay or partial ruin.

di-late' (di-lat'; di-), v.t. To enlarge or extend in bulk or size; expand. — v.i. 1. To dwell in narration; expatiate. 2. To expand.

di-lem'ma (di-lem'a; di-), n. A vexatious predicament; difficult choice or position.

dil'i-gent (-jent), a. 1. Assiduous; industrious; persevering. 2. Prosecuted with careful attention and effort.

di-lute' (di-lut'l di-), v.t. To make thinner by admixture; weaken by mixing, esp. with water; as, to dilute acid. — a. Diluted; weak.

di-min'ish (di-min'ish), v.t. & i. To make smaller or less; lessen; reduce in size or importance.

dip (dip), v.t. 1. To plunge or immerse, esp. temporarily or partly into or in a liquid or the like. 2. To take out as by lading. 3. To lower and raise quickly, as a flag.

di-plo'ma-cy (-ma-si), n. 1. Art of conducting negotiations between nations. 2. Dexterity in securing advantages; tact.

dip'lo-mat (dip'lo-mat), n. One employed or skilled in international diplomacy; a diplomatist.

di-rect' (di-rekt'), a. 1. Straight; leading by the shortest way to appoint or end. 2. Straightforward; not swerving from truth and openness.

di-rect'ly (-rekt'li), adv. 1. in a direct

manner or line. 2. Without delay; immediately.

di-rec'tor (di-rek'ter), n. 1. One that directs; a manager. 2. One of a body appointed to manage the affairs of a company or corporation.

di-rec'to-ry (di-rek'to-ri), n. 1. That which directs; esp., a body of directions or rules. 2. A book or list containing the names and addresses of the inhabitants of any place, or of classes of them.

dirt'y (-ti), a. 1. Soiled with dirt; unclean. 2. Of color, sullied; clouded.

dis'a-bil'i-ty (dis'a-bil'i-ti), n. State of being disabled; absence of competent power, etc.

dis-a'bled (-a'b'ld), p.a. Incapable; crippled.

dis'ad-van'tage (-ad-van'taj), n. 1. That which hinders success, or causes loss or injury. 2. Loss; detriment; injury; prejudice to fame, profit, or other good. — v.t. To injure the interest of.

dis'a-gree' (-a-gre), v.i. 1. To fail to agree; be unlike. 2. To differ in opinion. 3. To be unsuited.

dis'a-gree'a-ble (-a-b'l), a. Exciting repugnance; offensive; unpleasant in temper or mood.

dis'ap-pear (-a-per'), v.i. 1. To cease to appear; pass from view; vanish. 2. To cease to be; be lost.

dis'ap-point' (-point'), v.t. 1. To defeat of expectation or hope; balk. 2. To frustrate; foil; defeat.

dis'ap-point'ment (-ment), n. 1. Act of disappointing; state or emotion of being disappointed; frustration. 2. That which disappoints.

dis'ap-prove (dis'a-proov'), v.t. To pass unfavorable judgment on; censure.

dis'ar'ma-ment (-ar'ma-ment), n. Act of disarming; esp., reduction of an army or navy approximately to a peace footing.

dis'ar-ray' (-a-ra'), n. Disorder.

dis'a-vow' (dis'a-vou'), v.t. To refuse to own or acknowledge; disclaim; disown; deny.

dis-bur'den (-bur'd'n), v.t. 1. To rid of a burden; disencumber. 2. To put off a (burden); discharge.

dis-burse' (-burs'), v.t. To pay out; expend.

dis-card' (dis-kard'), v.t. To cast off as useless; throw or lay aside; turn away; reject.

dis-cern'ing, p.a. Acute; shrewd.

dis-close' (dis-kloz'), v.t. To lay open or expose to view; reveal; expose; divulge.

dis-col'or (dis-kul'er), v. To alter the natural color of, esp. for the worse; stain.

dis-com'fit (-kum'fit), v.t. To balk; throw into dejection.

dis-com'fort (-fert), v.t. To disturb the comfort of; make uneasy; pain. — n. 1. Want of comfort; pain; distress. 2. An inconvenience.

dis'con-cert' (-kon-surt'), v.t. 1. To throw into disorder or confusion. 2. To disturb; confuse.

dis'con-nect' (-ko-nekt'), v.t. To undo the connection of; disunite.

dis'con-tent' (dis'kon-tent'), a. Not content; dissatisfied. — n. Want of content; uneasiness; dissatisfaction. — v.t. To dissatisfy; displease.

dis'con-tent'ed (-ten'ted), p.a. Dissatisfied; uneasy in mind.

dis'con-tin'ue (-tin'u), v.t. & i. To interrupt the continuance of; break off; stop.

dis'cord (dis'kord), n. 1. Want of concord or agreement; disagreement. 2. A combination of musical sounds which strikes the ear harshly. 3. A harsh or confused noise; uproar.

dis'count (dis'kount; dis-kount'), v.t. 1. To deduct from an account, debt, charge, or the like. 2. To lend money on, deducting in advance the discount.

dis-cour'age (dis-kur'aj), v.t. 1. To lessen the courage of; dishearten; deject. 2. To dishearten one with respect to; deter one from.

dis-cour'age-ment (-ment), n. 1. Act of discouraging; state of being discouraged; depression. 2. That which discourages; a deterrent.

dis-course' (dis-kors'), n. 1. Conversation; talk. 2. Consecutive speech, written or unwritten; treatise; dissertation.

dis-cov'er-y (-er'i), n. 1. Act of discovering. 2. That which is discovered.

dis-cred'it (dis-kred'it), v.t. 1. To refuse credence to; disbelieve. 2. To destroy confidence in. 3. To deprive of credit or good repute; bring reproach upon.

dis-cre'tion (dis-kresh'un), n. 1. Freedom to decide or act; unrestrained exercise of choice or will. 2. Quality of being discreet; prudence.

dis-crim'i-na'tion (-na'shun), n. 1. Act of discriminating; state of being discriminated. 2. Quality of being discriminating; acute discernment.

dis-cuss' (dis-kus'), v.t. To examine or investigate by disputation; debate.

dis-cus'sion (dis-kush'un), n. Act of discussing; debate; investigation by arguments.

dis-dain' (-dan'), n. A feeling of contempt and aversion; scorn; arrogance; pride. — v.t. 1. To think unworthy; deem unsuitable or unbecoming. 2. To reject as not deserving one's notice; scorn.

dis'em-bark' (dis'em-bark'), v.t. & i. To remove or go ashore from on board a vessel; land.

dis'en-chant' (dis'en-chant'), v.t. To free from enchantment, or delusion.

dis'en-gage' (-gaj'), v.t. To release from that with which anything is engaged; extricate.

dis-fa'vor (dis-fa'ver), v.t. To withhold or withdraw favor from; regard with disesteem.

dis-fig'ure (-fig'ur), v.t. To mar the figure or appearance of.

dis-grace' (-gras'), n. 1. Condition of being out of favor. 2. State of being dishonored; shame; ignominy. 3. Cause of dishonor or shame.

dis-grun'tle (-grun't'l), v. To put in bad humor; render dissatisfied.

dis-guise' (-giz'), v.t. 1. To change the appearance of so as to conceal or mislead. 2. To hide or obscure by a counterfeit appearance; cloak; conceal; mask.

dis-gust' (-gust'), v.t. To provoke disgust or strong distaste in. — n. Aversion or repugnance produced by something loathsome.

dis-hon'est (dis-on'est), a. 1. Wanting in honesty or integrity. 2. Characterized by fraud; knavish.

dis-hon'or (-on'er), n. 1. Disgrace; shame; ignominy. 2. Indignity; insult. — v.t. 1. To disgrace; bring reproach or shame upon. 2. To refuse to accept or pay (a draft, check, etc.)

dis'il-lu'sion (dis'i-lu'zhun), n. Act of freeing from an illusion. — v.t. To free from illusion.

dis'in-fect' (-fekt'), v.t. To free from infection; treat with a disinfectant.

dis-in'ter-est-ed (dis-in'ter-es-ted), a. Not influenced by self-interest; free from selfish motive.

dis'lo-cate (dis'lo-kat), v.t. 1. To displace (esp. a bone from its natural connections); disjoint. 2. To disarrange, as plans.

dis-lodge' (dis-loj'), v.t. To drive from a place of rest, hiding, or defense.

dis-man'tle (dis-man't'l), 1. To strip of dress or covering. 2. To strip of furniture and equipments, guns, etc., as a house or a fort.

dis-or'der (dis-or'der), n. 1. Want of order; confusion; disarray. 2. Breach of public order; tumult. 3. Disease; ailment; illness; sickness. — v.t. To disturb the order or functions of; disarrange.

dis-or'gan-ize (-gan-iz), v.t. To destroy the organization of; throw into disorder; disarrange.

dis-par'i-ty (dis-par'i-ti), n. Inequality; difference in age, rank, condition, etc.

dis-pense' (dis-pens'), v.t. 1. To deal out; distribute. 2. To apply, as laws; administer.

dis-place' (-plas'), v.t. 1. To remove from its place. 2. To crowd out; take the place of. 3. To remove from an office or the like; discharge.

dis-play' (-pla'), v.t. 1. To unfold, spread out. 2. To spread before the view; manifest. 3. In printing, to make conspicuous by large type or varying length of lines. — n.

dis-please' (dis-plez'), v.t. To incur the disapproval of. — v.t. To give displeasure.

dis'po-si'tion (dis'po-zish'un), n. 1. Act or power of disposing. 2. Tendency; inclination. 3. Natural or prevailing spirit, or temper of mind.

dis-pute' (dis-put'), v.i. To contend in argument; discuss; debate; often, to argue irritably; wrangle. — v.t. 1. To

C
D

make (something) a subject of disputation; discuss. 2. To oppose by argument or assertion; controvert.

dis-qual'i-fy (dis-kwol'i-fi), v.t. 1. To render unfit; incapacitate. 2. To deprive of some power, right or privilege, as by law.

dis're-gard' (dis're-gard'), v.t. Not to regard, notice, or observe; hence, to slight as unworthy of regard. — n. A disregarding; neglect.

dis'sat-is-fac'tion (dis-sat'is-fak'shun), n. State of being dissatisfied, unsatisfied, or discontented.

dis-sen'sion (-sen'shun), n. Disagreement in opinion; contention; discord; quarrel.

dis-sent' (-sent'), v.i. To differ in opinion; disagree; — with from. — n. 1. Act of dissenting; disagreement. 2. Nonconformity to an established church, esp. that of England.

dis'si-dence (dis'i-dens), n. Disagreement; dissent.

dis-sim'i-lar'i-ty (-lar'i-ti), n. Difference in appearance or nature; unlikeness.

dis'si-pate (dis'i-pat), v.t. 1. To break up and drive off; disperse; dispel. 2. To scatter aimlessly or foolishly.

dis'so-lu'tion (dis'o-lu-shun), n. Act or process of dissolving or breaking up; disintegration; death.

dis-solve' (-zolv'), v.t. & i. 1. To separate into component parts; break up; disintegrate; hence, to destroy.

dis'tance (-tans), n. 1. The space between two objects.

dis'tant (-tant), a. 1. Separated; away. 2. Far off; remote. 3. Reserved or repelling in manners; not cordial.

dis-taste'ful (-fool), a. 1. Unpleasant to the taste. 2. Displeasing to the feelings; disagreeable.

dis-tem'per (-tem'per), n. 1. Ill humor. 2. illness; malady; esp., any of various infectious diseases of animals. — v.t. To derange or sicken.

dis-tinct' (-tinkt'), a. 1. Distinguished by nature; not the same; individual; distinctive. 2. That may be clearly seen or discerned.

dis-tinc'tion (tink'shun), n. 1. Act of distinguishing; discrimination; also, a difference. 2. State or quality of being distinguishable or distinct. 3. A distinguishing quality or mark. 4. A special recognition; eminence; honor.

dis-tract' (-trakt'), v.t. 1. To draw (the sight, mind, or attention) to a different object or in different directions; divert. 2. To agitate by conflicting passions; harass. 3. To unsettle the reason of; craze.

dis'tri-bu'tion (dis'tri-bu'shun), n. 1. Act of distributing; disposal. 2. That which is distributed.

dis'trict (dis'trikt), n. 1. A defined portion of a state, city, etc. 2. A region; quarter; tract.

dis-trust' (dis-trust'), v.t. To feel a lack or the absence of trust in; mistrust. — n. Lack of trust.

dis-turb' (-turb'), v.t. 1. To throw into disorder or confusion; stir up; unsettle. 2. To agitate the mind of; disquiet. 3. To turn from a regular or designed course; to cause to shift, stop, or go away.

ditch (dich), n. A trench dug in the earth, as for drainage.

dive (div), v.i. 1. To plunge into water, esp. head first.

di-vine' (di'vin'), a. 1. Of or pertaining to God. 2. Proceeding from God. 3. Addressed or appropriated to God; religious.

diz'zy (diz'i), a. 1. Giddy; hence, mentally confused or unsteady. 2. Causing, or tending to cause, giddiness.

dock, n. 1. An artificial basin to receive vessels, having gates to keep in, or shut out, the water.

dock'et (-et), n. 1. Law. An abridged entry of a proceeding in an action, or a register of such entries. 2. A schedule of matters for action in an assembly. U.S. — v.t.

doc'tor (dok'ter), n. 1. One holding the highest degree conferred by a university or college. 2. One licensed to practice medicine; a physician or surgeon. — v.t. 1. To treat as a physician does. Colloq. 2. To tamper with; falsify. Slang.

doc'trine (-trin), n. A principle, or the body of principles, in any branch of knowledge; tenet.

doc'u-ment (-u-ment), n. A writing conveying information, esp. an original or official paper.

do'ing (doo'ing), n. Anything done; hence, conduct; — usually in pl.

dom'i-nant (-nant), a. Ruling; prevailing; controlling.

dom'i-nate (-nat), v.t. To control; rule; govern. — v.i. To control; predominate.

do-na'tion (do-na'shun), n. Act of giving, or that which is given, as a present.

doom (doom), n. 1. Judgment; sentence. 2. That to which one is doomed; destiny or fate; hence, ruin; death. — v.t.

dor'mant (-mant), a. Sleeping; asleep; hence, inactive; in abeyance.

dote (dot), v.i. To be foolishly fond; love to excess.

dou'ble (dub'l), a. 1. Twofold; doubled; made or being twice as great, as large, as much, as many, as strong, as valuable, etc. 2. Being in pairs; coupled. 3. Twofold in relation, character, or action.

down'ward' (-werd), adv. 1. From a higher to a lower place, condition, etc. 2. From an earlier time. — a. Descending; inclined downward.

doze (doz), v.i. To sleep lightly; be drowsy or dull. — n. A light sleep; drowse.

draft (draft), n. 1. Act of drawing, or hauling; a load. 2. A current of any sort; current of air. 3. A preliminary sketch or outline.

drain (dran), v.t. & i. 1. To draw or flow off by degrees; draw off utterly; exhaust. 2. To make or become gradually dry or empty. — n.

dra'ma (dra'ma), n. 1. A composition intended to portray life or character, esp. one designed to be performed on the stage. 2. Dramatic art, literature, or affairs.

dras'tic (drak'tik), a. Acting rapidly and violently; extreme in effect; as, a drastic remedy.

draw'back' (-bak'), n. 1. Money paid back after collection. 2. Hindrance; objectionable feature.

draw'er (dro'er), n. 1. One who draws. 2. One who issues a draft. 3. A

boxlike receptacle as in a table, arranged to be drawn out. 4. pl. An undergarment for the legs and lower body.

dread (dred), v.t. & i. To fear greatly; regard or look forward to with great apprehension. — n. 1. Great fear, esp. of impending evil. 2. Reverential or respectful fear; awe. 3. An object of fear or awe. — a. Dreadful.

dread'ful (dred'fool), a. 1. Fearful; inspiring dread; terrible; as, a dreadful storm. 2. Awful; inspiring reverence; as, dreadful majesty.

dress (dres), v.t. To clothe; to clothe in formal dress.

drift (drift), n. 1. That which is forced, or urged along, esp. by wind, water, or ice. 2. State of being driven; act or motion of drifting. 3. Tendency of an act or process or esp. of an argument or the like; purport; meaning; aim. — v.u. & t.

drop (drop), n. 1. The quantity of fluid that falls in one spherical mass; liquid globule. 2. A small quantity of drink. b pl. Any medicine measured by drops.

du'bi-ous (du'bi-us), a. 1. Occasioning doubt; doubtful; undetermined; uncertain. 2. Of questionable character.

du'el (du'el), n. A combat between two persons, fought with deadly weapons by agreement, usually before witnesses (seconds) on each side.

dull (dul), a. 1. Slow of understanding; stupid. 2. Slow in action; sluggish; listless; inert. 3. Furnishing little pleasure or variety; uninteresting. 4. Not sharp. 5. Not bright or clear to the eye; dim. 6. Muffled; not clear, as sounds.

dumb (dum), a. 1. Destitute of speech; mute; silent. 2. Dull; stupid. Colloq.

du'ra-ble du'ra-b'l), a. lasting; enduring; as, a durable cloth.

du-ra'tion (du-ra'shun), n. State or quality of lasting; continuance.

dust (dust), n. 1. Fine, dry, powdery particles of earth; hence, any fine powder. 2. The earthy remains of bodies once alive, esp. of human bodies. 3. Fig., something worthless, or a low or mean condition. 4. A cloud of dust in the air. — v.t.

dwell'ing, n. Habitation; abode.

dwin'dle (dwin'l'l), v.i. To diminish; become less; waste away.

dy-nam'ic (di-nam'ik; di-), a. 1. Physics. a Of or pertaining to physical forces or energy. b Of or pert to dynamics; active. 2. Energetic; active; forceful.

dy'na-mite (di'na-mit), n. An explosive consisting of nitroglycerin absorbed in a porous material. — v.t. To shatter with dynamite.

E

each (ech), a. or a. pron. Every (individual of two or more) considered separately.

ea'ger (e'ger), a. 1. Spirited or strenuous. 2. keenly desirous to pursue, perform, or obtain; ardent.

ear (er), n. 1. The organ of hearing. 2. The external ear of man and most mammals.

ear'ly (ur'li), adv. In a time or position near the beginning of a period or a series; betimes. — a. Coming early; of remote past time.

earn (urn), v.t. To merit, or to acquire, by labor or performance, as wages.

earn'ing (ur'ning), n. Act or process of earning, or what is earned; esp., pl., money earned.

earth (urth), n. 1. The globe or planet which we inhabit; the world. 2. The land, in distinction from the air or water. 3. The softer part of the land, in distinction from rock; soil or dirt.

earth'ly (-li), a. 1. Of, like, or pertaining to, the earth; not heavenly or spiritual. 2. Possible; as, of what earthly use is it?

ease (ez), n. 1. State of being comfortable; freedom from pain, effort, trouble, etc. 2. Freedom from constraint, formality, difficulty, etc.; naturalness, as of manner. — v.t. & i.

ease'ment (ez-ment), n. 1. That which gives ease. 2. Law. Any of several rights which one person may have in the land of another.

East'er (es'ter), n. An annual church festival commemorating Christ's resurrection, occurring on a Sunday between March 21 and April 26.

eas'y (ez'i), a. 1. At ease; free form trouble, pain, care, anxiety, constraint, etc. 2. Causing, or attended with, little difficulty or discomfort. 3. Of persons, moods, etc.; a Not difficult to influence; tractable. b Not harsh or exacting; lenient. 4. Supportable with ease; not burdensome or oppressive. 5. Giving ease or comfort.

eb'on-y (-i), n.; pl. -ONIES (-z). A hard, heavy wood, generally black, yielded by various trees of Asia and Africa; also, any tree yielding this wood.

ech'o (ek'o), n.; pl. -OES (-oz). 1. Repetition of a sound due to the reflection of the sound ways. 2. Any repetition; also, one who repeats another's words, ideas, etc.

e-con'o-my (-mi), n.; pl. -MIES (-miz). 1. The management of affairs, as of a house, community, etc. 2. Thrifty administration; also, an act or means of saving; disposition or ability to save. 3. Structural principles; organization.

ec'sta-sy (ek'sta-si), n. 1. A mystic, prophetic, or poetic trance. 2. State of rapture.

edge (ej), n. 1. The thin cutting side of the blade of an instrument. 2. Sharpness; keenness. 3. Any sharp terminating border; margin.

ed'i-ble (ed'i-b'l), a. Fit to be eaten as food; eatable. — n. Anything edible.

ed'it (ed'it), v.t. To superintend or direct the publication of; revise for publication.

e-di'tion (e-dish'un), n. 1. The form in which a literary work or group of works is published. 2. All the copies of a work published at one time.

ed'i-to'ri-al (-to'ri-al), a. Of or pertaining to an editor. — n. An article in a newspaper or magazine giving the views of the editor.

ed'u-cate (ed'u-kat), v.t. To develop and cultivate mentally or morally; train; instruct; teach.

ed'u-ca'tion (-ka'shun), n. 1. Act or process of educating. 2. The sum of the qualities acquired through instruction and training.

ef-fem'i-na-cy (-fem'i-nas-si), n.

Womanish quality, as softness or weakness, unbecoming a man.

ef-fi'cien-cy (e-fish'en-si), n. Quality or degree of being efficient; efficient power or action.

ef'fort (ef'ort; -ert), n. 1. Exertion of power, physical or mental. 2. A production, as of oratory.

ef-fu'sion (ef-fu'zhun), n. 1. Act of pouring out or forth. 2. That which is poured out or forth; esp. an unrestrained utterance.

e'go-ism (e'go-iz'm; eg'o-), n. Excessive love and thought of self; — opposed to altruism.

e'go-tist (-tist), n. One who speaks much of himself or his own deeds or affairs.

e-gre'gious (e-gre'jus; -ji'us), a. Remarkable for bad quality; flagrant; gross.

ei'ther (e'ther; i-ther), a. & pron. 1. Each of two; the one and the other. 2. One of two; the one or the other. — conj. a disjunctive connection, used: a Before two or more words or phrases joined by the correlative or; as, either he is busy or he is away. b After an alternative to emphasize a negation; as, nor you, either.

e-ject' (e-jekt'), v.t. To throw, push, or drive out.

e-jec'tion (-jek'shun), n. Act of ejecting; state of being ejected; ejected matter.

e-lab'o-rate (e-lab'o-rat), a. Wrought out with great care or detail; complicated.

e-lapse' (e-laps'), v.i. To pass away, as time.

e-las'tic (e-las'tik), a. 1. Springing back; springy. 2. Of temperaments, etc., able to recover quickly; buoyant. — n. Fabric made elastic by the use of India rubber; also, India rubber in cords, strings, or bands.

e-la'tion (e-la'shun), n. A lifting up of the mind or spirit by success, or hope of success; exaltation.

el'bow (el'bo), n. 1. The joint or bend of the arm. 2. Any bend like an elbow.

el'der (el'der), n. A shrub, of the honeysuckle family, bearing broad clusters of white or pink flowers,

and black or red berries.

eld'er-ly (-li), a. Somewhat old.

e-lect' (e-lekt'), a. 1. Chosen; picked. 2. Chosen to an office, but not inducted. 3. Theol. Chosen by election.

e-lec'tri'cian (e-lek-trish'an), n. One versed in the science or uses of electricity.

e-lec-tric'i-ty (e-lek-tris'i-ti), n. 1. The agency or force to which are due numerous physical phenomena, as the electric spark, lightning, electromagnetism, etc. 2. Electrical science.

e-lec'tro-cute (e-lek'tro-kut), v.t. To execute (a criminal) by electricity.

el'e-gant (-gant), a. 1. Marked by niceties of manner, dress, or the like. 2. Characterized by grace, propriety, and refinement. 3. neat or simple and apt. 4. Keenly appreciative of what is elegant.

el'e-ment (-ment), n. 1. One of the simple substances (generally earth, air, fire, and water) formerly believed to compose the physical universe. 2. pl. Conditions of weather, usually implying violent weather.

el'e-men'tar-ry (el'e-men'ta-ri). a. 1. Consisting of a single element. 2. Treating of the first principles of anything; introductory.

el'e-phant (el'e-fant), n. Any of various well-known mammals, of Africa and India, having long tusks and the snout prolonged into a prehensile proboscis. They are the largest existing land animals.

el'e-vate (el'e-vat), v.t. 1. To lift up; raise; exalt; ennoble. 2. To exhilarate; raise the spirits of.

el'e-va'tion (-va'shun), n. 1. Act of elevating; height; exaltation. 2. An elevated place. 3. Height above sea level. 4. A drawing of an object that shows its vertical or upright parts.

el'e-va'tor (el'e-va'ter), n. One that raises anything; as: a A contrivance, as an endless chain with buckets, for raising grain to a loft. b A cage or platform for conveying persons, goods, etc., to or from different levels; a lift. c A building for elevating, storing, and discharging grain.

E
F

e-lic'it (e-lis'it), v.t. To draw out or forth; educe; to draw or entice forth; evoke.

el'i-gi-bil'i-ty (el'i-ji-bil'i-ti), n. Quality of being eligible; fitness; as, the eligibility of a candidate.

el'i-gi-ble (el'i-ji-b'l), a. Fitted or qualified to be chosen.

e-lim'i-nate (e-lim'i-nat), v.t. 1. To throw out; expel; exclude. 2. To ignore as unimportant or inapplicable. 3. To cause (an unknown quantity) to disappear from an equation.

e-lix'ir (e-lik'ser), n. 1. A supposed essence or substance with the power to prolong life indefinitely, sought by the alchemists. 2. An aromatic, sweetened, alcoholic preparation of a drug.

el'o-cu'tion (el'o-ku'shun), n. The art of public speaking or reading, esp. with reference to the graces of intonation, gesture, etc.

e-lon'gate (e-lon'gat), v.t. & i. To lengthen; extend.

e-lope' (e-lop'), v.i. To run away from one's spouse or home with a lover.

else (els), a., pron. Other; other one. — adv. 1. In a different place, time, or respect. 2. In another or a contrary case; otherwise.

e-lu'ci-date (e-lu'si-dat), v.t. To make clear or manifest; illustrate.

e-lude' (e-lud'), v.t. To avoid by dexterity or stratagem; evade; baffle.

e-lu'sive (-siv), a. Tending to elude; adroitly evading; of ideas, etc., not easily understood or defined; baffling.

e-man'ci-pate (e-man'si-pat), v.t. To set free, esp. from bondage; liberate.

e-man'ci-pa'tion (-pa'shun), a. Act or process of freeing; liberation; release; freedom.

e-mas'cu-late (-mas'ku-lat), v.t. To deprive of virile power or masculine vigor or spirit; weaken. — (-lat), a. Deprived of virility or vigor.

em-balm' (em-bam'), v.t. 1. To treat (a dead body), as with aromatic oils, etc., so as to prevent decay. 2. To keep in memory.

em-bank'ment (-ment), n. 1. Act of embanking. 2. A raised structure of earth, gravel, etc., to retain or hold back water, carry a roadway, etc.

em-bar'go (-bar'go), n. 1. An edict of a government prohibiting the departure or entry of ships of commerce at a port or ports. 2. Any prohibition imposed by law on commerce.

em-bark' (em-bark'), v.t. & i. 1. To put or go on shipboard for a voyage. 2. To engage, enlist, or invest (as persons, money, etc.), in any affair.

em-bar'rass (em-bar'as), v.t. 1. To confuse; disconcert; nonplus. 2. To impede; complicate. 3. To involve in financial difficulties.

em-bar'rass-ment (-ment), n. Embarrassed condition; that which embarrasses.

em'bas-sy (em'ba-si), n. 1. Function or position of an ambassador; the sending of ambassadors. 2. An ambassador and his suite. 3. The residence or office of an ambassador.

em-bel'lish (-bel'ish), v.t. 1. To make beautiful or elegant, as by ornaments. 2. To set out with fanciful enlargements; to heighten, as a story.

em-bit'ter (-bit'er), v.t. To make bitter or more bitter.

em'blem (em'blem), n. A visible sign of an idea; a figurative representation; a symbol.

em-bod'y ((-i), v.t. 1. To give a body to, as a spirit; incarnate. 2. Hence, to render concrete and definite. 3. To cause to become a body or part of a body; incorporate.

em-boss' (-bos'), v.t. 1. To ornament with raised work. 2. To raise in relief.

em-broil' (-broil'), v.t. To confuse or stir up by discord; involve in difficulties by strife.

e-merge' (e-murj'), v.t. To rise from or as from an enveloping fluid; come out into view.

e-mer'gen-cy (e-mur'jen-si), n. An unforeseen occurrence or condition calling for immediate action; exigency.

em'i-nence (em'i-nens), n. 1. That which is eminent; a height. 2. An elevated station; high rank; distinction. 3. [cap.] A title of honor, now applied only to cardinals.

em'i-nent (-nent), a. 1. Lofty, prominent. 2. Being above others by birth, merit, etc.; virtue; distinguished. 3. Conspicuous.

em'is-sa-ry (em'i-sa'ri), n. An agent employed to advance certain interests or to gain information; esp., a secret agent.

e-mit' (e-mit'), v.t. 1. To throw or give out or off. 2. To issue, as currency.

e-mo'tion (e-mo'shun), n. A feeling of joy, grief, fear, hate, love, awe, etc.

em'per-or (em'per-er), n. The sovereign or monarch of an empire.

em-pha'sis (em'fa-sis), n. 1. In reading or speaking, a force or stress of utterance given to important words or syllables. 2. Special impressiveness of expression or weight of thought.

em-phat'ic (em-fat'ik), a. 1. Uttered with emphasis; forcibly expressive; as, an emphatic tone or word. 2. Impressive; striking, as, an emphatic gesture.

em-ploy' (-ploi'), v.t. 1. to make use of; use. 2. To occupy; devote. 3. To give work to.

em-pow'er (-pou-er), v.t. To give power to.

emp'ty (-ti), a. 1. Containing nothing; without contents; vacant. 2. Without substance, effect, sense, feeling, sincerity, etc. —v.t. & i. To make or become empty; of a river, or the like, to discharge (itself).

em'u-late (em'u-lat), v.t. To strive to equal or excel (another); vie with; rival.

em'u-la'tion (-la'-shun), n. Endeavor to equal to excel; rivalry.

en-a'ble (en-a'b'l), v.t. To make able; give (one) power or ability (to be or do something).

en-act' (-akt'), v.t. 1. To make into an act or law; decree. 2. To act the part of; represent.

en'core' (an'kor'), adv. & interj. Once more; again; — used as a call for a repetition of a part of a play, concert, etc. — (pron. an'kor ';), n. The demand for repetition, as by applause; also, the repetition.

en-coun'ter (en-koun'ter), v.t. & i. To meet, esp. in opposition or with hostile intent. - n. A meeting, esp.

with hostile purpose; a combat; battle.

en-cour'age (en-kur'aj), v.t. 1. To inspire with courage, spirit, or hope; inspirit. 2. To give help or patronage to, as an industry; foster.

en-cour'age-ment (-aj-ment), n. 1. State of being encouraged. 2. That which encourages.

en-cum'ber (-kum'ber), v.t. 1. To impede in motion or action; retard; embarrass. 2. To render awkward, obstructive, or disagreeable, by superfluous parts, etc. 3. To place a burden on, as a debt or legal claim.

en-cy'clo-pe'di-a, n. A work in which the branches of learning are treated in separate articles.

end (end), n. 1. A limit or boundary; esp., an extreme region or part. 2. Extreme or last point or part; conclusion. 3. Issue; result; also, final state.

en-dan'ger (en-dan'jer), v.t. To bring into danger.

en-dear' (-der'), v.t. To make or hold dear.

en-deav'or (-dev'er), v.t. & i. To strive to achieve or reach; try; attempt.

end'ing (en'ding), n. 1. Termination; conclusion; also, death. 2. Gram. The final syllable or letter of a word, esp. when inflectional.

end'less (end'les), a. 1. Without end or ends; boundless; eternal; infinite. 2. Continuous by reason of the ends being united; as, an endless chain.

en-dur'ance (-ans), n. 1. State, quality, or act of enduring. 2. Ability to endure.

en'e-my (en'e'mi), n. 1. One who is hostile to another; hence, whatever does injury to one. 2. A military foe.

en-force' (-fors'), v.t. 1. To force; compel. 2. To put in force or effect, as a law. 3. To lay stress upon; emphasize.

en'gine (en'jin), n. 1. Any mechanical instrument. 2. A machine for converting physical force, as heat, into mechanical power. 3. A locomotive.

Eng'lish (in'glish), a. Of, pertaining to, or characteristic of, England or its inhabitants or citizens. — n. The language of the English.

E
F

en-grave' ('grav'), v.t. 1. To carve figures, letters, or devices on. 2. To form by incisions, as one wood, stone, or metal, esp. for printing. 3. To impress deeply.

en-gross' (-gros'), v.t. 1. To copy or write in a large hand; write a perfect copy of, as of a decree. 2. To take the whole of; absorb; monopolize.

en-hance' (-hans'), v.t. & i. To advance, augment, or elevate; heighten; intensify.

e-nig'ma (e-nig'ma), n. 1. An obscure or inexplicable saying; riddle. 2. Anything inexplicable.

en-large' (-larj'), v.t. & i. To increase in quantity, capacity, dimensions, or extent; extend.

en-light'en (-lit'n), v.t. To instruct; also, to give insight to.

en-list' (-list'), v.t. & i. 1. To enter on a list; enroll. 2. To engage for military or naval service. 3. To engage one's support and aid in behalf of.

en-liv'en (-liv'n), v.t. 1. To give life, action, or motion to; quicken. 2. To give spirit or vivacity to; animate.

en'mi-ty (en'mi-ti), n. Quality or state of being hostile; hatred; animosity.

e-nor'mi-ty (e-nor'mi-ti), n. Extreme or monstrous wickedness; an atrocious offense or crime.

e-nor'mous (-mus), a. 1. Exceeding the usual rule, norm, or measure; monstrous. 2. Greatly exceeding the usual size, number, or degree; immense.

e-nough' (e-nuf'), a. Satisfying desire; giving content; adequate; sufficient. — adv. In a degree or quantity that satisfies; sufficiently; hence, tolerably. — interj. Short for it is enough. — n. A sufficiency; an adequate quantity.

en-roll' (-rol'), v.t. To insert in a roll, list, or catalogue; hence, to record; also, to enlist (one's self).

en-sue' (en-su'), v.t. & i. To follow; pursue; come afterward or as a consequence.

en-tan'gle (-tan'g'l), v.t. 1. To tangle. 2. To involve; insnare; hence, to perflex; bewilder.

en'ter-tain' (-tan'), v.t. 1. To give hospitable reception or mainte- nance to. 2. To receive and take into consideration. 3. To harbor, as a grudge. 4. To amuse; divert. — v.i. To receive, or provide entertainment for, guests.

en-tice' (-tis), v.t. To draw on by exciting hope or desire; lure; allure.

en-tire' (-tir'), a. 1. Complete in all parts; whole. 2. Complete in one piece; continuous.

en'trance (-trans), n. 1. Act of entering; ingress. 2. Means or place for entering, as a door, gate, etc. 3. Power or permission to enter; entree.

e-nun'ci-ate (e-nun'shi-at; -si-at), v.t. To utter articulately; pronounce.

en'vi-ous (-us), a. Feeling envy; jealously pained by the excellence or good fortune of another; — with of, at, or against.

en-vi'ron-ment (-ment), n. 1. Act of environing. 2. Surrounding conditions, influences, or forces.

en'vy (en'vi), n. 1. A feeling of discontent and ill will at another's excellence or good fortune. 2. An object of envious notice.

ep'i-dem'ic (-dem'ik), a. Common to, or affecting at the same time, many in a community; general. — n. An epidemic disease.

ep'i-gram (ep'i-gram), n. 1. A short poem treating pointedly of a single thought or event, and now usually ending with a witticism, and often satirical. 2. A witting thought tersely expressed; also, concise and pointed expression.

ep'i-logue (ep'i-log), n. 1. The conclusion of a discourse. 2. A speech or short poem recited by an actor after a play.

ep'i-taph (ep'i-taf), n. An inscription on or at a tomb or grave in memory of the one buried there.

e'qual (e'kwal), a. 1. Exactly the same or equivalent in measure, amount, number, degree, value, quality, etc. 2. Uniform; equable.

e-quip (e-kwip), v.t. 1. To furnish for service; fit out. 2. To dress; array.

e-quip'ment (e-kwip'ment), n. 1. Act of equipping; state of being equipped. 2. Anything used in equipping.

eq'ui-ty (-ti), n. 1. State or quality of being equal or fair; fairness. 2. Law. An equitable claim or right.

e-quiv'o-cal (-o-kal), a. 1. Having two or more significations equally applicable; ambiguous; hence, suspicious; dubious. 2. Uncertain as an indication or sign; doubtful.

e-rad'i-cate (-kat), v.t. To pluck up by the roots; hence, to destroy utterly; extirpate.

e-rase' (e-ras'), v.t. To rub or scrape out, as written characters, etc.; efface.

e-rode' (e-rod'), v.t. To eat into or away; corrode; to wear away, as land by the action of water; to form (as a valley) by such action.

err (ur), v.i. To go astray; fall into error.

er-rat'ic (e-rat'ik), a. 1. Having no fixed course; irregular. 2. Eccentric; queer.

er-ro'ne-ous (e-ro'ne-us), a. Containing error; incorrect.

er'ror (er'er), n. 1. Belief in what is untrue. 2. A moral offense; fault. 3. A mistake.

es-cape' (es-kap'), v.i. 1. To get away, as by flight. 2. To issue from confinement or inclosure of any sort.

es'cort (es'kort), n. 1. A person or body of persons accompanying or attending another or others for protection, or as a mark of honor or courtesy. 2. Protection, care, or safeguard on a journey.

es'pi-o-nage (es'pi-o-naj; es-pi'-), n. The practice of spying on others, or the employment of spies.

es-say (es'a), n. 1. An effort; trial; attempt. 2. A literary composition dealing with its subject from a more or less limited or personal stand-point.

es-sence (-ens), n. 1. That which makes a thing what it is; a necessary constituent; element. 2. A substance having in a high degree the qualities or virtues of a plant, drug, etc., from which it is extracted. 3. Perfume, or the volatile matter constituting it.

es-sen'tial (e-sen'shal), a. 1. Having the character of an essence. 2. Most important; indispensable.

es-tate' (-tat'), n. 1. State or condition of being. 2. Social standing or rank. 3. A social or political class.

es-teem' (-tem'), v.t. 1. To appreciate

the worth of; to value. 2. To set a high value on; prize. 3. To consider; think; hold (a thing to be so and so). — n.

es-trange' (-tranj'), v.t. 1. To cause to be strange; to keep at a distance; withdraw. 2. To make indifferent or hostile; alienate.

e-ter'nal (e-tur'nal), a. 1. Of infinite duration; everlasting. 2. Incessant; perpetual.

eth'i-cal (eth'i-kal), a. Of or pertaining to moral action, motive, or character; also, treating of moral feelings or conduct; moral.

et'i-quette (et'i-ket), n. The system of conventional forms required by good breeding, or to be observed in official or social life.

eup'phe-mism (u'te-miz'm), n. A figure of speech in which an inoffensive word or expression is substituted for one considered unpleasant.

e-vade' (e-vad'), v.t. & i. To get away from by artifice; escape from cleverly; slip away; elude.

e-vap'o-rate (e-vap'o-rat), v.i. To pass off in vapor or change to vapor, as a fluid; hence, to pass off like vapor, or without effect. — v.t. 1. To cause to evaporate. 2. To expel moisture from, as by heat, leaving the solid portion; as, to evaporate fruit.

e-va'sion (e-va'zhun), n. Act of evading; also, a means of evading; a subterfuge.

eve'ning (ev'ning), n. The latter part and close of the day and early part of darkness or night.

ev'er (ev'er), adv. 1. At all times; always. 2. At any time; as, seldom if ever. 3. In any case; at all.

ev'er-y (ev'er-i), a. & a. pron. Each (one), without exception, of a group; as, his every word. — every other, each alternate; as, every other day.

ev'er-y-bod'y (-bod'i), n. Every person.

e-vict' (e-vikt'), v.t. Law. To put out or dispossess (a person) by legal process, or by virtue of a para-mount right; eject; as, to evict a tenant.

ev'i-dence (ev'i-dens), n. 1. State of being evident; clearness. 2. That which makes evident; proof. — v.t.

E

F

To render evident or clear.

ev'i-dent (-dent), a. Clear to the vision; satisfactory to the judgment.

e'vil (e'v'l), a. 1. Injurious or mischievous; not good. 2. Bad morally; wicked; vicious.

e-voke (e'vok'), v.t. To call forth.

e-volve' (e-volv'), v.t. To exhibit or produce by evolution; develop; deduce. — v.i. To become open, disclosed, or developed; unfold.

ex-act' (eg-zakt'), a. 1. Strict; undeviating; rigorous. 2. Marked by agreement with fact or a standard; precise or correct. 3. Capable of great nicety; as, exact instruments.

ex-ag'ger-ate (-zaj'er-at), v.t. 1. To enlarge beyond the truth; overstate. 2. To enlarge beyond this normal; as, an exaggerated development.

ex-am'ine (eg-zam'in), v.t. 1. To inquire or search into; investigate. 2. To interrogate closely, as in a judicial proceeding; try or test, as by question, as a student.

ex-as'per-ate (eg-zas'per-at), v.t. 1. To excite the anger of; irritate. 2. To aggravate.

ex-ca-vate (eks'ka-vat), v.t. 1. To hollow out by cutting or digging; to cut or dig out. 2. To form by hollowing, as a cellar. 3. To expose by digging.

ex-cel'lent (-lent), a. Very good of its kind; first-class; of great worth. — -**ly**, adv.

ex-cept' (-sept'), v.t. to take or leave out (anything) from a number or a whole as not belonging to it; exclude; omit. — v.t. To take exception; object. — prep. With exclusion of; excepting. —conj. Unless; if it be not so that.

ex-cerpt (ek'surpt), n. An extract; a selected or copied passage.

ex-change' (eks-chanj'), n. 1. Act or giving or taking one thing in return for another regarded as an equivalent.

ex-cit'a-ble (-sit'a-b'l), a. Capable of being excited; easily stirred up.

ex-cite' (ek-sit'), v.t. To call or stir to activity in any way, esp., to move to strong emotion.

ex-claim' (-klam'), v.i. & t. To cry out, utter, or speak in strong or sudden emotion.

ex-clu'sive (-siv), a. 1. Enjoyed to the exclusion of others. 2. Inclined to exclude outsiders. 3. Excluding; not comprising.

ex-com'mu-ni-cate (eks'ko-mu'ni-kat), v.t. To cut off, or shut out, from communion with the church, by ecclesiastical sentence.

ex-crete' (-kret'), v.t. To separate and eliminate or discharge (waste or harmful material) from the blood or tissues.

ex-cuse' (-kuz), v.t. 1. To offer excuse for; apologize for.

ex-ec'u-tive (eg-zek'u-tiv), a. Designed or fitted for execution, or carrying into effect; qualified for, or pertaining to, the execution of the laws or the conduct of affairs. — n. 1. Executive branch of a government. 2. Any person charged with administrative or executive work.

ex-empt' (-zempt'), a. Free or released from some liability to which others are subject; excepted. — v.t. To release from some liability.

ex'er-cise (ek'ser-siz), n. 1. Act of exercising; a putting into action, use, or practice. 2. Exertion for the sake of training or improvement.

ex-ert' (eg'zurt'), v.t. To put forth, as strength, ability, etc., put in vigorous action.

ex-hale' (eks'hal'; egz-), v.t. 1. To breathe out; emit, as vapor. 2. To draw out; evaporate; as, the sun exhales the dew. — v.i.

ex-haust' (eg'zost'), v.t. 1. To draw or drain off completely. 2. to empty by drawing out the contents; esp. to create a vacuum in. 3. To use up completely; tire or wear out. 4. To develop completely or discuss thoroughly. — n.

ex'hi-bi'tion (ek'si-bish'un), n. 1. Act of exhibiting. 2. That which is exhibited; also, any public show; a display, as of works of art.

ex-ist' (eg-zist'), v.i. 1. To have being; to be. 2. To continue to be; to live.

ex-or'bi-tant (-tant), a. Going beyond established limits or right or propriety; grossly excessive.

ex'or-cise (ek'sor-siz), v.t. To drive off (an evil spirit) by adjuration; hence, to deliver from an evil spirit.

ex-pand' (eks-pand'), v.t. & i. 1. To lay

open by extending; open wide. 2. To make to occupy more space; dilate; distend. 3. To express in greater detail; develop, as an argument.

ex-pan'sion (-shun), n. 1. Act or process of expanding; state of being expanded; enlargement. 2. Extent of expansion; an expanded thing or part.

ex-pect' (-pekt'), v.t. To look for (mentally); look forward to; to look for with some confidence.

ex'pec-ta'tion (eks'pek-ta'shun), n. 1. Act or state of expecting; anticipation. 2. That which is expected. 3. The prospect of anything good to come, esp. [pl.] of property or rank.

ex-pense' (-pens'), n. 1. That which is expended; outlay; hence, charge; cost. 2. A source of expenditure.

ex-pe'ri-ence (-pe'ri-ens), n. 1. The actual living through an event or events; actual enjoyment or suffering. 2. Skill or practical wisdom gained by personal knowledge, feeling, or action. 3. Something experienced. — v.t. To have the lot or fortune of; undergo; feel.

ex'pert (eks'purt), n. An expert or experienced person; hence, a specialist.

ex-pire' (ek-spir'), v.t. To breathe out; emit from the lungs. —v.i. 1. To emit the breath. 2. To die. 3. To come to an end; cease.

ex-ploit' (-ploit'), n. A deed or act; esp., a heroic act; a deed of renown.

ex-port' (eks-port'), v.t. To carry or send abroad in the way of commerce.

ex-po-sure (-po'zhur), n. 1. Act of exposing; state of being exposed. 2. Position as to points of compass, influences of climate, etc.

ex'qui-site (eks'kwi-zit), a. 1. Exciting intense delight or admiration by reason of rare beauty, excellence, or perfection.

ex-tend (esk-tend'), v.t. 1. To stretch or draw out; hence, to lengthen in space or time. 2. To straighten out, as a limb. 3. To enlarge, expand, as a surface, or as power, etc. 4. To hold out or reach forth. — v.i. To

stretch or stretch out; reach; be broad or comprehensive.

ex-tinct' (-tinkt'), a. 1. Extinguished; gone out. 2. No longer living or active; obsolete.

ex-tort' (-tort'), v.t. To obtain (something, as money or a confession) from a person by force, threats, violence, etc.; wring; exact.

ex'tra (eks'tra), a. or Adv. Beyond what is due, usual, or necessary; additional; hence, superior.

ex'tra-di'tion (-dish'un), n. Surrender of an alleged criminal by one state to another; surrender of a prisoner by one authority or another.

ex-treme' (-trem'), a. 1. Utmost; most remote. 2. Last; final. 3. Greatest in degree; such as cannot be exceeded. 4. Very great; hence, excessive; immoderate; radical. — n.

ex'tri-cate (-kat), v.t. To free, as from difficulties; disentangle.

ex-u'ber-ant (-ant), a. Characterized by abundance or superabundance.

ex-ult' (eg-zult'), v.i. To be in high spirits; rejoice exceedingly; triumph.

eye'glass' (i'glas'), n. 1. A lens of glass or plastic used to correct defects of vision.

eye'wit'ness (i'wit-nes), n. One who sees something done or happen and can testify to it.

F

fa'ble (fa'b'l), n. 1. A fictitious narrative or statement; untruth. 2. A story with a moral, esp. one in which animals apeak and act like human beings.

fab'ric (fab'rik), n. 1. A structure. 2. Texture. 3. Cloth woven or knot from fibers.

fab'u-lous (-lus), a. 1. Feigned, as a fable; fictitious. 2. Like a fable, esp. in exaggeration; astonishing.

face (fas), n. 1. The front part of the head; of man, the part of the head including from forehead to chin. 2. Expression; look. 3. Boldness; effrontery. 4. Presence; view. 5. The physical features of a country. 6. The surface of anything; front. 7. Any bounding plane of a polyhe-

E
F

dron. 8. The exact amount expressed on a note, bond, etc. — v.t.

fa'cial (fa'shal), a. Of or pertaining to the face.

fa-cil'i-tate (fa-sil'i-tat), v.t. To make easy or less difficult.

fac-sim'i-le (fak-sim'i-le), n. An exact copy or likeness.

fact (fakt), n. 1. A thing done or that comes to pass; event; occurrence; act; circumstance. 2. The quality of being actual or real.

fac'tious (-shus), a. 1. Given to faction, or dissension; seditious. 2. Due to, or characterized by, faction.

fac-ti'tious (fak-tish'us), a. Artificial; not natural.

fac'tor (fak'ter), n. 1. One who does business for another; agent. 2. Math. Any of the quantities which, multiplied together, form a product. 3. One of the elements that contribute to produce a result. — v.t. To resolve into factors.

fac'to-ry (fak'to-ri), n. 1. A trading station. 2. A building, or collection of buildings, for the manufacture of goods.

fac'ul-ty (fak'ul-ti), n. 1. Ability to act or do. 2. Special endowment; knack; talent. 3. One of the powers of mind or sense. 4. A department of instruction in a university. 5. The teachers in a university or college.

fad (fad), n. A hobby; craze.

fade (fad), v.i. 1. To grow weak; decay; wither. 2. To lose freshness or brightness; grow dim. 3. To vanish. — v.t. To cause to fade.

fail'ing, vb. n. A falling short; failure; fault.

fail'ure (fal'ur), n. 1. A failing; default; deficiency. 2. Omission to perform. 3. Want of success; state of having failed. 4. Breaking down; decline; decay. 5. A becoming insolvent or bankrupt. 6. One that has failed.

fair (far), a. 1. Pleasing to the eye; beautiful. 2. Free from spots, specks, dirt, or imperfection; unblemished. 3. Distinct; legible, as writing. 4. Characterized by frankness, honesty, or impartiality; open; just. 5. Open to legitimate pursuit; — chiefly in fair game. 6. Light; blond. 7. Without marked merit or defect; average; middling. 8.Not stormy; favorable; also, clear; cloudless. 9. Unobstructed; clear, as, a fair view. — adv. In a fair manner.

fair'ly, adv. In a fair manner; justly, plainly, etc.

faith (fath), n. 1. Firm belief or trust (in a person, thing, doctrine, etc.). 2. Recognition of spiritual realities and moral principles as supreme. 3. That which is believed; esp., a system of religious beliefs. 4. Fidelity; loyalty.

faith'ful (-fool), a. 1. Firm in adherence to promises and other engagements. 2. True in affection or allegiance. 3. Worthy of confidence; accurate, as a story.

fake (fak), v.t. To do, make, or work upon in some way, esp. so as to invent fictitiously, falsify, or the like. — v.i. To practice faking anything. — n. Any person or thing not as purported to be. All Colloq. or Slang.

fak'er (fak'er), n. Slang. One who fakes; as: a A peddler at fairs, etc. b A fraud; petty swindler.

fall (fol), v.i. 1. To pass downwards freely; drop; hence, to hang freely. 2. a To lose dignity, character, or the like. b To come to pass as if by descending; as, night falls. c To be uttered, as words. d To be lowered, as the glance. e To sound less loud or high.

fall'en (fol'n), p.a. Dropped; prostrate; degraded; ruined; shrunken; decreased; dead, etc.

fal'li-ble (fal'i-b'l), a. 1. Liable to err or to be deceived. 2. Liable to be erroneous, as rules.

false'ly, adv. In a false manner; erroneously.

fal'si-fy (-fi), v.t. To make false; also, to prove false; disprove. — v.i. To lie.

fal'ter (fol'ter), v.i. To move or act unsteadily or waveringly; hesitate.

fa-mil'iar (fa-mil'yar), a. 1. Closely acquainted; intimate. 2. Like an intimate friend; not formal. 3. Well-known; common; frequent. — n. An intimate; companion.

fa-mil'iar-ize (-mil'yar-iz), v.t. 1. To make well known or familiar. 2. To make (a person or one's self) familiar or intimate (with).

fam'i-ly (fam'i-li), n. 1. The body of persons who live in one house, and under one head; a household. — a. Those descended from a common progenitor; a tribe, clan, or race; kindred. b Lineage; esp., honorable lineage; noble stock; as, a man of family.

fam'ine (-in), n. 1. General scarcity of food; dearth; destitution. 2. Extreme scarcity of something; as, a coal famine. 3. Starvation.

fan (fan), n. 1. An instrument for producing currents of air by the motion of a broad surface. 2. Something fan-shaped.

fa-nat'i-cism (-siz'm), n. Excessive enthusiasm or unreasoning zeal, esp. as to religion.

fan'cy (fan'si), n. 1. The faculty by which the mind forms images of things not present; imagination. 2. An image formed in the mind; thought; idea. 3. A caprice; whim; impression. 4. Inclination; liking formed by caprice. — a.

fan'fare (fan'far'), n. A flourish of trumpets, etc.

fan-tas'tic (fan-tas'tik), a. Grotesque; quaint; whimsical; fanciful.

fan'ta-sy (fan'ta-si), n. 1. Imagination; fancy. 2. A product of imagination, as: a A mental image; phantasm; hallucination. b An ingenious or fanciful design or invention. 3. Whimsical or capricious mood.

farce (fars), n. 1. A light dramatic composition intended to excite laughter or absurdly extravagant incident. 2. Ridiculous or empty show; mockery.

far'-fetched', pa. Not naturally deduced or introduced; forced; as, a far-fetched joke.

fa-ri'na (fa-ri'na; -re'na), n. A kind of fine flour or meal of starchy material, as cereals, nuts, etc.

farm (farm), n. A tract of land devoted to agriculture.

far'sight'ed (-sit'ed), a. 1. Seeing to a great distance; sagacious. 2. Able to see distant objects more clearly than near ones.

fas'ci-nate (-nat), v.t. & i. 1. To influence by some powerful charm.

2. Captivate.

fash'ion (fash'un), n. 1. The make or form of anything. 2. The prevailing mode or style, esp. of dress. 3. Something fashionable; a fad.

fast (fast), v.i. To abstain from food or to eat sparingly, as by way of religious discipline. — n. 1. Abstinence from food, or from certain kinds of food. 2. A time of fasting.

fas'ten (fas'n), v.t. 1. To fix firmly; secure, as by a knot, lock etc. 2. To cause to hold fast; attach firmly.

fat (fat), a. 1. Fleshy; plump. 2. Oily; rich; resinous.

fa-tal'i-ty (fa'tal'i-ti), n. 1. State of being fatal. 2. That which is decreed by fate; destiny. 3. Fatal influence; mortality. 4. A calamity; disaster, esp. one resulting in death.

fa'ther (fa'ther), n. 1. A male parent. 2. A forefather. pl., ancestors. 3. A producer, author, or contriver. 4. [cap.] The Supreme Being and Creator; God. 5. As a title: a A dignitary of the church, as a bishop. b A confessor; — called also father confessor. c A priest. — v.t.

fault (folt), n. 1. A defect; an imperfection; a failing; flaw. 2. A moral failing less serious than a vice. 3. Negligence; also, culpability; responsibility; blame.

fa'vor (fa'ver), n. 1. Kind regard; commendation; approving disposition. 2. Act of countenancing; state of being countenanced. 3. A kind act; kindness.

fa'vor-ite (-er-it), a. Regarded with peculiar affection.

fawn (fon), n. A young deer.

fear (fer), n. 1. The painful emotion caused by a sense of impending danger of evil; dread. 2. The dread reverence felt toward God.

Feb'ru-a-ry (feb'roo-a'ri), n. The second month of the year, having 28 days, or, in leap year, 29.

fed'er-al (fed'er-al), a. 1. Pertaining to a state consolidated of several states retaining limited powers; as, a federal government.

feed (fed), v.t. To give food to.

feel (fel), v.t. 1. To perceive by touch. 2. To examine by touching; to test.

E
F

3. To be conscious of; experience.

feel'ing, p.a. 1. Sentient; that can feel; sensitive; sympathetic. 2. Having or expressing great sensibility.

fe'line (fe'lin), a. 1. Of or pertaining to the cat family. 2. Catlike; sly; stealthy; treacherous.

fell, v.t. 1. To cut, beat, or knock down. 2. To sew or hem down in a certain way. — n.

fel'low (fel'o), n. 1. A companion; comrade; associate; contemporary. 2. An equal in power, rank, character, etc. 3. One of two things used together. 4. A person; individual. 5. A man of low breeding or of little worth.

fel'o-ny (fel'o-ni), n. Any of various crimes more serious than misdemeanors.

fem'i-nine (fem'i-nin), a. 1. Female; of the female sex. 2. Of or pert. to a woman or women.

fem'i-nin'i-ty (-nin't-ti), n. Quality or nature of the female sex; womanliness.

fence (fens), n. 1. Art of fencing, or use of the sword. 2. An inclosing barrier, as of pickets, wire, stone, etc., as around a field. — v.t.

fend (fend), v.t. To keep or ward off. — v.i. To act on the defensive; resist; parry.

fe-ro'cious (fe-ro'shus), a. Fierce; savage; cruel.

fer'ry (fer'i), v.t. To transport over a river, strait, etc., in a boat. — v.i. To pass over water in a boat or by a ferry.

fer'tile (fur'til), a. 1. Producing in abundance; fruitful; prolific. 2. Capable of producing offspring, seed, or fruit.

fer'vent (-vent), a. 1. Hot; glowing; burning. 2. Warm in feeling; zealous.

fes'ti-val (-ti-val), n. 1. A time of feasting or celebration. 2. A periodical season of entertainment.

fetch (fech), v.t. 1. To bring, or to go and bring; get. 2. To perform; hence, to draw (a breath); heave (a sigh). 3. To attain; reach.

feud (fud), n. A quarrel; esp. an inveterate strife between families, clans, or the like.

few (fu), a. Not many; of small number.

fi-as'co (fe-as'ko), n. A complete or ridiculous failure, as of a play.

fib (fib), n. A falsehood concerning a trivial manner.

fi'ber (fi'ber), n. 1. A thread or threadlike substance.

fick'le (fik'l), a. Changeable; inconstant; as, fickle princes, winds, etc.

fi-del'i-ty (fi-del'i-ti; fi-), n. Faithfulness; careful observance of duty or obligations; esp.: a Loyalty. b Exactness; accuracy.

fidg'et (fij'et), v.i. To move about uneasily, as if restless. —v.t. To cause to fidget; make nervous.

fiend (fend), n. A malicious foe; one diabolically wicked; specif., the Devil; a demon.

fierce (fers), a. 1. Furious; violent; impetuous. 2. Vehement in anger; ferocious.

fi'er-y (fi'er-i), a. 1. Consisting of, or like fire. 2. Ardent; impetuous. 3. Heated; inflamed.

fig (fig), n. 1. A small pear-shaped fruit, pulpy when ripe, and eaten raw or preserved or dried with sugar; also, the tree which bears the fruit. 2. The value of a fig, almost nothing.

fight (fit), n. 1. A battle; combat. 2. Any contest. 3. Strength or disposition for fighting; pugnacity.

fig'ment (fig'ment), n. An invented statement, doctrine, etc.; a fiction.

fig'ure (fig'ur), n. 1. A numerical symbol; numeral; digit; as, 1, 2, 3, etc. 2. Value as expressed in numbers; price. Colloq. 3. Form; shape; outline.

fill (fil), v.t. 1. To make full. 2. Naut. (1) to dilate; distend, as a sail. (2) To trim (a yard) to the wind. 3. To furnish an abundant supply to; to pervade. 4. To feed; satisfy.

fil'ter (fil'ter) n. Anything porous through which liquid is passed to cleanse or strain it, or an apparatus containing such substance.

filth (filth), n. 1. Foul matter; repulsive dirt; nastiness. 2. Moral defilement; corruption.

fi'nal (fi'nal), a. 1. Pertaining to, or occurring at, the end; last. 2. Conclusive; decisive.

fi-nance' (fi-nans'), n. 1. Pecuniary

resources, esp. of a ruler or of a state; — usually in pl. 2. The conduct of monetary affairs. -v.t. To conduct the finances of; provide the capital for.

fi-nan'cial (fi-nan'shal), a. Pertaining to finance, or money matters.

fi'an-cier' (fin'an-ser'), n. 1. One having the administration of finance. 2. One skilled in financial operations.

find (find), v.t. 1. To meet with, come upon, or light upon; as: a To discover by study or experiment. b to gain; get; procure. c To attain to; arrive at; reach. 2. To arrive at, as a conclusion.

fin'ger (fin'ger), n. 1. One of the digits of the hand, esp. one other than the thumb. 2. Something like, or suggestive of, a finger, as a pointer.

fin'ish (fin'ish), v.t. 1. To arrive at the end of; end; terminate. 2. To complete; perfect. 3. To dispose of completely.

fire'proof' (-proof'), a. Relatively incombustible.

fire'work' (-wurk'), n. 1. A device for producing a display of light or a figure in fire; — usually in pl. 2. pl. A pyrotechnic exhibition.

firm (furm), a. 1. Fixed; hence, closely compressed; unyielding; as, firm flesh or wood. 2. Not easily moved; established; loyal. 3. Solid.

firm (furm), n. The name under which a company transacts business; partnership; commercial house.

firm'ly, adv. In a firm manner.

firm'ness, n. State of quality of being firm.

first (furst), a. Preceding all others, as in time or rank. — adv. 1. Before any or some other person or thing in time, space, rank, etc. 2. For the first time.

first'-class (furst'klas'), a. Of the best or highest class, rank, or quality. — adv. By a first-class conveyance; as, to travel first-class.

first'-hand' (-hand'), adv. Directly from the original source.

first'-rate' (-rat'), a. Very efficient or good.

fis'cal (fis'kal), a. 1. Pertaining to the public treasury or revenue. 2. Financial.

fish (fish), n. 1. Any completely aquatic, water-breathing vertebrate having the limbs (when present) developed as fins and, usually, a scaly body. 3. The flesh of fish, used as food.

fish'er-man (-er-man), n. One whose occupation is to catch fish.

fish'hook' (fish'hook'), n. A hook for catching fish.

fish'y (fish'i), a. 1. Consisting of, or having the qualities, taste, or odor of fish. 2. Improbable.

fist (fist), n. The hand clenched, esp. for a blow.

fit (fit), a. 1. Adapted to an end, object, or design; qualified. 2. Becoming; seemly; proper. 3. Prepared; ready.

fit'ful (fit'fool), a. Spasmodic; impulsive and unstable.

fit'ness, n. State or quality of being fit or fitted.

fiz'zle (fiz'l), v.i. 1. To fizz. 2. To burn with a fizz and then go out; hence; to fail ignominiously after a good beginning. Colloq.

flag, n. A light cloth bearing a device or devices to indicate nationality, party, etc.; or to give or ask information; a standard; banner, ensign.

flam-boy'ant (flam-boi'ant), a. 1. Gorgeous; showy.

flame (flam), n. 1. A body of burning gas or vapor. 2. State of blazing combustion; blaze; glow. 3. Burning zeal; passion; ardor. 4. A sweet-heart.

fla-min'go (fla-min'go), n. Any of several long-legged tropical or semi-tropical aquatic birds.

flap (flap), n. 1. Anything broad and limber or flat and thin, that hangs loose.

flare (flar), v.i. 1. To burn or blaze out with a sudden unsteady light. 2. to open or spread outward.

flash'y (flash'i), a. 1. Flashing; dazzling for a moment. 2. Showy; gaudy.

flat, a. 1. Having a surface level and smooth. 2. Lying spread out; prostrate; hence, laid low; ruined. 3. Having broad smooth surfaces and little thickness.

flat'ter-y (-i), n. Act of pleasing by artful compliments; false or

E

F

insincere praise; also, blandishment.

flaunt (flant; flont), v.i. & t. To wave, flutter, or move ostentatiously; parade or display obtrusively.

fla'vor (fla'ver), n. 1. Odor; fragrance. 2. That quality of anything which affects the taste; relish; savor. 3. A flavoring substance.

fleck (flek), n. A spot, as a freckle; a streak; speckle.

flee (fle), v.i. 1. To run away, as from danger. 2. To pass away swiftly; vanish. — v.t. To run away from; shun.

fleer (fler), v.i. & t. To laugh or grin coarsely; mock; gibe. — n. A derisive word or look.

flesh (flesh), n. 1. The softer parts of an animal body; animal food; meat.

flex (fleks), v.t. & i. To bend.

flex'i-ble (-b'l), a. 1. Capable of being flexed; pliable; not stiff. 2. Ready to yield; tractable; compliant. 3. Capable of being molded; plastic.

flick'er (flik'er), v.i. 1. To flutter. 2. To waver unsteadily like a dying flame; flutter.

flim'sy (flim'zi), a. Weak; slight; unsubstantial.

fling (fling), v.t. 1. To cast from or as from the hand; throw; hurl. 2. To throw off or down. 3. To send forth; emit. 4. To throw aside; cast off.

flip, v.t. 1. To toss; fillip; as, to flip a coin. 2. to flick; flirt.

float (flot), n. 1. Anything that floats on a fluid. 2. A flat-topped vehicle without sides for carrying a display; also, the vehicle with the display.

float'ing, p.a. 1. Buoyed on or in a fluid. 2. Shifting from place to place; not permanent. 3. Variable; not funded; as, a floating debt.

flood (flud), n. 1. A great flow of water; body of water overflowing land not usually covered; a deluge; inundation.

floor (flor), n. 1. The bottom of a room, on which one treads. 2. Hence, any ground surface, as of the sea. 3. The structure dividing a building horizontally into stories; hence, a story of a building.

flo'rist (flo'rist), n. A cultivator of, or dealer in, flowers.

flo-ta'tion (flo-ta'shun), n. Act of floating.

flour (flour), n. Finely ground meal of grain; esp., fine meal separated by bolting; hence, any fine soft powder.

flour'ish (flur'ish), v.i. 1. To grow luxuriantly; thrive. 2. To increase in wealth, honor, etc.; to be in one's prime. 3. To make ornamental strokes with the pen.

flow (flo), v.i. 1. To move or circulate, as a liquid; to run. 2. To proceed; issue forth. 3. To glide along smoothly; sound smoothly.

flow'er-pot' (-pot'), n. A vessel, esp. of pottery, for earth in which to grow plants.

fluc'tu-ate (fluk'tu-at), v.t. 1. To move as a wave; roll back and forth. 2. To waver; vacillate.

flu'ent (-ent), a. 1. Flowing, or capable of flowing, unstable. 2. Ready in the use of words; voluble; hence, flowing; smooth.

flu'id, n. A fluid substance; a liquid or gas.

flush (flush), v.i. 1. To flow and spread suddenly and freely; as, blood flushes into the face. 2. To turn red or hot; blush; glow.

flus'ter (flus'ter), v.t. To make hot and rosy, as with drinking; confuse.

flut'ter (flut'er), v.i. 1. To flap the wings rapidly, without flying. 2. To move with quick vibrations. 3. To move about agitatedly, with little result.

fly (fli), v.i. 1. To move in the air with wings. 2. To be driven through the air, as before the wind. 3. To move or pass swiftly.

foam (fom), n. The white substance, of minute bubbles, formed on liquids by agitation, fermentation, etc., froth; spume.

fog'gy (fog'i), a. 1. Filled with fog; misty. 2. Beclouded; muddled.

foil (foil), v.t. To defeat; baffle; frustrate; thwart.

folk'lore' (fok'lor'), n. Traditional customs, beliefs, etc., esp. such as are superstitious or legendary, current among the uneducated.

follow (fol'o), v.t. 1. To go or come after; attend. 2. To succeed in order of time, rank, etc. 3. To result from.

fond (fond), a. 1. Foolishly tender and loving, weakly indulgent. 2. Affectionate; tender.

food (food), n. 1. Nutriment taken into an organism for growth or repair and to maintain life. 2. Nutriment in solid form, as opposed to drink.

fool (fool), n. 1. One deficient in judgment; a simpleton. 2. A professional jester, formerly dressed in motley with cap and bells. 3. One made to appear foolish; butt; dupe. — v.i. To play the fool; jest; trifle. — v.t. To make a fool of; dupe.

fool'ish, a. 1. Exhibiting folly; unwise. 2. Proceeding from folly.

foot'ing, n. n. 1. Standing; stable position of the feet. 2. Place for the foot to rest on. 3. Relative position; condition; as, on a friendly footing. 4. Act of adding up, or amount of, a column of figures.

for-bear' (for-bar'), v.t. To do without; give up; abstain or refrain from.

forced (forst), p.a. 1. Compelled by force; compulsory; as, forced labor. 2. Done or produced laboriously; strained; as, a forced march.

for'ci-ble (for'si-b'l), a. 1. Effected by force. 2. Characterized by force, efficiency, or energy; strong; powerful.

fore'arm' (for-arm'), n. The part of the arm between the elbow and the wrist.

fore-bode' (for-bod'), v.t. & i. 1. To foretell; portend. 2. To have a premonition or presentiment of; augur despondingly.

fore-cast' (-kast'), v.t. & i. 1. To plan beforehand; project. 2. To foresee; calculate beforehand. 3. To predict.

fore-clo'sure (-klo'zhur), n. A proceeding which destroys a right to redeem a mortgaged property.

fore-gone' (-gon'), p.a. That has gone before; previous. — foregone conclusion. a A predetermined conclusion. b A result that was inevitable.

fore'head (for'ed), n. The part of the face above the eyes; the brow.

for'eign-er (-er), n. One not native, or not naturalized in the country under consideration; alien.

fore'man (for'man), n. The chief man; as: a The chairman of a jury. b The superintendent of a set of workmen.

fo-ren'sic (fo-ren'sik), a. Belonging to law courts or to public debate; rhetorical.

fore'sight' (for'sit'), n. 1. Act or power of foreseeing. 2. Care or provision for the future.

fore-tell' (for-tel'), v.t. & i. to tell beforehand; prophesy; foreshow.

for-ev'er (for-ev'er), adv. 1. Through eternity; eternally. 2. At all times, incessantly.

for'feit (for'fit), n. 1. A thing forfeited; a fine; penalty. 2. Forfeiture.

for-get' (for-get'), v.t. 1. To lose remembrance of; be unable to recall. 2. To omit or disregard unintentionally; hence, to neglect; slight. — v.i. To cease remembering.

for-give' (for-giv'), v.t. 1. to give up resentment or claim to requital for (an offense or wrong); pardon. 2. To cease to feel resentment against; pardon.

for-lorn' (for-lorn'), a. Deserted, forsaken; miserable; wretched; almost hopeless; desperate.

for'mer (for'mer), a. Preceding in time or order; previous; prior; foregoing.

for'mer-ly (-li), adv. In time past; heretofore.

for'mi-da-ble (-mi-da-b'l), a. Exciting fear or dread; alarming.

for-sake' (for-sak'), v.t. To desert; abandon.

fort (fort), n. A strong or fortified place, esp. one occupied only by troops; a fortification.

forth (forth), adv. 1. Forward; onward in time, place, or order. 2. Out, as from concealment.

for'ti-fy (for'ti-fi), v.t. 1. To strengthen; invigorate. 2. To strengthen by forts or batteries.

for'ti-tude (for'ti-tud), n. Firmness in confronting danger or enduring trouble.

for'tu-nate (for'tu-nat), a. 1. Coming by or bringing good fortune. 2. Favored by fortune; lucky.

for'tune (-tun), n. 1. The arrival of something, or that which arrives or happens, in a sudden or unexpected manner; luck, hap. 2. That which is to befall one; destiny.

for'ward (for'werd), a. 1. Near, at, or belonging to, the fore part. 2. Moving or leading to the front;

E

F

onward. 3. Advanced; precocious.

fos'ter (fos'ter), a. Affording, receiving, or sharing nourishment or nurture, through not related by blood; as, foster parent, child, brother, nurse, etc.

foun·da'tion (foun-da'shun), n. 1. Act of founding. 2. That on which anything is founded; groundwork. 3. An endowment. 4. An endowed institution or charity.

found'er, n. One who founds, or establishes.

foun'tain (foun'tin), n. 1. A spring of water. 2. An artificial jet of water or the structure from which it flows. 3. A reservoir for a liquid, as ink. 4. Spring; source; as, a fountain of wisdom.

fox (foks), n. Any of certain animals of the dog family, noted for craftiness.

frac'tion (frak'shun), n. 1. A fragment; scrap. 2. One or more parts of a unit, as the fraction 3/4 (read "three fourths," or "3 divided by 4").

frac'tion-al (-al), a. 1. Of or pert. to fractions or a fraction. 2. Relatively small; inconsiderable.

frag'ile (fraj'il), a. Easily broken, frail.

frag'ment (frag'ment), n. A part broken off.

fra'grance (fra'grans), n. Quality of being fragrant; a pleasing odor.

frail (fral), a. 1. Fragile; weak. 2. Liable to be led into sin.

frame'work' (fram'wurk'), n. The work of framing, or the completed work; the frame or skeleton.

fran'chise (fran'chiz; -chiz), n. 1. Freedom; exemption; privilege. 2. A constitutional or statutory right or privilege, as the right to vote.

fran'tic (fran'tik), a. Frenzied; distracted.

fra-ter'nal (fra'tur-nal), a. Of, pertaining to, or involving brethren; brotherly; of or pert. to a fraternity.

fra-ter'ni-ty (-ni-ti), n. 1. Brotherhood. 2. A society of men, often secret, for religious, social, or business purposes, or for mutual aid; a brotherhood.

frat'er-nize (frat'er-niz), v.i. & t. To associate, or bring into fellowship, as brothers.

freck'le (frek'l), n. A small yellow or brown spot in the skin.

free (fre), a. 1. Not in bondage to another; enjoying liberty; independent. 2. Exempt or released, as from a tax or duty. 3. Not combined with anything else; unattached.

free'dom (fre'dum), n. Quality or state of being free; as: a Liberty; independence. b Frankness; unreservedness. c Facility.

free'-hand', a. Done by the hand without support, instruments; measurements, etc.

free'hold (fre'hold'), n. Law. A right to hold land for life or so it descents to one's heirs.

free'ly (fre'li), adv. In a free manner.

free'think'er (-think'er), n. One who forms opinions independently of the authority of the church.

free trade. Trade or commerce free from any governmental influences, as duties or bounties, intended to change its natural course.

freeze (frez), v.i. 1. To become congealed or solidified by cold; harden into ice. 2. To become greatly chilled. 3. To adhere, by freezing.

freight (frat), n. 1. The compensation paid for the transport of goods. 2. That with which anything is laden for or as for transportation; lading; cargo.

freight'er (-er), n. 1. One who loads a ship. 2. One who receives and forwards freight. 3. A vessel used mainly to carry freight.

fren'zy (fren'zi), n. Any violent mental agitation approaching to distraction. — v.t. To affect with frenzy.

fre'quen-cy (-kwen'si), n. Fact or condition of returning or occurring frequently.

fresh (fresh), a. 1. Newly produced, gathered, or made. 2. Not salt. 3. Pure; refreshing; brisk. 4. Having the qualities unimpaired, as by age, use, fatigue, etc. 5. Full of vigor, etc.; newly made ready for use. 6. Novel; recent; lately made public; hence, additional; further.

fresh'man (fresh'man), n. A student during his first year, as in a college.

fri'ar (-er), n. R.C. Ch. A brother of a religious order, esp. of a mendicant order.

fric'tion (-shun), n. 1. Act of rubbing

one body on another. 2. A resistance to motion between two surfaces in contact. 3. A clashing between persons or parties in opinions or work.

Fri'day (fri'da), n. The sixth day of the week.

friend (frend), n. 1. One attached to another by esteem and affection. 2. One of the same nation, party, kin, etc. 3. A favorer; promoter.

friend'ship, n. State of being friends, amity.

fright (frit), n. 1. Sudden violent fear; sudden alarm. 2. A thing that frightens; something ugly or shocking.

fright'en (frit'n), v.t. To throw into a state of alarm or fright; affright; terrify.

fright'ful (-fool), a. Terrifying; shocking; dreadful; awful.

frig'id (frij'id), a. 1. Very cold. 2. Wanting warmth, vivacity, etc.; stiff and formal.

fringe (frinj), n. 1. A trimming consisting of projecting ends of a fabric twisted or plaited together, or of loose threads or strips, etc. 2. Something suggestive of a fringe; a border.

frisk (frisk), n. A frolic; fit of wanton gayety.

friv'o-lous (friv'o-lus), a. 1. Of little weight or importance. 2. Given to trifling or levity; interested esp. in trifles.

frog (frog), n. 1. Any of numerous well-known web-footed tailless amphibians of aquatic habits. 2. The triangular elastic horny pad in the middle of the sole of a horse's foot.

frol'ic (frol'ik), a. Frolicsome; merry.

fron'tier (fron'ter; frun'ter), n. That part of a country facing another country or an unsettled region.

frost'ing, n. 1. A composition of sugar, as with beaten egg, used to cover or ornament cake, pudding, etc. 2. A lusterless finish of metal or glass.

fro'zen (fro'z'n), p.a. Congealed with cold.

fru-i'tion (froo-ish'un), n. Use or possession of anything; pleasure from possession or use.

fruit'less, a. Not bearing fruit; barren; unprofitable; as fruitless effort.

frus'trate (frus'trat), a. Frustrated.

fud'dle (fud'l), v.t. To make foolish, as with drink; muddle. Colloq.

fudge (fuj), n. 1. Nonsense; bosh; — often an exclamation of contempt. 2. A kind of soft candy.

fu'el (fu'el), n. Anything that feeds fire; hence, that which increases passion or the like.

fu'gi-tive (fu'ji-tiv), a. 1. Fleeing, as from danger. 2. Not durable; liable to fade. 3. Of fleeting interest. — n. 1. One who flees from pursuit, danger, service, etc. 2. A refugee.

ful'fill', ful-fil' (fool'fil'), v.t. To accomplish or carry out, as a promise; satisfy, as a desire; perform; bring to pass.

full (fool), n. Complete measure; highest degree.

full'ness, n. State or quality of being full.

ful'ly (fool'i; -li), adv. In a full manner or degree.

ful'mi-nate (ful'mi-nat), v.i. & t. 1. To detonate; explode violently. 2. To issue (decrees, etc.) authoritatively; thunder forth (menaces).

fume (fum), n. 1. Aromatic smoke, as of incense. 2. A vaporous or odorous exhalation, exp. if offensive; reek; as, sulphurous fumes.

fu'mi-gate (fu-mi'gat), v.t. To apply smoke or vapor to, esp. for disinfecting.

fun (fun), n. Sport; playful action or speech.

func'tion (funk'shun), n. 1. The proper action of anything; office; duty. 2. A religious, public, or social ceremony or gathering, esp. if elaborate or formal.

func'tion-a-ry ('a-ri), n. One charged with the performance of a function.

fund (fund), n. 1. An accumulation or deposit or resources; stock; supply. 2. A sum of money, esp. one for a specific object; pl., pecuniary resources.

fun'da-men'tal (fun'da-men'tal), a. Of or pert. to the foundation; essential; basal.

fu'ner-al (fu'ner-al), n. Ceremonies in connection with a burial; obsequies.

E
F

fu·ne're·al (fu-ne're-al), a. Appropriate to a funeral; sad and solemn.

fun'gi·cide (-ji-sid), n. Any substance that destroys fungi.

fun'nel (fun'el), n. 1. A vessel shaped like a hollow cone, tapering into a tube, through which liquids, powders, etc., may be run into another vessel. 2. A flue; smoke-stack.

fun'ny (-i), a. 1. Droll; comical; laughable. 2. Strange; queer; odd. Colloq.

fur'bish (-bish), v.t. To burnish; renovate.

fur'lough (-lo), n. Leave of absence, esp. to a soldier.

fur'nish (-nish), v.t. 1. To equip; supply with furniture. 2. To provide; supply.

fur'ni·ture (fur'ni-tur), n. 1. That with which anything is furnished. 2. Household furnishings.

fur'row (fur'o), n. 1. A trench made by or as by a plow. 2. Any narrow channel, or groove; a wrinkle.

fur'ry (fur'i), a. 1. Covered with fur; dressed in fur; furred. 2. Consisting of or resembling fur.

fur'ther·ance (-ans), n. Act of furthering, or helping forward; promotion; advancement; progress.

fu'sion (fu'zhun), n. 1. A melting. 2. State of fluidity or flowing from heat. 3. Union or blending of things melted, or as if melted, together.

fuss (fus), n. A commotion; unneces-sary ado.

fuss'y (fus'i), a. 1. Disposed to fuss; overnice; fidgety. 2. Showing much detail or nicety.

fu'tile (fu'til). a. 1. Useless; vain. 2. Of no importance; trifling.

G

gain (gan), n. Increase or addition to what one has of advantage or benefit; profit.

gain'ful (-fool), a. Profitable; advantageous.

ga'la (ga'la), n. A festival.

gal'ax·y (gal'ak-si), n. [cap.] The Milky Way.

gale (gal), n. 1. A wind stronger than a stiff breeze, but not so strong as a hurricane.

gall (gol), n. 1. A bitter fluid secreted by the liver; bile, esp. that from the ox. 2. The gall bladder.

gal'lant·ry (gal'ant-ri), n. 1. Bravery; a gallant action or speech. 2. Civility or polite attention to ladies.

gall bladder. The sac which receives the bile.

gal'ler·y (gal'er-i), n. 1. A long narrow room, hall, or passage; hence, a room for showing pictures, shooting, taking photographs, etc.

gal'lon (gal'un), n. A measure of capacity, containing four quarts. The United States standard gallon contains 231 cubic inches. Abbr. gal.

gal'lop (gal'up), v.i. To go or ride at a gallop.

ga·lore' (ga-lor'), adv. In abundance; plentifully.

gam'ble (-b'l), v.i. To game; hazard something on a chance; wager.

gam'bling (-bling), n. The act of playing or gaming for stakes; hence, any wagering.

game (gam), n. 1. Sport of any kind; fun; also, playful ridicule. 2. A contest according to set rules for amusement or for a stake.

gang (gang), n. 1. A group; company. 2. A set of similar implements arranged to act together.

gang'plank' (gang'plank'), n. A portable platform or bridge, used in entering or leaving a vessel.

gap (gap), n. 1. An opening in anything made by or as by breaking or parting; any breach of continuity. 2. A mountain pass, cleft, or ravine.

gape (gap; gap; colloq. gap), v.i. 1. To open the mouth wide, as in surprise or yawning; to open widely. 2. To stare with open mouth.

gar'rage' (ga'razh'; gar'aj), n. A place for housing automobiles, or an airship or flying machine.

gar'bage (gar'baj), n. Animal or vegetable refuse.

gar'den (gar'd'n), n. Ground used for cultivating herbs, fruits, flowers, or vegetables; hence, a very fertile region.

gar'gle (gar'g'l), v.t. To rinse, as the throat, agitating the liquid by expulsion of the breath.

gar'lic (-lik), n. A European plant of the lily family. Also, its pungent bulb, used in cooking.

gar'ment (gar'ment), n. Any article of clothing.

gar'nish (-nish), v.t. 1. To decorate; adorn. 2. Law. To garnishee.

gar'nish-ment (gar'nish-ment), n. 1. Ornament; embellishment.

gas engine. An internal-combustion engine using gaseous fuel; broadly, any internal-combustion engine.

gash (gash), v.t. To make a gash in.

gasp (gasp), v.t. To catch the breath convulsively; labor for breath.

gas'tric (-trik), a. Of or pertaining to the stomach.

gath'er (gath'er), v.t. 1. To bring together; assemble; collect; accumulate. 2. To infer; conclude.

gath'er-ing, vb. n. A crowd; assembly; abscess.

gawk'y (-i), a. Foolish and awkward; clumsy.

gay (ga), a. 1. Excited with merriment; merry. 2. Bright; brilliant. 3. Given to social pleasures or indulgences; hence, loose; licentious.

gaze (gaz), v.i. To fix the eyes in a steady and intent look. — n. A fixed, intent look.

gem (jem), n. 1. A precious stone, esp. when cut and polished; a jewel.

gen'der (jen'der), n. Distinction of a word or words according to sex; also, the distinctive form itself, or a class so distinguished.

gen'e-al'o-gist (jen'e-al'o-jist), n. One who traces or studies genealogies.

gen'e-al'o-gy (jen'e-al'o-ji; je'ne-), n. A history of the descent of an individual or family from an ancestor; pedigree; lineage.

gen'er-al (-al), a. 1. Of or pertaining to the whole, or all; not local, or particular. 2. Not limited in meaning or application; not specific, or in detail.

gen'er-al-ize (jen'er-al-iz), v.t. To make general; reduced to general laws.

gen'er-al-ly (-l), adv. 1. In general, commonly; extensive. 2. In a general way; on the whole.

gen'er-ate (-at), v.t. 1. To beget; produce (offspring). 2. To originate,

esp. by a vital or chemical process.

gen'er-a'tion (-a'shun), n. 1. Act of generating. 2. A step in natural descent; those of the same stage in descent from an ancestor, or living at one period; also, the average lifetime of man.

ge-ner'ic (je-ner'ik), a. 1. Biology. Pertaining to a genus. 2. Pertaining to things of the same kind or class; characteristic of, or dealing with, groups rather than individuals.

gen'er-ous (jen'er-us), a. 1. Liberal; munificent. 2. Marked by generosity; ample; as a generous table.

gen'e-sis (-e-sis), n. 1. [cap.] The first book of the Bible; narrating the creation of the world. 2. Origin; mode of coming into existence.

ge'ni-al (je'ni-al; jen'yal), a. Favorable to growth or comfort; hence, sympathetically cheerful and cheering; jovial; kindly.

ge'ni-al'i-ty (je'ni-al'i-ti; jen-yal'-), n. Quality of being genial; cheerfulness; warmth.

gen'tile (jen'til), n. One not Jewish in nationality or faith; — in biblical use usually capitalized.

gen'tly ((-tli), adv. In a gentle manner.

gen'u-ine (jen'u-in), a. 1. Actually from the reputed source or author; authentic; real. 2. Of or pertaining to the original stock. 3. Sincere; frank.

ge-og'ra-phy (je-or'ra-fi), n. The description of the earth, its climate, products, inhabitants, etc.

ge-ol'o-gy (-ji), n. The science of the history of the earth and its life.

ge-om'e-try (-tri), n. The branch of mathematics treating of the relations and properties of solids, surfaces, lines, and angles.

ge-ra'ni-um (je-ra'ni-um), n. 1. Any of various plants with, usually, pink or purple flowers, and leaves of pungent odor. 2. Any of numerous cultivated plants of an allied genus, mostly with red, pink, or white flowers.

germ (jurm), n. 1. The earliest form of an organism; bud; seed; embryo. 2. Any microscopic organism, especially one that causes disease; microbe.

ger-mi-cid'al (jur-mi-sid'al), a. Destructive to germs, esp. disease

G
H

germs.

ger'mi-nate (-nat), v.i. & t. To sprout.

ges-ta'tion (jes-ta'shun), n. Pregnancy.

ges'ture (jes'tur), n. A bodily motion or posture intended to express or emphasize something.

get (get), v.t. 1. To come by; come to have; hence, to obtain, ascertain, learn, gain, win, etc.

ghast'ly (gast'li), a. 1. Horrible; shocking; as, ghastly wounds. 2. Ghostlike in appearance; deathly; pale; as, a ghastly face.

ghost (gost), n. 1. The soul; also, a disembodied soul; spirit; hence, an apparition; specter. 2. Any faint shadowy semblance; a phantom.

gi'ant (ji'ant), n. 1. A mythical manlike being or monster of huge stature. 2. A person, or an animal, plant, or thing, of extraordinary size or power.

gib'ber (jib'er; gib'er), v.i. & t. To speak rapidly and inarticulately; chatter.

gid'dy (gid'i), a. 1. Having a sensation of whirling in the head; dizzy. 2. Inducing giddiness. 3. Marked by inconstancy; flighty.

gift'ed, pa. Endowed with a gift; talented.

gi-gan'tic (ji-gan'tik), a. Like a giant.

gig'gle (gig'l), v.i. To laugh with short catches of the breath; laugh in an affected or silly manner.

gin (jin), n. A strong distilled alcoholic liquor flavored with juniper berries.

gin'ger-bread' (-bred'), n. 1. A kind of plain cake flavored with ginger. 2. Something tawdry and unsubstantial.

ging'ham (ging'am), n. A cotton or linen cloth, woven of dyed yarn, usually in stripes or checks.

gi'raffe' (ji-raf'), n. An African ruminant mammal. It is the tallest of quadrupeds.

girl (gurl), n. 1. A female child; a maiden. 2. A female servant.

gla'cier (gla'sher; glas'i-er), n. A body of ice, formed in a region of perpetual snow, and moving slowly down a mountainslope or valley, as in the Alps, or over an extended area, as in Greenland.

glad (glad), a. 1. Characterized by joy or pleasure; pleased; happy. 2. Expressive of, or exciting, gladness. 3. Characterized by brightness and beauty.

glad'den (glad'n), v.t. & i. To make, be, or become, glad.

glam'our (glam'er), n. Magic; a spell; a charm.

glance (glans), v.i. 1. To strike obliquely and fly off or turn aside. 2. To flash; gleam. 3. To look with a sudden, rapid cast of the eye.

glare (glar), v.i. 1. To shine dazzlingly. 2. To stare with fierce or piercing eyes.

glass (glas), n. 1. A hard, brittle, and, usually, transparent substance made by fusing together silica, as sand, an alkali, as potash or soda, and some other ingredient, as lime or lead oxide. 2. Collectively, articles made of glass.

glass'y (-i), a. 1. Resembling glass, as in smoothness. 2. Dull.

glaze (glaz), v.t. 1. To furnish or fit (a window, etc.) with glass. 2. To overlay with a surface of or like glass.

glide (glid), v.i. To move smoothly; pass silently and without apparent effort.

glim'mer-ing (glim'er-ing), vb. n. A faint, unsteady light; hence, a faint view or idea; inkling.

glimpse (glimps), n. 1. A faint appearance. 2. A short, hurried view.

globe (glob), n. 1. A spherical body; ball; sphere; orb. 2. The earth.

gloom (gloom), n. Partial or total darkness; deep shade; hence, low spirits.

gloom'y (gloom'i), a. 1. Dusky; dim. 2. Affected with or expressing gloom; melancholy.

glo'ri-fy (glor'ri-fi), v.t. 1. To make glorious; bestow honor and distinction upon. 2. To render homage to; adore.

glor'y (glo'ri), n. 1. Praise, admiration, or distinction, accorded by common consent, renown. 2. That which secures praise or renown. 3. Brilliancy; radiant beauty.

glos'sa-ry (glos'a-ri), n. A collection of glosses; a partial dictionary of a work, explaining the hard words, etc.

glove (gluv), n. A cover for the hand with a separate sheath for each finger.

glue (gloo), n. 1. A brownish gelatin, got by boiling skins, hoofs, etc., of animals, and used when heated with water as a cement. 2. Any of various sticky substances.

glut'ton-y -i), n. Excess in eating.

gnome (nom), n. One of an imaginary race of dwarfs dwelling in the inner parts of the earth.

go (go), v.i. 1. To pass from one place to another; proceed. 2. To depart.

goal (gol), n. 1. The bound or point where a race or journey is to end. 2. The final purpose, end, or aim.

goat (got), n. Any of certain hollow-horned ruminant animals closely allied to the sheep.

goat'ee' (go'te'), n. A beard on the chin, trimmed in a tuft like the beard of a he-goat.

gob'ble (gob'l), v.t. To swallow greedily; gulp.

go'-be-tween', n. One that goes between persons with messages, etc., an intermediary.

gob'lin (-lin), n. A sprite usually conceived as ugly or grotesque and as mischievous or evil.

god (god), n. 1. A being of more than human attributes and powers; a deity. 2. Any object thought to be endowed with divine powers; an idol. 3. [cap.] The Supreme Being.

god'child' (-child'), n. One for whom a person becomes sponsor at baptism.

god'ly (-li), a. Pious; reverencing God; devout; righteous.

god'par'ent (-par'ent), n. Godfather or godmother.

God'speed' (-sped'), n. Success; prosperous journeying; —contraction of "God speed you."

go'ing (go'ing), vb. n. 1. Departure. 2. Condition of the ground or of a road, etc., as for traveling.

gold (gold), n. 1. A precious metal of yellow color, — the most malleable and ductile metal, and one of the heaviest substances known. 2. Gold coin; riches. 3. The yellow color of the metal.

gold'en (gol'd'n), a. 1. Of or pertaining to gold. 2. Of the color of gold. 3. Precious; excellent. 4. Prosperous . and happy.

gold'fish' (-fish'), n. A small fish, of golden color.

golf (golf), n. A game in which a small, hard ball is struck with clubs so as to drive it into a series of holes.

good (good), a. 1. Having desirable qualities; sufficient or satisfactory. 2. Beneficial; fortunate. 3. Agreeable; pleasant; cheerful. 4. Morally excellent; virtuous; well-behaved.

good'ness, n. Quality or state of being good; excellence; virtue; kindness; beneficence.

gore, v.t. & i. To pierce or wound as with a horn.

gor'geous (gor'jus), a. Imposing through splendid or various coloring; magnificent; dazzling.

go'ril'la (go'ril'a), n. The largest anthropoid ape.

gos'sip (-ip), n. 1. An idle tattler. 2. Idle personal talk; groundless rumor.

Goth'ic (goth'ik), a. Pertaining to or designating a style of architecture characterized by pointed arches and steep roofs.

gov'ern (guv'ern), v.t. 1. To direct; control; restrain; manage. 2. Gram. To require to be (in a particular case or mood); to require (a particular case or mood).

gov'ern-ment (-ern-ment), n. 1. A governing, control; direction of affairs of state. 2. Mode or system of governing; as, a democratic government.

gown (goun), n. A loose, flowing outer garment; as: a the ordinary outer dress of a woman. 2. A nightgown.

grace (gras), n. 1. Good will; favor; disposition to show mercy, etc.

grade (grad), n. Rate of ascent or descent of a road, etc.; also, an incline.

grad'u-al (grad'u-al), a. Proceeding by steps or degrees.

grad'ua-te (-at), n. One who has been graduated.

gram'mar (gram'er), n. 1. The science or art treating of the classes of words, their inflections, syntax, etc. 2. Manner of speaking or writing, in reference to conformity to grammatical rules.

grand'child' (grand'child'), n. Child of one's son or daughter.

gran'deur (gran'dur), n. State or quality of being grand; magnificence.

grand'moth'er (grand'muth'er), n. Mother of one's father or mother; any female ancestor more remote than a mother.

grant (grant), v.t. 1. To agree to; accord. 2. To give. 3. To admit; concede.

grant'or (gran'tor; gran-tor'), n. Law. One by whom a grant is made.

gran'ule (gran'ul), n. A little grain; pellet.

grape (grap), n. 1. The berry of the grapevine. 2. A grapevine. 3. Grapeshot.

grape'fruit' (grap'froot'), n. A tropical fruit with bitter rind and acid pulp.

grave'vine (grap'vin'), n. A vine bearing smooth berries in clusters.

grap'ple (-'l), n. 1. A grapnel. 2. A seizing or seizure; close hug in contest.

grasp (grasp), v.i. To make the motion of seizing; clutch.

grate'ful (-fool), a. 1. Having a due sense of benefits received. 2. Affording pleasure; pleasing; gratifying.

gra-tu'i-tous (gra'tu'i-tus), a. 1. Given without recompense or pay; free. 2. Not based upon reason, cause, or proof; groundless; uncalled-for.

gra'tu'i-ty (-ti), n. Something given without recompense, or in return for a favor or service; a gift; a tip.

grave, n. An excavation in the earth as a place of burial; a tomb; sepulcher.

grav'el (grav'el), n. 1. Small stones and pebbles, often mingled with sand. 2. Small concretions in the kidneys or bladder; also, the disease indicated by them.

grave'yard' (-yard'), n. A cemetery.

grav'i-ta'tion (-ta'shun), n. 1. Act or process of gravitating. 2. The attraction by which all bodies or particles of matter tend toward each other.

grav'i-ty (-ti), n. 1. State of being grave; seriousness. 2. Gravitation; esp. the attraction of bodies toward the center of the earth.

gra'vy (gra'vi), n. 1. A liquid dressing for meat, etc. 2. The juice that drips from flesh during and after cooking.

greed'y (-i), a. 1. having a keen appetite; ravenous; voracious. 2. Having eager desire; avaricious.

green'back' (gren'bak'), n. Any United States legal-tender note having the back printed in green.

green'horn' (-horn'), n. An inexperienced person.

green'house' (-hous'), n. A building constructed chiefly of glass and used for growing tender plants.

greet (gret), v.t. To address, esp. with kind words; accost.

grid'dle (grid'l), n. A plate for cooking thin cakes of batter (griddlecakes) over a fire.

grief (gref), n. 1. Mental suffering, as from affliction, etc., or a cause of it. 2. A mishap; disaster; failure; — esp. in to come, or bring, to grief.

griev'ous (grev'us), a. 1. Distressing; hence, severe. 2. Atrocious. 3. Full of or expressing grief.

grime (grim), n. Soot or dirt, rubbed in.

grin (grin), v.i. To show the teeth, as in a smile of merriment, derision, etc.

groan (gron), v.i. 1. To utter a deep, moaning sound.

gro'cer (gro'ser), n. A dealer in tea, coffee, sugar, spices, fruits, and other foodstuffs.

gro'cer-y (-ser-i), n. 1. The commodities sold by grocers; — usually in pl. 2. A retail grocer's shop. U.S.

groom (groom), n. 1. A manservant, now, esp., one in charge of horses. 2. A bridegroom.

groove (groov), n. 1. A channel; furrow; rut. 2. A fixed routine.

gro-tesque' (gro-tesk'), a. 1. Characterized by fantastic exaggeration or combination, esp. of human and animal figures. 2. Absurdly incongruous or awkward.

ground (ground), n. 1. The surface of the earth. 2. A region, territory, or piece of land. 3. Land; estate; esp., pl. the gardens, lawns, etc., of a homestead.

group (groop), n. An assemblage of persons of things considered as a unit; cluster; aggregation.

grove (grov), n. A group of trees without underwood; a small wood.

grow (gro), v.i. 1. To spring up and mature; be developed; thrive; increase. 2. To increase by gradual assimilation of new matter into the living organism, as animals, plants, etc. 3. To come to be; become.

growth (groth), n. 1. Act of growing; development. 2. That which has grown or is growing.

grue'some (groo'sum), a. Inspiring fear or horror; horrid.

gruff (gruf), a. Of rough manner, speech, or countenance; surly.

grum'ble (grum'b'l), v.i. & t. To murmur with discontent; to growl; mutter.

guar'an-tee' (gar'an-te'), n. 1. A person to whom a guaranty is made; also, a guarantor. 2. A guaranty.

guard (gard), v.t. To protect; defend; shelter; watch over; restrain.

guard'i-an (gar'di-an), n. 1. One who guards or secures; a warden. 2. Law. One who has, or is entitled to, the care of the person or property, or both, of another.

guess (ges), v.t. & i. 1. To form an opinion of without certain knowledge; judge of at random; conjecture. 2. To hit on or solve by conjecture. 3. To suppose; believe. Colloq. n. A conjecture; surmise.

guest (gest), n. 1. A visitor; a person received and entertained in one's house. 2. Any person who lodges, boards, or receives refreshment, for pay, at a hotel, etc.

guide (gid), v.t. To act as a guide to; conduct; lead; pilot; regulate and manage; direct.

guilt'y (gil'ti), a. 1. Having incurred guilt; justly chargeable with a delinquency, crime, or sin. 2. Evincing, indicating, or involving guilt; sensible of guilt.

guise (giz), n. 1. Customary way of speaking or acting; fashion; behavior. 2. Appearance, esp. as to dress; aspect.

gulp (gulp), v.t. To swallow eagerly, or at one swallow.

gum'drop (-drop'), n. A confection of sweetened gum arabic, gelatin, or the like, molded in drops.

gump'tion (gump'shun), n. Shrewdness; common sense, cleverness. Colloq.

gun (gun), n. 1. A cannon. 2. Any portable firearm, esp. a rifle, carbine, or shotgun.

gun'ner (-er), n. 1. A Cannoneer. 2. One who hunts with a gun.

gust (gust), n. 1. A sudden blast of wind. 2. A sudden outburst, esp. of temper.

gus'to (-to), n. Taste; keen appreciation; zest.

gust'y (-ti), a. Windy; stormy.

gut'ter (gut'er), n. 1. A channel at the eaves of a house for carrying away rain. 2. A small channel at a roadside to lead off surface water.

G
H

H

ha (ha), interj. & n. An exclamation of surprise, joy, or grief, or, repeated, of laughter or triumph.

hab'it (hab'it), n. 1. Dress; garb; clothes. 2. a A costume indicative of rank, profession; esp., the dress of a religious order. b A lady's riding costume. 3. Bodily appearance, form, or condition. 4. A custom or practice.

hab'i-tat (hab'i-tat), n. Natural abode of a plant or animal; dwelling place.

ha-bit'u-al (ha-bit'u-al), a. 1. Of the nature of a habit; according to habit; customary. 2. Doing or acting by force of habit. 3. Usual; commonly used; accustomed.

hack (hak), v.t. To cut irregularly; haggle.

hae'mo-glo'bin (he'mo-glo'bin), n. The coloring matter of the red blood corpuscles of vertebrates.

hag (hag), n. 1. A witch. 2. An ugly old woman.

hag'gle (-'l), v.t. To cut roughly; hack.

hair'y (har'i), a. Bearing, or covered with, hair; hirsute; made of hair.

half (haf), a. 1. Consisting of a moiety, or half. 2. Consisting of about a half; part or degree; partially; imperfectly.

half'-heart'ed, a. Wanting in heart, spirit, zeal.

half'way' (haf'wa'), adv. In the middle;

partially. — a. Midway.

hall (hol), n. 1. The residence of a landed proprietor. Chiefly British. 2. A building of considerable size or stateliness and usually containing a place of assembly; as, a town hall. 3. An assembly room. 4. A university building. 5. Entrance room of a building; a corridor or passage.

hal'low (hal'o), v.t. To set apart for holy or religious use; consecrate.

Hal'low-een' (-en'), n. The evening of October 31.

hal-lu'ci-na'tion (ha-lu'si-na'shun), n. Perception of objects with no reality, or experience of sensations with no external cause; illusion.

halt (holt), n. A stop, as in marching; arrest of progress.

halve (hav), v.t. To divide into halves.

ham (ham), n. 1. The region back of the knee joint; in quadrupeds, the hock. 2. The thigh and buttock; — esp. in pl. 3. Thigh of an animal, esp. a hog, prepared for food.

ham'mer (-er), n. 1. An implement for pounding, beating, driving nails, etc. 2. Something like, or suggestive of, a hammer.

ham'mer-head' (-hed'), n. Any of certain sharks having a hammer-shaped head.

ham'mock (-uk), n. A hanging couch or bed, consisting of a wide strip of canvas, of netting, or the like, suspended by cords at both ends.

ham'per, v.t. To fetter; embarrass; encumber.

hand (hand), n. 1. The terminal part of the arm adapted, as in man and apes, as a grasping organ. 2. Personal possession; ownership; hence, control.

hand'bill' (-bil), n. Printed sheet to be handed out.

hand'cuff' (-kuf), n. A manacle.

hand'ful (-fool), n. 1. As much or many as the hand will grasp. 2. A small quantity or number.

hand'i-craft (-kraft), n. 1. Manual skill. 2. A trade requiring skill of hand.

hand'i-work' (-wurk'), n. Work done with the hands; hence, any work done personally.

hand'ker-chief (han'ker-chif), n. 1. A piece of cloth, usually square, carried for wiping the face, nose, etc. 2. A neckerchief; neckcloth.

hand'some (han'sum), a. 1. Ample. 2. Gracious; liberal; generous. 3. Having a pleasing appearance, with dignity and symmetry.

hand'writ'ing (-rit'ing), n. Form of writing peculiar to a particular hand or person.

hand'y (han'di), a. 1. Ready to hand; convenient. 2. Skillful with the hand; dexterous. 3. Naut. Easily managed; as, the yacht is handy.

hang'ing (hang'ing), n. 1. A suspending or state of being suspended. 2. Execution by hanging. 3. That which is hung, as drapery, tapestry, wall paper, etc.

hap'pen (hap'n), v.i. 1. To occur by chance or without previous design; fall out; hence, to come to pass. 2. To come (on) by chance.

hap'pen-ing, n. An occurrence; event.

hap'pi-ness (-nes), a. 1. Good fortune; prosperity. 2. A state of pleasurable content with one's condition of life. 3. Graceful aptitude; felicity.

hap'py (hap'i), a. 1. Favored by hap, or fortune; lucky; prosperous. 2. Contented; joyous. 3. Apt; felicitous. 4. Expressing happiness.

har'ass (har'as), v.t. To weary or distress with importunity, care, etc., or be repeated attacks.

har'bor (-er), n. 1. A place of security and comfort. 2. A portion of a body of water so protected to afford a refuge for vessels; port; haven.

hard (hard), a. 1. Not easily penetrated; firm; solid. 2. Difficult to impress or influence; unfeeling.

hard'-head'ed, a. Of sound judgment; shrewd.

hard'-heart'ed, a. Unfeeling; cruel.

hard'ly (hard'li), adv. 1. Severely; harshly. 2. With difficulty. 3. Scarcely; not probably.

hard'ship (-ship), n. That which is hard to bear, as privation, injury, etc.

har'dy (har'di), a. 1. Bold; audacious. 2. Inured to fatigue or hardships; robust. 3. Able to bear the cold of winter; — of plants.

hare'brained' (-brand'), a. Giddy; heedless.

ha'rem (ha'rem), n. The women's apartments in a Mohammedan residence; also, the occupants.

harm'ful (harm'fool), a. Hurtful; mischievous.

har-mon'ic (har-mon'ik), a. 1. Concordant; consonant. 2. Relating to harmony as distinguished from melody or rhythm.

har-mo'ni-ous (-mo'ni-us), a. 1. Symmetrical; congruous; in accord. 2. Marked by harmony.

har'mo-ny (har'mo-ni), n. 1. Just adaptation of parts to each other, giving unity or a pleasing whole; agreement; congruity. 2. Concord in facts, opinions, manners, interests, etc.

harsh (harsh), a. 1. Offensive to sense or feeling as being coarse, rough, discordant, astringent, sour, severe, etc., rasping; repellent. 2. Unfeeling; severe; cruel.

har'vest (har'vest), n. 1. Season of gathering grain and fruits; also, the gathering of a crop or crops. 2. Crop; yield, as of grain, fruit, etc.

hash (hash), v.t. To mince and mix; mangle.

haste (hast), n. 1. Quickness of motion; swiftness; dispatch. — applied to voluntary action. 2. undue celerity; hurry.

has'ten (has'n), v.t. To drive or urge forward; expedite; hurry.

hatch'et (-et), n. A small ax used with one hand.

hate (hat), v.t. To dislike intensely; detest; in a weakened sense, to dislike; as, to hate to write.

hate'ful (hat'fool), a. 1. Full of ill will. 2. Exciting hate.

haul (hol), v.t. & i. 1. To pull; drag; transport by drawing. 2. To shift the course of (a ship), esp. so as to sail closer to the wind.

have (hav), v.t. 1. To hold in possession or control; possess; own. 2. To possess mentally; know; understand.

ha'ven (ha'v'n), n. Harbor; port; place of safety.

hay (ha), n. Grass mowed or ready for mowing; grass cut and cured for fodder.

haz'ard (haz'ard), n. 1. Chance; accident. 2. Risk; danger; peril.

haze (haz), n. Light vapor or smoke in the air; hence, figuratively, obscurity; dimness.

he (he), pron. 1. The man or male being previously designated.

head (hed), n. 1. The part of the body containing the brain, mouth, etc. 2. The hair of the head. 3. Intellect; understanding.

head'long (hed'long), adv. 1. headforemost. 2. Rashly; impetuously. — a. 1. Rash; precipitate. 2. Plunging headforemost.

head'strong (-strong), a. 1. Not easily restrained; stubborn; self-willed. 2. Proceeding from or marked by willfulness.

health (helth), n. 1. State of being hale or sound; esp., freedom from physical disease. 2. A wish of health and happiness; as, to drink a health.

health'y (hel'thi), a. 1. Enjoying health. 2. Indicating or characteristic of health. 3. Conducive to health; wholesome; salutary.

hear (her), v.t. 1. To perceive by the ear; to gain knowledge by hearing. 2. To listen to; heed. 3. To hear for examination or judgment. 4. To grant, as a prayer.

hear-say' (her'sa'), n. Report; rumor.

heart (hart), n. 1. Anat. The organ which keeps the blood circulating. 2. The seat of life or strength; hence, mind; soul; spirit.

heart'bro'ken (-bro'k'n), a. Intensely grieved.

heart'burn' (-burn'), n. Burning sensation in the stomach, often with inclination to vomit.

heart'en (har't'n), v.t. To give heart to; encourage.

heart'i-ly (har'ti-li), adv. 1. From the heart; sincerely. 2. With zest or zeal; warmly. 3. Abundantly; completely; as, heartily tired of a thing.

heat (het), n. 1. A form of energy appearing in the effects of fire, the sun's rays, friction, etc. 2. high temperature; also, a period of heat. 3. Condition, or color as indicating temperature; degree to which a thing is heated.

hea'then (he'th'n), n. 1. An unconverted individual of a people that do

G
H

not acknowledge the God of the Bible; in the Bible, an idolater or a Gentile. 2. An unenlighted or irreligious person.

heave (hev), v.t. 1. To lift; raise, usually with exertion. 2. To cause to swell or rise, as the breast. 3. To force from the breast; utter with effort, as a groan. 4. To throw; cast.

heav'y (hev'i), a. 1. Lifted with labor; weighty. 2. Burdensome; oppressive. 3. Profound; intense; severe. 4. Burdened; bowed down, as with care.

hec'tic (hek'tik), a. 1. Having a fever characteristic of tuberculosis; consumptive. 2. Symptomatic of this fever; as, a hectic flush.

hedge'hog' (hej'hog'), n. 1. Any of certain insectivorous mammals having hair mixed with spines which they present outwardly by rolling themselves up. 2. In America, popularly, the porcupine.

heed (hed), v.t. To regard with care; take notice of.

height (hit), n. 1. Condition of being high. 2. Altitude; stature. 3. A hill or mountain. 4. Highest part; summit; hence, an extreme.

height'en (-'n), v.t. 1. To make higher; elevate. 2. To augment; intensify; as, a price, or a flavor.

hei'nous (ha'nus), a. Hateful; odious; atrocious.

heir (ar), n. One who inherits, or is entitled to inherit. — heir apparent, an heir whose right cannot be annulled if he survives the ancestor; — disting. from heir presumptive, whose right may be annulled by the birth of a nearer heir.

heir'loom (ar'loom'), n. Any piece of personal property owned by a family for several generations.

hell (hel), n. 1. Place of the dead or of souls after death; the grave; place or state of punishment for the wicked after death; the abode of evil spirits. 2. Hence, any place or state of misery or wickedness, esp. a prison or a gambling house.

hel'met (hel'met), n. 1. A defensive covering for the head. 2. Something resembling a helmet.

help (help), v.t. 1. To aid; assist. 2. To furnish with relief, as from distress;

succor. 3. To aid in bringing about.

help'ful (help'fool), a. Furnishing help; useful; salutary.

help'less, a. Destitute of help or strength; unable to help one's self.

hen (hen), n. The female of the domestic fowl, or of any various other birds.

hence (hens), adv. 1. From this place; away; from this world or life. 2. From this time. 3. From this reason; therefore.

her (hur), pron. & a. The objective and the possessive case of she.

her'ald (her'ald), n. 1. In olden times, an officer who bore messages between rulers or commanders, made announcements, officiated in tourneys, etc. 2. One who proclaims; a messenger; forerunner.

herd (hurd), n. 1. A number of beasts, esp. large ones, assembled together. 2. A crowd of common people; esp., with the, the rabble.

here (her), adv. 1. In this place. 2. In the present life or state. 3. To or into this place; hither. 4. At this point of time; now.

here'aft'er (her'af'ter), adv. In some future time or state.

he-red'i-ta-ry (he-red'i-ta-ri), a. 1. Descended, or capable of legally descending, from ancestor to heir. 2. Having title or possession by inheritance.

here-in' (her'in'), adv. In this.

here-of' (-ov'), adv. Of this, from this; hence.

here-'on (-on'), adv. On or upon this; hereupon.

her'e-sy (her'e-si), n. 1. Unorthodox religious opinion tending to promote schism. 2. An opinion opposed to the commonly received doctrine, and tending to dissension.

hers (hurz), pron. The form of the possessive her used when the governing noun does not follow.

her-self' (her-self'), pron. An emphasized form for her, she.

hes'i-ta'tion (hez'i-ta'shun), n. 1. Act of hesitating; doubt; vacillation. 2. A faltering in speech.

hey'day', n. Time of highest strength, vigor, or bloom; acme; as, the heyday of youth.

hic'cup (hik'up), n. A spasmodic

inspiration with closure of the glottis, producing a characteristic sound.

hid'den (hid'n), p.a. Concealed; secret.

hide (hid), v.t. 1. To conceal; put out of view; secrete. 2. To withhold from knowledge; keep secret.

hid'e-ous (hid'e-us), a. Revolting; horribly ugly or discordant; morally shocking or detestable.

hi'er-arch'y (hi'er-ar'ki), n. A body of officials (esp. ecclesiastical) in successive ranks, or government by such a body.

high (hi), a. 1. Lifted up; lofty; tall; elevated. 2. Geog. Far toward one of the poles; — chiefly in high latitude.

high'ly, adv. In a high degree; very much.

high'-strung, a. In a state of tense or quick sensibility; highly sensitive or nervous.

hi-la'ri-ous (hi-la'ri-us; hi-), a. Mirthful; noisy; merry.

hin'der (hin'der), v.t. 1. To keep back or behind; check; obstruct. 2. To prevent; embarrass; shut out.

hip'po-pot'a-mus (hip'o-pot'a-mus), n. A large animal common in the rivers of Africa. It is an amphibious, herbivorous mammal.

hire (hir), n. 1. The price paid for the use of a thing or a place, or for service or labor; pay. 2. Act of hiring something.

hit (hit), v.t. 1. To come upon (esp. a thing sought); meet with; reach, find. 2. To strike or touch (esp. an object aimed at).

hith'er (hith'er), adv. To this place.

hive (hiv), n. 1. A beehive; also, a hived swarm of bees. 2. Something suggestive of a beehive, as a place swarming with busy occupants.

hoard (hord), n. A store laid up; hidden supply; treasure.

hoarse (hors), a. 1. Harsh; discordant. 2. Having a grating voice; as, hoarse from a cold.

hob'by (hob'i), n. A subject to which one constantly reverts; favorite pursuit.

hoist (hoist), v.t. To raise; elevate; esp., to lift with tackle.

hoi'ty-toi'ty (hoi'ti-toi'ti), a. Thought-less; giddy; also, haughty.

hold, v.t. 1. To keep in a given situation, relation, or the like; retain; sustain; support. 2. To contain; have capacity for. 3. To maintain possession of, or authority over.

ho'li-ness (ho'li-ness), n. 1. State or character of being holy. 2. [cap.] A title of the Pope.

hol'low (hol'o), a. 1. Having a cavity within a solid substance; not solid. 2. Depressed; concave; sunken. 3. Reverberated from or as from a cavity.

hol'o-caust (hol'o-kost), n. a thorough destruction, esp. by fire, as of many human beings.

ho'ly (ho'li), a. 1. Set apart to the service of deity; hallowed; sacred.

hom'age (hom'aj), n. 1. A ceremony by which a man, in feudal times, acknowledged himself the vassal of a lord; relation so established. 2. Respect or reverential regard; deference; esp., obeisance.

home (hom), n. 1. One's dwelling place; abode of one's family. 2. One's native place or land. 3. The locality where a thing is usually or naturally abundant; habitat; seat.

hom'i-cid'al (hom'i-sid'al), a. Murderous.

hom'i-cide (hom'i-sid), n. The killing of one human being by another.

ho'mo-ge'ne-ous (ho'mo-je'ne-us; hom'o-), a. Of the same kind or nature; of similar elements.

hon'ey (hun'i), n. A sweet sticky fluid, the nectar of flowers as collected and worked up for food by certain insects, esp. bees.

hon'ey-bee' (-be'), n. Any of certain social honey-producing bees.

hon'ey-comb' (-kom'), n. 1. The mass of six-sided cells of wax built by bees. 2. Something likened to a bee's honeycomb.

hon'ey-moon (-moon'), n. The first month or so after marriage; esp., the holiday spent by a couple after marriage, before settling down.

hook (hook), n. 1. A curved or bent piece, as for catching something. 2. An implement for cutting or lopping, as a sickle.

hope (hop), n. 1. Desire, with expectation of getting what is

G
H

desired or belief that it is obtainable. 2. Trust. 3. Ground of hope. 4. That which is hoped for.

hope'less (a. 1. Without hope. 2. Affording no hope.

ho-ri'zon (ho-ri'zun), n. The apparent junction of earth and sky. Fig., limit or bounds of perception or experience.

hor'i-zon'tal (hor'i-zon'tal), a. Parallel to the plane of the horizon.

hor'ri-ble (-i-b'l), a. Exciting horror; dreadful; hideous.

hor'rid (-id), a. Hideous; shocking.

horse'man (hors'man), n. A rider on horseback; one skilled in the management or care of horses.

hor'ti-cul'ture (hor'ti-kul'tur), n. Cultivation of a garden or orchard; art or science of growing fruits, vegetables, or ornamental plants.

ho'sier-y (ho'zher'i), n. Stockings; goods knit or woven like hose.

hos'pice (hos'pis), n. An inn for travelers or strangers, esp. one belonging to a religious order.

hos'pi-ta-ble (-pi-ta-b'l), a. Extending, or marked by, hospitality.

hos'pi-tal (-tal), n. An institution in which the sick or injured are given medical or surgical care.

hos'tage (hos'taj), n. 1. A person given as a pledge. 2. Any pledge or guarantee.

hos'tile (hos'til), a. Like an enemy; showing ill will.

hot (hot), a. 1. Much above normal temperature; characterized by great or unusual heat. 2. Characterized by violent activity or emotion.

ho-tel' (ho-tel'), n. A house for entertaining strangers or travelers; inn.

hour (our), n. 60 minutes.

house (house), n. 1. A structure for human habitation. 2. With qualifying term, a building for some other purpose; as, henhouse, warehouse, etc. 3. A household.

house'break'ing , n. Act of breaking open and entering another's dwelling with felonious intent.

house'hold (-hold), n. those who dwell as a family; family.

house'warm'ing (-wor'ming), n. A festivity upon the occasion of occupying a new home.

huck'ster (-ster), n. A peddler; hawker.

hud'dle (hud'l), v.i. & t. 1. To crowd together, as from confusion, fear, etc. 2. To draw (one's self) into a heap; — esp. with up. 3. To do, make, or put, in haste or roughly.

hue (hu), n. Color; tint.

huff (huf), n. A fit of petulance or resentment; a sulky passion.

huge (huj), a. Very large; immense; vast.

hu-mane' (hu-man'), a. 1. Having feelings and inclinations creditable to man; benevolent. 2. Humanizing; refining.

hu-man'i-ty (hu-man'i-ti), n. 1. Quality or condition of being human; human nature. 2. Quality of being humane; kind feelings, dispositions, and sympathies.

hum'ble (hum'b'l), a. 1. Not proud or assertive; lowly; meek. 2. Of lowly condition, rank, etc.; unpretentious.

hu'mid (hu'mid), a. Damp; moist.

hu-mil'i-ate (-mil'i-at), v.t. To lower the dignity of; to humble; mortify.

hu-mil'i-a'tion (-a'shun), n. Act of humiliating, or state of being humiliated; mortification.

hu'mor-ous (-us), a. Characterized by humor; funny; facetious.

hun'ger (hun'ger), n. 1. A craving for food. 2. Any strong or eager desire.

hun'gry (-gri), a. 1. Feeling or showing hunger. 2. Poor; barren; as soil.

hunt (hunt), v.t. 1. To follow or search for (game); pursue (game). 2. To seek; pursue; follow; as, to hunt up evidence. 3. To drive; chase; persecute.

hurl (hurl), v.t. 1. To throw or cast violently. 2. To overthrow. 3. To utter vehemently.

hur-rah' (hoo-ra'; hu-ra'), interj. A word used as a shout of joy, triumph, applause, etc.

hur'ri-cane (hur'i-kan), n. A violent whirlwind, generally with rain, thunder, and lightning.

hur'ry (-i), v.t. To hasten; urge on; quicken.

hus-band (huz-band), n. A man who has a wife.

hy'brid (-brid), n. 1. The offspring of two animals or plants of different species or races. 2. Anything of heterogeneous origin or composition.

hy'drant (hi-drant), n. A discharge pipe with a valve and spout at which water may be drawn.

hy'dro-gen (hi'dro-jen), n. A gaseous element, colorless, tasteless, odorless, and inflammable, and lighter than any other known substance.

hy'gi-ene (hi'ji-en; ji'jen), n. Science of preserving health.

hy'per-crit'i-cal (-krit'i-kal), a. Too critical; captious.

hy'phen-ate (-at), v.t. To hyphen.

hyp'no-tism (hip'no-tiz'm), n. Induction of a state (called hypnosis, or hypnotic sleep) resembling sleep or somnambulism; loosely, hypnosis.

hyp'o-crite (hip'o-krit), n. One who feigns to be other and better than he is; a dissembler.

hy-poth'e-sis (-poth'e-sis; hi-), n. A principle or theory not proved, but assumed for argument, or to explain certain facts.

hys-te'ri-a (his-te'ri-a), n. A nervous affection marked by loss of control over the emotions, by imaginary sensations, and, often, paroxysms.

I

I (i), pron. The nominative case of the pronoun of the first person (by which a person denotes himself).

ice (is), n. 1. Frozen water. 2. A sweetened mixture, usually fruit juice and water, artificially frozen.

ice-berg' (is'burg') n. A large floating mass of ice, detached from a glacier.

i'ci-cle (i'ski-k'l), n. A hanging tapering mass of ice formed from dripping water.

i-de'a (i-de'a), n. 1. A pattern, standard, or ideal; hence, a plan or intention. 2. A mental image or picture. 3. A notion, opinion, or impression.

i-de'al (-al), a. 1. Existing in idea, or as a perfect pattern. 2. Visionary; unreal. 3. Pertaining to ideas or idealism.

i-den'ti-cal (i-den'ti-kal), a. 1. The same; the very same. 2. Exactly alike or equal.

id'i-o-cy (id'i-o-si), n. Extreme deficiency in intelligence; imbecility.

i'dle (i'd'l), a. 1. Without worth or basis; groundless; useless; vain. 2. Not occupied or employed; inactive. 3. Lazy; slothful.

i'dol (i'dol), n. 1. An image; object of worship. 2. Object of strong affection or devotion.

if (if), conj. 1. In case that; granting, allowing, or supposing that. 2. Whether.

ig-nite' (ig-nit'), v.t. To set on fire; light; kindle.

ig'no-min-y (ig'no-min-i), n. 1. Disgrace or dishonor; infamy. 2. Infamous conduct.

ig-nore' (ig-nor'), v.t. To refuse to notice; disregard willfully.

ill (il), a. 1. Unjust; unkind; harsh. 2. Harmful; bad; evil. 3. Incorrect; improper.

ill-bred', a. Badly brought up; impolite; rude.

il-le'gal (i-le'gal), a. Unlawful; illicit.

il-lic'it (i-lis'it), a. Not allowed; improper; unlawful.

il-lit'er-a-cy (i-lit'er-a-si), n. Illiterate quality or state; inability to read.

ill'ness (il'nes), n. Sickness; indisposition.

il-log'i-cal (i-loj'i-kal), a. Contrary to logic or sound reasoning.

il-lu'mi-nate (-nat), v.t. 1. To make light; light up; enlighten. 2. To make plain or clear. 3. To decorate with artificial lights.

il-lu'sion (i-lu'zhun), n. 1. A deceptive appearance. 2. State or fact of being deceived; false impression.

il-lus'trate (i-lus'trat' il'us-trat'), v.t. 1. To make clear or explain, as by figures or examples. 2. To provide or adorn, as a book, with pictures, etc.; also, to make clear or adorn.

im'age (im'aj), n. 1. A representation; effigy; statue. 2. A symbol; also, a type. 3. Picture drawn by the fancy; as, in image of farm life.

im-ag'i-na-ble (i-maj'i-na-b'l), a. Capable of being imagined; conceivable.

im-ag'ine (i-maj'in), v.t. 1. To form a mental picture of; conceive. 2. To

I
K

suppose; fancy.

im'be-cile (im'be-sil), a. 1. Feeble; esp., feeble-minded. 2. Stupid; idiotic.

im-mac'u-late (i-mak'u-lat), a. 1. Spotless; pure. 2. Without flaw or fault.

im'ma-ture' (-tur'), a. Not mature; not developed; crude.

im-meas'ur-a-ble (i-mezh'ur-a-b'l), a. Incapable of being measured; boundless.

im-me'di-ate (i-me'di-at), a. 1. With nothing between; acting without the intervention of anything; direct. 2. Not distant or separated; adjoining; hence, occurring without delay; done at once.

im-mense' (i-mens') a. Immeasurable; hence, vast; huge.

im-merse' (i-murs'), v.t. 1. To plunge into (a fluid, etc.); dip; sink. 2. To baptize by immersion. 3. To absorb; as, immersed in thought.

im'mi-grate (-grat), v.i. To come into a country for permanent residence.

im'mi-nent (-nent), a. Threatening to happen immediately; impending.

im-mo'bile (i-mo'bil), a. Immovable; fixed; also, motionless.

im-mor'tal (i-mor'tal), a. 1. Not mortal; undying; everlasting. 2. Of or pertaining to immortality.

im-mov'a-ble (i-moov'a-b'l), a. Incapable of being moved; as: (a) Stationary. (b) Steadfast; unyielding. (c) Emotionless.

im-mune' (i-mun'), a. Exempt; esp., protected against a particular disease, as by inoculation.

imp (imp), n. 1. A young or inferior devil; a little, malignant spirit. 2. Mischievous child or urchin.

im'pact (im'pakt), n. A striking together; collision; forcible contact.

im-pair' (im-par'), v.t. To make worse; diminish in quantity, value, excellence, or strength.

im-pal'pa-ble (im-pal'pa-b'l), a. That cannot be felt; intangible; also, extremely fine.

im-pa'tient (-shent), a. Not patient; uneasy.

im-peach' (-pech'), v.t. 1. To bring an accusation against; accuse. 2. To impute some fault to; call in question.

im-pec'ca-ble (im-pek'a-b'l), a. Not liable to sin or wrongdoing; free from fault or error.

im-pede' (im-ped'), v.t. To obstruct; hinder.

im-pend' (im-pend'), v.i. To hang or be suspended (over), threaten; be imminent.

im-pen'e-tra-ble (-pen'e-tra-b'l), a. 1. Incapable of being pierced. 2. Incomprehensible. 3. Not open, as to reason, sympathy, etc.

im-per'fect (im-pur'fekt), a. Not perfect; defective; incomplete.

im'per-fec'tion (im'per-fek'shun), n. Quality or state of being imperfect; deficiency; fault.

im-per'il (-per'il), v.i. To endanger.

im-per'son-ate (-at), v.t. To act the character of; personate.

im-per'ti-nent (-nent), a. 1. Not pertinent; not to the point; irrelevant. 2. Guilty of, or prone to; rudeness; insolent.

im-pet'u-ous (-pet'u-us), a. 1. Rushing with violence; furious; violent. 2. Hastily or rashly energetic.

im'pe-tus (im'pe-tus), n. 1. Force or energy of motion; momentum. 2. Impulse; incentive.

im-pinge' (-pinj), v.i. 1. To strike or dash (on, upon, against), esp. with sharp collision. 2. To encroach or infringe.

im-plant' (-plant'), v.t. To plant or set securely or deeply; instill or inculcate thoroughly.

im'ple-ment (im'ple-ment), n. An instrument, tool, or utensil.

im'pli-cate (-pli'kat), v.t. To involve; as, to implicate one in a crime.

im'pli-ca'tion (im'pli-ka'shun), n. 1. Act of implicating; state of being implicated. 2. That which is implied or involved; entanglement.

im-plic'it (im-plis'it), a. 1. Fairly to be understood, though not expressed; implied. 2. Unquestioning.

im-plore' (im-lor') v.t. To call upon or for earnestly; beseech; entreat.

im-ply (-pli), v.t. 1. To involve or include as a necessary logical consequence (something not expressly stated). 2. To express indirectly.

im-por'tance (im-por'tans), n. Quality

or state of being important; consequence; significance.

im-por'tant (-tant), a. 1. Having consequence; significant; weighty. 2. Consequential; pompous.

im'po-tent (-tent), a. Wanting in power, strength, or vigor; weak; inform.

im-pov'er-ish (-pov'er-ish), v.t. To make poor.

im-prac'ti-ca-ble (im-prak'ti-ka-b'l), a. Incapable of being practiced or used; unserviceable.

im-preg'na-ble (-preg'na-b'l), a. Able to resist attack; unconquerable.

im-preg'nate (-nat), v.t. 1. To make pregnant; fertilize. 2. To saturate; imbue.

im-press' (im-pres'), v.t. To levy for public service; esp., to force into the army or navy.

im-press', v.t. 1. To press, stamp, or print something in or upon. 2. a To cause a vivid impression of; stamp; imprint. b To affect or influence, esp. deeply.

im-pres'sion (-presh'un), n. 1. Act of impressing; state of being impressed. 2. Effect of impressing, as an indentation, stamp, or figure.

im-print' (-print'), v.t. 1. To impress; stamp. 2. To stamp or mark, as letters on paper, by means of type, stamps, etc.

im'pro-pri'e-ty (im'pro-pri'e-ti), n. 1. Quality or fact of being improper. 2. An improper act, use, sense, etc.

im-prove' (-proov'), v.t. 1. To make good use of. 2. To make better.

im-prove'ment (im-proov'ment), n. 1. Act of improving, or state of being improved. 2. A result of improving, or that which constitutes it.

im'pro-vise (im'pro-viz'), v.t. & i. 1. To compose, recite, sing, etc., without preparation; extemporize. 2. To make, do, or provide offhand.

im-pru'dent (-dent), a. Not prudent; indiscreet.

im'pu-dence (im'pu-dens), n. Quality of being impudent; insolence; effrontery; impertinence.

im-pu'ni-ty (-pu'ni-ti), n. Freedom from punishment, harm, or loss.

im-pure' (-pur'), a. Not pure; as: a Containing something unclean; dirty; unwholesome. b Adulterated. c Defiled; unholy. d Unchaste.

im-pute' (-put'), v.t. To charge or credit, as a fault or virtue; attribute.

in, adv. 1. Indicating a direction of entering; as, come in. 2. Indicating a position as to surroundings, inclosure, etc.

in-ac'cu-rate (-rat), a. Not accurate; inexact; incorrect; erroneous.

in-ac'tion (-ak'shun), n. Lack of action; idleness.

in'ap-pre'ci-a-ble (in'a-pre'shi-a-b'l), a. Not appreciable; too small to be perceived.

in'at-ten'tion (in'a-ten'shun), n. Want of attention; disregard; heedlessness.

in-au'gu-rate (-rat), v.t. 1. To admit or induct into an office formally. 2. To celebrate the first public use of. 3. To commence or enter upon; set in motion.

in'bred' (in'bred'), a. 1. Bred within; innate. 2. (pron. in-bred') Subjected to inbreeding.

in-breed' (in-bred'), v.t. 1. To produce within. 2. To breed with each other (animals closely related).

in-ca'pa-ble (-ka'pa-b'l), a. 1. Not capable. 2. Not susceptible. 3. Not to be brought to do.

in'ca-pac'i-tate (in'ka-pas'i-tat), v.t. To deprive of capacity; disable; disqualify.

in'ca-pac'i-ty (-ti), n. Want of capacity; inability, disability.

in-car'cer-ate (in-kar'ser-at), v.t. To imprison.

in-car'nate (-nat), a. Clothed with flesh; embodied in human form.

in'cense' (in'sens') n. Perfume from spices or gums burned in religious rites; any pleasing fragrance; also, the material used to produce such perfume.

in-cen'tive (-sen'tiv), a. Inciting. — n. That which incites; motive.

in'ci-dent (pent), n. 1. Liable to happen; happening or belonging, esp. as a subordinate feature. 2. Falling or striking, as a light ray on a surface.

in-cin'er-ate (in-sin'er-at), v.t. & i. To burn to ashes; cremate.

in-ci'sive (-si'siv), a. Cutting; sharp; hence, acute; clear-cut.

in-cite' (in-sit'), n. To spur or urge on.

I
K

in'cli-na'tion (in'kli-na'shun), n. 1. A leaning; propensity. 2. Act of inclining; nod. 3. Amount of deviation from the vertical or horizontal; slant; slope.

in-close' (-kloz'), v.t. 1. To shut up or in. 2. To insert (something) in the same parcel or envelope with another. 3. To surround.

in-clo'sure (in-klo'zhur), n. 1. Act of inclosing; state of being inclosed. 2. That which is inclosed. 3. That which incloses, as a fence.

in-clude' (in-klood'), v.t. To comprise; contain; comprehend; embrace.

in-clu'sive (-siv), a. 1. Inclosing; surrounding, containing. 2. Including the stated limit or extremes.

in-cog'ni-to (-ni-to), a. or adv. With (one's) identity concealed under an assumed name or title.

in'com'ing, a. Coming in; accruing, as profit; taking possession, as a tenant; about to begin, as a year; entering.

in'com-mu'ni-ca-ble (-mu'ni-ka-b'l), a. Incapable of being communicated or told.

in-com'pa-ra-ble (in-kom'pa-ra-b'l), a. 1. Beyond comparison; matchless. 2. Not suitable for comparison.

in-con'se-quence (in-kon'se-kwens), n. Quality or state of being inconsequent; irrelevance.

in-con'se-quent (-kwent), a. 1. Illogical. 2. Disconnected; irrelevant.

in'con-sist'en-cy (-sis'ten-si), n. 1. Quality or state of being inconsistent; incompatibility. 2. That which is inconsistent.

in-con'stan-cy (in-kon'stan-si), n. Want of constancy; fickleness; want of uniformity.

in'con-ven'ience (in'kon-ven'yens), n. 1. Quality or state of being inconvenient; discomfort. 2. That which is inconvenient.

in-cor'po-rate (in-kor'po-rat), a. 1. closely united or blended. 2. Incorporated.

in-crease' (in-kres'), v.i. 1. To become greater; grow; advance; wax. 2. To be fertile or prolific.

in'crease (in'kres), n. 1. That which results from increasing; addition; produce.

in'cre-ment (in'kre-ment), n. An increase.

in'cu-bus (in'ku-bus), n. 1. Nightmare. 2. Any person or thing that oppresses or burdens.

in'cul-ca'tion (in'kul-ka-shun), n. A teaching and impressing by repetitions or admonitions.

in-cum'bent (-bent), a. Required as a duty.

in-cur' (in-kur'), v.t. To become liable to; bring down upon one's self.

in-de'cen-cy (-de'sen-si), n. 1. Quality of being indecent. 2. Indecent act.

in-deed' (in-ded'), adv. In reality; truly; to be sure.

in-del'i-ble (in-del'i-b'l), a. That cannot be removed, or effaced.

in-dem'ni-fy (-dem'ni-fi), v.t. 1. To secure against loss or damage. 2. To repay or compensate, as for loss, damage, etc.

in-dem'ni-ty (-ti), n. 1. Protection or exemption from loss or damage. 2. Compensation for loss or injury sustained.

in'de-pend'ence (in'de-pen'dens), n. 1. State or quality of being independent. 2. Independent means; a competency.

in'de-scrib'a-ble (-shrib'a-b'l), a. Incapable of being described.

in'dex (in'deks), n. 1. The forefinger. 2. A pointer or indicator. 3. That which points out or discloses; indication.

In'di-an (in'di-an), a. 1. Of or pertaining to, or characteristic of, India, the Indies, or the Indians. 2. Of, pertaining to, or designating the aborigines, or Indians, of America.

in'di-cate (-kat), v.t. 1. To point out or to; make known; betoken. 2. In medicine, to show by symptoms; point to as the proper remedy.

in-dict' (-dit'), v.t. To charge with an offense; find an indictment against.

in-dict'ment (-dit'ment), n. 1. An indicting. 2. Law. The formal written statement of an offense as found by the grand jury.

in-dif'fer-ent (-ent), a. 1. Without choice or interest; unconcerned; heedless. 2. Having no marked tendency; neutral.

in'di-gence (in'di-jens), n. Poverty;

want.

in'dig-na'tion (in'dig-na'shun), n. Anger with contempt or loathing.

in-dig'ni-ty (in-dig'ni-ti), n. Any action toward another which shows contempt for him.

in'di-rec'tion (-rek'shun), n. Indirect course or means; unfair or dishonest practices.

in'dis-creet' (in'dis-kret), a. Lacking discretion.

in'dis-cre'tion (in'dis-kresh'un), n. Quality or state of being indiscreet; an indiscreet act.

in'dis-crim'i-nate (-rkim'i-nat), a. Confused; promiscuous.

in'dis-pose' (-poz'), v.t. 1. To render unfit or indisposed. 2. To render averse; disincline.

in'di-vid'u-al (in'di-vid'u-al), a. 1. Existing as a distinct entity; particular; single. 2. Having marked individuality. 3. Arising from, belonging to, or used by, an individual.

in'di-vid'u-al-ize (-vid'u-al-iz), v.t. 1. To make individual. 2. To treat or notice individually; particularize.

in'door' (in'dor'), a. Pertaining to the interior of a building; done, living, or given, within doors.

in-duce' (-dus'), v.t. 1. To lead on; influence, as by argument. 2. To bring on or about; cause. 3. To produce by induction, as an electric current.

in-duct' (-dukt'), v.t. To put formally in possession of a benefice or office; install.

in-dulge' (in-dulj'), v.t. To yield to the wishes of; humor.

in-dul'gence (-dul'jens), n. 1. Act, fact, or practice of indulging; gratification; esp., self-gratification. 2. Favor granted.

in-dus'tri-al (-dus'tri-al), a. 1. Engaged in, or derived from, industries. 2. Devoted to industrial training.

in'dus-try (in'dus-tri), n. 1. Steady application to labor or business. 2. Systematic labor. 3. Any branch of business.

in'ef-fi'cien-cy (in'e-fish'en-si), n. Want of efficiency; inability or failure to do something.

in-ert' (-urt'), a. 1. Powerless to move itself, or to resist motion actively. 2. Powerless for a desired effect, as a drug. 3. Inactive; sluggish.

in'ex-pe'ri-ence (-pe'ri-ens), n. Want or absence of experience.

in-fal'li-bil'i-ty (in-fal'i-bil'i-ti), n. Quality of being infallible.

in'fan-cy (-fan-si), n. 1. Early childhood. 2. Law. The status of one under 21 years.

in'fant (-fant), n. 1. A child in the first period of life; a babe. 2. Law. A person not of full age; a minor.

in-fect' (-fekt'), v.t. 1. To taint with any disease-producing substance or bacteria. 2. a To corrupt; deprave. b To imbue with some feeling.

in-fec'tion (-fek'shun), n. 1. An infecting, esp. with disease. 2. That which infects, or causes a disease.

in-fer' (-fur'), v.t. 1. To conclude; Colloq., to surmise. 2. To lead to as a conclusion; imply; indicate.

in-fe'ri-or (in-fe'ri-er), a. 1. Situated lower down; lower. 2. Of lower rank. 3. Of less importance or merit.

in'fi-del'i-ty (-del'i-ti), n. 1. Want of faith or belief in (a certain) religion. 2. Breach of trust; deceit; also, an unfaithful act.

in-fil'trate (in-fil'trat), v.t. 1. To cause to penetrate gradually. 2. To pass through or into as in filtering.

in'fi-nite (in'fi-nit), a. Unlimited; immeasurable.

in'fin-i-tes'i-mal (-fin-i-tes'i-mal), a. Infinitely small; very minute.

in-firm' (-furm), a. 1. Not firm or sound physically; feeble. 2. Weak; irresolute.

in-flame' (-flam), v.t. 1. To kindle or intensify, as passion. 2. to incense; enrage. 3. Med. To cause inflammation in.

in-fla'tion (-fla'shun), n. An inflating; inflated condition; as: a Distention. b Pomposity; great conceit. c Undue increase, as in prices.

in-flec'tion (-flek'shun), n. 1. Act of inflecting; a bending or bend. 2. Change in pitch or tone of the voice.

in-flu-ence (in'floo-ens), n. 1. An insensible or indirect altering of anything, or power to effect this. 2. Power due to position, wealth, etc. 3. That which exerts influence; an influential person.

in'flu-en'tial (in'floo-en'shal), a. Exerting or possessing influence; powerful.

in'flu-en'za (-za), n. An epidemic disease characterized by acute catarrh; grippe.

in'for-ma'tion (in'for-ma'shun), n. 1. Act of informing. 2. Knowledge; intelligence; news.

in-form'er (-for'mer), n. 1. One who imparts knowledge or news. 2. One who informs of breaches of law.

in-fre'quence (-fre'kwens), n. State of rarely happening; rareness.

in-fringe' (-frinj'), v.t. To commit a breach of.

in-gen'ious (in-jen'yus), a. 1. Possessed of ingenuity; inventive. 2. Showing cleverness or ingenuity.

in-gen'u-ous (-jen'u-us), a. Free from reserve, disguise, or pretense; open; frank; artless.

in'grate (in'grat), a. Showing ingratitude; ungrateful.

in-hab'it (-hab'it), v.t. To live in; occupy.

in-hab'it-ant (-tant), n. A permanent resident.

in-hale' (in-hal'), v.t. To draw into the lungs.

in-her'ent (-ent), a. Permanently existing as an attribute in something; belonging by nature; inseparable; essential.

in-her'it (-her'it), v.t. & i. 1. To take by descent or inheritance. 2. To come into possession of.

in-hu'man (-hu'man), a. Destitute of human kindness; cruel; unfeeling.

in-i'tial (in-ish'al), a. 1. Of or pertaining to the beginning. 2. Standing at the beginning; first.

in-i'ti-ate (-i-at), v.t. 1. To originate; begin. 2. To instruct in rudiments or principles. 3. To introduce into a society, club, etc., as by formal rites.

in'junc'tion (in-junk'shun), n. 1. An enjoining. 2. An order; precept. 3. Law. Judicial writ or process requiring a party to do or forbear some act.

in'ju-ry (in'joo ri), n. 1. Damage or hurt done or suffered. 2. An unjust act.

in'mate (in'mat), n. One of a family or community occupying a single dwelling; an occupant; also, one kept in an asylum, prison, etc.

in'nate (in'nat; in-nat'), a. Inborn; native; natural.

in'no-cent (-sent), a. 1. a Of persons: Guiltless; sinless; pure; also, blameless. b Of actions and things: Without evil influence or effect; harmless. 2. Guileless, ignorant, or simple.

in'no-vate (in'o-vat), v.i. To make changes.

in-nu'mer-a-ble (i-nu-mer'a-b'l), a. Too many to be counted.

in'of-fen'sive (in'o-fen'siv), a. Giving no offense; harmless.

in'quest (in'kwest), n. 1. Judicial or official inquiry, esp. before a jury; as, a coroner's inquest. 2. A body of men holding such an inquiry.

in-scrip'tion (-skrip'shun). 1. That which is inscribed. 2. A dedication, as of a book.

in'side' (in'sid'; in'sid), n. 1. The inner side, surface, or part; interior.

in-sid'i-ous (in-sid'i-us), a. Treacherous; sly; crafty.

in'sight' (in'sit'), n. 1. Discernment. 2. Apprehension of the inner nature of things.

in-som'ni-a (-som'ni-a), n. Sleeplessness.

in-spect' (in-spekt'), v.t. 1. To view critically; examine. 2. To view and examine officially.

in'spi-ra'tion (in'spi-ra'shun), n. 1. Act of breathing in. 2. In theology, a supernatural influence fitting men to receive and communicate divine truth; also, the truth so communicated.

in-spire' (in-spir'), v.t. 1. To inhale. 2. To give inspiration to. 3. To produce as by inspiration.

in'stance (in-stans), n. 1. Request. 2. An illustrative example. 3. Step in an action; occasion.

in'stant (-stant), a. 1. Pressing; urgent; earnest. 2. Present; current.

in-stead' (-sted'), adv. 1. In the place of.

in'sti-gate (-sti'gat), v.t. To urge forward; set on; incite.

in'stinct (in'stinkt), n. 1. Natural inward impulse; involuntary prompting to any action. 2. A natural aptitude; as, an instinct for order.

in'sti-tu'tion (-tu'shun), n. 1.An established social, political, or national law, custom, etc. 2. An organized society or corporation.

in-struct' (-strukt'), v.t. 1. To impart knowledge to; teach. 2. To give directions to; direct.

in'sub-or'di-nate (-sub-or'di-nat), a. Disobedient; mutinous.

in-sult' (in-sult'), v.t. To treat with insolence.

in-sur'ance (-ans), n. 1. An insuring against loss; the business of making insurance contracts. Called also assurance. 2. Premium paid for insuring anything. 3. Sum for which anything is insured.

in-tact' (in-takt'), a. Untouched; left entire.

in'take (in'tak'), n. 1. A taking in; thing taken in. 2. Place where a fluid is taken into a channel, etc.

in'tel-lect (in'te-lekt), n. 1. Power or faculty of knowing; the understanding. 2. A mind or intelligence; person of intellectual power.

in-tel'li-gence (in-tel'i-jens), n. 1. The intellect. 2. Mental quickness; sagacity. 3. Information communicated; news; advice; knowledge.

in-tense' (-tens'), a. 1. Extreme in degree; excessive; immoderate. 2. Strained or straining; high-wrought; profoundly earnest or intent.

in-ten'sive (-siv), a. 1. Of, pertaining to, or marked by, intensity. 2. Gram. Serving to give force or emphasis; as, an intensive verb.

in-tent' (-tent'), a. Directed with, or giving, keen attention; hence, earnest; intense; also, closely occupied.

in'ter-change' (in'ter-chanj'), n. 1. Mutual exchange. 2. Alternation.

in'ter-course (in'ter-kors), n. Communication; commerce; interchange of thought and feeling.

in'ter-est (in'ter-est), n. 1. Share in advantage, profit, and responsibility; as, an interest in a store. 2. Advantage; profit; benefit.

in'ter-im (in'ter-im), n. The meantime; interval between events, etc.

in'ter-ject' (-jekt), v.t. & i. To insert; interpose.

in'ter-lock' (-lok'), v.t. & i. To unite or engage with one another; lock into one another.

in'ter-mis'sion (-mish'un), n. 1. Act or state of intermitting; state of being intermitted; interruption. 2. A pause; interval.

in-ter'nal (-tur'nal), a. 1. Inclosed; inward; interior; also, designating that which is to be inwardly applied; as, internal medicine. 2. Pertaining to the inner nature; intrinsic.

in'ter-na'tion-al (in'ter-nash'un-al), a. Between or among nations.

in-ter'pret (in-tur'pret), v.t. To explain or tell the meaning of; translate; make clear.

in-ter'ro-gate (in-ter'o-gat), v.t. & i. To examine by questioning; question.

in'ter-rupt' (in'te-rupt'), v.t. 1. To break into or between; interfere with the course, current, or motion of. 2. To break the continuity or uniformity of.

in'ter-view (in'ter-vu), n. A meeting face to face; conference; esp., a meeting between a representative of the press and another person to get information for publication; also, the published account of such meeting.

in'ti-mate (in'ti-mat), a. 1. Deepseated; innermost. 2. Close in association or acquaintance; familiar; also, thorough. 2. closely united.

in-tim'i-date (in-tim'i-dat), v.t. To make timid or fearful; esp., to deter, as by threats; overawe; cow.

in-tol'er-ant (-ant), a. 1. Unable to endure. 2. Not tolerant; not tolerating difference of opinion, esp. as to religion; bigoted.

in-tox'i-cate (-kat), v.t. 1. To make drunk; excite or stupefy by strong drink or a narcotic. 2. To excite to enthusiasm, frenzy, or madness.

in-trigue' (in-treg'), v.i. & t. 1. To carry on a secret and improper love affair. 2. To plot; scheme.

in-trude' (in-trood'), v.t. To thrust or force in or on; esp., to force (one's self) in without leave or welcome.

in-trust' (-trust'), v.t. To confer a trust on; esp., to deliver something in trust to (another).

in'tu-i'tion (in'tu-ish'un), n. 1. Knowledge obtained without

I

K

conscious reasoning; ready insight. 2. Anything known by intuition.

in-val'u-a-ble (in-val'u-a-b'l), a. Valuable beyond estimation; inestimable; precious.

in-va'sion (-va'zhun), n. 1. Act of invading. 2. The first attack of anything hurtful.

in-vent' (-vent'), v.t. 1. To frame by thought or imagination; devise; contrive; as, to invent a yarn.

in-ven'tor (-ter), n. One who invents; contriver.

in-ves'ti-gate (-ves'ti-gat), v.t. To follow up by inquiry or observation.

in-vig'or-ate (-vig'or-at), v.t. To give vigor or life and energy to; refresh; animate.

in-vis'i-ble (-viz'i-b'l), a. Not visible; incapable of being seen.

in'voice (in'vois), n. 1. A priced list of merchandise sent to a purchaser, consignee, etc. 2. The lot or set of goods as shipped or received.

i-rate' (i-rat'; i'rat), a. Angry, incensed.

ir're-sist'i-ble (-zis'ti-b'l), a. That cannot be successfully resisted.

ir're-spec'tive (ir'e-spek'tiv), a. Disregarding particular persons, conditions, etc.

ir're-vers'i-ble (ir'e-vur'si-b'l), a. Incapable of being reversed.

ir'ri-gate (ir'i-gat), v.t. & i. To supply (land) with water by canals, etc., for nourishing plants.

ir'ri-ta-ble (ir'i-ta-b'l), a. Capable of being irritated.

is'land (i'land), n. 1. A tract of land surrounded by water, and smaller than a continent. 2. Something suggestive of an island in position.

is'sue (-u), n. 1. A passing or flowing out; egress; exit. 2. Progeny; offspring. 3. That which issues; outcome; result.

itch (ich), v.i. 1. To have an uneasy sensation in the skin, which inclines one to scratch the part affected. 2. To have a constant desire; long.

i'tem-ize (-iz), v.t. To state in items, or by particulars.

J

jab (jab), v.t. & i. To thrust abruptly with something sharp.

jack'al (-ol), n. Any of several wild dogs of the Old World.

jack'et (jak'et), n. 1. A short coat with skirts, usually with sleeves. 2. Any of various coverings.

jack'-o-lan'tern, n. A lantern made of a pumpkin, or the like, so as to show features of a human face.

jade (jad), n. A compact stone, commonly green, capable of a fine polish.

jag'ged (jag'ed), p.a. Having sharp notches; sharply pointed.

jail (jal), n. A prison, esp. one for persons held for minor offenses or pending judicial proceedings.

jan'i-tor (jan'i-ter), n. 1. A porter. 2. One having the care of a building, offices, apartments, etc.

Jan'u-a-ry (jan'u-a-ri), n. The first month of the year, having 31 days.

jar'gon (jar'gon), n. Confused, unintelligible language or utterance.

jaun'dice (jan'dis; jon'-), n. Med. A disease characterized by yellowness of the eyes, skin, etc.

jaw (jo), n. 1. One of the structures that border the mouth and serve to open and close it. 2. pl. Fig.: Mouth or entrance; as, the jaws of death.

jeal'ous (jel'us), a. 1. Apprehensively vigilant in care; anxious. 2. Disposed to suspect, rivalry in matters of interest or affection.

jeer (jer), v.i. & t. To utter, or to treat with, scoffing remarks; taunt. — n. A jeering utterance.

jel'ly (jel'i), n. A food preparation of a soft consistency due to its containing gelatin; similar preparation or substance.

jeop'ard-ize (-ar-diz), v.t. To expose to loss or injury; risk; jeopard.

jeop'ard-y (-di), n. 1. Hazard; danger. 2. Law. The danger that an accused person is subjected to when put on trial for a crime.

jerk (jurk), v.t. & i. To give a short sharp thrust, push, pull or twist. 2. To throw with a short quick motion.

jest (jest), n. 1. A jeer; taunt; thing said or done in banter or raillery; sport. 2. Laughing-stock.

Je'sus (je'zus), n. Bible. The son of Mary, and founder of the Christian religion.

Jew (ju; joo), n. A person of the

Hebrew race, or one whose religion is Judaism.

jew'el (ju'el; joo'el), n. 1. An ornament of gold, silver, or the like. 2. A precious stone; gem. 3. An object of special affection; a precious thing.

jif'fy (jif'i), n. A moment; instant. Colloq.

jig (jig), n. A brisk dance movement or a dance to it.

job (job), n. 1. A piece of work; esp., any definite piece of work. 2. A corrupt piece of official business. 3. A situation or employment. Colloq.

join (join), v.t. 1. To unite; connect; couple; combine. 2. a To associate one's self with; unite with. b To unite in marriage. 3. To engage in.

join'er (-er), n. 1. One that joins. 2. A mechanic who does the woodwork (as doors, stairs, etc.) necessary for the finishing of buildings.

joint (joint), n. 1. The part where two bones of an animal's body are joined, esp. so as to admit of motion. 2. The place or part where two things or parts are joined. 3. Any of the large pieces of meat as cut for roasting.

joke (jok), n. 1. Something witty or sportive; jest; witticism. 2. A laughing stock.

jok'er (jok'er), n. 1. One who jokes; a jester. 2. Card Playing. A card sometimes added to the pack, counting as a trump, usually the highest.

jolt (jolt), v.i. & t. To shake with short, abrupt risings and fallings, as a carriage on rough ground.

jos'tle (jos'l), v. To run against and shake; crowd against.

jour'nal (jur'nal), n. 1. A diary; an account of daily transactions and events, as a daybook or a log book. 2. A daily newspaper; hence, a periodical magazine.

jour'nal-ism (-iz'm), n. The business or profession of publishing, editing, or writing for, journals or newspapers.

jour'ney (-ni), n. Travel or passage from one place to another.

jour'ney-man (-man), n. One who has learned a trade and works, esp. by the day, for another.

jo'vi-al (jo'vi-al), a. Joyous; jolly;

merry.

joy (joi), n. 1. The emotion excited by acquisition or expectation of good; gladness; delight; happiness. 2. That which causes joy.

joy'ful (joi'fool), a. Full of joy; causing joy.

joy'less, a. Not having or causing joy; unenjoyable.

joy'ous (-us), a. Glad; joyful; affording or inspiring joy.

ju'bi-lant (joo'bi-lant), a. Shouting with joy; exulting.

ju'bi-lee (joo'bi-le), n. 1. The 50th (usually) anniversary of an event, or its commemoration. 2. A season or occasion of general joy. 3. Jubilation.

Ju'da-ism (joo'da-iz'm), n. The religious doctrines and rites of the Jews.

judge (juj), n. 1. An officer authorized to decide litigated questions; esp., the presiding magistrate in a court of justice. 2. An umpire.

judge'ment (juj'ment), n. 1. The pronouncing of a formal opinion or decision; opinion or decision given. 2. Law. Act of determining, as in courts, what is conformable to law and justice; the decree or sentence of a court.

ju-di'cial (joo-dish'al), a. 1. Of or pertaining or appropriate to the administration of justice, courts of justice, or a judge thereof. 2. Sanctioned, ordered, or enforced by a court. 3. Fitted for judging or deciding.

ju-di'ci-a-ry (-i-a-ri), a. Of or pertaining to courts, judges, or judicial procedure; judicial.

jug'gle (-'l), v.i. 1. To perform the tricks of a juggler. 2. To practice artifice or imposture.

ju'gu-lar (joo'gu-lar), a. Of or pertaining to the throat or neck.

juice (joos), n. 1. The fluid contents of plant or animal substance; pl., all the fluids in the animal body. 2. Any liquid extracted from a body.

ju'jut'su (joo'joot'soo), n. The Japanese art of self-defense without weapons.

Ju-ly' (joo-li'), n. The seventh month of the year, having 31 days.

junc'tion (junk'shun), n. 1. Act of

joining; state of being joined; union; coalition. 2. Place or point of meeting, as of railroad lines.

jun'ior (joon'yer), a. 1. Younger. Abbr. Jr. or jr.; as, John Smith, Jr. 2. Lower in standing or in rank; later in office. 3. Composed of juniors.

junk (junk), n. 1. Pieces of old cordage used to make gaskets, mats, oakum, etc. 2. Old metal, glass, paper, etc. 3. Hard salted beef supplied to ships.

ju'ris-pru'dence (-proo'dens), n. 1. The science or philosophy of law. 2. Law, or a system of laws.

ju'ry (-ri), n. 1. Law. A body of men legally chosen to inquire into any matter of fact, and to render a verdict, according to the evidence. 2. A committee to determine relative merit or award prizes at a competition.

jus'tice (jus'tis), n. 1. Quality of being just. 2. The principle or practice of just dealing; rectitude; integrity. 3. Uprightness; equitableness; fairness.

jus'ti-fi'a-ble (jus'ti-fi'a-b'l), a. Capable of being justified, or shown to be just.

jus'ti-fi-ca'tion (-fi-ka'shun), n. A justifying, also, that which justifies; defense; vindication.

jus'ti-fy (-fi), v.t. 1. To prove or show to be just; vindicate. 2. To pronounce free from guilt or blame; exonerate. 3. To adjust or arrange exactly.

jute (joot), n. 1. The glossy fiber of either of two East Indian plants, used for sacking, twine, etc. 2. Either plant producing this fiber.

ju've-nile (joo've-nil; -nil), a. 1. Young; youthful; immature or undeveloped. 2. Of or pertaining to youth.

K

ka-lei'do-scope (ka-li'do-skop), n. An instrument containing loose pieces of colored glass, etc., and mirrors arranged to show symmetrical forms.

kan'go-roo' (kan'ga-roo'), n. A herbivorous leaping marsupial of Australia.

kay'ak (ki'ak), n. An Eskimo canoe, usually of sealskin.

keen (ken), a. 1. Sharp; having a fine edge or point. 2. Sharply painful; bitter; cutting. 3. Eager.

keep (kep), v.t. 1. To observe; perform, as duty; celebrate. 2. To preserve or maintain. 3. To hold; retain; detain.

ken'nel (-el), n. A house for a dog or dogs.

ker'nel (kur'nel), n. 1. A whole grain or seed of a cereal, as of corn.

ketch'up (kech'up), n. Catchup.

ket'tle (ket'l), n. A metallic vessel for boiling liquids; esp., a teakettle.

key, n. 1. An instrument to move the bolt of a lock. 2. Something resembling a key in form or function; as, a watch key. 3. In a piano, typewriter, etc., a lever, actuating the mechanism or regulating the action. 4. Music. A system of tones based on their relation to a keynote.

key'board' (ke'bord), n. Bank, row, or set of keys as of a piano, typewriter, etc.

kick (kik), v.i. & t. 1. To strike, thrust, or hit, with or as with the foot or feet. 2. To object strenuously or grumblingly. 3. Of a firearm, to recoil, or recoil against when fired.

kid (kid), n. 1. A young goat. 2. Flesh or skin of a kid; also, a thing made of such skin; as: a A kind of leather. b pl. Kid gloves.

kid'nap (kid'nap'), v.t. To carry (any one) away by unlawful force.

kid'ney (kid'ni), n. Either of the pair of glandular organs that excrete urine.

kill (kil), v.t. 1. To deprive of life; slay. 2. To deprive of vital or active quality; destroy.

ki-mo'no (ki-mo'no; Jap. kim'o-no), n. A kind of loose Japanese gown, or one imitating it.

kind (kind), n. 1. A natural group, class, or division. 2. A class; sort; description.

kin'der-gar'ten (kin'der-gar-ten), n. A school for beginning the education of children by utilizing their normal aptitude for exercise, play, etc.

kind'-heart'ed (kind'har-ted), a. Humane; sympathetic.

kind'ness (kind'nes), n. 1. State or

quality of being kind; beneficence.
2. A kind act.

kin'dred (kin'dred), n. 1. Relationship;
affinity; kinship. 2. Collective pl. The
family or stock to which one
belongs.

king (king), n. 1. A male sovereign;
monarch.

king'dom (-dum), n. 1. A state or
territory subject to a king or queen;
sphere of control; domain. 2. A
division of natural objects; as, the
animal kingdom.

kiss (kis), v.t. & i. 1. To touch or press
with the lips, as a mark of greeting,
forgiveness, etc. 2. To touch gently
or lightly.

kitch'en (kich'en), n. 1. A room
appropriated to cookery. 2. Cooking
department; cuisine.

kitch'en-ette' (kich'en-et'), n. A room
combining a very small kitchen and
a pantry.

kit'ten (kit'n), n. A young cat.

knack (nak), n. 1. A clever way of
doing something; an ingenious
device. 2. Skill; dexterity.

knead (ned), v.t. 1. To work and press
into a mass, usually with the hands,
as dough. 2. To treat or form as by
kneading.

knee (ne), n. 1. The joint, or the
region of the joint, in the middle part
of the leg. 2. Something suggestive
of the bent knee.

kneel (nel), v.i. To fall or rest on the
knees or a knee.

knick'knack' (-nak'), n. A trifle or toy.

knife (nif), n. A cutting instrument
consisting of a thin blade fastened
to a handle. — v.t. To cut, stab, etc.,
with a knife.

knight (nit), n. In feudal times, a
mounted man-at-arms; esp., one
who was admitted to a special
military rank and bound to
chivalrous conduct.

knit (nit), v.t. 1. To form, as a textile
fabric, by interlacing yarn or thread
in loops with needles. 2. To bring or
bind together as by knitting; unite
firmly. 3. To draw together; wrinkle.

knock (nok), v.i. 1. To strike a sharp or
resounding blow, as with something
hard or heavy or with the fist; rap;
hit. 2. To drive or be driven against
something; collide.

know (no), v.t. 1. To perceive;
recognize; recognize as distinct;
distinguish. 2. To perceive or
apprehend as true; perceive with
understanding and conviction. 3. To
be convinced or assured of.

know'ing, p.a. 1. Informed; intelligent;
as, a knowing dog. 2. Artful;
cunning; shrewd; as, a knowing
look.

knowl'edge (nol'ej), n. 1. Familiarity
from actual experience; practical
skill. 2. Acquaintance with fact;
hence, scope of information. 3. Act
or state of knowing; clear perception of fact, truth, or duty.

ko'sher (ko'sher), a. Ceremonially
clean, according to Jewish law; —
used of food, esp. meat.

Kriss Krin'gle (kris krin'g'l). Santa
Claus.

L

la'bel (la-bel) n. A slip of silk, paper,
parchment, metal, etc., affixed to
anything, and indicating the
contents, ownership, destination,
etc.

la'bor (-ber), n. 1. Toil; exertion; work.
2. Hired workers, as a body or
class. 3. An act of laboring; a work;
task. 4. Travail; childbirth.

lab'o-ra-to-ry (lab'o-ra-to-ri), n. A
place devoted to experimental
study in natural science, or to
testing, analyzing, or preparing
drugs, chemicals, explosives, etc.

la'bor-er (-ber-er), n. One who labors;
esp., one who does physical labor
or work that requires strength rather
than skill.

la-bo'ri-ous (la-bo'ri-us), a. 1.
Requiring labor; toilsome. 2.
Diligent; industrious.

lac'er-ate (las'er-at), v.t. To tear; rend;
mangle. Hence: To afflict; harrow.

lack (lak), n. Deficiency; want; need.

lack'a-dai'si-cal (lak'a-da'zi-kal), a.
Affectedly languishing.

lad'der (lad'er), n. An appliance,
consisting of two long side pieces
joined at intervals by rungs, forming
steps for ascent or descent.

lag (lag), n. A falling behind or
retardation, as in a current.

la-goon' (la-goon'), n. A shallow channel or lake, esp. one near the sea.

la'i-ty (la'i-ti), n. 1. The people, as distinguished from the clergy; laymen. 2. Those not of a certain profession.

lake, n. A considerable inland body of standing water; also, an expanded part of a river.

lamb (lam), n. 1. A young sheep. 2. A person like a lamb, as in being innocent. 3. Lamb's flesh.

lame (lam), a. 1. Disabled in the leg or foot; crippled. 2. Fig., halting; defective, as, a lame argument.

la-ment' (la-ment'), v.i. To express or feel sorrow; weep; wail; mourn greatly.

lamp (lamp), n. A vessel with a wick, for burning oil or the like to produce light; hence, any of various devices for producing light or heat; as, an arc lamp, incandescent lamp, etc.

land (land), n. 1. The solid part of the surface of the earth. 2. Any part of the surface of the earth, as a country, estate, etc.; hence, a nation; a people.

land'hold'er (land'hol'der), n. A holder or owner of land.

land'ing, n. 1. Act of one that lands. 2. A place for landing, as from a ship, a carriage, etc. 3. A platform at the end of a flight of stairs.

land'lord' (-lord'), n. 1. One who holds and lets real estate to another. 2. Master of an inn, etc.

land'mark' (-mark'), n. 1. A mark to designate the boundary of land. 2. Any conspicuous object on land that serves as a guide.

land'scape (land'skap), n. 1. A portion of land comprehended in one view, esp. in its pictorial aspect. 2. A picture representing natural scenery.

lan'guage (lan'gwaj), n. 1. The body of words and forms of speech used by a considerable community. 2. Any means of expressing feeling or thought. 3. Form, manner, or style of expression, esp. verbal expression.

lan'guid (-gwid), a. 1. Drooping or flagging from exhaustion; weak. 2. Sluggish; apathetic; listless.

lan'guish (-gwish), v.i. 1. To become languid; to lose strength or animation. 2. To droop or pine with longing.

la-pel' (la-pel'), n. That part of the front of a coat continuing the collar.

lar'ce-ny (lar'se-ni), n. Law. The unlawful taking away of personal property with intent to deprive the rightful owner of it; theft.

large (larj), a. Having power, size, capacity, or scope greater than is usual; big; great.

lar'yn-gi'tis (lar'in-ji'tis), n. Inflammation of the larynx.

lar'ynx (lar'inks), n. The modified upper part of the trachea, or windpipe; the organ of voice.

last, a. 1. Being or remaining after all others; final, hindmost; farthest. 2. Most recent. 3. Lowest in rank or degree.

last'ing, p.a. Existing or continuing a long while; enduring.

late (lat), a. 1. Coming or doing after the usual or proper time; tardy. 2. Far advanced toward the end or close. 3. Lately, deceased, or gone out of office.

late'ness (lat'nes), n. State or quality of being late.

lat'er-al (lat'er-al), a. Of or pertaining to the side; situated at, directed toward, or coming from, the side.

lat'i-tude (lat'i-tud), n. 1. Freedom; independence. 2. Geog. Distance, north or south, from the equator. 3. A region or locality.

laugh (laf), v.i. To show mirth, satisfaction, or derision, by laughter.

laugh'ter (-ter), n. The movement of the muscles of the face, esp. of the lips, with interrupted (often noisy) expulsion of air from the lungs, indicating merriment, satisfaction, or derision.

laun'dry (-dri), n. 1. A place where laundering is done. 2. Articles sent to a laundry to be washed. Colloq.

law (lo), n. 1. A binding custom or rule of conduct, or the whole body of such customs and rules; also, the regulation or state of society brought about by their enforcement.

law'ful (-fool), a. 1. Conformable to law; legitimate. 2. Authorized or established by law.

law'less (lo'les), a. Without law; hence, not restrained or controlled by law; unruly; disorderly; licentious.

law'yer (lo'yer), n. One versed in the laws, or a practitioner of law, as an attorney, counselor, etc.

lax (laks), a. 1. Not tense, firm, or rigid; loose; slack. 2. Not strict or stringent; vague.

lay, v.t. 1. To bring down, as with force. 2. To calm; allay; suppress. 3. To put or set down in a recumbent position; deposit.

lead'er (led'er), n. One that leads; as: 1. A guide, conductor. 2. A chief; commander.

leak (lek), n. 1. A crack or hole which (contrary to intention) admits or lets out fluid. 2. Act of leaking; leakage.

lean (len), v.i. 1. To incline or bend so as to receive support. 2. To incline or bend from the vertical. 3. To incline in opinion or desire.

leap (lep), v.i. 1. To spring clear of the ground; jump; vault. 2. To spring; bound, move swiftly.

leap'frog (lep'frog), n. A play among boys, in which one stoops down and another leaps over him.

learn (lurn), v.t. 1. To gain knowledge of, or skill in, by study or instruction; fix in the mind. 2. To ascertain; hear.

lease (les), v.t. 1. To grant or convey by lease; let. 2. To hold or take a lease of.

least (lest), a. Shortest; slightest; lowest.

leave (lev), n. 1. Permission; leave of absence, as from military duty. 2. A formal parting.

lec'ture (lek'tur), n. 1. A discourse; esp., a formal discourse for instruction. 2. A reprimand.

left, a. 1. Designating, or pertaining to, that side of the body on which, in man, muscular action is generally weaker than on the other side. 2. Situated to the left.

left'-hand'ed (-han'ded), a. 1. Having the left hand more serviceable than the right. 2. Done, made with, or adapted to, the left hand instead of the right.

leg'a-cy (leg'a-si), n. A gift of property, esp. personal property, by will.

le'gal-ize (le'gal-iz), v.t. To make legal.

leg'end (lej'end; le'jend), n. 1. An unauthentic story coming down from the past; a tradition. 2. An inscription, motto, or title, as on a coin.

leg'i-ble (lej'i-b'l), a. Capable of being read or deciphered; plain.

leg'is-late (lej'is-lat), v.i. To make or enact a law or laws.

leg'is-la'tor (-la'ter), n. One who makes laws for a state or community; a member of a legislature.

lem'on-ade' (-ad'), n. A beverage consisting of lemon juice mixed with water and sweetened.

lend (lend), v.t. 1. To allow the temporary use of. 2. To afford; grant. 3. To devote or accommodate (one's self or itself), to.

length (length), n. 1. The longest, or longer, dimension of any object; extent from end to end. 2. Extent in time, number, or quantity.

le'ni-ence (le'ni-ens), n. Lenient action, clemency.

le'ni-ent (le'ni-ent), a. Mild; clement; merciful; not rigorous or severe.

Lent (lent), n. A season of fasting, consisting of the 40 week days preceding Easter.

leop'ard (lep'erd), n. 1. A ferocious cat of Asia and Africa. 2. The jaguar.

lep'ro-sy (-ro-si), n. An infectious disease marked by affections of the skin, ulcerations, and disturbances of sensation. It is nearly always fatal.

le'sion (le'zhun), a. A hurt; injury.

less'en (les'n), v.t. & i. 1. To make or become less; reduce. 2. To represent as less; disparage.

les'son (les'n), n. 1. A portion of Scripture red at divine service. 2. A reading or exercise assigned for study.

let, v.t. 1. To leave; abandon. Archaic, exc. with alone or be. 2. To cause; make. Obs., except in to let (one) know.

leth'ar-gy (leth'ar-ji), n. 1. Morbid drowsiness; profound sleep. 2. A state of inaction or apathy.

let'tuce (let'is), n. A garden plant of the chicory family, the leaves of which are used as salad.

lev'el (lev'el), n. 1. Horizontal condition; uniform altitude. 3. A horizontal surface.

le'ver (le'ver), n. A bar used to exert force at one point of its length, by applying a force at a second point and thus turning the bar at a third (fixed) point called a fulcrum.

lev'i-ty (lev'i-ti), n. Lack of gravity; frivolity; flippancy.

lev'y (lev'i), n. Act or process of levying or that which is levied.

lewd (lud), a. Lustful; unchaste.

li'a-bil'i-ty (li'a-bil'i-ti), n. An obligation for which one is liable, e.g. debt.

li'a-ble (li'a-b'l), a. 1. Bound in law or equity; responsible; answerable. 2. Exposed to some undesirable contingency; — with to.

li'bel (li'bel), n. 1. Law. Any representation wrongfully published and tending to expose another to public hatred, contempt, or ridicule; also, the act of so publishing it. 2. Any false and defamatory representation.

lib'er-al (lib'er-al), a. 1. Not servile or mean; esp., not narrowly restricted. 2. Bestowing, or bestowed, in a large and noble way; generous; ample. 3. Not strict or rigorous; free.

lib'er-al-ism (-iz'm), n. Liberal principles.

lib'er-ty (lib'er-ti), n. 1. Freedom. 2. Exemption from arbitrary or despotic control. 3. Freedom from restraint; power to do as one pleases; state of being disengaged.

li'bra-ry (li'bra-ri), n. 1. A building devoted to books, or an establishment for their custody and control. 2. A collection of books.

li'cense (li'sens), n. 1. Authority or permission given to do or forbear any act. 2. Any permitted unusual freedom of action. 3. Excess of liberty; disregard of law or propriety.

lick (lik), n. 1. A stroke of the tongue in licking. 2. A place where natural salt is found and where wild animals resort to lick it up.

lid (lid), n. 1. That which covers the opening of a vessel, box, etc.; a movable cover. 2. An eyelid.

lie (li), n. A falsehood uttered or acted to deceive; hence, anything which misleads or deceives.

life (lif), n. 1. The quality or state of being alive; animate, existence. 2. A living being; esp., a person; also, living beings or organisms collectively; as, animal life.

life'less, a. Destitute of life; hence, spiritless; dull.

life'like (lif'lik'), a. Like a living being or a real object; resembling life.

lift (lift), v.t. 1. To bring, or cause to move, up higher; raise, elevate. 2. To exalt in rank, condition, estimation, spirits, etc. 3. To steal. Colloq.

light (lit), n. 1. That by which objects are rendered visible, or by which we see. 2. The sun's light; daylight; also, day; especially, dawn. 3. That which furnishes light, as the sun, a candle, a lamp, etc.

light'-foot'ed, a. Having a light step; nimble.

light'-head'ed (-hed'ed), a. 1. Dizzy; delirious, as with fever. 2. Thoughtless; frivolous.

light'-heart'ed, a. Free from anxiety; gay; merry.

light'ning (lit'ning), n. The flashing of light caused by a discharge of atmospheric electricity; hence, the discharge itself.

light'weight' (lit'wat'), n. One of less than average weight.

lik'a-ble (lik'a-b'l), a. Such as attracts liking.

like (lik), a. 1. Having the same, or nearly the same, appearance or characteristics; similar. 2. Indicative of. 3. Inclined toward.

like, v.t. To have a liking for; enjoy.

like'li-hood (lik'li-hood), n. Probability.

like'ly (-li), a. 1. Appearing like truth; probable; credible. 2. Such as to render something probable. 3. Suitable.

like'wise (-wiz'), adv. & conj. In like manner; also, moreover; too.

lik'ing (lik'ing), n. State of being pleased with a thing or person; hence, inclination; desire.

lim'ber (lim'ber), a. 1. Easily bent; flexible; pliant. 2. Supple; lithe.

lim'bo (lim'bo), n. A place or condition of restraint or confinement, or of neglect or oblivion.

lim'it (lim'it), n. That which terminates, circumscribes, or confines; bound;

border.

lim'i-ta'tion (lim'i-ta'shun), n. 1. A limiting. 2. That which limits; restriction; qualification.

li'mou-sine' (le'moo-zen'), n. A large automobile with permanent top like a coupe.

limp (limp), a. Lacking stiffness; flexibic.

limp, v.i. To walk lamely.

line (lin), v.t. 1. To cover the inner surface of, as of a cloak. 2. To put something in the inside of; fill. 3. To serve as the lining of.

lin'en (lin'en), n. 1. Thread or cloth of flax; collectively, linen fabrics, articles of linen. 2. Garments usually or chiefly of linen, esp. shirts, collars and cuffs.

lin'ge-rie' (lan'zh'r-re'), n. Linen goods; linen or muslin underclothes, esp. of women.

lin'gual (-gwal), a. Of or pertaining to the tongue.

lin'i-ment (lin'i-ment), n. A medicinal preparation thinner than an ointment, to rub on the skin.

li-no'le-um (li-no'le-um), n. A floor cloth with a surface of hardened linseed oil and ground cork.

lip (lip), n. 1. Either of the two fleshy folds which surround the mouth. 2. An edge, as of a hollow vessel or cavity.

li'queur' (le'kur'), n. An aromatic spirituous liquor, usually sweetened.

liq'ui-date (lik'wi-dat), v.t. 1. To discharge; pay off, as a debt. 2. To settle the accounts and distribute the assets of (a corporation or estate).

liq'uor (lik'er), n. 1. An alcoholic beverage, esp. if strong or distilled.

list (list), n. 1. A strip forming the body or selvage of cloth. 2. A roll or catalogue, as of names.

lis'ten (lis'n), v.i. To hearken; hence, to give heed; yield to advice.

list'less (list'les), a. Having no desire or inclination; indifferent.

lith'o-graph (-o-graf), v.t. To produce, copy, or portray by lithography.

li-thog'ra-phy (li-thog'ra-fi), n. Art or process of putting writing or designs on stone (or zinc, aluminium, etc.) with a greasy material, and of

producing prints therefrom.

lit'i-gate (-gat), v.t. To make the subject of a lawsuit.

li-ti'gious (li-tij'us), a. 1. Inclined to engage in lawsuits; contentious; quarrelsome. 2. Of or pertaining to litigation.

lit'tle (lit'l), a. 1. Small in size or extent; diminutive. 2. Short in duration; brief. 3. Small in quantity or degree.

live'li-hood (liv'li-hood), n. Means of supporting life; maintenance.

live'ly (liv'li), a. 1. Full of life; vigorous; active; animated. 2. Enlivening. 3. Vivid; brilliant.

liv'ing (-ing), n. 1. State of one that lives. 2. Manner or rule of life. 3. Possibility of living, esp. comfortably.

liz'ard (liz'ard), n. Any of numerous small four-legged, long-bodied reptiles, with tapering tail, and scaly skin.

load (lod), n. 1. That which is carried; a burden; hence, the quantity proper to carry, as in a cart. 2. That which burdens the mind. 3. The charge of a firearm.

loaf (lof), n. A regularly shaped or molded mass of bread, cake, or sugar.

loan (lon), n. 1. A lending; permission to use. 2. That which one lends or borrows, esp. money.

loath (loth), a. Filled with disgust or aversion.

loathe (loth), v.t. To dislike greatly; abhor.

lob'ster (-ster), n. A large edible crustacean.

lo-cal'i-ty (lo-kal'i-ti), n. 1. Fact or state of being local. 2. A place.

lo-cate (lo'kat), v.t. 1. To designate the site or place of, as a mining claim. 2. To establish in a certain place; settle; place. 3. To search for and discover the place of.

lo-ca'tion (lo-ka'shun), n. 1. A locating. 2. Situation; place, as of residence or settlement.

lock'er (-er), n. A drawer; compartment, chest, or closet, that may be locked.

lock'up' (lok'up'), n. A jail.

lo'co-mo'tion (lo'ko-mo'shun), n. Act or power of moving from place to

L
M

place.

lo'cust (lo'kust), n. 1. Any grasshopper having short antennae; any of certain species that often travel in vast swarms and destroy vegetation.

lodge (loj), n. 1. A small or temporary dwelling house; a hut; booth; tent; hence, any abode, as for a caretaker on an estate, etc.

lodg'ing (-ing), n. 1. Dwelling; esp., temporary abode; quarters. 2. pl. A room or rooms in another's house, as a place of residence.

loft (loft), n. A room or floor above another; esp., an attic room or an attic.

log'ger-head' (log'er-hed'), n. 1. A blockhead. 2. A very large marine turtle. — to be at loggerheads, to contend or quarrel.

log'ic (loj'ik), n. 1. The science, art, or laws of exact reasoning or thinking. 2. A treatise on logic. 3. Reasoning; esp., sound reasoning.

loin (loin), n. That part of the body, on either side, between hip bone and false ribs.

loi'ter (loi'ter), v.i. To be slow in moving; saunter.

lone'ly, a. 1. Without company; alone; lone. 2. Solitary; unfrequented. 3. Lonesome.

lone'some (-sum), a. 1. Secluded from society; unfrequented; solitary; hence, causing loneliness or depression. 2. Conscious of, and depressed by, solitude.

lon-gev'i-ty (lon-jev'i-ti), n. Length of life.

long'hand' (long'hand'), n. The characters used in ordinary writing;

long'ing (long'ing), n. An eager desire.

long'-suf'fer-ing, a. Bearing injuries or trials with patience.

look (look), v.i. 1. To direct the eyes for seeing. 2. To direct the attention; give heed; take care. 3. To expect.

look'out' (look'out'), n. 1. A watching for an object or event; also, the place from which such observation is made. 2. One engaged in watching.

loon (loon), n. A rogue; also, a boor.

loose (loos), a. 1. Not fastened so as to be fixed, rigid, firm, or tight. 2.

Free, esp. from confinement. 3. Not dense, close, or compact.

lord (lord), n. 1. One who has authority; a master; ruler. 2. A titled nobleman.

lorn (lorn), a. Forsaken; desolate; forlorn.

loss (los), n. 1. State or fact of being destroyed; ruin. 2. Act or fact of suffering deprivation; esp., unintentional parting with something. 3. Act or fact of failure to win, or utilize.

lost (lost), p.a. 1. Ruined. 2. Parted with; gone out of one's possession. 3. Having wandered from, or unable to find, the way; also, no longer visible.

lot'ter-y (lot'er-i), n. A scheme for distributing prized by lot, esp. such a scheme in which lots, or chances, are sold.

lov'a-ble (luv'a-b'l), a. Worthy of love.

love (luv), n. 1. A feeling of strong personal attachment; ardent affection. 2. Strong liking; fondness. 3. Tender and passionate affection for one of the opposite sex.

love'less, a. Without love; unloved or unloving.

love'lorn (-lorn'), a. Forsaken by one's love.

love'ly (-li), a. 1. Beautiful; esp., having a delicate beauty. 2. Beautiful in character.

lov'er (luv'er), n. One who loves; esp. one in love with one of the other sex.

low (lo), a. 1. Having small elevation; not high or tall. 2. Below the normal level, surface, etc. 3. Near the horizon. 4. Of relatively little importance; humble in station.

low'ly (-li), a. 1. Low in rank; modest; humble; meek. 2. Low in position or development.

loy'al (loi'al), a. 1. Faithful, as to the lawful government or to a friend; true. 2. Of or showing loyalty; as, loyal expressions.

lu'bri-cant (lu-bri-kant), a. Lubricating.

lu'cid (lu'sid), a. 1. Shining; bright. 2. Clear. 3. Designating, or marked by, a sane or normal state of the faculties.

luck'y (-i), a. 1. Favored by luck; fortunate.

lu'cra-tive (lu'kra-tiv), a. Yielding profit, esp. financial profit.

lu'di-crous (lu'di-krus), a. Adapted to excite laughter; ridiculous.

lug'gage (-aj), n. That which is lugged; esp. a traveler's baggage.

luke'warm' (luk'worm'), a. Moderately warm; tepid; indifferent.

lull'a-by' (lul'a-bi'), n. A soothing refrain, as to quiet a baby.

lum-ba'go (lum-ba'go), n. Rheumatic pain in the loins and the lower part of the back.

lum'ber (-ber), n. 1. Old or refuse household stuff. 2. Timber, esp. that sawed into boards, plants, etc.

lump (lump), n. 1. A piece or mass of indefinite or irregular shape. 2. A swelling. 3. A whole aggregation.

lu'na-cy (-si), n. 1. Unsoundness of mind.

lu'na-tic (-na-tik), a. 1. Affected with lunacy; crazy. 2. For insane persons; as, a lunatic asylum.

lunch (lunch), n. 1. A luncheon. Colloq. 2. Food for a lunch.

lung (lung), n. One of the (usually two) compound saclike organs forming the respiratory organ of air-breathing vertebrates.

lunge (lunj), n. 1. A sudden thrust, as with a sword. 2. A plunging forward; leap.

lurk (lurk), v.i. 1. To lie hidden, as in ambush. 2. To exist secretly. 3. To move furtively.

lus'cious (lush'us), a. 1. Grateful to taste or smell, esp. from sweetness; delicious. 2. Sweet to excess; cloying.

lust (lust), n. 1. Sensuous, esp. sexual, desire. 2. Longing desire; — usually in a bad sense; as, lust of gain.

lus'ter (lus'ter), n. 1. Fact or quality of shining with reflected light; shine or sheen; gloss. 2. Brilliancy; glitter. 3. A chandelier or the like.

lux'u-ry (luk'shoo-ri), n. 1. Indulgence in costly gratifications of the tastes; a mode of life marked by this. 2. Anything which pleases the senses, and is also costly.

M

mac'a-ro'ni (mak'a-ro-ni), n. 1. A pasta made in slender tubes and cooked for food (ex. macaroni and cheese).

ma-che'te (ma-she'tee), n. A large heavy knife, used for cutting cane, etc. Sp. America.

mad (mad), a. 1. Disordered in intellect; insane. 2. Rashly foolish; senseless. 3. Frenzied; furious. Colloq., angry; vexed.

mad'am (mad'am), n. A form of polite address to a lady.

mad'den (-'n), v.t. & i. To make or become mad.

mad'ly (mad'li), adv. In a mad manner; wildly.

mad'man (-man), n. A lunatic.

mag'a-zine' (mag'a-zen'), n. 1. A storehouse or warehouse; esp., a place for keeping military stores. 2. A periodical publication containing various articles.

mag'ic (maj'ik), n. 1. The art which pretends to produce effects by the aid of supernatural beings or by a mastery of secret forces in nature.

mag-nan'i-mous (mag-nan'i-mus), a. 1. Great of mind; raised above what is low or mean. 2. Dictated by or exhibiting nobleness of soul.

mag'net (mag'net), n. Any body which has polarity and the property of strongly attracting iron and some other substances.

mag'net-ize (-iz), v.t. 1. To give magnetic properties to; convert into a magnet. 2. To attract by magne-tism; captivate.

maid (mad), n. 1. An unmarried girl or woman; a maiden; a virgin. 2. A female servant.

maid'en (-'n). A maid.

mail, n. 1. a Matter, as letters, parcels, etc., conveyed under public authority from one post office to another. b The system of appli-ances used in the postal service.

maim (mam), v.t. To mutilate; cripple; disable.

main (man), n. 1. A broad stretch or expanse; esp. 2. Chief part; essential point.

main'ly, adv. Principally; chiefly.

L
M

main-tain' (man-tan'; men-), v.t. 1. To hold or keep in any state, esp. in efficiency or soundness; keep up. 2. To continue in or with; carry on. 3. To bear the expense of; support.

ma-jor'i-ty (ma-jor'i-ti), n. 1. Status of being of full legal age. 2. The greater of two numbers regarded as parts of a whole; more than half of any total; also, the excess of this greater number over the remainder.

make (mak), v.t. 1. To form or constitute, or cause to be, in external nature; as, to frame, fashion, prepare, construct, fabricate, manufacture, compose, etc. 2. To form mentally or ideally.

make'shift' (mak'shift'), n. Temporary expedient.

make-up', n. 1. The way in which anything is put together.

mal'e-dic'tion (mal'e-dik'shun), n. 1. A proclaiming of evil against some one; a cursing; a curse. 2. Slander.

mal'for-ma'tion (mal'for-ma'shun), n. Irregular, abnormal, or wrong formation or structure.

mal'ice (mal'is), n. 1. Enmity of heart; malevolence. 2. Law. State of mind shown by intent to commit an unlawful act.

ma-lign' (-lin'), a. 1. Having an evil disposition; malevolent; malignant. 2. Tending to injure; evil; baleful; sinister.

ma-lig'nant (-nant), a. 1. In medicine, tending or threatening to produce death; virulent. 2. Having a baleful influence; malign. 3. Disposed to do harm or inflict suffering; malicious.

mal'nu-tri'tion (mal'nu-trish'un), n. Faulty nutrition.

ma-ma' (ma-ma'; ma'ma), n. Mother; — usually a child's word.

man (man), n. 1. A human being. 2. The human race; mankind. 3. The male human being; esp., an adult male person.

man'date (-dat), n. An authoritative command; order; injunction.

man'da-to-ry (man'da-to-ri), a. Containing, or of the nature of a mandate; obligatory.

ma-neu'ver (ma-noo'ver; -nu'ver), n. 1. A military or naval evolution. 2. A stratagem; artifice.

man'gle (man'g'l), v.t. To cut or hack with repeated strokes at random. 2. To spoil, mutilate, or injure in making, doing, or performing.

man'hole' (man'hol'), n. A hole through which a man may get access to a drain, etc.

ma'ni-a (ma'ni-a), n. 1. Violent derangement of mind; insanity. 2. Excessive excitement or enthusiasm; a "craze"; a "rage", as, a stamp mania.

ma'ni-ac (-ak), a. 1 Raving with madness; mad. 2. Frantic; violent.

man'i-fest (-fest), a. Evident to the senses, esp. the sight; obvious to the understanding.

man'i-fest, n. A list or invoice of a ship's cargo, to be exhibited at the custom house.

ma-nip'u-late (ma-nip'u-lat), v.t. & i. 1. To treat, work, or operate with the hands, or by mechanical means, esp. with skill. 2. To treat or manage with the mind, esp. skillfully.

man'kind', n. 1. (man'kind') The human race. 2. (man'kind') Men, as disting. from women.

man'ly (-li), a. Having qualities becoming to a man; manlike, esp. brave or noble; masculine.

man'ner (man'er), n. 1. Species; kind; sort. 2. A way of acting; way, mode; habit; custom. 3. Behavior; conduct.

man'sion (man'shun), n. A large and stately residence.

man'slaugh'ter (-slo'ter), n. The killing of a human being, esp. unlawfully but without malice.

man'u-fac'ture (-tur), n. 1. The making of wares or material products by hand or machinery. 2. Anything manufactured.

man'y (men'i), a. The comparative and superlative are supplied by more, most. Consisting of a great number; numerous.

map (map), n. A representation (usually flat) of the earth's surface or a part of it.

ma-raud'er (-er), n. A freebooter; plunderer.

march, v.t. 1. To advance in step or in military order, as soldiers. 2. To walk in a grave or steady manner.

Mar'di Gras' (mar'de gra'). The day (Tuesday) before Lent begins; — in some cities, a day of merrymaking.

mare (mar), n. The female of the horse kind.

mar'gin (mar'jin), n. 1. A border; edge; brink; verge; limit. 2. A reserve, as of money, to meet unforeseen conditions. 3. That part of a page outside of the main body of text.

mar'i-tal (mar'i-tal), a. Of or pertaining to marriage.

mark, n. 1. A thing aimed at; a goal or target. 2. A significant token; symptom; sign; esp., an indication of character; a trait. 3. Limit or standard of action or fact.

mar'ket-a-ble (mar'ket-a-b'l), a. 1. Fit to be offered for sale in a market. 2. Of or pert. to buying or selling; current in the market.

ma-roon' (ma-roon'), v.t. To put (a person) ashore on a desolate island or coast and abandon him.

mar'riage (mar'ij), n. 1. The state or condition of being married; the relation existing between husband and wife; wedlock. 2. Act of marrying, or rite used in marrying; a wedding.

mar'ry, v.t. 1. To unite in wedlock; join in matrimony. 2. To dispose of in wedlock. 3. To take as husband and wife; wed.

mar'tyr (mar'ter), n. 1. One who suffers death for refusing to renounce his religion. 2. One who sacrifices life, station, etc., for principle, or to sustain a cause.

mar'vel (mar'vel), n. 1. That which causes wonder or astonishment. 2. Wonder; astonishment.

mar'vel-ous (-us), a. Exciting marvel; astonishing.

mas'cot (mas'kot), n. A person, animal, or thing supposed to bring good luck.

mas'cu-line (-ku-lin), a. 1. Gram. Of or pertaining to or designating the class of words that denotes males. 2. Having the qualities of a man; virile; of a woman, mannish.

mash (mash), n. 1. Crushed malt, or meal of grain, steeped and stirred in hot water to form wort. 2. A mixture of meal, bran, or the like, and hot water, fed warm to animals.

ma'son (ma's'n), n. 1. One who builds with stone, brick, etc., or prepares stone for building.

Mass (mas), n. The service or liturgy of the Eucharist; The Lord's Supper; — now used chiefly of the Roman Catholic service.

mas'sa-cre (mas'a-ker), n. The atrocious killing of a considerable number of human beings.

mas-sage' (ma-sazh'), n. A method or the act of treating the body by rubbing, etc., as for remedial purposes.

mas'ter (mas'ter), n. 1. A man having another living being subject to his will. 2. One who uses, or controls, anything inanimate.

mas'ter-piece' (mas'ter-pes'), n. Anything done or made with extraordinary skill; a chief-d'oeuvre.

mat'a-dor (mat'a-dor; -dor), n. The man appointed to kill the bull in bullfights.

match, n. 1. A person or thing equal or similar to another. 2. An exact counterpart. 3. A pair suitably associated.

mate, n. 1. A companion; comrade. 2. A match, an equal. 3. A husband or wife; also, one of a pair of animals.

ma-te'ri-al-ist, n. 1. An adherent of materialism. 2. One absorbed in material interests.

ma-te'ri-al-ize (-te'ri-al-iz), v.t. 1. To invest with material characteristics; to express through the medium of material objects. 2. Spiritualism. To make (a spirit) visible in or as in material form. — v.i. To appear as a material form.

ma-ter'nal (ma-tur-nal), a. 1. Of or pertaining to a mother; motherly. 2. Derived or received from, or connected through, one's mother.

math'e-mat'ics (-mat'iks), n. The science of the relations between quantities or magnitudes and operations.

mat'ri-cide (mat'ri-sid; ma'tri-), n. 1. The murder of a mother by her child. 2. One who murders one's own mother.

mat'ri-mo'ni-al (mat'ri-mo'ni-al), a. Of or pert. to marriage; conjugal; nuptial.

ma'tron-ly (-li). a. Like, or befitting, a matron; hence, sedate; grave.

mat'ter (-er), n. 1. That of which any

L
M

physical object is composed; material. 2. Pus. 3. Physics. Whatever occupies space.

mat'ter-of-fact', a. Adhering to facts; commonplace; dry.

mat'tress (-res), n. A bed stuffed with hair, moss, or the like, and tufted or otherwise fastened.

ma-ture' (ma-tur'), a. 1. Full-grown; ripe; fully developed. 2. Completely worked out; perfected. 3. Having run to the limit of its time; due, as a note.

maun'der (mon'der; man'-), v.i. 1. To move languidly or idly. 2. To mutter; mumble.

May, n. The fifth month of the year, having 31 days.

may'be (ma'be), adv. Perhaps.

maze (maz), n. 1. Confusion of thought; perplexity. 2. A confusing network, as of paths.

me (me), pers. pron. The objective (dative or accusative) case of I.

mead'ow (med'o), n. A piece of land devoted to grass; specif., low level grass land.

mea'ger (me'ger), a. 1. Having little flesh; thin; lean. 2. Destitute of richness, strength, or the like; poor.

mel'o-dra'ma (mel'o-dra'ma; mel'o-dra'ma), n. Any romantic drama marked by sensational situations and a happy ending.

mel'o-dy (mel'o-di), n. 1. An agreeable succession of sounds; musical quality. 2. Music. a A rhythmical succession of single tones; a tune. b The chief voice part in a harmonic composition; the air.

mel'on (-un), n. 1. Muskmelon. 2. Watermelon.

mem'ber (mem'ber), n. 1. A part or organ of the animal body; esp., a limb. Archaic. 2. In botany, a part of a plant body. 3. One of the persons composing a society, community, or party.

me-men'to (me-men'to), n. A thing to awaken memory; reminder; souvenir.

mem'oir (mem'wor), n. 1. pl. A history composed from personal experience; often, esp., an account of episodes in one's own life. 2. A biography.

me-mo'ri-al (me-mo'ri-al), a. 1.

Serving to preserve remembrance; commemorative. 2. Of or pertaining to memory.

mem'o-ry (-ri), n. 1. The act, capacity, or function of mentally reproducing and recognizing previous experience. 2. The sum total of a mind's experience as actually or possibly remembered.

men'ace (men'as), n. A threat or threatening.

mend (mend), v.t. & i. 1. To free from defects; to alter (anything) for the better; correct; also, to repair. 2. To improve, better, or ameliorate.

me'ni-al (me'ni-al; men'yal), a. Pertaining or appropriate to servants; servile; sordid; low.

men'tal (men'tal), a. Of or pertaining to the mind; intellectual.

men-tal'i-ty (men-tal'i-ti), n. 1. Mental quality or power. 2. Mind considered as a characteristic.

men'tion (-shun), n. A brief speaking or notice.

men'tor (-tor), a. A wise and faithful counselor or monitor.

mer'can-tile (mur'kan'til; -til), a. Of or pertaining to merchants, or trade.

mer'chan-dise (-chan-diz), n. The objects of commerce; wares; goods.

mer'chant (-chant), n. 1. One who traffics on a large scale, esp. abroad. 2. A retailer. U.S.

mer'ci-ful (-si-fool), a. Full of mercy; compassionate; mild.

mer'ci-less, a. Destitute of mercy; pitiless.

mer'cy (mur'si), n. 1. Forbearance from inflicting harm, esp. in punishment; clemency. 2. Compassionate treatment of the unfortunate.

merg'er (mur'jer), n. An absorption of one estate or interest in another.

mer'it (mer'it), n. 1. Due reward or punishment (usually reward). 2. Quality, state, or fact of deserving well or ill.

mer'i-to'ri-ous (-i-to'ri-us), a. Deserving of reward or honor.

mer'maid (mur-mad), n. A fabled sea creature, typically with a woman's body and a fish's tail.

mer'ry (mer'i), a. Pleasing, delightful; mirthful; sportive.

mer'ry-go-round', n. Any of various revolving contrivances for amusement.

mer'ry-making (-mak'ing), a. Festive; jolly.

mes-mer'ic (mez-mer'ik), a. Of, pertaining to, or induced by, mesmerism; hence, fascinating.

mes'sage (mes'aj), n. Any communication sent from one to another.

mes'sen-ger (mes'en-jer), n. 1. One who bears a message or does an errand. 2. A forerunner.

Mes-si'ah (me-si'a), n. Also -as. The expected king and deliverer of the Hebrews; the Christ.

mess'y (mes'i), a. Like a mess; disordered; untidy.

met'a-mor'pho-sis (-fo-sis), n. 1. Change of form, structure, or substance; also, the form resulting from this. 2. A marked change in the form of an animal after the embryonic stage, as when a tadpole changes to a frog.

met'a-phor (met'a-for), n. A figure of speech by which a word or phrase literally denoting the kind of object or idea is applied to another to suggest a likeness; as in "the ship plows the sea."

met'a-phys'ics (-fiz'iks), n. That division of philosophy which includes the science of being and the theory of knowledge.

me'te-or (me'te-or), n. A meteoroid heated to incandescence by friction in passing through the earth's atmosphere; a shooting star.

meth'od (meth'ud), n. 1. Mode of procedure; manner; way. 2. Orderly arrangement; plan or design, as of an author.

me-tic'u-lous (me-tik'u-lus), a. Unduly or excessively careful of small details.

met'ro-pol'i-tan (met'ro-pol'i-tan), a. Of, pertaining to, or designating, a metropolis or metropolitan.

met'tle (met'l), n. Quality of temperament; spirit.

Mex'i-can (mek'si-kan), a. Of or pertaining to Mexico or its people.

mez'za-nine (mez'a-nin; -nen), n. Also mezzanine floor or story. A low story between two high ones.

mi'cro-scope (mi'kro-skop), n. Optical instrument for making enlarged images of minute objects.

mid (mid), a. 1. Denoting or being the middle part; as, in mid ocean. 2. Middle in position; middle; — chiefly in combination.

mid'day' (mid'da'), n. Middle of the day, noon.

mid'dle (mid'l), a. Equally distant from given extremes; mean.

mid'dle-aged' (mid'l-ajd'), a. Being of an age between youth and old age.

mid'dle-man (-man), n. An agent or broker between two parties, esp. a dealer who buys of the producer and sells to the retailer.

midg'et (mij'et), n. A very diminutive person.

midst (midst), n. 1. The interior or central part or place; middle. 2. The position or condition of being surrounded or beset; the press.

mid'sum'mer (mid'sum'er), n. Middle of summer; esp., the summer solstice.

mid'wife' (mid'wif'), n. A woman who assists women in childbirth.

mid'win'ter (mid'win'ter; mid'win'-), n. The middle of winter; esp., the winter solstice.

might'y (-i), a. 1. Possessing might; potent; powerful. 2. Accomplished or marked by might. 3. Extraordinary; great. Chiefly Colloq.

mi'grate (mi'grat), v.i. To go from one country or region to another with a view to residence. 2. To pass periodically from one region or climate to another, as various birds.

mi'gra-to-ry (mi'gra-to-ri), a. 1. Migrating, or disposed to migrate. 2. Roving; nomad. 3. Of or pert. to migration.

mild (mild), a. Gentle; kind; soft; clement; moderate; temperate.

mil'dew (mil'du), n. A parasitic fungus or the whitish down or discoloration which it produces on plants, paper, clothing, etc.

mile'age (mil'aj), n. 1. An allowance for traveling expenses at a certain rate per mile. 2. Aggregate length or distance in miles.

mil'i-tant (mil'i-tant), a. Engaged in warfare; fighting; also, combative.

milk (milk), n. 1. The fluid secreted by the mammary glands of female mammals. 2. A liquid resembling milk, as the juice of the coconut, etc.

milk'maid' (milk'mad'), n. A woman who milks cows or works in a dairy.

mill, n. 1. A building with machinery for grinding grain into flour; hence, a machine for grinding. 2. Any of various machines used in working up raw material.

mil'lion (-yun), n. 1. The number of ten hundred thousand, or a thousand thousand, — written 1,000,000. 2. An indefinitely large number.

mil'lion-aire' (-ar'), n. One whose wealth amounts to a million or millions of dollars, pounds, etc.

mim'ic (mim'ik), a. Of the nature of, pert. to, or formed by, imitation or mimicry.

mince'meat' (mins'met'), n. A mixture, chopped fine, of raisins, apples, suet, spices, etc., with or without meat, used to fill mince pies.

mind (mind), n. 1. Remembrance. 2. Consciousness; thought. 3. Understanding; intellect; also, sanity.

mind'ful (mind'fool), a. Bearing in mind; regardful; attentive.

min'gle (min'g'l), v.t. 1. To combine or join by intermixture or diffusion; mix; associate or unite. 2. To make or prepare by mixing; concoct.

min'i-a-ture (min'i-a-tur), n. 1. Any very small painting, esp. a portrait, as on ivory. 2. A representation on a small scale.

min'i-mize (-miz), v.t. To reduce to the smallest part or proportion possible.

min'i-mum (min'i-mum), n. 1. The least quantity or amount assignable, admissible, etc. 2. The lowest point or amount reached.

min'is-try (min'is-tri), n. 1. Ministration; as, the ministry of angels. 2. The office, duties, or functions of a minister. 3. The clergy.

mi'nor (mi'ner), a. 1. Inferior; less; smaller; as, of minor importance. 2. Music. Less by a half step than the major.

mi-nor'i-ty (mi-nor'i-ti), n. 1. The smaller in number of two aggregates; — opposed to majority. 2. Quality or state of being a minor.

min'u-et' (min'u-et'), n. A kind of slow graceful dance, or music suited to such a dance.

min'ute (min'it), n. 1. The sixtieth part of an hour or a degree; sixty seconds. 2. A moment. 3. A memorandum, note, or draft, as of instruction. b pl. An official record of proceedings.

mi-nute' (mi-nut;; mi-), a. 1. Very small; little; slight. 2. Of trivial importance; trifling. 3. Marked by or attentive to small details.

mir'a-cle (mir'a-k'l), n. 1. A wonderful thing; a marvel. 2. An event or effect in the physical world deviating from the known laws of nature.

mi-rac'u-lous (mi-rak'u-lus), a. 1. Of the nature of a miracle. 2. Marvelous; wonderful.

mi-rage' (me-razh'), n. An optical effect, as on ocean or desert, in which a reflected image is seen, commonly inverted, while the real object may or may not be in sight.

mirth (murth), n. Gladness or gayety, as shown by laughter; jollity.

mis'ad-ven'ture (mis'ad-ven'tur), n. Mischance; ill luck; a mishap; accident; disaster.

mis'al-li'ance (-a-li'ans), n. An improper or undesirable alliance, esp. in marriage.

mis'be-hav'ior (-hav'yer), n. Bad behavior.

mis-car'riage (-kar'ij), n. 1. Mismanagement; failure. 2. Failure to carry properly. 3. Premature bringing forth of young.

mis-car'ry (-i), v.t. 1. To fail of intended result. 2. To suffer miscarriage (of young).

mis'cel-la'ne-ous (mis'e-la'ne-us), a. 1. Mixed; consisting of diverse things. 2. Having various qualities; many-sided; as, a miscellaneous writer.

mis'chief (mis'chif), n. 1. Harm; esp., trouble or vexation caused by some one; as, to make mischief. 2. A cause or source of harm or vexation.

mis'chie-vous (mis'chi-vus), a. Causing, or full of, mischief; injurious; esp., inclined to the causing of, or involving, petty injury or annoyance; naughty.

mis'con-ceive' (mis'kon-sev'), v.t. & i. To conceive wrongly.

mis-con'duct (mis-kon'dukt), n. Wrong or improper conduct; misbehavior.

mis'con-struc'tion (mis'kon-struk'shun), n. Act of misconstruing; wrong interpretation.

mis-con'strue (mis-kon'stroo; mis'kon-stroo'), v.t. to construe wrongly.

mis-deed' (-ded'), n. An evil deed.

mis'de-mean'or (-er), n. A crime less than a felony.

mis'di-rect' (-di-rekt'), v.t. To direct wrongly.

mi'ser (mi'zer), n. A covetous person; esp., one having wealth who lives miserably to increase it.

mis'er-a-ble (miz'er-a-b'l), a. 1. In a state of misery; wretched; as, she seems miserable; — often as a figure of speech. 2. Causing misery, or discomfort; pitiably poor; as, a miserable lot.

mi'ser-ly (mi'zer-li), a. Pertaining to, like, or characteristic of, a miser; very covetous.

mis'er-y (miz'er-i), n. 1. A state of great distress; privation; poverty. 2. A wretched circumstance; misfortune.

mis-fit' (mis-fit'), n. 1. Act of state of fitting badly. 2. Something that fits badly, as a garment.

mis-for'tune (-for'tun), n. Bad fortune; mishap.

mis-give' (mis-giv'), v.t. To give doubt and apprehension to; as, her heart misgave her.

mis-hap (-hap'), n. Mischance.

mis-lead' (-led'), v.t. To lead into a wrong way; lead astray; deceive.

mis-place' (mis-plas'), v.t. To put in a wrong place or on an improper or unworthy object.

mis-rep're-sent' (mis-rep're-zent'), v.t. & i. To represent falsely, improperly, or imperfectly.

mis'sion (mish'un), n. 1. A sending, or being sent, by authority on some service or function. 2. Persons sent; envoys.

mis-spell' (mis-spel'), v.t. To spell incorrectly.

mis-take' (mis-tak'), v.t. 1. To take in a wrong sense; misunderstand; as a remark. 2. To take erroneously, as one person or thing for another.

mis'tress (mis'tres), n. 1. A woman having authority or ownership, female head of a family, etc. 2. A woman skilled in anything. 3. A sweetheart.

mis-trust' (-trust'), n. Want of confidence or trust.

mis'un-der-stand'ing, n. 1. Mistake of meaning; error. 2. Disagreement; quarrel.

mit'i-gate (mit'i-gat), v.t. To render mild or milder; soften; appease; lessen; moderate.

moan (mon), n. A low prolonged sound, indicative of pain or grief.

mo'bile (mo'bil; -bel), a. 1. Movable; marked by ease of movement. 2. Moving or flowing freely. 3. Changing readily.

mock (mok), v.t. 1. To treat with scorn or contempt; deride; ridicule. 2. To disappoint; deceive; delude. 3. To imitate; mimic.

mock'er-y (mok'er-i), n. 1. Insulting or contemptuous action or speech. 2. A subject of derision. 3. An insincere or contemptible imitation.

mod'el (mod'el), n. 1. A miniature representation of a thing. 2. A copy; image. Now Colloq. 3. A pattern of a thing to be made; hence, something worthy of imitation.

mod'er-ate (-er-at), a. Kept within due bounds; limited.

mod'er-a'tor (mod'er-a'ter), n. 1. An arbitrator; mediator. 2. A presiding officer.

mod'ern (mod'ern), a. Of or pert. to present or recent time.

mod'ern-ism (-er-niz'm), n. Modern practice; esp., a modern usage, characteristic, etc.

mod'est (-est), a. 1. Placing a moderate or low estimate on one's own capabilities or merits. 2. Evincing, or arising from, modesty.

mod'i-fy (mod'i-fi), v.t. 1. To limit or reduce in extent or degree; moderate. 2. To change somewhat in form or qualities; alter somewhat.

moist (moist), a. Slightly wet; damp; humid; not dry.

mois'ten (mois'n), v.t. To make moist or damp.

mold (mold), n. A fungous growth or discoloration produced on organic matter, esp. when damp or decaying.

mold'ing, n. 1. Act or process of shaping in or on a mold, or of making molds. 2. Anything cast, or appearing as if cast, in a mold. 3. A narrow surface, sunk or projecting, used for decoration.

mole (mol), n. A spot or small permanent prominence on the human body, esp. a dark-colored one.

mole, n. Any of numerous small animals having minute eyes, small concealed ears, and very soft fur. They live almost entirely underground.

mo-lest' (mo-lest'), v.t. To interfere with hostilely or vexatiously.

mo'les-ta'tion (mo'les-ta'shun; mol'es-), n. Act of molesting; state of being molested; annoyance.

molt (molt), v.i. To shed or cast off the feathers, outer layer of the skin, or the like, which are replaced by new growth.

mo'ment (mo'ment), n. 1. A minute portion of time; an instant. 2. Importance, as in influence or effect; consequence.

mo-men'tum (-tum), n. 1. Mech. The quantity of motion in a moving body, being proportioned to the mass multiplied by the velocity. 2. Impetus.

mon'arch-y (mon'ar-ki), n. 1. The state or territory ruled by, or the government exercised by, a monarch. 2. The system of government in which a single person is sovereign.

mon'as-ter-y (-as-ter-i), n. A house of religious retirement for persons under religious vows, esp. monks.

mon'e-ta-ry (mon'e-ta-ri; mun'-), a. 1. Of or pertaining to the coinage or currency. 2. Of or pertaining to money; pecuniary.

mon'i-tor (mon'i-ter), n. 1. One who admonishes. 2. A pupil or student selected for special duties, usually disciplinary.

monk (munk), n. One of a religious community of men living apart from the world and bound by vows of chastity, obedience, and poverty.

mon'o-chrome (-krom), n. Painting or drawing in a single color.

mon'o-cle (-k'l), n. An eyeglass for one eye.

mo-nog'a-mous (mo-nog'a-mus), a. Upholding, or practicing, monogamy; of or pert. to monogamy.

mo-nog'a-my (-mi), n. Single marriage; esp., marriage with but one person at the same time.

mon'o-logue (-log), n. 1. A dramatic part or composition for a single performer. 2. A soliloquy.

mo-nop'o-lize (-liz), v.t. To gain a monopoly of.

mon'o-tone (-ton), n. 1. Continuous utterance in one unvaried pitch. 2. Monotony of style. 3. Something uttered or written in one tone or strain or marked by monotonous recurrences.

mon-soon' (mon-soon'), n. A periodic wind, esp. in the Indian Ocean and off the south coast of Asia. Also, the rainy season accompanying the southwest monsoon in India.

mon'ster (mon'ster), n. 1. A fabulous or actually existing animal of strange or horrible form. 2. Any huge animal or thing. 3. An animal or plant departing greatly from the usual type.

mon'u-ment (mon'u-ment), n. 1. A structure serving as a memorial.

mood, n. State or temper of mind; disposition.

mood'y (mood'i), a. 1. Subject to moods of depression, bad temper, or the like; gloomy. 2. Expressing moodiness or ill humor; as, a moody face.

moon (moon), n. 1. The satellite of the earth. 2. A lunar month; a month; as, three moons ago. 3. Any satellite, or secondary planet.

moon'shine (-shin'), n. 1. Moonlight. 2. Show without substance or reality; empty show. 3. Liquor smuggled or illicitly distilled. Colloq.

mop (mop), n. 1. An implement for washing floors, etc. made of cloth or yarn, fastened to a handle. 2. Something likened to a mop, as a mass of hair.

mope (mop), v.i. To be dull and spiritless.

mor'al (mor'al), a. 1. Of or pert. to questions of right and wrong. 2. Righteous; virtuous; just. 3. Capable of being governed by, or of influencing, the sense of right.

mor'al-ist (mor'al-ist), n. 1. One who moralizes; a teacher or student of morals. 2. One who practices moral duties or leads a moral life.

mo-ral'i-ty (mo-ral'i-ti), n. 1. Moral quality; virtue. 2. a Moral discourse or instruction. b A kind of allegorical play (popular esp. in the 16th century), in which actors personify faith, death, vice, etc.

mor'al-ize (mor'al-iz), v.t. 1. To explain in a moral sense. 2. To make moral.

mor'bid (mor'bid), a. 1. Not sound and healthful; diseased; sickly; given to gloomy or unwholesome ideas. 2. Relating to disease.

more-o'ver (mor-o'ver), adv. Beyond what has been said; further; besides; also.

morgue (morg), n. A place where bodies of persons found dead are exposed for identification.

morn'ing (mor'ning), n. Early part of the day.

mor'tal (mor'tal), a. 1 Subject to death. 2. Deadly; fatal; causing death, physical or spiritual. 3. So severe as to be thought of as threatening death.

mor-tal'i-ty (mor-tal'i-ti), n. 1. Condition, quality, or nature of being mortal. 2. The death of large numbers; esp., number or rate of deaths.

mort'gage (mor'gaj), n. A conditional conveyance of property, as security for the payment of a debt, etc., to become void upon settlement of the obligation.

mort'ga-gee' (-ga-je'), n. The person to whom property is mortgaged.

mor'ti-fy (mor'ti-fi), v.t. To deaden by religious or other discipline, as the carnal affections; hence, to abase; humble.

mor'tu-a-ry (mor'tu-a-ri), a. Of or pertaining to the burial of the dead or death or mourning.

mos-qui'to (mos-ke'to), n. Any of certain two-winged insects, having a long proboscis adapted, in the females only, for puncturing the skin. Some species transmit the organisms that produce malaria, yellow fever, etc.

most'ly (most'li), adv. For the greatest part.

moth'er, n. 1. A female parent. 2. Source or origin. 3. used as a title of an abbes or the like.

mo'tion (mo'shun), n. 1. Act, process, or state of changing place; movement. 2. Mental act or impulse. 3. A proposal, esp. a formal one in a deliberative body.

mo'tive (mo'tiv), n. That which incites to action or moves the will.

mount, v.i. 1. To rise; ascent. 2. To get up (on something, as a platform); esp., to seat one's self on an animal for riding. 3. To rise or increase in amount.

moun'tain (moun'tin), n. Any elevation higher than a hill, and often abrupt, but without great extent of surface at its summit.

mourn (morn), v.i. & t. To express or to feel sorrow; esp., to lament some one's death.

mouse (mous), n. Any of numerous species of small rodents.

mouth (mouth), n. 1. The opening through which an animal receives food; also, the cavity containing the tongue and teeth. 2. An opening suggestive of a mouth. 3. A wry face; a grimace.

mouth'ful (mouth'fool), n. 1. As much as the mouth holds, or as is put into the mouth at one time. 2. A small quantity.

move (moov), v.t. 1. To change the place or position of; shift. 2. To set or keep in motion; stir; drive; actuate. 3. To excite to action; impel.

Mr. (mis'ter). Written form of the title Mister.

Mrs. (-is; -iz). Written form of the title Mistress.

much (much), a. Great in quantity, extent or duration.

muck'y (-i), a. Filthy with much; miry.

mud (mud), n. Soft, wet earth; mire.

mud'dy (-i), a. 1. Abounding in mud; smeared, dashed, or turbid with or as with mud. 2. Not clear or bright; cloudy.

mug (mug), n. A kind of earthen or metal drinking cup.

mug'gy (mug'i), a. Warm, damp, and close; as, muggy weather.

mulch (mulch; mulsh), n. Any substance, as straw, used to protect the root of plants from heat, cold, or drought.

mul'ti-ple (-p'l), a. Containing more than one; manifold. — Product of one number multiplied by another.

mul'ti-ply (mul'ti-pli), v.t. 1. To increase in number. 2. Math. To find the product of by multiplication. — v.i.

mul'ti-tude (-tud), n. 1. A crowd; a large assembly. 2. A great number of persons or things.

mum'ble (mum'b'l), v.i. & t. 1. To speak thickly or obscurely with the lips partly closed; mutter. 2. To chew softly with closed lips, or with little use of the teeth. — n. A mumbling.

mum'my (mum'i), n. A corpse treated with preservatives after the manner of the ancient Egyptians.

mumps (mumps), n. Med. An infectious disorder marked by inflammation of the parotid glands.

mun'dane (mun'dan), a. Of or pertaining to the world; worldly; earthly. — -ly, adv.

mu-nic'i-pal (mu-nis'i-pal). a. 1. Enjoying a local self-government; — said of a corporation such as a town, borough, or city. 2. Of or pertaining to such a corporation; as, municipal buildings.

mur'der (mur'der), n. Law. The offense of unlawfully killing a human being with premeditated malice.

murk (murk), n. Darkness; gloom.

murk'y (mur'ki), a. Dark; obscure; gloomy.

mur'mur (mur'mur), n. 1. A low, confused, indistinct sound, as of running water. 2. A low, muttered complaint.

mus'cle (mus'l), n. 1. a An organ or mass of tissue whose special function is to exert physical force. b The peculiar tissue of such an organ. 2. Muscular strength or development. Colloq.

mus'cu-lar (mus'ku-lar), a. 1. Of or pert. to muscles. 2. Having well-developed muscles; strong.

muse (muz), v.i. & t. To meditate; ponder.

mus'ic (mu'zik), n. 1. Melody or harmony generally. 2. The science or art of pleasing, expressive, or intelligible combination of tones.

mu'si-cal (mu'zi-kal), a. 1. Of or pertaining to music. 2. Having the pleasing qualities of music; melodious; harmonious. 3. Fond of music.

mus-tache' (mus-tash'), n. The beard growing on the upper lip; also, either side of this hair.

mus'tard (mus'tard), n. 1. A plant of the cabbage family, with yellow flowers, and narrow pods. 2. A pungent powder of ground mustard seed.

mus'ty (mus'ti), a. 1. Moldy; sour. 2. Spoiled by age; stale.

mu'ta-ble (mu'ta-b'l), a. 1. Capable of, or subject to, mutation. 2. Unstable; fickle.

mu-ta'tion (mu'ta-shun), n. Alteration in form or qualities.

mute (mut), a. 1. Not speaking; silent; speechless. 2. Incapable of speaking; dumb; also, unaccompanied by speech or sound.

mu'ti-late (mu'ti-lat), n. 1. To cut off or remove a limb or essential part of; maim. 2. To destroy or remove a material part of, so as to render imperfect.

mut'ter (mut'er), v.i. To speak indistinctly or with a low voice and lips partly closed; esp., to grumble complainingly or angrily; growl.

mu'tu-al (mu'tu-al), a. 1. Reciprocally acting or related; interchanged. 2. Possessed, experienced, or done by two or more at the same time.

my (mi), pron. & a. Of or belonging to me.

my-o'pa (mi-o'pi-a), n. Med. Near-sightedness.

myr'tle (mur't'l), n. 1. A shrub with evergreen leaves and white or rosy flowers, followed by black berries.

my-self' (mi-self'), pron. An emphasized form for I or me.

mys-te'ri-ous (mis-te'ri-us), a. Of or pertaining to mystery; containing or implying a mystery; obscure.

mys'ter-y (mis'ter-i), n. A profound secret; something unknown or concealed; something beyond human comprehension.

mys'tic (mis'tik), n. A believer in mysticism.

mys'ti-cism (-ti-siz'm), n. 1. Mystic character or quality. 2. The doctrine that reality or God may be known in an immediate insight differing from all ordinary sensation or reasoning.

mys'ti-fi-ca'tion (-fi-sk'shun), n. Act of mystifying, or state of being mystified.

mys'ti-fy (-fi), v.t. 1. To involve in mystery; make obscure.

myth (mith), n. 1. A legendary story, esp. one serving to explain some practice, belief, or the like, esp. in connection with religion. 2. A person or thing whose existence is imaginary or not verifiable.

N

nag, v.t. & i., To annoy by persistent scolding or urging.

na-Ive (na'ev'), a. Unaffectedly simple; ingenuous; artless.

na'ked (na'ked), a. 1. Having on no clothes or covering; nude; bare; uncovered. 2. Destitute; bare of means. 3. Defenseless; unprotected.

name (nam), n. 1. The title by which any person or thing is known or designated. 2. A descriptive appellation; epithet. 3. Reputation; fame.

name'sake (-sak'), n. One that has the same name as another; esp., one named after another.

nap, v.i. To have a short sleep; doze; be in a careless, unguarded state.

nar-cot'ic (-kot'ik), a. Having the properties of, or operating as, a narcotic.

nar-rate' (na-rat'), v.t. To tell; relate; detail.

nar'ra-tive (nar'a-tiv), n. 1. That which is narrated; story. 2. Art or practice of narrating.

nar'row-ly (nar'o-li), adv. 1. With minute scrutiny; closely; carefully. 2. With little margin or space; barely. 3. Not broadly; illiberally.

nas'ty (nas'ti), a. 1. Disgustingly dirty; foul. 2. Morally filthy; obscene; indecent. 3. Seriously harmful or dangerous; bad.

na'tion (na'shun), 1. A people connected by ties of blood and generally having a common language, customs, etc. 2. The body of inhabitants of a country united under a single government.

na'tive (na'tiv), a. 1. Born with one; inherent,. 2. That was the place of one's birth; as, native land, etc. 3. Of minerals, etc., natural; not artificially prepared.

na-tiv'i-ty (na-tiv'i-ti), n. 1. Birth; the circumstances attending birth. 2. [cap.] the birth of Christ.

nat'u-ral (nat'u-ral). a. 1. Of, from, or by, birth; innate; inborn. 2. Born out of wedlock; illegitimate. 3. In accordance with human nature.

nat'u-ral-ly, adv. In a natural manner.

na'ture (na'tur), n. 1. That which is the source or essence of life; creative force. 2. The universe. 3. Kind; sort.

naugh'ty (no'ti), a. Mischievous; wayward; disobedient; — used of children or in sportive censure.

nau'se-a (no'she-a; -se-a), n. 1. Seasickness; hence, any sickness of the stomach with a desire to vomit; qualm. 2. Extreme disgust; loathing.

na'vy (na'vi), n.; pl. -VIES (-viz). 1. A fleet of ships. 2. The war vessels of a nation. 3. The naval establishment of a nation, including yards, shops, men, ships, etc.

near (ner), adv. 1. At, within, or to a little distance (in place or time). 2. Within little; almost; nearly. 3. Closely.

near'ly, adv. In a near manner or degree.

near'sight'ed (-sit'ed), a. Seeing distinctly at short distances only; shortsighted.

neat (net), a. 1. Free from admixture or adulteration. 2. Simple and becoming; tasteful. 3. Clever; finished; adroit.

nec'es-sa-ry (nes'e-sa-ri), a. 1. Impossible to be otherwise or to be done without; indispensable. 2. Not to be avoided; inevitable. 3. Acting from necessity or compulsion;

N O

involuntary.

ne-ces'si-tate (ne-ses'i-tat), v.t. To make necessary; to force; compel.

nec'tar (nek'tar), n. 1. Classic Myth. The drink of the gods; hence, any delicious beverage. 2. A sweet liquid secreted by plant nectaries.

need (ned), n. 1. A state requiring supply or relief; necessity; lack of anything desired or useful. 2. Poverty; destitution.

nee'dle (ne'd'l), n. 1. A small pointed instrument for sewing, with an eyehole for thread. 2. A slender rod used in knitting; also, a hooked instrument for crocheting, etc.

need'less (ned'les), a. Not needed; unnecessary.

nee'dle-work (-wurk), n. Work done with a needle; also, the occupation of sewing.

need'y (ned'i), a. Poverty-stricken; necessitous.

neg'a-tive (neg'a-tiv), a. 1. Expressing or implying negation; refusing assent. 2. Not positive or direct.

neg-lect' (neg-lekt'), v.t. To disregard; as: a To omit to notice; slight; as, to neglect a rule. b To be remiss in attending to; as, to neglect a duty.

ne-go'ti-ate (-at), v.t. 1. To sell; as, to negotiate securities. 2. To procure, or arrange for, by negotiating.

neigh'bor (na'ber), n. 1. A person who lives near another. 2. A person or thing near another.

neph'ew (nef'u; nev'u), n. the son of a brother or of a sister.

ne-phri'tis (ne-fri'tis; nef-ri'tis), n. Med. Inflammation of the kidneys; Bright's disease.

nerv'ous (nur-vus), a. 1. Possessing or manifesting vigor of mind; forcible; spirited. 2. Of, pertaining to, or affecting the nerves.

nest (nest), n. 1. The bed or receptacle prepared by a bird for its eggs and young. 2. Any snug retreat. 3. An abode; haunt.

nes'tle (nes'l), v.i. 1. To make and occupy a nest. 2. To lie close and snug, as a bird in her nest.

net'work' (net'wurk'), n. 1. A fabric of intersecting threads, cords, or wires, with spaces, or meshes, between them. 2. Any system of similarly crossing lines.

neu-ral'gi-a (nu'ral'ji-a), n. Med. A very acute pain which follows the course of a nerve.

neu-rot'ic (nu-rot'ik), a. Med. Of or pert. to the nerves; nervous.

neu'ter (nu'ter), a. 1. Gram. a Of neither masculine nor feminine gender. 2. Biol. a Sexless.

neu'tral-ize (nu'tral-iz) v.t. To destroy the peculiar properties or opposite dispositions of; make neutral; counteract; nullify.

nev'er (nev'er), adv. 1. Not ever; at no time. 2. Not in any degree; or way, under any condition, etc.; — in emphatic negation; as, never fear.

new (nu), a. 1. Having existed but a short time; recent; not old. 2. a Recently discovered; hence, strange; unfamiliar. b Other than the former, or old; fresh. 3. Not habituated; unaccustomed.

new'fan'gled (nu'fan'g'ld; nu'fan'-), a. 1. Inclined to novelties; given to new fashions. 2. Newly made; novel; — used disparagingly.

news'boy', n. A boy who distributes or sells newspapers.

news'pa'per (-pa'per), n. A paper printed and distributed at stated intervals to convey news, etc.

next (nekst), adv. Nearest; having nothing similar intervening; immediately succeeding.

nib'ble (nib'l), v.t. & i. To bite lightly or gently; eat in small bits.

nice (nis), a. 1. Fastidious; overdainty; finial; also, refined; cultured; discriminating. 2. Exacting, scrupulous; punctilious.

niche (nich), n. A hollow or recess, generally in a wall, as for a statue.

nick'el (nik'l), n. 1. Chem. A hard, malleable, ductile metal of the iron group, resistant to oxidation. 2. A coin of or containing nickel; esp., a five-cent piece. Colloq., U.S.

nick'name' (-nam'), n. 1. A name given in derision or sportive familiarity. 2. A familiar diminutive name.

nic'o-tine (nik'o-tin; -ten), n. A poisonous alkaloid, the active principle of tobacco.

niece (nes), n. A daughter of one's brother or sister.

night (nit), n. 1. The time from sunset

to sunrise, esp. when it is dark. 2. Nightfall. 3. The darkness of night; — often used figuratively.

night'ly, a. Of or pertaining to night; happening, done, or used by night, or every night.

night'time' (-tim'), n. The time from dusk to dawn.

nil (nil), n. Nothing; thing of no account.

nim'ble (nim'b'l), a. 1. Light and quick in motion; lively; swift. 2. Of the mental faculties, alert; acute.

nin'ny (nin'i), n. A fool; simpleton.

nip'per (nip'per), n. 1. One the nips. 2. Any of various devices for nipping, as small pincers; — usually in pl. 3. One of the large claws of a crab or lobster.

nip'ple ('i), n. 1. The protuberance of a breast; teat; pap. 2. Any small teatlike projection.

nit (nit), n. The egg of a louse or other parasitic insect; also, the young insect.

no (no), adv. 1. Not. 2. Not any; not at all. 3. Not so.

no'ble (no'b'l), a. 1. Of persons, possessing eminence, elevation, dignity, or the like; illustrious; of deeds or acts, great; famous. 2. Grand, esp. in appearance; stately; imposing. 3. Possessing very high or excellent qualities or properties.

nod (nod), v.i. & t. 1. To bow or incline the head in assent, salutation, etc., or involuntarily from drowsiness or sleep. 2. To signify by nodding the head.

noise (noiz), n. 1. Loud or confused shouting; clamor. 2. Any sound, esp. if without musical quality.

noise'less, a. Making or causing no noise or stir; silent.

noi'some (noi'sum), a. 1. Noxious; harmful; unwholesome. 2. Offensive, esp. to the smell; disgusting.

nois'y (noiz'i), a. 1. Making, or given to making, a noise. 2. Marked by noise.

nom'ad (nom'ad; no'mad), n. One of a wandering race or tribe.

nom'i-nate (-nat), v.t. To name as a candidate for election or appointment; propose by name.

non'cha-lant (-lant), a. Lacking in warmth of feeling, enthusiasm, or interest; indifferent; careless.

non-com'bat-ant (non-kom'bat-ant), n. Any person connected with a military or naval force whose duties do not include fighting, as a chaplain.

non'con-form'ist (non'kon-for'mist), n. One who does not conform to an established church, esp. [often cap.] that of England; a dissenter.

non'de-script (non'de-skript), a. Not easily described; of no particular class or kind.

none (nun), pron. 1. No one; not one. 2. Not any. As subject, none with a plural verb is the commoner construction unless a singular idea is clearly intended.

non'ex-ist'ence (non'eg-zis-tens), n. Absence of existence; nonentity.

non'sense (non'sens), n. 1. That which is not sense, or has no sensible meaning; absurdity. 2. Trifles; things of no importance or value.

noo'dle (noo'd'l), n. A simpleton; blockhead.

noon (noon), n. 1. Midday; twelve o'clock in the daytime. 2. The highest point; culmination.

noose (noos), n. 1. A loop with a running knot, which binds the closer the more it is drawn. 2. Fig.: A tie, bond, or snare.

nor'mal (nor'mal), a. The ordinary or usual condition, degree, or the like; average; mean.

north'ern-er (-ther-ner), n. One born or living in the north, or [cap.] U.S., the North.

nose (noz), n. 1. That part of the face, or head, containing the nostrils. 2. The smelling organ. 3. Sense of smell; also, scent.

nos'tril (nos'tril), n. Either of the external openings of the nose.

no'ta-bil'i-ty (no'ta-bil'i-ti), n. 1. A person of note. 2. Quality of being notable.

no'ta-ble (no'ta-b'l), a. Worthy of note or notice; remarkable; hence, distinguished.

noth'ing (nuth'ing), n. 1. Not anything; no thing, nought. 2. What is of no significance. 3. Arith. Absence of magnitude or quantity.

no'tice (no'tis), n. 1. Intelligence;

information; intimation or warning, esp. if formal. 2. A written or printed sign, announcement, or the like, communicating information or warning. 3. Act of noting, remarking, or observing; cognizance.

no'ti-fi-ca'tion (no'ti-fi-ka'shun), n. 1. An intimation; notice. 2. The written or printed matter which gives notice, as an advertisement.

no'ti-fy (no'ti-fi), v.t. 1. To give notice of, make known, publish. 2. To give notice to.

no-to'ri-ous (no-to'ri-us), a. Generally known; well-known; — now almost always implying evil or wickedness.

not'with-stand'ing (not'with-stan'ding), adv. conj. Nevertheless; yet; although. — prep. Without prevention from or by; in spite of.

nour'ish (nur'ish), v.t. To supply with whatever promotes growth, development, etc.; feed; foster.

nov'el-ty (nov'el-tri), n. 1. Quality or state of being novel; newness; freshness. 2. Something novel; an innovation.

nov'ice (nov'is), n. 1. One who has entered a religious house on probation. 2. One new in any business, profession, or calling; beginner.

now (nou), adv. & conj. 1. At the present time; at this moment. 2. Hence: a In the time immediately to follow. b Very lately; a moment ago.

nox'ious (nok'shus), a. Hurtful; injurious; unwholesome.

nude (nud), a. Bare; naked; un-clothed.

nui'sance (nu'sans), n. That which annoys or gives trouble and vexation or that is offensive.

null (nul), a. 1. Of no legal or binding force; invalid; void. 2. Of no consequence or value.

nun (nun), n. A woman under certain religious vows, esp. one living in a convent.

nurse (nurs), n. 1. A person who nurses a child or cares for an invalid.

nur'ture (nur'tur), n. 1. A nourishing or nursing. 2. That which nourishes; food.

nut'ty (nut'i), a. 1. Abounding in or producing nuts. 2. Having a flavor like that of nuts.

O

oak (ok), n. a Any of a very large genus of trees and shrubs. b The wood of these trees.

oar (or), n. 1. A long, slender wooden implement for propelling or steering a boat. 2. An oarsman. — v.t. To propel with or as with oars.

o-a'sis (o-a'sis; o'a-sis), n.. A fertile or green spot in a waste or desert.

oat (ot), n. The grain or seed of a certain cereal grass, or the plant.

ob'du-rate (ob'du-rat), a. Hardened in feelings; stubbornly wicked.

o-be'di-ence (o-be'di-ens), n. Act of obeying.

o-be'di-ent (-ent), a. Willing to obey.

o-bese' (o-bes'), a. Very fat.

o-bey (-ba'), v.t. 1. To execute the commands of. 2. To submit to the authority of.

o-bit'u-a-ry (-bit'u-a-ri), a. Of or pertaining to the death of a person or persons. — n. A notice of a death, with a biographical sketch.

ob'ject (ob'jekt), n. 1. A material thing. 2. That which is set before the mind so as to be apprehended or known. 3. End; aim.

ob'li-ga'tion (-ga'shun), n. 1. Any duty imposed by law, promise, or contract, by social relations or by kindness, etc. 2. State of being indebted for an act of favor; also, the act itself.

o-blige' (o-blij'), v.t. 1. To constrain; put under obligation to do or forbear something. 2. To bind by a favor rendered; hence, to do a favor to; accommodate.

ob-lit'er-ate (-lit'er-at), v.t. To erase.

ob-liv'i-on (-liv'i-un), n. 1. A forgetting. 2. State of being forgotten.

ob-nox'ious (ob-nok'shus), a. Objectionable.

ob-scene' (ob-sen'), a. 1. Foul. 2. Offensive to chastity or modesty.

ob-scen'i-ty (-sen'i-ti), n.; pl. -TIES (-tiz). Obscene language or acts.

ob-scure' (ob-skur'), a. 1. Shaded, or darkened. 2. Indistinctly seen. — v.t. To make dim.

ob-serv'a-ble (ob-zur'va-b'l), a. 1.

That must or may be observed. 2. Capable of being observed.

ob'ser-va'tion (ob'zer-va'shun), n. 1. Act, faculty, or habit of observing. 2. Fact of being observed or seen. 3. A remark.

ob-serv'a-to-ry (ob-zur'va-to-ri), n. 1. A place equipped with instruments for observing natural phenomena. 2. A place or building affording a wide view.

ob-serve' (-zurv'), v.t. 1. To take notice of by appropriate conduct. 2. To see. 3. To remark. — v.i. 1. To take notice. 2. To remark. **ob'sess'** (ob-ses'), v.t. To beset or dominate.

ob'so-lete (ob'so-let), a. No longer in use.

ob'sta-cle (ob'sta-k'l), n. Obstruction.

ob'sti-nate (-nat), a. 1. Stubborn. 2. Not easily overcome.

ob-struct' (ob-strukt'), v.t. 1. To block. 2. To be in the way of. 3. To cut off the sight of (an object).

ob-struc'tion (-struk'shun), n. Hindrance; barrier.

ob-tain' (ob-tan'), v.t. To procure.

ob-trude' (ob-trood'), v.t. To thrust impertinently upon another. — v.i. To intrude.

ob'vi-ous (ob'vi-us), a. Easily seen or understood.

oc-ca'sion-al (-al), a. Incidental.

oc-cult' (o-kult), a. Hidden; supernatural.

oc'cu-pant (-pant), n. One who occupies.

oc'cu-pa'tion (-pa'shun), n. 1. Act or process of occupying. 2. One's principal business in life.

oc'cu-py (-pi), v.t. 1. To dwell in. 2. To fill. 3. To employ.

oc-cur'rence (o-kur'ens), n. An event.

o-cean (o'shan), n. 1. The whole body of salt water on the surface of the globe. 2. One of the large bodies of water into which the great ocean is regarded as divided. 3. An immense or limitless expanse or quantity.

o'clock (o-klok). Of (by) the clock.

oc'ta-gon (ok'ta-gon), n. Polygon of eight sides.

Oc-to'ber (-to'ber), n. The tenth month of the year, having thirty-one days.

odd (od), a. 1. Not paired with another. 2. Not divisible by 2

without a remainder. 3. Extra.

odds (odz), n. pl. & sing. 1. Probability. 2. An equalizing allowance given to a contestant or opponent that is at a disadvantage. 3. Quarrel.

o'dor (o'der), n. Any smell or scent, fragrant or otherwise.

of (ov; unaccented ov), prep. 1. From. 2. As a result of. 3. Belonging or related to.

off (of), adv. Away so as not to be on, against, or near.

off-col'or, a. 1. Not of proper or natural color. 2. Of doubtful propriety.

of'fend' (o'fend'), v.i. To sin. — v.t. To displease; make angry.

of-fen'sive (o-fen'siv), a. 1. Making attack. 2. Insulting. 3. Disagreeable. — n. State or posture of one who makes attack.

of'fer (of'er), n. 1. To sacrifice. 2. To tender. 3. To propose. 4. To try to inflict, make, or do. — n. Act of offering or proposing.

of'fice (of'is), n. 1. A service. 2. Special, proper, or assigned service. 3. A ceremony.

of'fi-cer (-i-ser), n. One who holds an office.

of-fi'cial (o-fish'al), a. Authorized; authoritative. — n. One holding, or invested with, an office.

of-fi'ci-ate (-i-at), v.i. To perform divine service; to act as an officer in performing a duty.

off'spring' (of'spring'), n. Issue; progeny.

of'ten (of'n), adv. Frequently.

oil'y (-i), a. 1. Of or like oil. 2. Covered with oil.

old (old), n. Aged.

o'men (o'men), n. Foreboding. — v.t. To presage.

om'i-nous (om'i-nus), a. Foreboding evil.

o-mis'sion (o-mish'un), n. 1. An omitting. 2. That which is omitted.

o-mit' (o-mit), v.t. To leave out.

om-nis'cient (-ent), a. Having universal knowledge.

on, adv. In or into a position.

once (wuns), adv. 1. One time and no more. 2. At any one time; ever. — n. One time or occasion.

one (wun), a. 1. Being a single unit, being, or thing. 2. Denoting a

N O

person or thing indefinitely. 3. Denoting a particular thing or person.

one'self' (wun'self'), pron. A reflexive and emphatic form for the indefinite pronoun one.

on'ly (on'li), a. 1. Single. 2. Alone because of superiority. — adv. 1. Exclusively. 2. Without there being others.

o'pen (o'p'n), a. 1. Not shut or closed. 2. Available. 3. Public. 4. Sincere.

op'er-a (op'er-a), n. A drama wholly or mostly sung, with orchestral accompaniment and appropriate costumes, scenery, and action.

op'er-a-tive (op'er-a'tiv), a. 1. Capable of acting. 2. Effective.

o-pin'ion (o-pin'yun), n. 1. A belief. 2. A formal judgment by an expert.

op'por-tune' (op'or-tun'), a. Fit; timely.

op'por-tu'nism (op'or-tu'niz'm), n. The taking advantage, as in politics, of opportunities, often with little regard for principles or consequences.

op'por-tu'ni-ty (-ni-ti), n.; pl. -TIES (-tiz). Fit or convenient time.

op-pose' (o-poz'), v.t. 1. To set against. 2. To confront.

op'po-site (op'o-zit), a. 1. Set against. 2. Contrarily turned or moving. 3. Diametrically different. — n. That which is contrary.

op-press' (o-pres'), v.t. 1. To weigh heavily on. 2. To crush by abuse of power.

op-pres'sive (o-pres'iv), a. 1. Unreasonably burdensome. 2. Hard to be borne.

op'ti-cal (op'ti-kal), a. 1. Relating to optics. 2. Relating to vision.

op-ti'cian (op-tish'an), n. One who makes, or deals in, optical glasses and instruments.

op'ti-mism (-ti-miz'm), n. 1. Doctrine that everything is ordered for the best. 2. Disposition to take the most hopeful view.

op'ti-mis'tic (-mis'tik), a. Hopeful.

op'tion (op'shun), n. 1. Act of choosing. 2. Power or right of choosing. 3. That which is offered for choice.

o'ral (o'ral), a. 1. Spoken. 2. Of or pertaining to the mouth.

o-ra'tion (o-ra'shun), n. An elaborate discourse.

or'chard (or'cherd), n. A grove of fruit trees.

or'der-ly, a. 1. In order. 2. Observant of order or rule. 3. Performed in good order. — adv. Methodically. — n. 1. Mil. A noncommissioned officer or soldier who attends a superior office. 2. A hospital attendant.

or'di-nance (-nans), n. 1. That which is decreed or ordained. 2. Established rules. 3. A prescribed practice.

or-gan'ic (or-gan'ik), a. 1. Of or pertaining to an organ or a system of organs. 2. Pertaining to, or derived from, living organisms. 3. Pertaining to, or inherent in, a certain organization or structure; constitutional.

or'gan-i-za'tion (-i-za'shun), n. 1. Act or process of organizing. 2. State or manner of being organized.

or'gan-ize (or'gan-iz), v.t. To arrange or constitute in interdependent parts; systematize.

or'i-gin (-jin), n. 1. The first existence or beginning; birth; hence, parentage; ancestry. 2. That from which anything primarily proceeds.

o-rig'i-nal (o-rij'i-nal), a. 1. Of or pert. to the origin or beginning; primitive; primary. 2. Not copied or reproduced; novel; fresh. 3. Independent and creative; inventive. — n. 1. That of which something else is a copy. 2. An eccentric person.

or'na-ment (or'na-ment), v.t. To adorn; deck; embellish.

or-nate' (or-nat'; or'nat), a. Elaborately adorned. — -ly, adv. — -ness, n.

or'phan-age (-aj), n. 1. State of being an orphan. 2. an institution for the care of orphans.

or'tho-dox (or'tho-doks), a. 1. Sound in opinion or doctrine; hence, holding the Christian faith as formulated in the church creeds; — opp. to heretical and heterodox. 2. Approved; conventional.

or'tho-pe'dics (-pe'diks), n. Correction or prevention of deformities, esp. in children.

os'cil-late (os'i-lat), v.i. 1. To swing backward and forward like a pendulum. 2. To fluctuate between fixed limits. — **os'cil-la'tor**, n.

os'si-fi-ca'tion (-i-fi-ka'shun), n. 1. State of being ossified. 2. That which is ossified, as a bone.

os'tra-cism (os'tra-siz'm), n. 1. Gr. Antiq. A method of temporary banishment by popular vote. 2. Exclusion by general consent from common privileges, favor, etc.; as social ostracism.

os'tra-cize (-siz), v.t. To exile, banish, or exclude, by ostracism.

oth'er (uth'er), a. 1. (That) which remains of two, as distinguished from that which is specified; (the) remaining. 2. Second.

oth'er-wise' (uth'er-wiz'), adv. 1. In another way, or in other ways; contrarily. 2. In different circumstances. 3. In other respects. — a. Different.

ought (ot), v. Orig. pref., later also p.o. of OWE; now only an auxiliary in the pref. form, except in the illiterate "had ought." To be bound or obliged, as by duty or moral obligation, or by what is necessary, fit, or naturally to be expected.

our (our), pron. & a. Of or belonging to us.

our-selves' (our-selvz'), pron. An emphasized form for we, us. The singular our-self' is used chiefly in regal or formal style.

out (out), adv. Outside of, or away from within, a space; from the interior, or beyond the limits or boundary; not in. Hence: 1. Away from a usual, or particular place. 2. Beyond possession, control, or occupation. 3. Beyond the limit of existence, continuance, or supply; to a conclusion; completely.

out'break' (out'brak'), n. A bursting forth.

out'build'ing (out'bil'ding), n. A building near, and subordinate to, a main house; an outhouse.

out'burst' (-burst), n. An outbreak.

out'cast' (out'kast'), n. One who is cast out; an exile; hence, a vagabond. — a. Cast out; rejected; thrown away; hence, exiled; degraded.

out-class' (out-klas'), v.t. To excel or surpass.

out'come' (out'kum'), n. Result; consequence.

out'cry' (-kri'), n. 1. A loud cry; clamor. 2. An auction; the crying of wares for sale in the streets.

out'doors' (out'dorz), adv. Out of the house; out of doors. —(out'dorz'), n. The world out of doors.

out'law' (out'lo), n. 1. One excluded from the benefit or protection of the law. 2. A lawless person; a fugitive from the law. — v.t. 1. To deprive of the benefit or protection of law; proscribe. 2. To remove from legal jurisdiction or enforcement; as, to outlaw a debt.

out'line' (-lin'), n 1 a The line that marks the outer limits of an object or figure; contour; — commonly in pl. b The style of drawing in which contours are unshaded. c A sketch in outline. 2. A preliminary sketch in words; rough draft. — v.t.

out-live' (out-liv), v.t. To live longer than.

out'look (out'look), n. 1. A lookout. 2. The view had by one looking out; scope of vision; prospect.

out'ly'ing (-li'ing), a. Lying or being at a distance from the central part or main body; remote.

out-pour' (-por'), v.t. & i. To pour out.

out'put' (out'poot'), n. 1. The product of one or more mines, machines, mills, etc., in a given time. 2. Hence, yield of any commodity.

out'rage (-raj), n. Injurious and wanton wrong; gross violation of right or decency. — v.t. 1. To treat with violence or abuse. 2. To ravish.

out-ra'geous (out-ra'jus), a. Of the nature of outrage or an outrage; excessive; violent; atrocious. — - **ly**, adv. — -**ness**, n.

out'right' (out'rit), adv. 1. Forthwith; at once. 2. Wholly; entirely.

out'spo'ken (out'spo'k'n), a. Speaking, or spoken, freely or boldly. — -**ly**, adv. — -**ness**, n.

out-stand'ing, a. That stands out; uncollected or unpaid.

out-vote' (out-vot'), v.t. To outnumber in voting.

out'ward (out'werd), a. 1. Out; outer; exterior. 2. Of or pertaining to the physical character; external; hence, formal.

N

O

out-weigh' (-wa), v.t. To exceed in weight.

out-wit' (-wit'), v.t. To surpass in cunning; get the better of by cunning.

o'va-ry (o'va-ri), n.; pl. -RIES (-riz). 1. Anat. & Zool. The female organ in which ova or eggs are produced. 2. Bot. An enlarged (usually the basal) portion of the pistil.

o-va'tion (o-va'shun), n. An enthusiastic popular reception or tribute.

ov'en (un'n), n. A chamber or structure for baking, heating, or drying, esp., now, in a store.

o'ver-alls' (-olz'), n. pl. Loose trousers worn over others to protect them.

o'ver-bal'ance (-bal'ans). v.t. 1. To exceed equality with; outweigh. 2. To cause to lose balance. — n. Excess of weight or value.

o'ver-bear' (-bar'), v.t. 1. To bear down, as by excess of weight, force, etc.; overcome; suppress. 2. To domineer over. — v.i. To be too prolific.

o'ver-bur'den (-bur'd'n), v.t. To load with too great weight or too much care, etc.

o'ver-cast (-kast'), v.t. 1. To cast or cover over; hence, to cloud; darken. 2. (pron. o'ver-kast') To take long, loose stitches over (the raw-edges of a seam) to prevent raveling; sew over and over.

o'ver-charge' (-charj'), v.t. 1. To charge or load too heavily; fill too full. 2. To charge excessively in price.

o'ver-coat' (o'ver-kot'), n. A coat worn over the other clothing; greatcoat; topcoat.

o'ver-come' (-kum), v.t. To get the better of; surmount; conquer. — v.i. To be victorious.

o'ver-do' (-doo'), v.t. 1. To do too much; exaggerate. 2. To overtask; exhaust. 3. To cook too much, as meat. — v.i. To do too much.

o'ver-draw' (-dro'), v.t. 1. To exaggerate. 2. Banking. To make drafts upon in excess of the drawer's balance; as, to overdraw an account.

o'ver-due' (o'ver-du), a. Delayed beyond the proper time of arrival or payment, etc.

o'ver-es'ti-mate (-es'ti-mat), v.t. To estimate too highly. —**o'ver-es'ti-mate** (-mat), n.

o'ver-haul' (o'ver-hol'), v.t. 1. To haul or drag over; hence, to examine thoroughly for correction or repair. 2. Chiefly Naut. To gain on; overtake.

o'ver-head (o'ver-hed'), a. 1. Operating or situated above or overhead. 2. Passing over the head.

o'ver-hear' (-her'), v.t. 1. To hear (something) not intended to be heard or not addressed to one. 2. To hear (a speaker) whose remarks are not addressed to one or not intended for one.

o'ver-look' (-look'), v.t. 1. To look down on; hence, to rise above; overtop. 2. To supervise; watch over. 3. To look over and beyond (anything) without seeing it; hence, to pass over without notice, censure, or punishment.

o'ver-night' (o'ver-nit'), adv. In the evening before; also, during the night.

o'ver-pow'er (-pou'er), v.t. 1. To excel or exceed in power; vanquish; subdue. 2. To affect intensely or overwhelmingly.

o'ver-reach' (-rech'), v.t. 1. To reach above or beyond. 2. To miss by reaching too far. 3. To get the better of; outwit; cheat.

o'ver-rule' (-rool'), v.t. 1. To rule or decide to the contrary of or against. 2. To bring over, as by persuasion. — v.i. To be superior in ruling; also, to prevail by influence, character, etc.

o'ver-shad'ow (-shad'o), v.t. 1. To throw a shadow, or shade, over; darken; obscure. 2. Figuratively. To dominate; be more important than.

o'ver-sight' (-sit'), n. 1. Watchful care; superintendence. 2. An overlooking; omission or error due to inadvertence.

o'ver-take' (o'ver-tak'), v.t. 1. To come or catch up with. 2. To come upon suddenly or unexpectedly; surprise.

o'ver-time' (-tim'), n. time beyond a limit; esp., extra working time. — adv. After the proper or regular time.

o'ver-work' (-wurk'), v.t. To cause to work too much or too long; as, to overwork a horse. — v.i. To work beyond one's strength.

o'ver-wrought' (-rot'), p.a. 1. Wrought upon to excess; too excited. 2. Overworked. 3. Overdone.

owe (o), v.t. 1. To be under an obligation to restore, pay, or render (something) in return; be indebted to. 2. To have or bear (a certain feeling); as, to owe a grudge. 3. To be indebted for. — v.i. To be in debt.

own (on). a. Belong to one's self or itself; peculiar; — after a possessive case or pronoun, as my, our, your, his, her, its, their, to intensify the idea of interest or ownership.

own, v.t. 1. To possess; have as property. 2. To admit.

own'er-ship, n. State or fact of being an owner.

ox'i-da'tion (ok'si-da'shun), n. Act or process of oxidizing; state or result of being oxidized.

ox'y-gen (ok'si-jen), n. A colorless, tasteless, odorless, gaseous element occurring in the free state in air, of which it forms about 21 per cent by volume. Oxygen is the most abundant element.

oys'ter (ois'ter), n. Any of certain marine bivalve mollusks, many of which are edible.

P

pace (pas), n. 1. A step. 2. The length of a step in walking. 3. Rate of movement; speed.

pa-cif'ic (pa-sif'ik), a. Tending to make peace; of or pertaining to peace; peaceful; peaceable.

pac'i-fy (pas'i-fi), v.t. To make to be at peace; appease; clam; soothe.

pack, n. 1. A bundle prepared to be carried, esp. on the back.

pack'age (pak'aj), n. 1. Act or process of packing. 2. A bundle; a parcel.

pack animal. An animal used in carrying packs.

pack'et (pak'et), n. 1. A small pack or little bundle. 2. Naut. A vessel conveying mails, passengers, and goods, and having fixed sailing days.

pact (pakt), n. An agreement; a compact.

pad'dle (pad'l), n. 1. A broad-bladed implement used without a fixed fulcrum to propel and steer canoes and other boats.

page (paj), n. One side of a leaf of a book, etc.

pag'i-na'tion (paj'i-na'shun), n. Act or process of paging a book, etc., page numbering.

paid (pad), p.a. 1. Receiving pay; hired. 2. Delivered to discharge an obligation; discharged, as a debt.

pail (pal), n. A vessel for holding or carrying liquids, commonly circular, having a bail, and often a cover.

pain (pan), n. 1. Punishment for crime; penalty. Obs., exc. in phrases, as "on pain of death." 2. A distressing feeling due to derangement or functions, disease, or bodily injury.

pain'ful (pan'fool), a. 1. Full of, or affected with, pain; grievous. 2. Requiring toil; difficult.

pain'stak'ing (panz'tak'ing), a. Taking pains; careful in doing; assiduous.

paint'ing, vb.n. 1. Act of one who paints. 2. The art of depicting objects or scenes in color on a surface with pigments.

pal'ace (pal'as), n. 1. The official residence of a sovereign, also, Eng., of an archbishop or bishop. 2. A large, stately, or splendid house or building.

pal'at-a-ble (pal'at-a-b'l), a. Agreeable to the taste; savory.

pal'ate (-at), n. 1. The roof of the mouth. The front part is the hard palate, the back part is the soft palate, or velum. 2. The sense of taste.

pale (pal), a. 1. Wanting in color; dusky white; ashen. 2. Not bright or brilliant; faint.

pa'le-on-tol'o-gy (-ji), n. The science dealing with the life of past geological periods, as shown by fossil remains of animals and plants.

pal'ette (pal'et), n. A painter's tablet, with thumb hole at one end, on which to lay and mix pigments.

pall'bear'er (pol'bar-er), n. One of those who attend the coffin at a

P
R

funeral.

pal'li-ate (-i-at), v.t. 1. To reduce in violence; mitigate. 2. To extenuate; excuse.

palm (pam), n. 1. The part of the hand, on the side opposite the knuckles, between the bases of the fingers and the wrist.

Palm Sunday. The Sunday next before Easter.

pal'pi-tate (-pi-tat), v.i. To pulsate violently; — esp. of the heart.

pal'sy (pol'zi), n. Paralysis.

pam'per (-per), v.t. To treat indulgently.

pam'phlet (-flet), n. A book of a few sheets of printed matter, commonly with a paper cover.

pan (pan), n. 1. A vessel or dish for domestic uses, commonly broad and shallow, and often open.

pan'cake' (pan'kak'), n. A griddlecake; flapjack.

pan'der (pan'der), n. 1. A go-between in love intrigues. 2. A minister to the lusts of others. — v.i. To act as pander; cater; as, to pander to low taste.

pan'el (pan'el), n. 1. A list of persons summoned as jurors; hence, the whole jury. 2. A compartment, portion, or section of a wall, ceiling, or other surface, as of a door or window.

pan'ic (pan'ik), a. Of, pertaining to, or coming from, a panic.

pan'sy (pan'zi), n. A garden plant and flower, a species of violet.

pant (pant), v.i. 1. To breathe quickly or in a labored manner, as from exertion. 2. To long eagerly; yearn.

pan'ther (pan'ther), n. 1. The leopard. 2. In America, the cougar; also, the jaguar.

pan'try (pan'tri), n. A room or closet for bread and other provisions.

pa'pa' (pa-pa'), n. Father; — a child's word.

pa'pa-cy (pa'pa-si), n. 1. The office of the Pope or Rome. 2. The popes collectively. 3. The Roman hierarchy.

pa'pal (-pal), a. 1. Of or pertaining to the Pope or Rome; as, the papal crown. 2. Of or pertaining to the Roman Catholic Church; as, papal ritual.

pa-pa'ya (pa-pa'ya), n. The edible fruit of a palm-like tropical American tree.

paper money. Government notes, bank notes, etc., that circulate as a substitute for coin.

pa-poose' (pa-poos'), n. A young child of North American Indian parents.

pa'pri-ka (pa'pre-ka), n. The dried ripened fruit of various peppers; also, the mildly pungent red condiment prepared from it.

par'a-chute (par'a-shoot), n. An umbrella-like device for making a descent, as from a balloon.

pa-rade' (pa-rad'), n. Any march or procession, esp. a formal one.

par'a-dise (-dis), n. A place of bliss; a state of happiness.

par'al-lel (-lel), a. 1. Geom. Lying or extended in the same direction, and in all parts equally distant. 2. Having the same direction or tendency; like in essential parts.

pa-ral'y-sis (pa-ral'i-sis), n. Med. Loss or impairment of function in any part of the body, esp., loss of the power of voluntary motion, or sensation.

par'a-lyt'ic (par'a-lit'ik), a. Of, pertaining to, resembling, or affected with, paralysis.

par'a-mount (-mount), a. Higher or highest in rank or jurisdiction; chief; superior.

par'a-pher-na'li-a (-fer-na'li-a), n. pl. 1. Personal belongings. 2. Furnishings or apparatus.

par'a-phrase (par'a-fraz), n. A free rendering of a text, etc., giving the meaning in another form.

par'a-site (-sit), n. 1. A hanger-on; sycophant. 2. Biol. A plant or animal living in, on, or with, some other living organism (called its host) at whose expense it obtains its food, or the like.

par'a-sol (-sol), n. A light portable sunshade.

par'boil (par'boil'), v.t. To boil partially.

par'cel (-sel), n. 1. Law. A portion; part. 2. A bundle; package.

parcel post. That branch of a postal service dealing with parcels.

par'don (par'dun; -d'n), v.t. 1. To free from penalty for a fault. 2. To remit the penalty of; forgive. 3. To excuse.

pare (par), v.t. 1. To cut or shave off the superficial substance or ends of. 2. To cut or shave, as the outside part, from anything.

par'ent-age (-en-taj), n. 1. Descent from parents; birth. 2. State or fact of being a parent.

pa-ren'the-sis (-the'sis), n. One of the curved lines (), inclosing a parenthetic word or phrase. Also, these curves collectively.

par'ish (par'ish), n. 1. The district committed to one pastor. Brit. 2. The members of a parish collectively. 3. A local church; loosely, the territory in which the members live.

pa-rish'ion-er (pa-rish'un-er), n. One who belongs to, or is connected with, a parish.

par'i-ty (par'i-ti), n. 1. Equality; close correspondence. 2. Equality in purchasing power between different kinds of money at a given ratio.

park (park), n. 1. A tract of land, either ornamentally laid out or kept in its natural state, as for game, riding, or, esp., recreation.

par'ley (par'li), n. Oral conference, esp. with an enemy.

par'lor (par'ler), n. A room primarily for conversation, for reception of guests, etc.

par'o-dy (par'o-di), n. A writing mimicking the language of or sentiment of an author; travesty; also, a burlesque of a musical composition.

par-quet' (par-ka; -ket'), n. A flooring, esp. of parquetry.

par'ra-keet (par'a-ket), n. Any of certain parrots, esp. those of small size and with a long tail.

par'ri-cide (par'i-sid), n. 1. One who murders a person to whom he stands in a sacred relation, as a father or mother. 2. Act or crime of a parricide.

par'rot (-ut), n. A bird of the order including the parrakeets, cockatoos, macaws, etc., distinguished es. by a stout, hooked bill.

pars'ley (pars'li), n. A garden herb, the leaves of which are used to flavor soups, as a garnish, etc.

pars'nip (-nip), n. A plant allied to the carrot; also, its long tapering root,

poisonous in the wild state, but made edible and palatable by cultivation.

par'son (par'sn'), n. 1. The rector of a parochial church. 2. Any clergyman. Colloq.

par'son-age (-aj), n. The house appropriated by a parish for the minister.

part (part), n. 1. One of the portions into which anything is divided; a piece.

part'ed (par'ted), pa. Divided; cleft.

par'tial (-shal), a. 1. Inclined to one party more than the other; biased. 2. Having a liking (for).

par-tic'i-pant (par-tis'i-pant), a. Sharing.

par'ti-cle (-k'l), n. 1. A minute portion of matter; a bit. 2. Any very small portion.

par-tic'u-lar (par-tik'u-lar), a. 1. Relating to a portion of anything; separate; specific. 2. Of or pert. to a single person, class, or thing; not general; personal.

par-tic'u-lar-ize (-tik'u-lar-iz), v.t. To give as a particular, or as the particulars; mention particularly.

par-tic'u-lar 'ly, adv. 1. In a particular manner; individually; severally. 2. Especially.

part'ing (par'ting), p.a. 1. That parts: a Departing; fig., dying. b Dividing. 2. Given, etc., when departing; farewell; as, a parting kiss.

par'ti-san, par'ti-zan, n. A devoted adherent.

part'ly, adv. In part; not wholly.

part'ner (part'ner), n. 1. An associate; sharer; companion. 2. a A husband or a wife. b Either of a couple who dance together.

part'ner-ship, n. 1. State of being a partner; association; participation.

par'ty (par'ti), n. 1. A body of persons forming one side in a contest, etc.; esp. one of the parts into which a people is divided on public questions; as, the Democratic party. 2. A detachment, as of troops.

pass, n. 1. Act of passing; passage. 2. State of things; condition. 3. Permission or license to pass, or to go and come.

pass'a-ble (pas'a-b'l), a. 1. Capable of being passed, as a road, or

P
R

penetrated, as a forest. 2. Generally receivable; current.

pass'ing (pas'ing), a. 1. Going by, beyond, through, or away. 2. Fleeting.

pas'sion (pash'un), n. Intense emotion; often, rage or love; also, enthusiasm; eager desire.

pas'sion-ate (-at), a. 1. Capable or susceptible of passion; easily excited, esp. to anger. 2. Affected with, or marked by, passion; ardent.

Passion Week. The week before Easter.

pas'sive (pas'iv), a. 1. Not active, but acted on or receiving impressions.

pass'-key', n. A master key; also, a private key.

pass'port (pas'port), n. 1. An official document permitting one to pass or travel about unmolested. 2. That which secures admission or acceptance.

pass'word' (pas'wurd'), n. A word to be uttered by one before he is allowed to pass; watchword.

past (past), a. 1. Of or pertaining to a former time or state; gone by; elapsed; last; foregoing.

pas'time' (pas'tim'), n. That which amuses, and serves to make time pass agreeably; amusement: diversion; recreation.

pas'tor (-ter), n. A priest; a minister.

pas'try (pas'tri), n. Articles of food made of paste, or with a crust of paste.

pas'tur-age (pas'tur-aj), n. 1. A pasturing; the grazing of cattle. 2. Grazing round; pasture.

pas'ture (-tur), n. Growing grass or grass land for sheep, cattle, etc., to feed upon; pasturage.

pat (pat), v.t. To strike, esp. gently, with a flat surface, with the hand, or the like.

patch'work' (pach'wurk'), n. Work of pieces sewed together, esp. pieces of various colors and figures; hence, a jumble; hodgepodge.

pat'ent (pat'ent), n. Legal protection for unique inventions, processes, and machines.

pa-ter'ni-ty (-ni-ti), n. 1. Fatherhood. 2. Derivation or descent from a father; male parentage.

path (path), n. 1. A beaten way,

footway. 2. A way or track in which anything moves; also, a course or way of life, thought, etc.

pa-thet'ic (pa-thet'ik), a. Affecting or moving the tender emotions, especially pity or grief.

pa-thol'o-gist (pa-thol'o-jist), n. One skilled in, or a student of pathology.

pa'tience (pa'shens), n. State or quality of being patient; perseverance.

pa'tient (pa'shent), a. 1. Undergoing pains, trials, etc. without complaint. 2. Lenient; forbearing.

pa'tri-arch (pa'tri-ark), n. 1. The father and ruler of a family or tribe. 2. A venerable old man.

pa'tri-ot (pa'tri-ot; pat'ri-), n. One who lives his country and zealously supports it.

pa'trol' (-trol'), v.i. & t. To go the rounds of, or traverse as for guarding.

pa-trol'man (-man), n. One who patrols; a policeman who patrols a certain beat.

pa-tron (pa-trun), n. 1. One who protects or supports; defender. 2. A regular customer. 3. A guardian saint; a tutelary deity.

pat'ter, v.t. To strike or move with a quick succession of pat.

pau'per (po'per), n. 1. One without means except from charity. 2. A very poor person.

pause (poz), n. 1. A temporary stop or res; interruption; cessation. 2. Temporary inaction; hesitation.

pave (pav), v.t. 1. To lay or cover with stone, brick, etc. 2. To make smooth or easy; prepare.

paw (po), n. The foot of a quadruped having claws.

pawn, n. 1. A surety or pledge; gage. 2. State of being pledged.

pawn'bro'ker (-bro'ker), n. One whose business is lending money on pledged personal property.

pay'a-ble (pa'a-b'l), a. That may, can, or should be paid; justly due.

pay'ment (pa'ment), n. Act of paying; that which is paid; pay; recompense; requital.

peace (pes), n. A state of quiet; freedom from disturbance; calm; esp.: a Public quiet, order, and security. b Harmony between persons or nations.

peace'ful (-fool), a. 1. Pacific; peaceable; as, peaceful words. 2. Possessing or enjoying peace.

peach (pech), n. The well-known fruit, a drupe, of a low tree of the plum family; also, the tree.

pea'nut (pe'nut), n. A trailing plant of the bean family, widely cultivated in warm regions, whose pods ripen underground; also, its nutlike seed.

pear (par), n. The fleshy fruit of a tree related to the apple; also, the tree.

pearl (purl), n. 1. A dense shelly concretion, formed as an abnormal growth in some mollusks. It is used as a gem. 2. The color of a pine pearl; a pale bluish gray. 3. Mother-of-pearl.

peb'ble (peb'l), n. A small stone rounded by the action of water.

pe-can' (pe-kan), n. A species of hickory of the southern U.S.; also, its nut.

peck (pek), v.t. 1. To strike with the beak. 2. To make (a hole), with or as with a beak.

pec'u-late (pek'u-lat), v.i. & t. To steal or misappropriate moneys intrusted to one's care; embezzle.

pe-cul'iar (pe-kul'yar), a. 1. One's own; belonging to an individual; particular; special. 2. Singular; queer.

pe-cu'li-ar'i-ty (pe-kul'li-ar'i-ti), n. Quality or state of being peculiar; that which is peculiar; also, a singularity; odd traits.

ped'al (ped'al), n. A lever acted on by the foot; treadle.

ped'dle (ped'l), v.i. 1. To travel about with wares for sale. 2. To do a small business.

pe-des'tri-an (pe-des'tri-an), a. 1. Going or performed on foot. 2. Of or pert. to walking; hence, slow or dull.

peek (pek), v.i. To look slyly, or with the eyes half closed; peep.

peel (pel), v.t. 1. To strip off the skin, bark, or rind of; sometimes, to pare. 2. To strip or tear off, as the bark of a tree, etc.

peep (pep), v.i. 1. To cry, as a young chick, a mouse, etc.; cheep. 2. To speak with a small thin voice.

peep, v.i. 1. To peer through or as through a crevice. 2. To begin to come from or as if from concealment; emerge partially.

peer (per), v.i. To look narrowly, curiously, or intently.

pel-la'gra (pe-lag'ra; -la'gra), n. A skin disease, caused by a microbe, accompanied by disturbance of the digestive and nervous systems.

pel'vis (-vis), n. Anat. The basin-like structure formed by the hip bones, coccyx, and sacrum.

pen (pen), n. 1. A small inclosure for animals.

pen, n. An instrument with a split point for writing with fluid ink; also, such a pen and its holder.

pe'nal (pe'nal), a. Of or pertaining to punishment or penalties; as, a penal code.

pen'ance (-ans), n. Action performed to show penitence and as reparation for sin.

pen'cil (pen'sil), n. A slender cylinder of black lead, colored chalk, slate, etc., commonly incased in wood, for drawing or writing.

pend'ing, p.a. Not yet decided; as, a pending suit.

pen'e-trate (pen'e-trat), v.t. 1. To enter into; pierce. 2. To pervade; permeate. 3. To move deeply.

pen'e-trat'ing (-trat'ing), p.a. 1. Sharp; penetrative. 2. Acute; discerning; sagacious.

pen'guin (pen'gwin; pen'-), n. Any of certain flightless aquatic birds of the Southern Hemisphere, with flipperlike wings.

pen-in'su-la (pen-in'su-la), n. A portion of land nearly surrounded by water; also, any piece of land jutting out into the water.

pen'i-tent (-tent), a. Feeling sorrow for sins or offenses; repentant.

pen'i-ten'tia-ry (-sha'ri), a. 1. Of or pertaining to penance. 2. Used for punishment, discipline, and reformation. 3. Making one liable to punishment in a penitentiary. U.S.

pen'man-ship, n. Art or practice of using the pen in writing; style or manner of writing.

pen'ny-wise', a. Wise in small matters; saving small sums while losing larger.

pe-nol'o-gy (pe-nol'o-ji), n. The study of punishment for crime; the

P
R

science that treats of the management of prisons and reformatories.

pen'sion (-shun), n. 1. A stated allowance made to one retired from service. 2. A payment regularly made to one not an employee, as for good will.

pen'sion-er (-er), n. One in receipt of a pension.

Pen'te-cost (-te-kost), n. 1. A solemn festival of the Jews, celebrated the fiftieth day after the second day of the Passover. 2. Whitsunday.

pent'house' (pent'hous'), n. A shed or roof attached to, and sloping from, a wall or building.

pe'on (pe'on), n. A common laborer of any kind; — often, in reference to Latin America, esp. Mexico, implying bondage, as for debt.

peo'ple (pe'p'l), n. sing. & pl. 1. A body of persons united by a common character, culture, or sentiment. 2. A race, tribe, or nation. 3. The persons of a particular group.

pep'per (pep'er), n. 1. A pungent condiment made from dried berries of several East Indian plants. 2. Any plant yielding pepper, (def. 1), esp. the common, or black, pepper, a climbing shrub.

pep'per-mint (-mint), n. 1. A pungent mint; also, its oil or essence. 2. A peppermint lozenge.

pep'tic (-tik), a. 1. Pertaining to gastric digestion. 2. Of or pertaining to pepsin.

per (pur), prep. Through; by means of; by.

per'cale' (per-kal'; per'kal'), n. A fine, smooth-finished cotton fabric, often printed.

per-ceive' (-sev'), v.t. 1. To obtain knowledge of through the senses; see, hear, or feel. 2. To apprehend by the mind, discern.

per-cent'age (per-sen'taj), n. A certain rate per cent; allowance, duty, rate of interest, or commission on a hundred; loosely, a part or proportion.

per-cep'ti-ble (per-sep'ti-b'l), a. That may be perceived.

perch, n. 1. A horizontal pole or other support for birds to roost on; hence, any elevated seat or station. 2. A

measure equal to a rod.

per-chance' (per-chans'), adv. 1. By chance. 2. Perhaps; possibly.

per'co-late (pur'ko-lat), v.t. & i. 1. To filter, as a liquor. 2. To ooze through; permeate.

per'emp-to-ry (per'emp-to-ri; per-emp'-), a. 1. Taking away a right of action, debate, etc. Hence, conclusive; absolute. 2. Admitting no denial or refusal; imperative.

per-en'ni-al (per-en'i-al), a. 1. Lasting or continuing through the year. 2. Unceasing; enduring.

per'fect (pur'fekt), a. 1. Having all the properties naturally belonging to it; complete; sound; right; faultless; righteous, etc. 2. Utter; downright.

per-fect'i-ble (per-fek'ti-b'l), a. Capable of becoming, or being made, perfect.

per-fid'i-ous (-fid'i-us), a. 1. Guilty of perfidy; false to trust. 2. Involving, or marked by, perfidy.

per'fi-dy (pur'fi-di), n. Breach of faith or allegiance; faithlessness; treachery.

per'fo-rate (pur'fo-rat), v.t. & i. To pierce through; to make a hole through.

per-form' (-form'), v.t. 1. To execute (anything); accomplish; do. 2. To discharge; fulfill. 3. To render, as a play; act on the stage; as a part.

per-form'ance (-for'mans), n. 1. Act of performing; execution; achievement. 2. A thing done; esp., an action of a public character.

per-fume' (-fum'), v.t. To fill with an agreeable odor, as of incense, flowers, etc.; scent.

per-haps' (per-haps'), adv. By chance; it may be.

per'il (per'il), n. Danger; exposure to injury or destruction.

pe'ri-od (pe'ri-od), n. 1. A portion of time determined by some recurrence, as by the completion of a revolution of a planet. 2. A certain series of years, months, days, etc.; cycle; age; era; epoch.

per'ish (per'ish), v.i. To be destroyed; hence, to waste away; pass away; die.

per'i-win'kle, n. A kind of trailing evergreen herb with blue or white flowers.

per'jure (pur'jur), v.t. To make guilty of perjury; — used reflexively.

per'ju-ry (-ju-ri), n. False swearing; voluntary violation of an oath or vow.

perk (purk), v.i. 1. To behave jauntily or smartly. 2. To become erect, brisk, or lively; — usually with up.

per'ma-nent (-nent), a. Continuing in the same state; abiding; fixed; stable.

per'me-ate (-at), v.t. & i. 1. To pass through the pores or interstices of; as, water permeates sand. 2. To enter and spread through; pervade.

per-mit' (-mit'), v.t. 1. To consent to; tolerate. 2. To grant (one) express license to do an act; authorize.

per'mit (pur-mit), n. Warrant; license.

per-ni'cious (per-nish'us), a. Destructive; ruinous; injurious; hurtful.

per'pe-trate (pur'pe-trat), v.t. To do or commit; — usually in a bad sense; as, to perpetrate a crime.

per-pet'u-al (per-pet'u-al), n. Continuing for an unlimited time; continuous.

per-plex' (per-pleks'), v.t. To trouble with ambiguity, suspense; or anxiety; confuse.

per-plexed' (-plekst'), pa. Doubtful; puzzled; bewildered.

per'se-cute (pur'se-kut), v.t. To harness; esp., to afflict or kill because of belief or religion.

per'se-cu'tion (-ku'shun), n. 1. Act or practice of persecuting. 2. State of being persecuted.

per'se-ver'ance (pur'se-ver'ans), n. Act of persevering; persistence; steadfastness; constancy.

per'se-vere' (pur'se-ver'), v.i. To persist in any business or enterprise undertaken.

per'si-flage' (per'se-flazh'; pur'si-flazh), n. Frivolous or bantering talk; light raillery.

per-sist' (-sist'), v.i. 1. To continue steadfastly. 2. To endure or remain.

per-sist'ence (-sis'tens), n. Quality or state of being persistent.

per-sist'ent (-sis'tent), a. 1. Inclined to persist; having staying qualities. 2. Existing continuously; enduring.

per'son (pur'sun; s'n), n. 1. A human being. 2. The bodily form of a human being; outward appearance. 3. Individual personality.

per'son-al (-al), a. 1. Of or pertaining to a particular person; not general. 2. Done in person; direct from one person to another. 3. Pertaining to the person, or body.

per'son-ate (-at), v.t. To assume the character of; act the part of.

per-son'i-fi-ca'tion (per-son'i-fi-ka'shun), n. 1. Act of personifying; that which personifies. 2. A figure of speech in which an inanimate object or abstract idea is endowed with personal attributes.

per-son'i-fy (per-son'i-fi), v.t. 1. To regard, treat, or represent as a person. 2. To be the embodiment of; impersonate; typify.

per'son'nel' (per'so'nel), n. The body of persons in some (esp. public) service.

per'spi-ca'cious (pur'spi-ka'shus), a. Of acute vision; mentally keen.

per-spic'u-ous (per-spik'u-us), a. Clear to the understanding.

per'spi-ra'tion (pur'spi-ra'shun), n. 1. Act or process of perspiring. 2. The fluid secreted by the sweat glands; sweat.

per-spire' (per-spir'), v.i. & t. Physiol. To excrete, esp. fluids, through the skin; sweat.

per-suade' (-swad'), v.t. To induce (a person) to believe or do something; convince.

per-sua'sion (-zhun), n. 1. Act of persuading. 2. Power of persuading; persuasiveness. 3. State of being persuaded.

per'ti-na'cious (pur'ti-na'shus), a. Holding obstinately to any opinion or design; resolute; obstinate.

per'ti-nent (-nent), a. Related to the subject or matter in hand; apposite; relevant.

per-turb' (per-turb'), v.t. To disturb greatly; trouble; disquiet; derange.

per-verse' (-vurs'), a. 1. Turned away from the right; wicked. 2. Obstinate in the wrong; stubborn. 3. Wayward; petulant; as, a perverse child.

pes'si-mist (-mist), n. One who looks on the dark side of things.

pest (pest), n. 1. A pestilence. 2. Something that is troublesome or destructive; a nuisance.

P
R

pes'ter (pes'ter), v.t. To harness with petty vexations; annoy; worry; tease.

pes'ti-lence (pes'ti-lens), n. Any contagious or infectious epidemic disease that is virulent and devastating; esp., bubonic plague.

pet'tish (pet'ish), a. Fretful; peevish.

pet'ty (pet'i), a. Of small importance; inconsiderable; also, inferior; subordinate.

pew (pu), n. One of the long, fixed benches or seats in a church.

phan'tasm (fan'taz'm), n. 1. A product of phantasy; as: a A mental image of a real object. b A phantom. 2. Apparition of a person; living or dead, in a place where his body is known not to be.

phan'ta-sy (fan'ta-si), n. Power of creating mental images; an image so created.

phar'ma-cy (far'mas-si), n. 1. Art or practice of preparing drugs, and of dispensing medicines. 2. A drug store; apothecary's shop.

phe-nom'e-nal (-nal), a. Of the nature of, or pert. to, a phenomenon or phenomena.

phe-nom'e-non (-non), n. 1. Any observable fact or event. 2. Something unaccountable or very notable or exceptional.

phi-lan'thro-py (-pi), n. 1. Love to mankind; desire and readiness to do good to all men. 2. Philanthropic act, agency, or the like.

phi-los'o-pher (fi-los'o-fer), n. 1. One versed in, or devoted to, philosophy. 2. One who meets or regards all changes of fortune calmly.

phon'ic (fon'ik; fo'nik), a. Of, pertaining to, or of the nature of, sound, usually of vocal sounds.

pho'no-graph (fo'no-graf), n. An instrument of recording and reproducing speech, music, etc.

pho'to-en-grav'ing (fo'to-en-grav'ing), n. A photomechanical process for reproducing pictures, etc.; also, a print so made.

pho-tog'ra-phy (fo-tog'ra-fi), n. Art or process of producing images on sensitized surfaces by the chemical action of light.

phrase (fraz), n. 1. A brief expression; Gram., two or more words having in the sentence the force of a single part of speech; as, an adverbial phrase. 2. A short, pithy expression.

phys'ic (fiz'ik), n. 1. Art of healing diseases; practice of medicine. 2. An internal medicine. 3. A cathartic.

phys'i-cal (-i-kal), a. 1. Of or pert. to nature or the laws of nature; material. 2. Of or pert. to natural science.

phy-si'cian (fi-zish'an), n. One skilled in physic, or the art of healing; a doctor of medicine.

phy-sique' (fi-zek'), n. Physical or bodily structure, constitution, or appearance.

pi-an'ist (pi-an'ist; pe'a-nist), n. A performer, esp. a skilled performer, on the piano.

pick'et (pik'et), n. 1. A pointed or sharpened stake or pale, as for making fences. 2. Mil. a Detached body of soldiers, or a soldier, serving to guard an army from surprise.

pick'ing (-ing), n. 1. Act of one that picks. 2. That which is or may be picked or picked up; a scrap; pl., portions picked up or out.

pick'le (pik'l), n. 1. Brine or vinegar for preserving food; also, an article of food, or (usually in pl.) food, so preserved. 2. A difficult situation; predicament; as, to be in a pickle.

pick'pock'et (pik'pok'et), n. One who steals purses or other articles from pockets.

pic'nic (pik'nik), n. An excursion or outdoor pleasure party in which the members partake of refreshments carried, usually, by themselves.

pic'ture (pik'tur), n. 1. A representation, esp. as a work of art, produced by painting, drawing, engraving, photography, etc. 2. A transitory visible image.

piece (pes), n. 1. A fragment; a part separated; portion. 2. A distinct or limited part or quantity; a bit. 3. A quantity, as a length, weight, or size, usually fixed, in which various articles or products are made or put up.

piece'meal' (pes'mel'), adv. 1. Piece by piece; little by little; by degrees. 2. In pieces.

piece'work' (pes'wurk'), n. Work done

or paid for by the piece or job.

pier (per), n. 1. A support for a bridge span. 2. A supporting pillar, or structure, as of an arch or lintel.

pierce (pers), v.t. 1. To run into or through as a pointed instrument does; stab. 2. To perforate. 3. To force a way into or through.

pig (pig), n. 1. A young swine; also, any swine. 2. Metal. A casting, esp. of iron or lead, run directly from the smelting furnace into a troughlike mold.

pi'geon (pij'un), n. A well-known stout-bodied, short-legged bird.

pig'gish (pig'ish), a. Like a pig; greedy; stubborn; filthy.

pig'-head'ed (-hed'ed), a. Stupidly obstinate.

pil'fer (pil'fer), v.i. & t. To practice petty theft; filch.

pil'grim (pil'grim), n. 1. A journeyer; wayfarer. Rhetorical. 2. One who travels to some holy place as a devotee.

pil'lage (pil'aj), n. 1. Act of pillaging or plundering, esp. in war; plunder. 2. Spoil; booty.

pil'low (pil'o), n. 1. Anything used to support one's head when reposing; esp., a sack filled with feathers or other soft material. 2. Any of various things likened to a pillow.

pil'low-case' (-kas'), n. A removable case or covering, usually of white linen or cotton, for a pillow.

pim'ple (pim'p'l), n. Any small pointed elevation of the skin; pustule.

pin'a-fore' (pin'a-for'), n. A sleeveless overdress worn esp. by children or girls to protect the dress.

pine (pin), v.i. 1. To languish; lose vigor or flesh, esp. under distress or anxiety; droop. 2. To languish with desire; long intensely.

pine, n. 1. A cone-bearing tree of many species, and having needle-shaped leaves (pine needles). 2. Wood of the pine. 3. Pineapple.

pi'quant (-kant), a. Stimulating to the taste, curiosity, etc.; tart; pungent.

pique (pek), n. A feeling of hurt or resentment due to a slight or injury, esp. to one's pride.

pis'til (pis'til), n. The seed-bearing organ of a flower.

pis'tol (-tul), n. A firearm for use with one hand.

pitch'er (-er), n. A vessel for holding and pouring liquids, usually with a handle.

pitch'er, n. One who pitches.

pitch'fork (pich'fork'), n. A fork used in pitching hay, grain, etc.

pit'e-ous (pit'e-us), a. 1. Evincing pity; tender. 2. Fitted to excite pity or sympathy; miserable; lamentable.

pit'i-ful (-fool), a. 1. Full of pity; compassionate. 2. Piteous; lamentable. 3. Paltry.

pit'y (pit'i), n. 1. A feeling for the sufferings of others; compassion. 2. A reason or cause of pity; grief, or regret.

pla'ca-ble (pla'ka-b'l), a. Capable of being pacified.

plac'id (plas'id), a. Calm; peaceful; quiet.

pla'gi-a-rize (-riz), v.t. & i. To steal and use as one's own (the ideas, words, etc., of another).

plague (plag), n. 1. Any afflictive evil. 2. a nuisance. Colloq. 3. Any malignant, esp. infectious, disease, esp., an acute infectious fever.

plain (plan), a. 1. Flat; plane (which see). 2. Open; clear; as, in plain sight. 3. Open to the mind; manifest; also, candid.

plain'tiff (plan'tif), n. Law. One who commences a personal suit for an injury to his rights.

plan (plan), n. 1. A draft or form, properly one drawn on a plane; as a map; esp., a top view. 2. A method of procedure or arrangement; a scheme.

plan'ner (plan'er), n. One who plans; a projector.

plan-ta'tion (plan-ta'shun), n. 1. A group, usually large, of plants or trees under cultivation.

plant'er (plan'ter), n. 1. One that plants. 2. One who owns or cultivates a planation.

plas'ma (plaz'ma), n. The watery part of blood, lymph, or milk.

plat'form (plat'form), n. 1. A level, usually raised, surface; a flooring, for speakers. etc. 2. A declaration of principles on which a party stands.

pla-toon' (pla-toon'), n. A subdivision of a company, troop, etc., commanded by a lieutenant.

P
R

plat'ter, n. A large dish for serving meat, etc.

plau'si-ble (plo'zi-b'l), a. 1. Superficially fair, reasonable, or valuable; specious; as, a plausible excuse. 2. Fair-spoken; as, a plausible man.

play (pla), v.i. 1. To move, operate, or have effect in a lively or brisk and irregular, or alternating manner, or in a jet or stream. 2. To busy or exercise one's self for diversion; sport; frolic.

plead (pled), v.i. 1. Law. To make a plea, or conduct a cause, in court. 2. To argue for or against a thing. 3. To entreat or appeal earnestly.

plead'ing, n. Law. The successive statements by which the plaintiff sets forth his cause, and the defendant his defense.

please (plez), v.i. 1. To afford or give pleasure; be agreeable. 2. To be pleased or willing; like; choose.

pledge (plej), n. 1. A security for the performance of an act; a guarantee. 2. A toast; a health. 3. A promise or agreement to do or forbear something.

plen'ti-ful (-ti-fool), a. 1. Yielding or containing plenty. 2. Marked by, or existing in, plenty; copious.

plen'ty (-ti), n. 1. Full supply; an abundance. 2. Abundance; copiousness.

plight, v.t. 1. To put in danger of forfeiture; pledge; — never applied to property or goods. 2. To bind by a pledge; betroth.

plod (plod), v.i. 1. To walk heavily; trudge. 2. To toil monotonously; drudge.

plow (plou), n. 1. An implement for making a furrow in, and turning up, the earth, as in tilling it. 2. Any implement suggestive of a plow.

pluck (pluk), v.t. 1. To pull or pick off or out; pick. 2. To pull; drag; — with out, off, up, etc. 3. To jerk; twitch; hence, to twang.

plum (plum), n. 1. The well-known fruit of any of various species of a tree allied to the peach; also, the tree. 2. A raisin, esp. one used in cooking.

plun'der (plun'der), v.t. 1. To pillage; spoil, rob. 2. To take or appropriate by force or wrongfully.

plunge (plunj), v.t. To thrust or force, as into liquid or a cavity; immerse; submerge.

poach (poch), v.t. 1. To cook (an egg) by breaking it into boiling water. 2. To trespass on, esp. for game or fish; steal (game).

pock'et (pok'et), n. 1. A bag or pouch carried by a person; esp., a small bag inserted in a garment; hence, purse; money. 2. A cavity or receptacle; as, a coal pocket.

pock'et-knife' (-nif'), n. Knife with folding blades for carrying in the pocket.

po'em (po'em), n. A piece of poetry; opposed to prose.

po'et (po'et), n. An author of, or one skilled in making, poetry.

po'et-ry (po'et-ri), n. Embodiment in rhythmical language, usually metrical, of beautiful thought, imagination, or emotion; also, poems collectively.

poign'an-cy (poin'an-si; -yan-si), n. Quality or state of being poignant.

point (point), n. 1. Tapering sharp end, as of a needle, finger, etc. 2. Something having a tapering end, as a promontory or cape, etc.

poi'son (poi'z'n), n. 1. Any agent which, introduced into the animal organism, may produce a morbid, noxious, or deadly effect. 2. That which taints or destroys moral purity or character.

pok'y (-i), a. Slow; dull; petty.

po'lar (po'lar), a. 1. Of or pertaining to a pole, as of the earth; lying near, or proceeding from, one of the poles.

pole'cat (-kat'), n. 1. A European animal of which the ferret is a variety. 2. A skunk. U.S.

po-lem'ic (po-lem'ik), a. Of or pert. to controversy; controversial.

po-lice' (po-les'), n. The department of government charged with enforcement of the laws and maintenance of public order, etc.

po-lice'man (-man), n. A member of a body of police; a constable.

pol'i-cy, n. 1. A certificate of insurance. 2. A form of lottery.

pol'ish (pol'ish), v.t. 1. To make smooth and glossy, usually by friction. 2. To make elegant, cultured, or polite; refine.

po-lite' (po-lit'), a. Marked by refinement or culture; courteous; civil.

pol'i-tic (pol'i-tik), a. 1. Political; as, the body politic. 2. Sagacious in promoting a policy; prudent; in a bad sense, artful; cunning.

po-lit'i-cal (po-lit'i-kal), a. 1. Of or pertaining to polity, or politics. 2. Having, or conforming to, a system of government.

pol'len (pol'en), n. The powdery fertilizing substance formed in the anther of seed plants.

pol-lute' (po-lut'), v.t. To make impure; defile; profane.

pol-lu'tion (po-lu'shun), n. Act of polluting, or state of being polluted; defilement.

po-lyg'a-mist (-a-mist), n. One who practices polygamy.

po-lyg'a-my (-mi), n. State of having plurality of wives or (rarely) husbands at the same time.

pol'y-pus (pol'i-pus), n. A kind of tumor of the mucous membrane, as in the nose.

pol'y-tech'nic (-tak'nik), a. Pertaining to many arts and sciences.

po-mol'o-gy (po-mol'o-ji), n. Science and practice of fruit growing.

pomp (pomp), n. 1. A show of magnificence; sometimes, esp. in the pl., vain display. 2. A procession marked by magnificent display.

pom'pous (pom'pus), a. Marked by excessive self-importance.

pon'cho (pon'cho), n. A kind of cloak like a blanket with a slit for the head.

pond (pond), n. A small body of still water.

pon'der-ous (-us), a. 1. Heavy; massive. 2. Heavy in spirit; dull.

pon'tiff (-tif), n. 1. A high priest. 2. A bishop; esp., the Pope.

pon-tif'i-cal (pon-tif'i-kal), a. Of or pertaining to a pontiff; esp., papal.

poor (poor), a. 1. Wanting in money or goods; needy. 2. Destitute of some normal or desirable quality.

poor'house' (poor'hous'), n. An almshouse.

pope (pop), n. [Often cap., esp. when used of a particular pope.] The (or a) bishop of Rome, the head of the Roman Catholic Church.

pop'er-y (pop'er-i), n. Papal doctrines and practices; — used opprobriously.

pop'lar (pop'lar), n. Any of certain trees with handsome foliage.

pop'u-lace (pop'u-las), n. The common people.

pop'u-lar (pop'u-lar), a. 1. Of or pert. to the common people. 2. Suitable to the public in general.

pop'u-late (pop'u-lat), v.t. To inhabit or furnish with inhabitants; to people.

porch (porch), n. A covered entrance to a building. 2. A veranda.

pore (por), v.i. To look or gaze intently, esp. in reading; also, to mediate or ponder intently.

pore, n. A minute opening, as in the skin.

pork (pork), n. The flesh of swine, used for food.

port, n. 1. A harbor; haven. 2. Place to which vessels may resort to discharge or receive cargo.

port'a-bil'i-ty (por'ta-bil'i-ti), n. Quality of being portable.

port'a-ble (por'ta-b'l), a. Capable of being borne; easily transported.

por'tal (-tal), n. A door, gate, or entrance.

por-tend' (por-tend'), v.t. To indicate (events, etc.) as in the future; foretoken; — now esp. of unfavorable signs.

por'ter (por'ter), n. 1. A doorkeeper. 2. An attendant on a sleeping car or parlor car. U.S.

port-fo'li-o (port-fo'li-o; fol'yo), n. 1. A portable case for holding loose papers, prints, etc. 2. The office and functions of a minister of state.

por'tion (por'shun), n. 1. A part of anything. 2. An allotted part; share.

por'trait (por'trat), n. A pictorial representation of a person, esp. of the face; a likeness, esp. one from life.

por-tray (por-tra'), v.t. 1. To represent by drawing, painting, etc.; delineate; depict. 2. To describe in words; represent dramatically.

pose, v.t. 1. To lay down; propound. 2. To place in a fixed position; arrange posture and drapery of.

pos'i-tive (poz'i-tiv), a. 1. Definitely or formally laid down or imposed; hence, explicit; definite; also,

P
R

Colloq., downright; absolute. 2. Confident; certain.

pos-sess' (po-zes'), v.t. 1. To have and hold as property; own. 2. To have as a property, attribute, etc.; have. 3. To gain; seize; win.

pos'si-bil'i-ty (pos'i-bil'i-ti), n. 1. Quality or state of being possible. 2. That which is possible.

post'age (pos'taj), n. Charge for conveyance of anything by public post.

postage stamp. A government stamp to be put on articles sent by mail, in payment of postage.

pos'tal (pos'tal), a. Of or pertaining to the post office or mail service.

post card, n. A private card admitted to the mails when bearing an adhesive postage stamp.

post'date' (post'dat'), v.t. To date after the real time, or time of making, as a check.

post-grad'u-ate (post-grad'u-at), a. Of, pertaining to, or designating, studies pursued after graduation.

post'hu-mous (pos'tu-mus; post'hu-mus), a. 1. Born after the death of the father, as a son. 2. Published after the death of an author. 3. Being, arising, or continuing after one's death.

post'mark' (-mark'), n. Any mark officially put on mail, as the date or the cancellation.

post-na'tal (-na'tal), a. Subsequent to birth.

post-pone' (post-pon'), v.t. To defer to a future or later time; put off.

post'script (post'skript), n. A paragraph added to a letter after it is concluded; an addition appended to a completed book or composition.

pos'ture (pos'tur), n. 1. Relative arrangement of parts; bearing; attitude. 2. State or situation.

pot (pot), n. 1. A metallic or earthen vessel of rounded form. 2. A pot (vessel) with its contents.

po-ta'to (-to), n. 1. The sweet potato. 2. The edible starchy tuber of an American plant of the nightshade family; also, the plant.

pot-ten'cy (po-ten'si), n. Quality or state of being potent; power; efficiency; capability.

po'tent (po'tent), a. Having great power; mighty; powerful.

po-ten'tial (po-ten'shal), a. 1. Existing in possibility only; latent. 2. Gram. Expressive of possibility; as, the potential mood.

poth'er (poth'er), n. bustle; bother.

pot'luck' (pot'luk'), n. Whatever may chance to be in the pot, or may be provided for a meal.

pot'pie' (pot'pi), n. A meat pie boiled in a pot.

pot'pour'ri (po'poo're'), n. A medley or mixture.

pot'ter-y (-i), n. 1. A place where earthen vessels are made. 2. Art of the potter. 3. Ware made from clay, etc., molded and hardened by heat; esp., the coarser ware so made.

poul'try (pol'tri), n. Domestic fowls.

pound (pound), n. An inclosure for confining stray animals.

pour (por), v.t. & i. To send or issue in or as in a stream or flood; emit, discharge, or escape, freely.

pout (pout), v.i. To thrust out the lips, as in sullenness.

pov'er-ty-strick'en, a. Very poor or destitute.

pow'der (pou'der), n. 1. Substance in fine dry particles; dust. 2. Any of various solid explosives, as gunpowder.

pow'er (-er), n. 1. Ability to act; faculty of doing or performing something. 2. Exerted energy; vigor; force. 3. Control; authority; influence.

pow'er-ful (-fool), a. Full of or having power; potent; influential.

pow'er-less, a. Destitute of power; unable to produce effect.

prac'tice (-tis), v.t. 1. To do, carry on, act, or exercise; to do or perform often or habitually. 2. To follow or work at, as a profession, etc. 3. To perform repeatedly, for proficiency.

praise (praz), v.t. 1. To express approbation of; laud; applaud. 2. Of God or a god, to glorify by homage, esp. in worship or song.

prank, n. A gay or sportive action or trick; a frolic.

pray (pra), v.t. 1. To entreat; implore. Archaic. 2. To ask earnestly for; supplicate for.

preach (prech), v.i. 1. To proclaim, esp. the gospel; deliver a sermon.

2. To give serious advice, as on morals.

pre-ca'ri-ous (pre-ka'ri-us), a. 1. Depending on the will of another; uncertain. 2. Taken for granted; unfounded. 3. Insecure; dubious.

pre-cau'tion (pre-ko'shun), n. 1. Previous caution or care. 2. A measure taken beforehand to ward off evil or secure good or success.

pre-cede' (-sed), v.t. & i. To be or go before in rank, order, etc.

prec'e-dent (pres'd-dent), n. Something done or said that may serve as an example or rule to authorize or justify a subsequent act of like kind.

pre'cept (pre'sept), n. Any command-ment, instruction, or order for conduct, esp. moral conduct; a working rule or direction.

pre'cinct (pre'sinkt), n. 1. An inclosure bounded by walls or other limits or by an imaginary line; esp., pl., environs. 2. A boundary or limit. 3. A district within certain boundaries, esp. one for governmental purposes, as for police control.

pre-cip'i-tate (-tat), a. 1. Acting with unwise haste; overhasty. 2. Done without due deliberation; hurried. 3. Falling or rushing with steep descent.

pre-ci'sion (-un), n. Quality or state of being precise; exactness; accuracy; definiteness.

pre-clude' (-klood'), v.t. 1. To put a barrier before; close; hinder, stop. 2. To prevent or obviate by anticipation.

pre'con-ceive' (pre'kon-sev'), v.t. To conceive, or form an opinion of, beforehand.

pre-da'cious (pre-da'shus), a. Living by preying on other animals; predatory.

pred'a-to-ry (pred'a-to-ri), a. 1. Of, pertaining to, or marked by, plundering. 2. Predacious.

pred'e-ces'sor (pred's-ses'er; pre'de-), n. One that has preceded another in any state, position, office, etc.

pre-des'ti-na'tion (-na'shun), n. 1. A predestinating; state of being predestined; fate; destiny. 2. In theology, the foreordaining of men to everlasting happiness or misery.

pre-de-ter'mine (pre'de-tur'min), v.t. & i. To determine beforehand.

pre-dic'a-ment (pre-dik'a-ment), n. Condition; situation; esp., an unfortunate or trying position.

pre-dict' (pre-dikt'), v.t. & i. To tell beforehand; foretell; prophesy; presage.

pre'dis-pose' (pre'dis-poz'), v.t. To dispose or incline beforehand; give a tendency to.

pre-dom'i-nate (-nat), v.t. To be superior in number, strength, influence, or authority.

pre-emp'tion (-emp'shun), n. Act or right of purchasing before others.

pre'ex-ist' (pre'eg-zist'), v.t. To exist before.

pref'er-ence (-ens), n. 1. Act of preferring; state of being preferred. 2. That which is preferred.

pref'er-en'tial (-en'shal), a. Of, or of the nature of, preference; giving or having a preference.

pre-fix' (pre-fiks'), v.t. To put or fix before, or at the beginning of, another thing.

preg'nan-cy (preg'nan-si), n. State of being pregnant; of the mind, fertility; inventiveness.

pre'his-tor'ic (pre'his-tor'ik), a. Of or pertaining to the period before written history begins.

pre-judge' (pre-juj'), v.t. To judge before full and sufficient examina-tion; judge beforehand.

pre-lim'i-na'ry (pre-lim'i-na-ri), a. Introductory; prefatory.

pre'ma-ture' (pre'ma-tur'; pre'ma-tur), a. Happening, arriving, or per-formed before the proper or usual time.

pre-med'i-tate (pre-med'i-tat), v.t. & i. To revolve in the mind, or deliber-ate, beforehand.

pre-mise' (pre-miz'), v.t. To set forth beforehand, or as introductory; offer previously, as in explanation.

pre'mi-um (pre'mi-um), n. 1. A reward or recompense; a prize to be won in a competition. 2. Something offered or given for the loan of money; bonus. 3. The consideration given for a contract of insurance.

pre'mo-ni'tion (pre'mo-nish'un), n. 1. Previous warning. 2. Presentiment.

pre-oc'cu-py (-pi), v.t. 1. To occupy

P
R

before another, as a country. 2. To engage, occupy, or engross the attention of, beforehand.

pre-pare' (-par'), v.t. 1. To fit or adapt for a particular purpose; make ready. 2. To make; compound.

pre-pay' (pre-pa'), v.t. To pay, or to pay the charge on, in advance.

pre-pon'der-ant (-ant), a. Superior in influence, force, etc.; predominant.

pre-pos'ter-ous (pre-pos'ter-us), a. Contrary to nature, reason, or common sense; utterly foolish; absurd.

pre-req'ui-site (pre-rek'wi'zit), a. Previously required; necessary to a proposed end.

pre-scrip'tion (pre-skrip'shun), n. 1. A prescribing; thing prescribed; direction. 2. Med. A written direction for the preparation and use of a medicine; also, the medicine.

pres'ence (prez'ens), n. 1. Act, fact, or state of being present. 2. The immediate vicinity of a person; proximity. 3. The whole of one's personal qualities; personality.

pres'ent (prez'ent), n. Anything presented or given; a gift.

pres'ent-ly (prez'ent-li), adv. 1. At once. 2. Soon; shortly; before long.

pre-serve' (pre-zurv'), v.t. 1. To defend from injury; protect; save. 2. To save from decay; as by the use of sugar, salt, etc., as, to preserve fruit.

pre-side' (pre-zid'), v.i. 1. To occupy the place of authority or control, as of chairman. 2. To exercise superintendence, guidance, or control.

press'ing, a. Urgent; exacting.

pres'sure (presh'ur), n. 1. A pressing; compression. 2. A constraining force or impulse. 3. Affliction; distress; burden. 4. Urgency. 5. Action of a force against some opposing force.

pre-sume' (-zum'), v.t. 1. To take upon one's self; esp., to do without authority; venture. 2. To take for granted; infer.

pre'sup-pose' (pre'su'poz'), v.t. To suppose or assume beforehand.

pre-tend' (pre-tend'), v.t. 1. To represent, esp. falsely; feign. 2. To put forward as a reason, pretext, or excuse.

pre-tend'er, n. One who pretends; one who claims a title (to something); a dissembler.

pre-tense', pre-tence' (pre-tens'), n. 1. A claiming; claim made; pretension. 2. A holding out to others something false or feigned; deception. 3. False or hypocritical show, etc.; pretext.

pre'text (pre'tekst; pre-takst'), n. That which is assumed to conceal a purpose or condition; pretense; disguise.

pret'ty (prit'i), a. 1. Pleasing by delicacy or grace; pleasing, but not grand. 2. Pleasing to the mind; entertaining. 3. Good; fine.

pret'zel (pret'sel), n. A kind of salted biscuit.

pre-vail' (pre-val'), v.i. 1. To gain the victory; triumph. 2. To have effect, power, or influence. 3. To persuade; induce.

pre-vent' (-vent'), v.t. To intercept; hinder; frustrate.

pre'vi-ous (pre'vi-us), a. Going before in time; prior.

prey (pra), n. Any animal seized by another to be devoured; hence, a person given up or seized as a victim.

price'less, a. Of inestimable worth; invaluable.

pride (prid), n. 1. Quality or state of being proud; as: a Excessive self-esteem; conceit. b Lofty self-respect; a reasonable or justifiable feeling of elation. 2. Proud behavior; arrogance; disdain.

priest (prest), n. 1. One set apart or authorized to perform religious or sacred functions. 2. A person ordained to the Christian ministry; minister.

prim (prim), a. Formally neat or precise; stiffly decorous or nice.

pri'ma-ry (-ri), a. 1. First in order; primitive; original. 2. First in dignity or importance; chief; principal. 3. First, as preparatory to something higher.

prime (prim), a. 1. Primary; original. 2. First in rank, dignity, etc.; chief. 3. First in excellence.

print'er (prin'ter), n. One who prints or works at printing; a typesetter or a pressman.

pri'or (pri'er), a. Preceding in time or order; antecedent.

pri'va-cy (pri'va-si), n. 1. Seclusion. 2. A place of seclusion. 3. Secrecy.

pri'vate (pri'vat), a. 1. Of or concerning an individual person, company, or interest; personal; not public. 2. Sequestered; secret; secluded; solitary.

prob'a-ble (prob'a-b'l), a. 1. Supported by evidence, but leaving some room for doubt; likely. 2. Giving ground for belief; but not proving.

prob'lem (prob'lem), n. 1. A matter difficult of solution. 2. Math. Anything required to be done.

pro-ce'dure (pro-se'dur), n. 1. Law. The mode of conducting litigation. 2. An action in a course of conduct; a proceeding.

pro-ceed' (pro-sed'), v.i. 1. To go forward or onward; advance; continue. 2. To issue or come forth as from a source; come (from). 3. To go on in an orderly or regulated manner.

pro-claim' (-klam), v.t. To make known by public announcement.

pro-cras'ti-nate (pro-kras'ti-nat), v.t. & i. To put off from day to day; defer; postpone.

pro-cure' (pro-kur'), v.t. 1. To bring into possession; get. 2. To contrive.

prod'i-gal (prod'i-gal), a. Given to prodigality; recklessly profuse.

pro-di'gious (pro-dij'us), a. Extraordinary in bulk, extent, quantity, or degree; vast; immense.

pro-duc'tive (-tiv), a. 1. Having the quality or power of producing; also, fertile. 2. Producing; causing to exist.

pro-fane' (pro-fan'), a. 1. Not sacred or holy. 2. Treating sacred things irreverently; irreverent; blasphemous.

pro-fess' (pro-fes'), v.t. 1. To declare openly, as one's belief, action, etc., avow; acknowledge. 2. To set up a claim of; pretend. 3. To pretend to knowledge of.

prof'it (prof'it), n. 1. Accession of good; valuable results; benefit; gain. 2. Excess of returns or income over expenditure in a given

transaction, etc.

pro-found' (pro-found'), a. 1. Opening or reaching to a great depth; deep. 2. Intellectually deep; thorough. 3. Deeply felt; intense.

pro'gram (pro'gram), n. 1. A brief outline of the order for, or of the subjects of, any public exercise, performance, etc. 2. Hence, the selections or features of a performance collectively. 3. A plan of future procedure.

prog'ress (prog'res or, esp. British, pro'gres), n. 1. A moving or going forward; an advance. 2. Growth, development, or course.

pro-ject' (pro-jekt'), v.t. 1. To throw or cast forward; shoot forth. 2. To contrive; scheme. 3. Geom. To throw forward (as a point, line, etc.) so as to depict on a given surface.

pro'logue (pro'log; prol'og), n. A preface, as to a drama, etc.

pro-long' (pro-long'), v.t. 1. To extend in space or length. 2. To lengthen in time; draw out.

prom'i-nent (-nent), a. 1. Projecting beyond the surface. 2. Distinctly manifest. 3. Standing out from the crowd; eminent.

pro-mis'cu-ous (pro-mis'ku-us), a. 1. Mingled; confused. 2. Distributed or applied indiscriminately.

pro-mote' (pro-mot'), v.t. 1. To contribute to the growth or prosperity of; further; encourage. 2. To exalt in station or rank; advance.

pro-mot'er (-mot'er), n. 1. One that promotes; encourager. 2. One who initiates the organization of a company, the sale of bonds, stocks, etc.

prompt (prompt), a. 1 Ready and quick to act. 2. Done or rendered readily or immediately.

proof (proof), n. 1. Any effort or process designed to establish or discover a fact or truth; test; trial; check. 2. Quality or state of having been proved or tried.

prop'a-gate (prop'a-gat), v.t. 1. To cause to continue or multiply by generation. 2. To extend the action of; diffuse; transmit. 3. To spread from person to person; disseminate.

proph'et (prof'et), n. 1. One inspired by God to speak in His name,

P
R

announcing future events. 2. One who foretells events. 3. [cap.] pl; with the. Certain books of the Old Testament.

pro-pi'ti-ate (-pish'i-at), v.t. To appease and render favorable; conciliate.

pro-pos'al (-poz'al), n. 1. Act of proposing; presentation. 2. That which is proposed, offer.

pro-pose' (-poz'), v.t. 1. To offer for consideration or adoption. 2. To purpose; intend.

pro-pri'e-ta-ry (-pri'e-ta-ri), n. 1. A proprietor; owner. 2. A body of proprietors.

pros'e-cute (pros'e-kut), v.t. 1. To follow or pursue with a view to reach, execute, or accomplish, carry on.

pros'pect (pros'pekt), n. 1. That which is seen; view; scene. 2. Relative aspect; outlook. 3. Act of looking forward; anticipation.

pro-spec'tive (pro-spek'tiv), a. 1. Looking forward in time; acting with foresight. 2. that is in prospect; expected.

pros'per (pros'per), v.t. To render successful.

pros'per-ous (pros'per-us), a. 1. Favorable; as, a prosperous wind. 2. Making gain, or increase; successful; as, a prosperous voyage.

pro-tect' (pro-tekt'), v.t. 1. To shield from damage or injury; defend; guard. 2. Econ. To foster by a protective tariff.

pro-tec'tor (-ter), n. One that protects; defender; guardian; patron.

pro-test' (pro-test'), v.t. 1. To declare solemnly; affirm. 2. To make a certain formal written declaration to protect the holder of a dishonored bill of exchange or note.

proud (proud), a. 1. Feeling or manifesting pride; as: a Arrogant; haughty. b Having proper self-respect or self-esteem. c Exulting (in); elated.

prove (proov), v.t. 1. To try, as by experiment or by a standard; test. 2. To establish or ascertain by argument or evidence; demonstrate. 3. To establish the genuineness or validity of; verify.

pro-vide' (-vid'), v.t. 1. To look out for in advance; procure beforehand; prepare. 2. To supply; afford. 3. To furnish; supply.

prov'i-dence (prov'i-dens), n. 1. Foresight; care; esp., divine foresight, care, or guidance; hence [cap.], God. 2. A manifestation of God's care over his creatures. 3. Prudence; economy.

pro-vi'sion (-vizh'un), n. 1. Act of providing; preparation. 2. That which is provided; esp., a stock of food.

prov'o-ca'tion (prov'o-ka'shun), n. Act of provoking to anger; annoyance; incitement.

prow'ess (prou'es), n. 1. Distinguished bravery; valor. 2. A brave or valorous act or feat.

prox-im'i-ty (prok-sim'i-ti), n. Quality or state of being next; immediate nearness.

prox'y (prok'si), n. 1. Authority to act for another; agency. 2. A person authorized to act for another. 3. A writing authorizing another to act in the signer's stead.

prude (prood), n. A woman of excessive, esp. affected, modesty or propriety.

pru'dent (-dent), a. 1. Sagacious in adapting means to ends; discreet; sensible; dictated by prudence. 2. Provident.

prune (proon), n. A plum; now, any plum that may be, or has been, dried without fermentation.

pry, v.i. To look closely; inspect impertinently; peep; peer.

psalm (sam), n. A sacred song or poem. Hence: [Often cap.] One of the hymns comprising a certain book (**the Psalms**) of the Old Testament.

psy'chic (si'kik), **psy'chi-cal** (-ki-kal), a. 1. Of or pertaining to the soul. 2. Of or pertaining to the mind; mental.

psy-chol'o-gy (-ji), n. Science of mind, its nature and functions.

pub'li-ca'tion (-ka'shun), n. 1. Act of publishing; state of being published; proclamation. 2. That which is published, esp. a book, pamphlet, etc.

pub'lic-ly (pub'lik-li), adv. 1. Without concealment; openly. 2. In respect

puddle 133 pajamas

of the community.

pud'dle (pud'l), n. A small pool of dirty water.

pudg'y (puj'i), a. Short and stout.

pu'er-ile (pu'er-il), a. Childish.

puff'y (puf'i), a. 1. Swollen with air, or any soft matter. 2. Inflated; bombastic. 3. Gusty.

pug-na'cious (pug-na'shus), a. Disposed to fight; fighting.

pull (pool), v.t. 1. To exert force on so as to cause, or tend to cause, motion toward oneself; draw; move or operate in this way.

pul'mo-na-ry (pul'mo-na-ri), a. 1. Pertaining to the lungs. 2. Having lungs.

pulp (pulp), n. The fleshy or pithy part of a vegetable or animal body, organ, or part, as the flesh of a fruit, the pith of a plant stem, etc.; hence, any moist soft mass of undissolved matter.

pul'pit (pool'pit), n. A place, usually elevated, in a church, where the clergyman stands while preaching or conducting the service.

pul'sate (pul'sat), v.i. To throb, as a pulse; beat, as the heart.

pump'kin (pump'kin; colloq. and commonly pun'kin), n. A certain gourdlike fruit widely cultivated; also, the vine producing it.

pun (pun), n. A play on words of the same sound but different meanings or on different applications of a word.

punch, v.t. To thrust or strike, esp. with the fist.

punc'ture (punk'tur), n. 1. Act of puncturing. 2. A hole made by a point, as of a pin.

pun'gent (-jent), a. 1. Causing a sharp sensation; biting. 2. Sharply painful; poignant. 3. Caustic.

pun'ish (pun'ish), v.t. 1. To impose punishment on; chasten. 2. To inflict a penalty for (an offense) on the offender. 3. To deal with roughly or harshly. Colloq. or Slang.

pu'ni-tive (pu'ni-tiv), a. Of or pertaining to punishment.

pu'ny (pu'ni), a. Imperfectly developed; insignificant; petty.

pup (pup), n. A young dog or seal.

pu'pil (-pil), n. The contractile aperture in the iris of the eye.

pup'pet (pup'et), n. 1. A small image in human form; doll. 2. A similar figure, often jointed, moved by the hand or by strings or wires; marionette. 3. One acting as another wills; a tool.

pur-chase (-chas), v.t. To get by paying money or its equivalent; buy.

pure (pur), a. 1. Separate from all foreign matter; clear; unmixed. 2. Free from defilement; innocent; chaste. 3. Genuine; perfect.

pu'ri-tan (pu'ri-tan), n. 1. One who is extremely scrupulous in his religious life. 2. [cap.] One who, in the 16th and 17th centuries, advocated simpler forms of faith and worship than those established by law.

pu'ri-ty (-ti), n. Condition of being pure; freedom from foreign or contaminating matter.

pur'pose (-pus), v.t. & i. To propose, as an aim, to one's self; intend; design; resolve.

pur-su'ant (-su'ant), a. Done in consequence (of anything); hence, according.

push (poosh), v.t. 1. To press against in order to impel; move or endeavor to move by pressure. 2. To press or urge forward; prosecute; extend; as, to push the war into the interior.

put (poot), v.t. 1. To push, thrust; as, to put a knife into. 2. To throw or cast, esp. with a certain pushing overhand motion; as, to put the shot. 3. To drive or force; incite; urge; constrain.

pu'ta-tive (pu'ta-tiv), a. Reputed; supposed.

pu'tre-fy (pu'tre-fi), v.t. & i. To render or become putrid; cause to rot.

pu'trid (pu'trid), a. 1. Decomposed; rotten; as, putrid flesh. 2. Indicating, or proceeding from, decay; as, a putrid smell.

pyg'my (pig'mi), n. A dwarf; a short; insignificant person.

pa-ja-mas (pa-ja'maz), n. pl. A suit, consisting of loose trousers or drawers and a jacket, for wear in the dressing room and during sleep.

P
R

Q

quack, n. 1. A boastful pretender to medical skill. 2. A charlatan.

quad-ren'ni-al (-ren'i-al), a. 1. Comprising, or lasting through, 4 years. 2. Occurring once in 4 years.

quad'ru-ple (-p'l), a. & adv. Fourfold.

quad'ru-plet (-plet), n. A collection of four of one kind; esp., pl., four children born at one birth.

quaint (kwant), a. 1. Curious and fanciful; affected. 2. Strange, esp. old-fashioned, but pleasing in character; appearance, etc.

qual'i-fied (kwol'i-fid), p.a. 1. Fitted; competent; fit. 2. Limited or modified.

qual'i-fy (-fi), v.t. 1. To modify; limit. 2. To soften; abate. 3. To fit, as for office.

qual'i-ty (-ti), n. 1. A property, characteristic, or attribute. 2. Proper or essential being; character; nature; kind. 3. Special or temporary character.

qualm (kwam), n. 1. A sudden attach of illness, faintness, or pain, esp. of nausea. 2. A sudden misgiving. 3. A scruple of conscience; compunction.

quan'ti-ty (-ti), n. 1. The being so much with reference to a possible more or less. 2. Amount or portion; bulk; extent, etc. 3. An indefinite, usually a considerable, amount.

quar'an-tine (kwor'an-ten), n. The term during which an arriving ship suspected of infection is restrained from intercourse with the shore; hence, such restraint, or the measures taken to enforce it; also, the place where prohibited vessels are stationed. Now, any forged stoppage of travel or intercourse on account of disease.

quar'rel (kwor'el), n. A breach of concord; disagreement; esp., an angry dispute; altercation.

quart (kwort), n. A measure of capacity, both in dry and in liquid measure; one fourth of a gallon; one eighth of a peck; 2 pints. Abbr. qt.

quar'ter-ly (-ter-li), adv. By quarters; once in a quarter of a year.

quar'ter-mas'ter (-mas'ter), n. 1. Mil. A commissioned officer charged with providing quarters, clothing, etc., for troops. 2. Naut. A petty officer who attends the helm, etc.

qua-ver (kwa'ver), v.i. To tremble; shake; esp., to cause the voice to vibrate.

queen (kwen), n. 1. The wife of a king. 2. A female monarch. 3. A woman eminent in power or attractions; — also used of cities, countries, etc.

queer (kwer), a. 1. Differing in some odd way from the ordinary; singular; peculiar. 2. Suspicious; questionable. Colloq. 3. Qualmish; faint.

quench (kwench), v.t. 1. To extinguish; make an end of. 2. To cool suddenly, as heated metal.

que'ry (kwe'ri), n. 1. A question; an inquiry. 2. An interrogation point [?].

quest (kwest), n. A seeking; search; adventure; in medieval romance, a knightly expedition, as that in search of the Holy Grail (see GRAIL); also, the knights engaged in the expedition.

ques'tion (kwes'chun), n. 1. Act of asking; interrogation; inquiry. 2. Discussion; debate; hence, objection; doubt. 3. Investigation, esp. a judicial one.

quib'ble (kwib'l), n. A shift or turn from the point in question; an evasion; equivocation.

quick (kwik), a. 1. Living; animate. Archaic. 2. Characterized by life or animation. 3. Speedy; hasty.

quick'en (-n'), v.t. 1. To make alive; revive; excite; stimulate. 2. To hasten; accelerate.

quick'sand (-sand'), n. Sand easily yielding to pressure; esp., a mass of loose sand mixed with water into which a person or object readily sinks.

qui'et (kwi'et), a. 1. In a state of rest or calm; still; hushed. 2. Not excited or anxious; calm; placid. 3. Not turbulent; gentle.

quilt (kwilt), n. 1. A bed coverlet of two thicknesses of material with a filling of wool, cotton, etc. 2. Anything quilted or like a quilt.

quin-tet' (kwin-tet'), n. 1. Music. A composition for five voices or instruments; also, the set of five performers. 2. Any set of five.

quip (kwip), n. 1. A smart, sarcastic turn or jest; gibe; witty sally. 2. A quibble. 3. A droll or eccentric action; also, something odd or strange.

quit (kwit), v.t. 1. To discharge, as an obligation; requite; repay. 2. To conduct; acquit; — used reflexively. Archaic. 3. To have done with; stop; leave; forsake; yield.

quit'claim' (kwit'klam'), n. Law. A release or relinquishment of a claim; a deed of release.

quite (kwit), adv. 1. Completely; wholly; entirely. 2. Positively; really; also, loosely, to a considerable extent or degree; as, it is quite near.

quit'tance (kwit'ans), n. 1. Discharge from a debt or an obligation. 2. Recompense; requital.

quiv'er (kwiv'er), v.i. To shake or move with slight and tremulous motion; tremble; shiver.

quiz (kwiz), n. 1. To ridicule; banter; question closely. 2. To examine or coach by questions. U.S.

quo'ta (kwo'ta), n.; pl. -TAS (-taz). A (certain) proportional part or share.

quot'a-ble (kwot'a-b'l), a. Capable or worthy of being quoted.

quo-ta'tion (kwo-ta'shun), n. 1. Act of quoting, or citing. 2. That which is quoted, or cited. 3. Commerce. The naming of the current price of any security or commodity; also, the price named.

R

race (rac), n. 1. Career; course of life. 2. A contest of speed. 3. A strong or rapid current of water, or its channel. — v.i. 1. To go swiftly, esp. in competition. 2. To run too fast under a diminished load, as an engine. — v.t. 1. To cause to contend in a race. 2. To run a race with.

race, n. 1. The descendants of the same ancestor; a family, tribe, or people; breed; as, the human race. 2. State of being one of a particular race.

ra'cial (ra'shal), a. Of or pertaining to a race or family of men.

rack'et, n. Confused, clattering noise; din; noisy talk or sport.

rac'y (ras'i), a. 1. Having a strong flavor indicating origin, as a wine. 2. Vigorous or spirited.

ra'di-ance (-ans), n. State or quality of being radiant; brilliancy; vivid brightness.

ra'di-ate (-at), v.i. 1. To emit rays; shine. 2. To issue in or as in rays, or direct lines, as heat. — v.t. To emit in rays, as heat.

rad'ish (rad'ish), n. The edible pungent root of a common garden plant; also, the plant.

raf'fi-a (raf'i-a), n. A kind of palm fiber.

raf'fle (raf'l), n. A kind of lottery. — v.i. To engage in a raffle. — v.t. To dispose of by means of a raffle.

raft (raft), n. A float of logs, etc., fastened together. — v.t. To transport on or as a raft.

rag (rag), n. 1. A shred; tatter. 2. [Usually in pl.] Mean or tattered attire.

rage (raj), n. 1. Violent passion or feeling; anger; fury; frenzy. 2. The subject of eager desire. 3. Enthusiasm, esp. at its height. — v.i. 1. To be furious with anger. 2. To act with fury. 3. To prevail without restraint, as the plague.

rag'ged (rag'ed), a. 1. Rough; jagged. 2. Unfinished; irregular. 3. Worn into tatters. 4. Wearing ragged clothes.

raid (rad), n. 1. A predatory incursion; foray. 2. An attack or invasion, to make arrests, seize property, or plunder. — v.t. To make a raid on or into.

rail'road' (ral'rod'), n. A permanent road or way having a line or lines of rails providing a track for cars; such a road or line together with the lands, buildings, rolling stock, etc., pertaining thereto. — v.t. 1. To transport by railroad. 2. To send or put through rapidly.

rain (ran), n. 1. Water falling in drops from the clouds. 2. A shower or continued fall of, or as of, rain. — v.i. 1. To fall as or like rain. 2. To send down rain. — v.t. 1. To pour down. 2. To yield or shed copiously.

rain'bow' (ran'bo'), n. A bow or arc exhibiting the several colors of the spectrum, and formed opposite the

P
R

sun by refraction and reflection of the sun's rays in drops of rain, or in spray, mist, etc.

raise (raz), v.t. 1. To cause to rise up. a to awaken; arouse. b Revivify. 2. To cause to arise, grow up, or come into being; as: a To build up; erect. b To bring or get together; collect. c to breed; propagate; grow. d To utter. 3. To elevate; heighten; intensify. 4. To cause to rise or become light, as bread. 5. To end, as if by lifting away, as a siege.

rai'sin (ra'z'n), n. A dried grape of a special type.

ral'ly (ral'i), v.t. 1. To collect and bring to order, as troops in confusion; reunite. 2. To revive; rouse. — v.i. 1. To assemble in order; unite in action; also, to renew order or united effort. 2. To revive; recover strength. — n. 1. Act or process of rallying. 2. A mass meeting.

ram (ram), n. 1. A male sheep. 2. An engine of war used for butting, or battering. — v.t. 1. To butt or strike against violently. 2. To fill or compact by pounding or driving.

ram'ble (ram'b'l), n. An excursion or stroll merely for recreation. — v.i. 1. To go from place to place without definite object. 2. To talk or write discursively. 3. To extend or grow at random.

ram'i-fi-ca'tion (-i-fi-ka'shun), n. 1. Act or process of ramifying. 2. A small branch or offshoot. 3. A division.

ramp'age (ram'paj; ram'paj'), n. Violent or riotous behavior; a state of excitement or passion.

ram'pant (-pant), a. 1. Ramping; rearing up with forelegs or paws extended. 2. Threatening, extravagant, or unrestrained in action, etc. 3. Exuberant; unchecked.

ranch (ranch), n. 1. An establishment, with its estate, for the grazing and rearing of horses, cattle, or sheep. 2. A large farm.

ran'cid (ran'sid), a. Having a rank smell or taste, as of old oil.

ran'dom (ran'dum), n. Going by chance.

ran'som (-sum), n. Redemption of a captive by paying a price; the price paid or demanded. — v.t. 1. To

redeem from captivity by paying a price. 2. To deliver; redeem.

rant (rant), v.i. To be noisy and bombastic in talk or declamation. — n. Ranting speech.

rap'ture (rap'tur), n. 1. Transport. 2. An expression of ecstasy.

rare (rar), a. Not thoroughly cooked.

rare'ly (rar'li), adv. Seldom.

ras'cal (ras'kal), n. A mean, trickish fellow.

rash, a. 1. Overhasty in counsel or action. 2. Due to too much haste or too little reflection.

rasp'ber-ry (raz'ber-i), n. The fruit of any of various brambles; also, the plant bearing it.

rat (rat), n. Any of certain rodents allied to the mice, but larger.

rate, n. 1. Quantity, amount, or degree of a thing measured per unit of something else; proportional amount. 2. A fixed ratio; proportion; also, a charge or price fixed by a ratio, scale, or standard. 3. Relative condition or quality; rank; class; kind.

rath'er (rath'er), adv. 1. More properly. 2. Somewhat. 3. More readily or willingly.

rat'i-fy (rat'i-fi), v.t. To approve and sanction; confirm; establish.

ra'tion (ra'shun; rash'un), n. An allowance of provisions.

ra'tion-al (rash'un-al), a. 1. Having reason or understanding; reasoning. 2. Of or pert. to reason. 3. Agreeable to reason.

rat'tan' (ra-tan'), n. 1. a Any of certain climbing palms with remarkably long stems. b A portion of one of these stems. 2. A rattan cane or switch.

rat'tle-snake' (-l'snak'), n. Any of certain venomous American snakes having horny joints at the end of the tail which rattle sharply when shaken.

rau'cous (ro'kus), a. Hoarse; harsh.

rav'age (rav'aj), n. Desolation by violence; waste. — v.t. To lay waste.

rave (rav), v.i. To talk or act wildly.

rav'en-ous (-us), a. Voracious.

rav'ing (rav'ing); p.a. Talking or acting wildly; delirious; as, a raving lunatic.

rav'ish (rav'ish), v.t. 1. To seize and carry away by violence. 2. To transport with joy or delight. 3. To violate.

raw (ro), a. 1. Not cooked. 2. In the natural state or nearly so. 3. Crude. 4. Deprived of skin.

ray (ra), n. 1. A line of light; hence: Any line of radiant or radioactive energy. 2. A thin line like a ray, esp., one of a number diverging from a center.

ra'zor (ra'zer), n. A keen-edged instrument used in shaving the face or head.

reach (rech), v.t. 1. To stretch out, as a limb. 2. To pass to another. 3. To touch or seize, esp. with the hand. 4. To extend to. 5. To arrive at; come to; attain. 6. To hit or touch with a missile. 7. To influence. — v.i.

re-act' (re-akt'), v.i. 1. To return an impulse; resist action by an opposite force. 2. To respond to a stimulus. 3. To act in a contrary direction or manner.

read (red), v.t. 1. To interpret (as a riddle, etc.); hence, to foresee; foretell. 2. To look at characters or words with understanding. 3. To learn of by perusal. 4. To discern by observation of signs. 5. To attribute (a meaning, explanation, etc.) to what is read.

read'i-ly (red'i-li), adv. 1. Cheerfully. 2. Quickly.

read'i-ness, n. 1. State of being ready. 2. Ease or facility of performance.

read'ing (red'ing), n. 1. Act of one who reads. 2. A public recital; also, a lecture. 3. Study of books. 4. Form in which anything is written; version.

read'y (red'i), a. 1. Prepared for immediate action or use. 2. Immediately liable; likely. 3. Willing; disposed. 4. Quick. 5. At hand.

re-al'i-ty (re-al'i-ti), n. 1. State or quality of being real. 2. That which is real.

reap (rep), v.t. 1. To gather, as a harvest, by cutting. 2. To obtain or receive as a reward, or as the fruit of labor. 3. To clear of a crop by reaping. — v.i. To reap something.

rea'son-a-ble (-a-b'l), a. 1. Having the faculty of reason; rational. 2. Governed by reason; just; rational.

3. Not excessive.

re'as-sur'ance (re'a-shoor'ans), n. Renewed assurance.

re-bate' (re-bat'), v.t. To deduct from; allow a discount to.

re-bel'lious (-yus), a. 1. Engaged in rebellion; disposed to rebel; insubordinate. 2. Resisting treatment or operation; refractory; as, a rebellious disease.

re-bound' (re-bound'), v.i. To spring back on collision or impact. — n. Act of rebounding.

re-buff' (re-buf'), n. 1. A brusque refusal; snub. 2. A repulse. —v.t. To administer a rebuff to.

re-buke' (-buk'), v.t. To reprimand; reprove; censure. — n. A sharp reproof.

re-call' (re-kol'), v.t. 1. To call or summon back. 2. To call back to mind; recollect. 3. To revoke; annul; retract. — n. 1. Act of recalling, or a signal used to recall, or summon back. 2. The right or procedure by which a public official may be removed from office by popular vote.

re-cede' (re-sed'), v.i. 1. To move back or away; retreat; retire; as, the water receded. 2. To withdraw a claim, pretension, or proposal.

re-ceipt' (re-set'), n. 1. A formula according to which things are to be taken or combined; a recipe. 2. That which is received, in distinction from what is expended; — usually in pl. 3. Act of receiving; reception. 4. A writing acknowledging the receiving of goods or money.

re-ceive' (-sev'), v.t. 1. To take, as something that is offered, sent, paid, or the like; accept. 2. To permit to enter, as into one's house; hence, to greet. 3. To admit; hence, to hold. 4. To get, acquire; hence, to experience. 5. To support; catch; bear. —v.i. 1. to be a recipient. 2. To receive visitors.

re'cent (re-sent), a. Of late origin, existence, or occurrence.

re-cep'tion (re-sep'shun), n. 1. Act of receiving; state of being received; admission. 2. Act or manner of receiving, esp. visitors; an occasion of receiving guests. 3. Acceptance.

rec'i-pe (res'i-pe), n. A formula for

some combination or preparation; a receipt.

re-cit'al (re-sit'al), n. 1. Act of reciting; rehearsal. 2. A telling in detail; narration; story. 3. Music. A performance by one person.

re-cite' (re-sit'), v.t. & i. 1. To repeat, as a lesson. 2. To tell over.

reck'less (rek'les), a. Rashly negligent; utterly heedless.

rec'og-ni'tion (rek'og-nish'un), n. Act of recognizing; state of being recognized; formal avowal.

rec'og-nize (rek'og-niz), v.t. 1. To avow knowledge of; consent to admit, hold, etc. 2. To acknowledge formally. 3. To know again; identify as previously known. 4. To acknowledge acquaintance with, as by salutation. 5. To show appreciation of (services, etc.).

re'col-lect (re'ko-lekt'), v.t. 1. To collect again, as something scattered; also, to gather; rally; recover. 2. To compose (one's self).

rec'ol-lect' (rek'o-lekt'), v.t. 1. To call to mind; remember. 2. Reflexively, to compose (one's self); recover command of (one's self).

rec'om-mend' (rek'o-mend'), v.t. 1. To commit; consign. 2. To commend to favorable notice. 3. To make acceptable; attract favor to. 4. To advise.

rec'om-pense (rek'om-pens), v.t. 1. To render an equivalent to, for service, loss, etc.; compensate. 2. To give compensation for. — n. Compensation.

rec'on-cile (-sil), v.t. 1. To cause to be friendly again. 2. To adjust, as a quarrel; settle. 3. To bring to acquiescence or content. 4. To make consistent.

re-cord' (re-kord'), v.t. To commit to writing, printing, inscription, or the like; register; enroll.

rec'ord (rek'ord; -ord), n. 1. A recording or being recorded; reduction to writing as evidence. 2. Esp.: a An official writing recording public acts. b An authentic official copy of a document. 3. Testimony. Archaic. 4. Something written or transcribed to perpetuate a knowledge of events.

re-count' (re-kount'), v.t. To count

again. — (re-kount'; re-kount), n. A counting again.

re-coup' (re-koop'), v.t. 1. To get compensation for; as, to recoup a loss. 2. To reimburse; indemnify.

re-cov'er (re-kuv'er), v.t. 1. To get again; esp., to regain, as lost property. 2. Law. To gain as a compensation, or return; obtain title to by a judicial decision. 3. To make up for; retrieve. 4. To rescue; deliver.

re-crim'i-na'tion (re-krim'i-na'shun), n. Act of recriminating; a counter accusation.

re-cruit' (re-kroot'), v.t. 1. To supply with new men, as an army; also, to muster; raise. 2. To reinvigorate. — v.i. 1. To enlist new soldiers. 2. To gain new supplies of anything wasted; gain health. — n. Mil. A new enlisted soldier.

re-cu'per-ate (-ku'per-at), v.t. To recover. — v.i. To recover health or strength.

re-cur' (re-kur'), v.i. 1. a To go or come back in thought or discourse. b To come again to mind; come up again for consideration. 2. To occur again, as a fever.

re-deem' (re-dem'), v.t. 1. To buy back; hence, to recover, as pledged property. 2. To ransom or liberate as from captivity. 3. In theology, to deliver from the bondage of sin and its penalties. 4. To fulfill, as a promise.

re-duce' (re-dus'), v.t. 1. Med. To restore to its proper place or condition, as a displaced part. 2. To bring into a certain order, or classification. 3. Arith. To change the denominations of (a quantity) or the form of (an expression) without changing the value. 4. To bring to a certain condition by grinding, etc.

re-dun'dant (-dant), a. 1. Exceeding what is natural or necessary; superabundant. 2. Characterized by redundance; pleomastic.

reef (ref), n. A ridge of rocks or sand at or near the surface of the water.

re-fer' (-fur'), v.t. 1. To assign, as to a class, cause, source, motive. 2. To send or direct elsewhere, as for aid, information, decision, etc.; submit to another.

ref'er-ence (ref'er-ens), n. 1. A referring; state of being referred. 2. Relation; respect. 3. a That which alludes to something. b A specific direction of the attention, as to a book; also, the book referred to. 4. One that is referred to; as: a One of whom inquiries can be made as to another. b A written statement of the qualifications of an employee given by the employer.

re-fine' (re-fin'), v.t. 1. To reduce to a fine or pure state. 2. To purify from what is coarse, vulgar, etc. — v.i. 1. To become pure. 2. To affect nicety or subtlety. 3. To improve in fineness.

re-flect' (-flekt'), v.t. 1. To bend or throw back, esp. after striking. 2. To give back an image. 3. To bring or cast as a result. — v.i. 1. To throw or turn back the thoughts (upon anything); contemplate. 2. To cast reproach, discredit, etc. 3. To throw back light, heat, etc.

re-form' (re-form'), v.t. To amend or improve by change of form, by removal of faults or abuses, etc.; correct; improve. — v.i. To amend or correct one's character or habits. — n. Amendment of what is defective, vicious, etc., or a case of it.

re-form'a-to-ry (-to-ri), a. Tending to, or intended for, reformation. — n. A penal institution for promoting the reformation of young offenders.

re-frain' (-fran'), v.i. To hold back or aloof; forbear; abstain.

re-frig'er-a'tor (-a'ter), n. A box or room for keeping food, etc., cool, usually by means of ice.

ref'uge (ref'uj), n. 1. Shelter or protection from danger or distress. 2. One that protects from danger, distress, or calamity; an asylum.

re-fund' (re-fund'), v.t. & i. To give back; repay.

re-fuse' (-fuz'), v.t. & i. 1. To decline to accept; reject. 2. To decline to submit to; decline to do or give; deny.

re-fute' (re-fut'), v.t. To disprove; prove to be false or erroneous.

re-gain' (-gan'), v.t. 1. To gain anew; recover. 2. To get back to.

re-gard' (re-gard'), v.t. 1. To keep in view; view; observe; gaze upon. 2. To take into account; consider. 3. To esteem; care for.

re-gard'less, a. Having no regard.

re-gen'er-ate (-at), a. 1. In theology, spiritually reborn; become Christian. 2. Restored; reformed; redeemed. — (-at), v.t.

reg'i-cide (rej'i-sid), n. 1. One who kills a king, esp. his own king. 2. The killing of a king.

reg'i-ment (-ment), n. Mil. An organized body of soldiers under a colonel.

re'gion (re'jun), n. 1. A large tract of land; district; tract. 2. A part or division of the body.

reg'is-ter, n. 1. A written account or record; a book containing regular entries of items or details; also, an entry therein. 2. The compass of a voice or instrument. 3. A device to admit or exclude heated air, or to regulate ventilation. 4. That which registers, or records. — v.i.

re-gret' (-gret'), v.t. To experience regret on account of; grieve at. — n. 1. Pain or distress of mind on account of something past, with a wish that it had been different. 2. An expression of regret; — usually in pl.

reg'u-lar (reg'u-lar), a. 1. Conformed to some established rule, law, principle, or type; symmetrical.

re-gur'gi-tate (re-gur'ji-tat), v.t. & i. To pour, gush, or cast back or out again, esp. from the stomach; eructate.

re-hearse' (-hurs'), v.t. 1. To repeat, as a statement; recite aloud formally; enumerate. 2. To drill in preparation for a public performance. — v.i. To recite something for practice.

re-it'er-ate (re-it'er-at), v.t. To repeat; say or do over again or repeatedly.

re-ject' (re-jekt'), v.t. 1. To refuse to acknowledge, receive, etc.; decline to accept. 2. To cast off; throw away, as useless, etc.; discard. 3. To refuse to grant or consider.

re-joice' (-jois'), v.t. To give joy to; gladden. — v.i. To feel joy.

re-ju've-nate (re-joo've-nat), v.t. To make young or vigorous again.

re-lapse' (re-laps'), v.i. To slip or fall

P
R

back into a former state or practice, as from convalescence. — n. A relapsing; state of having relapsed.

re-la'tion (-la'shun), n. 1. Act of relating, or telling; recital; narration. 2. State of being related or of referring; connection. 3. Reference; respect; — esp. in in relation to. 4. Connection by blood or affinity; kinship. 5. A relative; kinsman; kinswoman. 6. State of mutual or reciprocal interest; also, pl., dealings; affairs.

re-lax' (-laks'), v.t. 1. To make lax; slacken; loosen. 2. To make less severe, rigorous, or tense; abate. — v.i. 1. To become lax, weak, or loose. 2. To remit attention or effort.

re-lease' (re-les'), v.t. 1. Law. To remit. 2. To set free. 3. To relieve, as from pain, penalty, etc. — n. 1. Deliverance or relief from care, pain, trouble, etc. 2. Discharge from obligation or responsibility. 3. Act of liberating or freeing.

re-lent' (re-lent'), v.i. To become less hard, harsh, cruel, or the like; to become compassionate.

re-lent'less, a. Unmoved by sympathy; unyielding; unpitying.

rel'e-vant (-vant), a. Bearing upon, or applying to, the case in hand.

re-li'ance (-ans), n. 1. Act of relying; state of being reliant; confidence. 2. Anything on which to rely; dependence, ground of trust.

rel'ic (rel'ik), n. Remains; esp., sacred or venerated remains; memorial.

re-lief' (re-lef'), n. 1. Act of relieving; state of being relieved; removal of any evil or burden. 2. Release from duty. 3. That which or one who gives aid or comfort. 4. In sculpture, the projection of figures, etc., from a background; a work of art so produced.

re-li'gious (-lij'us), a. 1. Possessing, or conforming to, religion; pious; godly. 2. Bound by monastic vows. 3. Of or pertaining to religion. 4. Scrupulous; strict.

re-lin'quish (-lin'kwish), v.t. 1. To withdraw from; abandon. 2. To give up, as a right.

re-luc'tance (re-luk'tans), n. State or quality of being reluctant; repugnance; aversion.

re-luc'tant (-tant), a. Disinclined; loath; unwilling.

re-ly' (re-li'), v.i. To rest with confidence; trust; depend; —with on.

re-main' (re-man'), v.i. 1. To be left after another, or a part, or others have been removed, destroyed, or subtracted. 2. To be left as not included or comprised. 3. To stay behind while others withdraw. 4. To endure; continue. — n. 1. The portion remaining; esp., a A fragment; relic; remainder; — chiefly in pl. b pl. A dead body; relics. 2. pl. Posthumous works or productions, esp. literary.

re-mark' (re-mark'), v.t. 1. To notice; observe. 2. To state; say. — n. Act of remarking or noticing; a casual observation or statement.

rem'e-dy (rem'e-di), n.; pl. -DIES (-diz). 1. That which relieves or cures a disease. 2. That which corrects or counteracts an evil; corrective; cure. — v.t. To apply a remedy to; cure; correct.

re-mem'ber (re-mem'ber), v.t. 1. To have (an idea) come into the mind again; recollect. 2. To hold in mind; as, remember to go. 3. To recall to the mind of another; as, remember me to him. — v.i. To exercise or have the power of memory.

re-mit (re-mit'), v.t. 1. To forgive, as sin; pardon. 1. To refrain from inflicting or enforcing; as, to remit a penalty. 3. To send, esp. to a distance, as money due. — v.i. 1. To abate. 2. To send money, as in payment.

re-morse' (re-mors'), n. Tormenting distress excited by a sense of guilt; repentant regret.

re-mote' (-mot'), a. 1. Far away; distant. 2. Not connected or closely related; not obvious; as, a remote resemblance.

re-move' (-moov'), v.t. 1. To move away; cause to change the place of; displace; shift. 2. To take or put away. — v.i. To depart.

ren'der (ren'der), v.t. 1. To give or inflict in return or requital. 2. To give; deliver; transmit. 3. To yield; surrender. 4. To state; deliver; as, to render an account.

ren'dez-vous (ran'de-voo), n. 1. A

place appointed for a meeting. 2. A meeting by appointment. — v.i. & t. To meet, esp. by appointment.

re-new' (re-nu'), v.t. 1. To make new again; restore. 2. To begin again; resume; as, to renew one's efforts. 3. To revive; reestablish; rebuild. — v.i. 1. To become new. 2. To begin again.

re-nounce' (re-nouns'), v.t. 1. To give up, abandon, or resign. 2. To repudiate.

rent, n. Periodical payment for the use of property. — v.t. 1. To pay rent for. 2. To grant possession of for rent. — v.i. To be leased or let.

re-pay (re-pa'), v.t. 1. To pay back; pay back to; as, to repay money or a creditor. 2. To glve or do something for, in requital. 3. To recompense, as a kindness. — v.i. To make payment or requital.

re-peal' (-pel'), v.t. To recall. — n. Revocation.

re-peat (-pet'), v.t. 1. To say or utter again. 2. To make or do again. 3. To say over from memory; recite; also, to utter after another. — v.i. To say or do what has been said or done.

re-pel' (-pel'), v.t. 1. To drive back, repulse. 2. Physics. To force, or tend to force, apart by mutual action at a distance. 3. To cause aversion in.

re-pent' (re-pent'), v.i. & t. 1. To feel penitence or regret for past conduct. 2. To change the mind with regard to one's conduct, from regret or dissatisfaction.

rep'e-ti'tion (-e-tish'un), n. 1. Act of repeating; iteration; reiteration. 2. Act of reciting, as something learned; also, recital; mention.

re-place' (re-plas'), v.t. 1. To place again; restore to a former place. 2. To take the place of; supply the want of. 3. To refund; repay; restore.

re-plen'ish (re-plen'ish), v.t. To refill.

re-ply' (re-pli'), v.i. 1. To answer in words; respond; rejoin. 2. To do something as a response to something done. — v.t. To return as an answer. — n. Answer; response.

re-pose' (-poz'), v.t. To place, rest, or set (trust, hope, etc.).

re-pose' (re-poz'), v.t. To lay at rest.

—n. Rest.

rep're-sent' (rep're-zent'), v.t. 1. To bring clearly before the mind; present. 2. To state in order to affect action or judgment. 3. To portray or depict; exhibit.

re-press' (re-pres'), v.t. 1. To check; curb, as a desire. 2. To press back; quell; subdue.

re-prieve' (re-prev'), v.t. 1. To postpone execution of sentence on respite. 2. To relieve temporarily. — n. 1. A reprieving; state of being reprieved. 2. A respite; temporary escape.

rep'ri-mand (rep'ri-mand), n. A severe reproof. — v.t. To reprove severely or formally.

re-proach' (-proch'), v.t. To charge with a fault; rebuke; censure. — n. 1. A cause of blame, censure, disgrace, or discredit; hence, disgrace or the like. 2. Censure, rebuke, or blame.

re'pro-duce' (re'pro-dus'), v.t. To produce again; as: a To produce again by generation or the like. b To repeat. c To make an image, a copy, etc. of; portray. d To present or exhibit again; as, to reproduce a witness. — v.i. To reproduce its kind.

rep'tile (rep'til), n. Any of a class of air-breathing vertebrates including alligators, lizards, and turtles.

re-pug'nance (-pug'nans), n. An aversion.

rep'u-ta'tion (-ta'shun), n. 1. Estimation in which one is held; repute. 2. Good reputation; good name; as, a man of reputation.

re-quest' (-kwest'), n. 1. Act of asking for something desired; expression of desire; solicitation. 2. That which is asked for. 3. A state of being asked for or sought after; demand. — v.t. 1. To ask for (something); solicit. 2. To ask (one) to do something; as, to request one to go.

re-scind' (re-sind'), v.t. To abrogate; annul; to vacate or make void, as a law; repeal.

res'cue (res'ku), v.t. To free from confinement, violence, danger, or evil. — n. Act of rescuing.

re-sem'ble (-b'l), v.t. To be like or similar to.

P
R

re-sent' (re-zent'), v.t. To feel, express, or exhibit indignant displeasure at.

re-served' (-zurvd'), p. a. 1. Restrained in words or actions. 2. Set aside for future use.

res'er-voir (rez'er-vwor), n. 1. A place where anything, esp. water, is kept in store. 2. A reserve; a store.

re-side' (re-zid'), v.i. 1. To dwell permanently or for a considerable time. 2. To be present; inhere; be as an attribute or element.

res'i-dence (rez'i-dens), n. 1. Act or fact of residing in a place for some time. 2. The place or house where one resides; dwelling place.

res'i-due (rez'i-du), n. That which remains after a part is taken or designated; remnant; remainder.

re-sign' (re-zin'), v.t. To yield to another; surrender. — v.i. To surrender a position.

re-sil'i-ent (-ent), a. 1. Rebounding; recoiling; returning to the original position or shape. 2. Possessing power of recovery; elastic; buoyant.

re-sist' (re-zist'), v.t. 1. To withstand. 2. To strive against. —v.i. To make opposition; offer resistance.

re-solve' (re'zolv'), v.t. 1. To separate (into component parts or elements). 2. To change or convert by resolution or formal vote. 3. To answer or solve, as a problem; explain; clear up. 4. To declare or decide by a formal vote.

re-source' (-sors'), n. 1. That resorted to for supply or support. 2. pl. Funds; available means. 3. Ability to meet a situation.

re-spect' (re-spekt'), v.t. 1. To relate to; be concerned with. 2. To consider worthy of esteem; hence, to refrain from obtruding upon. — n. 1. Relation; relationship; reference; regard. 2. A point regarded; a particular; detail. 3. Regard; consideration. 4. Favor; partiality; discrimination.

re-spect'a-ble (-spek'ta-b'l), a. 1. Worthy of respect; of good repute. 2. Considerable; also, moderate, in size, excellence, or number 3. Decent in behavior or character; also, presentable.

res'pi-ra'tion (res'pi-ra'shun), n. Act or process of respiring, or breathing, by which an animal takes in oxygen and gives off the products formed by oxidation in the tissues.

rest (rest), n. 1. Sleep. 2. Freedom from activity. 3. Peace of mind or spirit.

rest'less, a. 1. Deprived of rest; uneasy. 2. Not affording rest. 3. Never resting; unquiet.

re-strain' (-stran'), v.t. 1. To check; curb. 2. To limit; restrict.

re-sult (re-zult'), v.i. To arise as a consequence. — n. Consequence.

re-sume' (-zum'), v.t. 1. To assume or take again; put on anew. 2. To enter upon, or being, again. 3. To take up again.

res'ur-rect' (rez'u-rekt'), v.t. To raise from the dead.

re-sus'ci-tate (re-sus'i-tat), v.t. & i. To revive, esp. from apparent death or unconsciousness.

re-tail' (re-tal'; re-tal), v.t. 1. To sell in small quantities or to the consumer. 2. To sell again or to many.

re-tain' (re-tan'), 1. To keep in possession. 2. To employ (as a lawyer) by paying a preliminary fee. 3. To remember.

re-tal'i-ate (re-tal'i-at), v.t. & i. To return the like for.

re-tard' (-tard'), v.t. 1. To make slow; delay; hinder. 2. To put off; postpone. — n. Retardation; delay.

re-ten'tion (re-ten'shun), n. 1. Act of retaining; state of being retained. 2. Act of retaining; or ability to retain, things in the mind; memory.

ret'i-cent (-sent), a. Inclined to keep silent; uncommunicative.

re-tire' (re-tir'), v.t. 1. To withdraw; remove. 2. To withdraw from circulation, or from the market. 3. To cause to retire. — v.i. 1. To retreat. 2. To withdraw. 3. To go to bed. 4. To withdraw from office, etc.

re-trac'tion (-shun), n. 1. Withdrawal of something advanced, claimed, said, or done. 2. Act of retracting; state of being retracted.

ret'ri-bu'tion (ret'ri-bu'shun), n. That which is given in compensation; esp., condign punishment.

re-trieve' (-trev'), v.t. 1. To find and bring in (killed or wounded game). 2. To recover; regain. 3. To restore;

revive. 4. To make good; repair. —
v.i. To retrieve game.

re-turn' (re-turn'), n. 1. To go or come
back again to a place or condition.
2. To go back or revert in thought,
narration, or argument. 3. To come
back, as in possession; revert, as
an estate. 4. To reply; respond.

re-un'ion (re-un'yun), n. 1. Reuniting.
2. An assembling of persons who
have been separated.

re-veal' (re-vel'), v.t. 1. To make
known; unveil; disclose. 2. To
communicate by supernatural
instruction or agency.

re-venge' (re-vej'), v.t. To inflict harm
or injury in return for; avenge. — n.
1. Act of revenging; vengeance. 2.
An opportunity of getting satisfaction.

rev'er-ence (rev'er-ens), n. 1.
Profound respect mingled with fear
and affection; veneration. 2. A token
of respect or veneration; an
obeisance.

re-view' (re-vu'), v.t. 1. To view,
examine, or study again. 2. To
examine critically. 3. To look back
on. — v.i. To write reviews; be a
reviewer. — n.

re-voke' (re-vok'), v.t. To annul by
recalling.

re-volt' (re-volt'; -volt'), v.t. To affect
with disgust or loathing; nauseate.
— v.i. 1. To renounce allegiance;
rebel. 2. To be disgusted, or grossly
offended.

re-ward (-word'), v.t. 1. To give as a
reward. 2. To make a return, or give
a reward, to (a person) or for (a
service, etc.); requite; recompense.
— n.

rhet'o-ric (ret'o-rik), n. 1. The art of
expressive speech or of discourse.
2. Artificial elegance of language.

rid'dle, n. An enigma. — v.t. To
explain. — v.i. To speak ambigu-
ously or enigmatically.

ride (rid), v.i. 1. To be carried on or as
on the back of an animal. 2. To be
borne in or on a vehicle. 3. To float;
of a vessel; to float at anchor or
when moored. 4. To be borne
along.

rid'i-cule (rid'i-kul), n. Remarks
designed to excite laughter with a
degree of contempt for the subject

of the remarks. — v.t. To treat with
ridicule.

right, n. 1. That which is right or
correct; esp., obedience to duty or
authority. 2. That, as a power or
privilege, to which one has a just or
lawful claim. 3. The side or part on
or toward the right side.

right'ful (-fool), a. 1. Consonant to
justice; just. 2. Having a right or just
claim according to law. 3. Belonging
or possessed by right.

rig'id (rij'id), a. 1. Firm. 2. Strict.

ri'ot (ri'ut), n. 1. Disorderly behavior;
uproar; tumult. 2. Profligate living;
revelry. 3. A tumultuous disturbance
of the public peace by an unlawful
assembly of three or more persons.
—v.i. To engage in a riot; act
riotously.

rise (riz'; ris), n. 1. Act of rising; state
of being risen; ascent. 2. Distance
through which anything rises. 3. A
piece of land higher than its
surroundings.

risk (risk), n. Hazard; peril; exposure
to loss or injury. — v.t. 1. To expose
to risk; hazard. 2. To incur the risk
of danger of.

rit'u-al (rit'u-al), a. Of or pertaining to
rites or a ritual. — n. 1. Established
form of worship; religious ceremonial. 2. Hence, a code of ceremonies observed.

ri'val (ri'val), n. One of two or more
striving to reach or get that which
only one can possess; competitor.
— a. Having the same pretensions
or claims; standing in competition.

road, n. An open way or public
passage for vehicles, persons, and
animals; highway.

roast (rost), v.t. Primarily, to cook by
exposure before a fire; also, to cook
(as meat) in a close oven. — v.i. To
undergo the process of being
roasted.

robe (rob), n. 1. An outer garment of a
flowing and elegant style; hence, a
dress of rank, office, etc.; pl. dress;
costume. 2. A skin of an animal
used as a wrap, as in driving. — v.t.
& i. To put on a robe or robes;
dress; array.

ro-bust' (ro-bust'), a. Having or
evincing strength or vigorous
health; strong; vigorous; sturdy;

P
R

hearty.

rogue (rog), n. 1. A knave; cheat. 2. In playful use, one who is mischievous or frolicsome.

room (room), n. 1. Extent of space, great or small; compass; esp., unobstructed space. 2. An apartment or chamber. 3. Possibility of admission; opportunity; as, room for doubt. — v.i. To occupy a room or rooms.

rope (rop), n. 1. A large, stout cord of twisted or braided strands. 2. A row or string of things united by braiding, twining, etc. 3. A viscous or glutinous formation in a liquid. — v.t. 1. To bind or tie with a rope. 2. To divide off by a rope. 3. To lasso.

rot (rot), v.i. To decompose. — v.t. To cause to rot. — n. Process of rotting.

ro'tate (ro'tat), v.i. & i. To turn, as a wheel, round an axis; revolve.

rot'ten (rot'n), a. 1. Putrid; decayed. 2. Unsound, as if rotted; not firm; as, rotten iron.

rough (ruf), a. 1. Having an uneven surface. 2. Coarse. 3. Boisterous; tempestuous.

round (round), n. 1. Anything round, as a circle, globe, or ring. 2. A circular dance. 3. A course ending where it began; a circuit; beat.

route (root), n. The course or way which is, or is to be, traveled. — v.t. To forward or transport by a certain route.

rou-tine' (roo-ten'), n. A regular course of action; customary or mechanical procedure.

roy'al (roi'al), a. 1. Kingly. 2. Characteristic of or befitting a king.

rude (rood), a. 1. Characterized by roughness; rough; harsh; severe. 2. Lacking delicacy or refinement; uncultured; impudent. 3. Unskillful; raw; ignorant.

ru'in (roo'in), n. 1. Destruction. 2. Ruination. 3. That which is fallen down and become worthless from injury or decay. 4. State of decay or worthlessness. — v.t. & i. To bring, fall, go, or come to ruin.

rule (rool), n. 1. A regulation. 2. A controlling principle.

ru'mor (roo'mer), n. 1. A popular report. 2. A story current without known authority for its truth. — v.t. To tell by rumor.

run (run), v.i. 1. To hasten. 2. To move rapidly by springing steps so that for an instant in each step neither foot touches the ground.

run, n. 1. Act of running. 2. a Continuation or course. b A continuing urgent demand, as on a bank for money. c Games, etc. The making of a number of successful shots, strokes, or the like, successively, or the score so made.

ru'ral (roo'ral), a. Of or pertaining to the country or country life; rustic.

rus'tic (rus'tik), a. 1. Rural. 2. Awkward. 3. Befitting the country. — n. An inhabitant of the country.

S

sa'bo'tage' (sa'bo'tazh'), n. Malicious waste or destruction of an employer's property by workmen during labor troubles.

sac'cha-rin (sak'a-rin), n. A coal-tar product several hundred times sweeter than cane sugar.

sa'chet' (sa'sha'), n. A scent bag, or perfumed pad.

sack, n. A bag. — v.t. To bag.

sac'ra-ment (sak'ra-ment), n. 1. One of the solemn religious ceremonies, as baptism, the Eucharist, etc. 2. [Often cap.] The Eucharist.

sa'cred (sa'kred), a. 1. Set apart to religious use. 2. Relating to religion. 3. Inviolable.

sac'ri-fice (sak'ri-fish; -fiz), n. 1. An offering to a deity. 2. Anything consecrated and offered to God or to a divinity. 3. Destruction, surrender, or loss incurred for the sake of something; also, the thing sacrificed.

sad'dle (-l'), n. 1. A seat for a rider on a horse's back, a bicycle, etc. — v.t. 1. To put a saddle on. 2. To load.

safe (saf), a. 1. Free from harm or risk. 2. Conferring safety.

safe, n. A place or receptacle for safe-keeping.

safe'guard (saf'gard'), n. 1. Protection. 2. A safe-conduct. — v.t. To protect.

sa-ga'cious (sa-ga'shus), a. Shrewd;

wise.

sage (saj), n. 1. A half-shrubby, aromatic mint, used to flavor meats, etc. 2. The sagebrush.

sage (saj), a. 1. Wise. 2. Proceeding from wisdom. — n. A profoundly wise man.

sail'boat' (sal'bot'), n. A boat usually propelled by a sail.

sail'or (-er), n. One who sails.

saint (sant), n. 1. A holy or godly person. 2. One of the blessed dead in heaven. 3. One canonized by the church. — v.t. To make a saint of.

saint'ed (san'ted), p.a. 1. Sacred. 2. Canonized.

sake (sak), n. Cause; account.

sal'a-ble (sal'a-b'l), a. Capable of being sold; marketable.

sal'a-man'der (sal'a-man'der), n. Any of numerous harmless amphibians superficially resembling lizards, but having a soft, moist skin.

sal'a-ry (sal'a-ri), n.; pl. -RIES (-riz). A regular recompense paid for services. — v.t. To pay a salary to.

sa-li'va (sa-li'va), n. The secretions of the glands discharging into the mouth.

sal'i-vate (-vat), v.t. To produce saliva.

sal'u-ta'tion (-ta'shun), n. Act of saluting; also, that which is uttered or done in saluting.

sa-lute' (-lut'), v.t. 1. To greet. 2. To show deference to by assuming a prescribed position; as, to salute an officer. — v.i. To make a salute.

sal'vage (sal'vaj), n. Act of saving a vessel or goods from peril; also, the property so saved, or recompense paid for the saving of it.

sal-va'tion (sal-va'shun), n. 1. Act of saving or delivering from evil. 2. In theology, deliverance from sin and its consequences.

same (sam), a. 1. Being identical. 2. Equal.

sanc'tu-a-ry (-tu-a-ri), n. 1. A consecrated and sacred place. 2. A sacred and inviolable place of refuge.

sand (sand), n. A loose granular material resulting from disintegration of rocks. — v.t. To sprinkle or mix with sand.

san'dal (san'dal), n. 1. Kind of shoe covering the sole of the foot only.

sand'pa'per (sand'pa'per), n. Paper coated on one side with sand, used for smoothing and polishing. — v.t. To smooth or polish with sandpaper.

sand'wich (-wich), n. Two pieces of bread having a layer of meat, cheese, or the like, between them. — v.t. To make into a sandwich; also, to insert something between things that are unlike it.

sane (san), a. 1. Mentally sound. 2. Proceeding from a sound mind.

san'guine (-gwin), a. 1. Red; ruddy. 2. Cheerful; hopeful. 3. Warm; ardent.

san'i-ta'tion (-ta'shun), n. Hygiene.

san'i-ty (san'i-ti), n. State or quality of being sane.

sap (sap), n. The juices of a plant.

sap'phire (saf'ir), n. 1. A pure variety of corundum; esp., a blue transparent variety; prized as a gem. 2. The color of the gem; bright blue.

sar'casm (sar'kaz'm), n. A bitter taunt; also, bitter and contemptuous irony.

sar-cas'tic (sar-kas'tik), a. Marked by, or of the nature of, sarcasm; given to the use of sarcasm.

sar-don'ic (sar-don'ik), a. Strained; forced; hence, sneering; bitterly sarcastic; — only of laughter, a smile, etc.

sa-tan'ic (sa-tan'ik), a. Of, pertaining to, or resembling, Satan; devilish.

sat'ire (sat'ir), n. 1. A literary composition, originally in verse, holding up abuses, vice, etc., to ridicule. 2. Biting wit.

sat'is-fac'to-ry (-to-ri), a. Giving satisfaction.

sat'u-rate (sat'u-rat), v.t. To cause to become completely penetrated or soaked.

sauce (sos), n. 1. A condiment or composition of appetizing ingredients eaten with food as a relish. 2. Stewed or preserved fruit. — v.t. 1. To season. 2. To be saucy to.

sau'cer (so'ser), n. 1. Small dish to hold a cup. 2. Something shaped like a saucer.

sav'age (sav'aj), n. 1. Rugged. 2. Untamed. 3. Uncivilized. 4. Cruel; inhuman. — n. 1. A person untaught, uncivilized, or without cultivation. 2. A person of brutal cruelty.

S
T

save (sav), v.t. 1. To make safe. 2. In theology, to deliver from sin and its penalty. 3. To hoard. 4. To spare. — v.i. To avoid expense.

sav'ing (sav'ing), p.a. That saves; as: a Rescuing. b Economizing. c Making reservation or exception. — v.b. n. 1. a Preservation from danger or loss. b Economy in outlay. 2. That which is saved. — prep. or conj. Except.

sav'ior (sav'yer), n. 1. One who saves, or delivers. 2. [cap.] Jesus Christ.

sa'vor (sa'ver), n. 1. Taste and odor. 2. Specific flavor or quality. — v.i. 1. To have a taste or smell. 2. To partake of the quality or nature. — v.t. 1. To season. 2. To appreciate.

sa'vor-y (-i), a. 1. Pleasing to taste or smell. 2. Pleasing morally.

say (sa), v.t. 1. To declare. 2. To repeat. 3. To assert. 4. To suppose. — v.i. To speak. — n. 1. That which is said or to be said. 2. One's turn or right to speak or decide in an affair.

scab (skab), n. An incrustation over a wound.

scaf'fold (skaf'old), n. A platform, as for exhibiting or supporting something, or for executing a criminal. — v.t. To furnish or uphold with a scaffold.

scald (skold), v.t. 1. To burn with hot liquid or steam. 2. To cause to come to a boil. 3. To subject to the action of a boiling liquid. — n. A burn by hot liquid or steam.

scale (skal), n. An instrument for weighing. — v.t. 1. To weigh in scales. 2. To weigh.

scan'dal (skan'dal), n. 1. Injury to reputation, or rumor or general comment causing it. 2. Heedless or malicious defamatory talk. 3. That which causes scandal.

scan'dal-ize (-iz), v.t. To horrify or shock by some action considered immoral or improper.

scant (skant), 1. Scarcely sufficient. 2. Having a small or insufficient supply. — v.t. To limit.

scape'goat' (skap'got'), n. A person or thing bearing blame for others.

scar (skar), n. 1. A mark remaining after a wound or ulcer is healed. 2.

A mark where a fallen leaf was attached. — v.t. & i. To mark with or form a scar or scars.

scarce (skars), a. Deficient in quantity; hence, infrequent; rare. — adv. Scarcely.

scare (skar), v.t. To frighten. — v.t. To be scared. — n. Fright or a fright.

scat'ter (skat'er), v.t. & i. 1. To dissipate. 2. To strew.

scav'en-ger (skav'en-jer), n. Any animal that devours refuse.

scen'er-y (sen'er-i), n. 1. The painted scenes or hangings of a stage, with their accessories. 2. The general aspect of a landscape.

sce'nic (se'nik; sen'ik), a. 1. Of or pertaining to the stage. 2. Affording attractive scenery.

scent (sent), v.t. 1. To smell. 2. To fill with odor. — n. 1. Fragrance. 2. A perfume. 3. The odor left by an animal in passing. 4. Sense of smell.

scheme (skem), n. 1. A systematic plan. 2. A plan or theory of action. — v.t. & i. To plan; plot.

schol'ar (skol'er), n. 1. A student. 2. One who holds a scholarship. 3. A learned person.

schol'ar-ship, n. 1. Character or qualities of a scholar. 2. A foundation for the support of a student.

school, n. 1. A place for instruction. 2. The body of pupils in a school. 3. A sect or denomination in philosophy, medicine, etc. — v.t. 1. To educate in a school. 2. To train.

school'ing, n. 1. Instruction in school. 2. Discipline. 3. Pay for instruction.

sci'ence (si'ens), n. 1. Knowledge, as of principles or facts. 2. Knowledge systematized and formulated with reference to general truths or general laws. 3. Knowledge relating to the physical world. 4. Any branch of systematized knowledge.

sci'en-tist (sc'en-tist), n. One learned in science.

scis'sors (siz'erz), n. pl. A cutting instrument.

scold (skold), v.i. & t. To rebuke harshly.

scope (skop), n. Range or extent of view, intent, action, etc.

scorch (skorch), v.t. To parch by heat or burn superficially. —v.t. To be burnt on the surface.

scorn (skorn), n. Extreme contempt. — v.t. To hold in, or reject with, disdain. — v.i. To scoff.

scor'pi-on (-un), n. Any of numerous insects allied to the spiders, having a narrow tail with a venomous sting at the tip.

scour (skour), v.i. To run swiftly. — v.t. To pass over swiftly.

scourge (skurj), v.t. & t. 1. To whip. 2. To punish or afflict severely. — n. 1. A lash or whip. 2. A means of inflicting punishment or suffering; a cause of calamity or affliction.

scowl (skoul), v.i. To wrinkle the brows, as in frowning; look sullen, angry, or threatening. — n. A frown.

scram'ble (skram'b'l), v.i. 1. To move or clamber with or on hands and feet or knees. 2. To struggle with others for something. — n. A scrambling.

scrap'book (-book'), n. A blank book in which pictures, clippings, etc., may be pasted.

scrape (skrap), v.t. 1. a To rub over the surface of with a sharp or rough instrument. b To remove in this way. 2. To collect by or as by a process of scraping. 3. To draw harshly or roughly over a surface. - v.i. 1. To scrape anything. 2. To occupy one's self with getting goods laboriously. 3. To draw back the foot along the ground or floor when making a bow. — n. 1. Act or sound of scraping. 2. A disagreeable predicament.

scraw'ny (skro'ni), a. Thin; bony.

scream (skrem), v.i. To cry out with a shrill voice. — v.t. To utter as or with a scream. — n. Act or sound of screaming.

screen (skren), n. 1. Anything in the nature of a protective partition or curtain. 2. A surface on which an image is thrown by a magic lantern, etc. 3. A coarse sieve. — v.t. 1. To shelter. 2. To sift through a screen.

scrib'ble (skrib'l), v.t. To write hastily or carelessly. — v.i. To scrawl. — n. Hasty or careless writing.

scribe (skrib), n. One who writes.

scrim'mage (skrim'aj), n. A confused struggle.

Scrip'tur-al (skrip'tur-al), a. Pertaining to, contained in, or according to, the Scriptures.

scrip'ture (-tur), n. 1. [cap.] The Bible. 2. Any sacred writing.

scroll (skrol), n. 1. A roll of paper or parchment. 2. Something, as an ornament, in form resembling a roll of paper.

scru'ple (skroo'p'l), n. 1. A minute portion. 2. Hesitation from difficulty in determining what is right or proper. — v.i. & t. To have scruples.

scru'pu-lous (skroo'pu-lus), a. Full of or having scruples.

scru'ti-nize (skroo'ti-niz), v.t. & i. To examine closely.

sculp'tor (skulp'ter), n. One who sculptures.

sculp'ture (-tur), n. Act or art of sculpturing. — v.t. To form with the chisel or other tool on, in, or from, wood, stone, metal, etc.

scum (skum), n. 1. Extraneous matter risen to, or formed on, the surface of liquids. 2. Refuse; low people.

sea (se), n. 1. One of the larger bodies of salt water. 2. A large inland body of water. 3. The ocean as a whole. 4. The swell of the ocean.

sea gull. Any gull frequenting the sea.

seal (sel), n. A marine carnivorous mammal, of various species, chiefly of the colder regions, hunted for its fur, hide, etc. —v.i. To hunt seals.

seam (sem), n. 1. The fold or line formed by sewing together pieces of cloth, etc. 2. A line of junction. 3. Geol. A thin stratum. 4. A scar. — v.t. 1. To form a seam upon or of. 2. To line; scar.

seam'stress (sem'stres), n. A needlewoman.

se'ance (sa'ans; sa'ans'), n. 1. A session. 2. A meeting to receive spirit communications.

search (surch), v.t. 1. To look over or through, in order to find something. 2. To inquire after. 3. To probe. 4. To examine. — v.i. To seek; investigate. — n. Act of searching.

search warrant. Law. A warrant authorizing a search of a house, etc., as for stolen goods.

sea'sick'ness, n. Nausea caused by the pitching or rolling of a vessel.

sea'son (se'z'n), n. 1. One of the divisions of the year, as spring,

S
T

summer, autumn, and winter. 2. A period of the year set off as by special activity. — v.t. 1. To fit or adapt for use or a given condition; as: a to habituate. b To cure. 2. To render palatable. 3. To moderate. — v.i. To become fit for use or adapted to a condition.

sea'son'ing, n. 1. Act or process by which anything is seasoned. 2. That which is added to give zest or relish.

seat (set), n. 1. The place, part, or thing on which one sits; anything made to sit in or on. 2. Location. 3. A right to sit. — v.t. 1. To place on a seat. 2. To cause to occupy a post, site, or situation. 3. To furnish with seats. **sea'wor'thy** (se'wur-thi), a. Fit for a sea voyage.

se-cede' (se-sed'), v.i. To withdraw from fellowship.

se-clude' (-klood), v.t. To shut up apart from others; place in solitude.

sec'ond (sek'und), a. 1. Immediately after the first in place or time. 2. Next to the first in value, power, rank, etc. — n. 1. One that is second. 2. One who attends another to support and aid him. — v.t. 1. To act as the second of. 2. In parliamentary practice, to support.

sec're-ta-ry (sek're-ta-ri), n. 1. One who attends to orders, letters, etc., for an organization or an individual. 2. An officer of state in charge of a department. 3. A writing desk.

se-cre'tive (-tiv), a. Disposed to secrecy.

sec'tion-al (-al), a. 1. Of or pertaining to a section. 2. Consisting of sections.

sec'u-lar (-u-lar), a. Of or pert. to this world; worldly.

se-cure' (se-kur'), a. 1. Confident. 2. Confident in opinion. 3. Safe. 4. Free from uncertainty. — v.t. 1. To make safe. 2. To put beyond hazard of losing. 3. To make fast. 4. To get.

se-date' (-dat'), a. Undisturbed by passion or caprice.

sed'en-ta-ry (-en-ta'ri), a. 1. Stationary. 2. Accustomed to sit much.

sed'i-ment (sed'i-ment), n. 1. The matter which settles to the bottom from a liquid. 2. Geol. Material deposited, as by water.

se-duce' (se-dus'), v.t. To lead aside or astray; corrupt.

se-duc'tive (-tiv), a. Tending to seduce; tempting.

see, v.t. 1. To perceive with the eye. 2. To comprehend. 3. To make sure. — v.i. 1. To have or use the sense of light. 2. To discern. 3. To be attentive.

seek (sek), v.t. 1. To look for. 2. To ask for. 3. To try to acquire or gain. — v.i. To make search or inquiry.

seem (sem), v.i. To appear.

se'er (se'er; ser), n. 1. One that sees. 2. One who foresees or foretells events.

seg're-gate (seg're-gat), a. Separate. — (-gat), v.t. To separate or set apart.

seize (sez), v.t. 1. To take possession of by force. 2. To lay hold of suddenly or forcibly. 3. To grasp with the mind. — v.i. To take, or take possession.

sei'zure (se'zhur), n. 1. Act of seizing. 2. Sudden attack.

sel'dom (sel'dum), adv. Rarely.

se-lect' (se-lekt'), a. Taken from a larger number by preference. — v.t. To take by preference.

self (self), a. 1. Same. 2. Having its own or a single nature or character.

self'ish (sel'fish), a. Caring unduly for one's self.

sell (sel), v.t. 1. To transfer property for a consideration. 2. To make a matter of bargain and sale. — v.i. 1. To sell commodities. 2. To be sold.

sem'blance (-blans), n. 1. Image. 2. Seeming. 3. Resemblance.

se-mes'ter (se-mes'ter), n. Either of the two terms into which the period of instruction is divided in many colleges.

sem'i-co'lon (sem'i-ko'lon), n. Punctuation. The mark [;] indicating a separation between parts of a sentence more distinct than that marked by a comma.

sem'i-nar' (sem'i-nar'), n. A group of students engaged, under an instructor, in original research.

sen-sa'tion (sen-sa'shun), n. 1. A feeling produced by an external object (stimulus). 2. Any feeling. 3. A state of excited interest or feeling.

sen-sa'tion-al (-al), a. 1. Of or

pertaining to sensation or sensa-
tionalism. 2. Melodramatic.

sense (sens), n. 1. Meaning. 2.
Perception through the intellect. 3.
Sound perception and reasoning. 4.
Moral perception or appreciation. 5.
The faculty of receiving mental
impressions through certain organs
of the body. — v.t. To understand.

sen'si-ble (sen'si-b'l), a. 1. Capable of
being perceived. 2. Capable of
receiving impressions from external
objects. 3. Perceiving, or having
perception. 4. Wise.

sen'so-ry (sen'so-ri), a. 1. Of or pert.
to sensation. 2. Pertaining to sense.

sen'su-al (sen'shoo-al), a. 1. Carnal;
fleshly. 2. Devoted to the pleasures
of sense.

sen'tence (sen'tens), n. 1. An opinion;
judgment. 2. Gram. A combination
of words complete as expressing a
thought, and in writing marked at
the close by a period, question
mark, or exclamation point. — v.t.
To pass or pronounce judgment on.

sen'ti-ment (sen'ti-ment), n. 1.
Feeling. 2. A mental attitude,
thought, or judgment prompted by
feeling. 3. Refined feeling.

sen'ti-men'tal (-men'tal), a. 1. Of the
nature of, or marked by, sentiment.
2. Affectedly or excessively tender
or emotional.

sen'ti-nel (sen'ti-nel), n. A guard;
sentry.

sep'a-rate (-rat), v.t. 1. To divide. 2. To
intervene. — v.i. 1. To part. 2. To
divide. — (-rat), a. 1. Separated. 2.
Unconnected. 3. Single.

sep'a-ra'tion (-ra'shun), n. A
separating.

Sep-tem'ber (sep-tem'ber), n. The
ninth month of the year, containing
thirty days.

se'quel (se'kwel), n. 1. That which
follows. 2. Consequence.

se'quence (se'kwens), n. 1. State of
being sequent; succession. 2. An
effect, result. 3. Order of events in
time; as, in chronological sequence.

se-ques'ter (se-kwes'ter), v.t. 1. Law.
To separate (property) from the
owner for a time, until a demand is
satisfied. 2. To cause to retire or
withdraw into obscurity; seclude;
also, to separate.

ser'e-nade' (ser'e-nad'), n. Music. a
Music as sung or played in the
open air at night, esp. for gallantry,
under the windows of ladies. b A
piece of music suitable for such
performance. — v.t. & i. To entertain
with a serenade; perform a
serenade.

se-rene' (se-ren'), a. 1. Bright. 2.
Calm.

se'ri-al (se'ri-al), a. Of, pertaining to,
or arranged in, a series, rank, or
row; appearing in successive parts
or numbers. —n. 1. A serial
publication. 2. A tale, or other
writing, published in successive
numbers of a periodical.

se'ri-ous (se'ri-us), a. 1. Grave in
disposition; earnest. 2. Important;
weighty. 3. Attended with danger.

ser'mon (sur'mun), n. 1. A public
religious discourse grounded on
Scripture. 2. A serious address; a
lecture on conduct or duty; —often
depreciatory.

ser'pent (sur'pent), n. 1. A snake. 2. A
subtle, treacherous person.

serv'ant (sur'vant), n. 1. One
employed by another, esp. for
menial offices. 2. Law. An agent
subject to control of his principal.

serve (surv), v.t. 1. To work for; be in
the employment of, as an inferior,
domestic, slave, helper, etc., in a
religious sense, to obey and
worship. 2. To wait upon, as at table
or in a shop. 3. To bring forward,
arrange, or distribute, as food. —
v.i. 1. To be or act as a servant or a
slave. 2. To perform domestic
offices; prepare and dish up food,
etc. 3. To do duty as a soldier, etc.

ser'vi-tude (-tud), n. 1. Condition of a
slave; bondage. 2. Penal service. 3.
Condition of a servant or servitor;
menial service.

ses'sion (sesh'un), n. The sitting, or
time of sitting, of a court, legislature, etc.

set'back' (set'bak'), n. A setting back,
reverse.

set'tle-ment (-ment), n. 1. Act of
settling; state of being settled. 2.
That which settles, or is settled,
established, or fixed. 3. A settled
place of abode; a colony. 4. Law. A
disposition of property for the

S
T

benefit of some one.

sev'er (-er), v.t. & t. 1. To separate, as one from another; divide; part, esp. by cutting, rending, etc. 2. To cut or break open or apart; disjoin.

sev'er-al (-al), a. 1. Individual; single; separable. 2. Diverse; various. 3. Consisting of more than two, but not many.

sew (so), v.t. To unite or fasten by stitches. — v.i. To work with needle and thread.

sex (seks), n. 1. Character of being male or female, or of pertaining to the distinctive function of the male or female. 2. One of the two divisions of organisms distinguished as male and female.

sex'u-al (sek'shu-al), a. Pertaining to sex or the sexes.

shab'by (shab'i), a. 1. Torn or much worn. 2. Clothed with worn or seedy garments. 3. Mean.

shack (shak), n. A hut; shanty. Colloq.

shack'le (shak'l), n. 1. A manacle; fetter; — usually in pl. 2. That which prevents free action, as if by fetters. 3. Any of various fastening devices, as a link for coupling cars. — v.t. To bind or fasten with a shackle; chain.

shade (shad), n. 1. Comparative obscurity owing to interception of the rays of light. 2. Darkness; obscurity. 3. A retired or secluded place. 4. That which intercepts, or shelters from, the sun's direct rays; screen. — v.t. 1. To shelter; screen. 2. To obscure; dim. 3. To paint in obscure colors; darken. 4. To make with gradations of light or color. — v.i. To undergo or exhibit minute difference or variation, as of color, meaning, etc.

shad'ow (shad'o), n. 1. Shade within defined limits; partial darkness in a space from which rays are cut off by a body, or any image thus made on an intersecting surface. 2. Darkness; obscurity. 3. A shaded or darker portion of a picture. 4. A reflected image, as in water. — v.t. 1. To cut off light from; shade. 2. To mark with gradations light or color; shade. 3. To represent faintly, mystically, etc.

shag'gy (-i), a. 1. Rough with or as with long hair or wool. 2. Thick and

rough, tangled, or irregular in surface, as hair.

shak'y (shak'i), a. 1. Liable to shake. 2. Easily shaken; unsound. 3. Questionable; uncertain; unreliable. Colloq.

shal'low (shal'o), a. 1. Not deep. 2. Superficial. — n. A shoal.

sham (sham), n. A fraud. — a. False. — v.t. & i. To feign.

sham'ble (-b'l), v.i. To walk unsteadily.

shame'ful (-fool), a. 1. Bringing shame or disgrace; disgraceful. 2. Exciting shame; indecent.

sham'rock (sham'rok), n. A three-leaved plant used as a national emblem by the Irish.

share'hold'er (-hol'der), n. A holder of a share or shares.

shark (shark), n. 1. Any of numerous voracious fishes, esp. abundant in warm seas. 2. A rapacious person.

shat'ter (shat'er), v.t. 1. To break at once into pieces; rend into splinters. 2. To disorder; derange; impair. — v.i. To break into fragments.

shave (shav), v.t. 1. To cut or pare, as by the sliding movement of a razor; cut off (hair) close to the skin with a razor. 2. To cut off thin slices from 3. To skim along or near the surface of. — v.i. To remove hair with a razor; be hard and severe in a bargain; practice extortion; cheat. — n. 1. A thin slice; shaving. 2. Act of shaving, esp. the beard.

she (she), pron. 1. The female previously referred to. 2. A woman; a female person or animal.

shear (sher), v.t. 1. To cut, clip, or sever something from, esp. wool from sheep. 2. To clip. — n. A machine for shearing metal.

shears (sherz), n.pl. Any of various instruments consisting of two blades so fastened together that the edges slide one by the other, used for cutting cloth, etc.; large scissors.

shed (shed), n. A slight structure for shelter or storage, as for a wagon or airplane or for wood.

sheen (shen), n. Brightness; splendor.

shelf (shelf), n. A thin, flat, usually long and narrow, piece set horizontally, as on a wall, to set things on; a ledge.

shel'ter (-ter), n. 1. That which covers

or defends. 2. State of being covered and protected. — v.t. 1. To be a shelter for; shield; protect. 2. To take or betake to cover, or safety. — v.i. To take shelter.

shep'herd (shep'erd), n. A herder of sheep. — v.t. To tend, guard, lead, or drive as a shepherd.

sher'bet (shur-bet), n. A water ice.

sher'iff (sher'if), n. The chief executive officer of a shire or country, esp. charged with execution of the laws and preservation of the peace.

shift (shift), v.t. 1. To move or remove; transfer. 2. To exchange; change. — v.i. 1. To change position. 2. To manage. 3. To practice indirection or evasion. — n. 1. Act of shifting; as: a Change. b A turn. 2. The change of one set of workmen for another.

shim'mer (shim'er), v.i. To shine with a faint, tremulous light. — n. A glimmer.

ship'ment (-ment), n. Act of shipping goods for transportation, also, the goods.

shirt (shurt), n. A loose undergarment for the upper part of the body.

shiv'er, v.t. To tremble; quiver; shake, as from cold or fear. — n. A shivering.

shod'dy (shod'i), n. 1. A fibrous material got by shredding refuse woolen or cotton goods. 2. A cloth entirely or largely of shoddy; an inferior person or thing claiming superiority. — a. Wholly or in part of shoddy.

shoe'horn' (-horn'), n. A curved piece, as of horn, to aid in sliding on a shoe.

shoot (shoot), v.t. 1. To send out or forth, esp. rapidly or suddenly; to cast; throw; emit; discharge. 2. To let fly, or project, with force from a bow, gun, or the like. 3. To discharge (a gun, etc.). 4. To hit, kill, or wound with a missile. — v.i. 1. To drive or rush swiftly. 2. To dart with a piercing sensation. 3. To bud. 4. To cause a bow, gun, etc., to discharge a missile. — n. 1. a A shooting match. b A hunt. 2. A sending out of new growth; also, the new growth.

shop (shop), n. 1. A building or apartment where goods are retailed; store. 2. A place where mechanics or artisans work. 3. [Often in pl.] Any factory. — v.i. To visit shops in order to buy or inspect goods.

shop'lift'er (-lif'ter), n. One who steals from a shop.

short'age (shor'taj), n. A deficiency or deficit.

short'en (shor't'n), v.t. 1. To make short or shorter; abridge. 2. To make brittle; as pastry, with butter, lard, etc. — v.i. To become short or shorter.

short'hand' (short'hand'), n. A rapid method of writing by substituting characters, abbreviations, or symbols, for letters, words, etc., stenography.

short'ly, adv. 1. In a short or brief time or manner. 2. In few words; briefly. 3. Abruptly curtly.

short'sight'ed (short'sit'ed), a. 1. Nearsighted. 2. Lacking foresight.

short'-wind'ed (-win'ded), a. Having a quick, difficult respiration, or unable to make much violent exertion without having such respiration.

shoul'der (shol'der), n. 1. The projecting part of the human body formed by the bones and muscles where the arm joins the trunk. 2. A projection, or part suggestive of the human shoulder. — v.t. & i. 1. To push with the shoulder. 2. To assume the burden of.

shout (shout), v.i. To utter a sudden and loud cry. — v.t. To utter with a shout. — n. A vehement outcry.

shove (shuv), v.t. To push. — v.i. To move off, along, or onward by pushing or jostling. — n. Act of shoving; push.

show (sho), v.t. 1. To exhibit or present to view; display. 2. To tell; disclose; reveal. 3. To direct; guide. 4. To make apparent or clear. 5. To bestow; confer. — v.i. 1. To present an appearance; look. 2. To be noticeable. 3. To make an appearance; exhibition. 2. That which is shown; display; exhibition. 3. Parade; pomp.

shrewd (shrood), a. 1. Biting. 2. Artful.

3. Clever in practical affairs.

shriek (shrek), v.i. To utter a sharp, shrill sound or cry. — v.i. To utter in or with a shriek or shrieks. — n. A sharp, shrill outcry; scream.

shrimp (shrimp), n. 1. Any of numerous small, mostly marine, crustaceans. Many are used as food. 2. A little wrinkled or puny person.

shrine (shrin), n. 1. A case or box for sacred relics. 2. Tomb of a saint. 3. Place consecrated to some deity or saint. — v.t. To enshrine.

shriv'el (shriv'l), v.i. & t. To draw into wrinkles; shrink.

shrug (shrug), v.t. & i. To draw up or contract (the shoulders), esp. in dislike; doubt, etc. — n. Act of shrugging.

shud'der (shud'er), v.i. To tremble involuntarily; shiver. — A shuddering.

shun (shun), v.t. To avoid; keep clear of.

shut (shut), v.t. 1. To close to ingress or egress. 2. To forbid entrance into; bar. 3. To preclude; exclude. 4. To fold together; close up parts of.

shy (shi), a. 1. Easily frightened, timid. 2. Bashful; coy. 3. Wary; suspicious.

sick (sik), a. 1. Affected with disease. 2. Having, or attended by, nausea. 3. Disordered.

sick'ly (-li), a. 1. Somewhat sick. 2. Characteristic or indicative of sickness. 3. Marked by or producing disease. 4. Appearing as if sick; pale.

side'walk' (-wok'), n. A walk for foot passengers at the side of a street or road; foot pavement.

siege (sej), n. The besetting of a fortified place by an army.

sigh (si), v.i. 1. To make a deep, audible respiration, esp. from fatigue, grief, sorrow, etc. 2. To lament. 3. To make a sound like sighing, as wind. — Act of sighing.

sight (sit), n. 1. Power or act of seeing. 2. That which is seen; a spectacle; something worth seeing. 3. Visibility; open view; range of vision. — v.t. 1. To get sight of; see. 2. To look at through or as through a sight. 3. To direct by means of a sight or sights; as, to sight a rifle. —

v.i. To take aim by a sight.

sig'nal (sig'nal), n. A sign made to give notice of something, as of a command or danger. — a. Noticeable; extraordinary. — v.t. & i. To communicate or to notify by a signal or signals.

sig'na-ture (-tur), n. 1. A person's name written with his own hand.

sig-nif'i-cant (-kant), a. Fitted or designed to signify something; having a meaning; full of meaning; expressive or suggestive.

si'lent (si'lent), a. 1. Making no utterance; mute; taciturn. 2. Free from sound or noise; still. 3. a Unuttered; unexpressed. b Pron. Not pronounced; as e in fire.

sil'hou-ette' (sil'oo-et'), n. An outline figure of an object filled in, usually in black; a profile of this kind, as in a shadow. — v.t. To represent by, or project so as to form, a silhouette.

silk (silk), n. 1. A fine, strong, lustrous fiber produced by various insect larvae, usually to form a cocoon; esp., that of silkworms, used for weaving into fabrics; also, thread or fabric made of it. 2. The silky styles on an ear of Indian corn.

sil'ly (sil'i), a. 1. Weak in intellect; foolish. 2. Stupid.

sim'i-lar (-lar), a. 1. Nearly corresponding; having a general likeness. 2. Geom. Having the same shape, differing only in size and position; — said of figures.

sim'mer (sim'er), v.i. & t. To boil gently; cook in liquid heated almost or just to boiling.

sim'ple (-p'l), a. 1. Single; uncompounded; uncombined; elementary; esp., Bot., having only one blade, or not compound, as a leaf. 2. Free from intricacy; easy to understand or solve; plain. 3. Unadorned; plain, not luxurious. — n. 1. Something not mixed or compounded. 2. A medicinal plant.

sim-plic'i-ty (sim-plis'i-ti), n.; pl. -TIES (-tiz). 1. Quality or state of being simple; clearness; plainness. 2. Artlessness. 3. Lack of sagacity.

sim'pli-fy (sim'pli-fi), v.t. To make simple; show an easier way of doing, making, etc.

si'mul-ta'ne-ous (si'mul-ta'ne-us;

sim'ul-), a. Existing, happening, or done, at the same time.

sin (sin), n. 1. Transgression of the law of God. 2. An offense; misdemeanor. — v.i. To violate the divine law by transgression or neglect; violate any rule of duty. — v.t. To do or commit sinfully; to commit (a sin).

since (sins), adv. 1. a From a definite past time until now. b Subsequent to a certain past time and before the present. 2. In the time past; before this or now; ago. — prep. From the time of; subsequently to; after. — conj. 1. From and after the time when. 2. Seeing that; because.

sin-cere' (sin-ser'), a. Genuine; true; real.

sin'ful (-fool), a. Tainted with sin.

sing (sing), v.i. 1. To utter vocal sounds with musical inflections or melodious modulations. 2. To produce harmonious or pleasing sounds, as a brook. 3. To make a small, shrill sound. — v.t. 1. To utter with musical inflections or modulations. 2. To chant; intone. 3. To celebrate in song or in verse.

sin'gu-lar (sin'gu-lar), a. 1. Gram. Denoting one person or thing; as, the singular number. 2. Separate from others; alone; hence: a Unique; unparalleled. b Unusual; strange. c Eminent; exceptional. d Odd; whimsical. — n. Gram. The singular number, the inflectional form denoting it, or a word in that form.

sir (sur), n. 1. A title prefixed [cap.] to the Christian name of a knight or a baronet. 2. A respectful title used in addressing a man without using his name.

si'ren (si'ren), n. 1. An enticing, dangerous woman. 2. A kind of compressed-air fog signal.

sis'ter (sis'ter), n. 1. A female considered in her relation to another having the same parents. 2. A woman closely associated with another or others, as in the same sisterhood, order, etc.

sis'ter-in-law', n. Sister of one's husband or wife; also, the wife of one's brother.

sit (sit), v.i. 1. To rest on the haunches or buttocks. 2. To perch; rest with the feet drawn up, as birds. 3. To be situated; lie, rest, or bear. — v.t. 1. To set on, as a horse. 2. To cause to be seated.

sit'u-a'tion (-a'shun), n. 1. Manner or position in which an object is placed; locality; site. 2. Position as regards conditions and circumstances; state. 3. Position of employment; office.

siz'a-ble (siz'a-b'l), a. Of suitable size; usually, of considerable bulk.

size, n. 1. Extent of surface or volume. 2. A conventional relative measure of dimension. — v.t. To adjust or arrange according to size.

skel'e-ton (skel'e-tun), n. 1. The bones collectively. 2. Framework or outline of anything.

skep'tic (skep'tik), n. One whose attitude is critical or is marked by doubt. — a. Skeptical.

sketch (skech), n. 1. An outline; rough draft; a slight preliminary draft. 2. A simply constructed literary composition, as a short story. — v.t. To outline; make a rough draft of. — v.i. To make a sketch or sketches.

ski (ske), n. One of a pair of long strips of wood bound one on each foot for gliding over snow. — v.i. To use ski.

skill (skil), n. Knowledge of, and expertness in, execution or performance.

skim, v.t. 1. To clear (a liquid) from scum or floating substance; also, to take off by skimming. 2. To pass swiftly or lightly over. 3. To read or examine superficially and rapidly. — v.i. 1. To pass lightly or hastily; glide along evenly and smoothly, esp. near the surface. 2. To skip or ricochet over a surface, as of water.

skin'ny (skin'i), a. 1. Of the nature of skin. 2. Emaciated.

skull (skul), n. The skeleton of the head or a vertebrate; the cranium and parts united with it.

sky (ski), n. 1. The upper atmosphere. 2. The heavens. 3. Heaven.

slack (slak), a. 1. Slow. 2. Sluggish. 3. Remiss; inattentive. 4. Inactive; dull. 5. Lax; not tense. — n. The part of anything (as a rope) that hangs loose. — adv. Slackly.

slam (slam), v.t. & i. 1. To shut

S
T

violently; bang. 2. To put in or on some place, or strike, forcibly and noisily. — n. Act of slamming, or the noise so made.

slan'der (slan'der), n. Defamation, oral or written. — v.t. To utter slander against.

slap (slap), n. A blow, esp. one from or as from the open hand; also, a rebuff; insult. — v.t. 1. To slap.

slash (slash), v.t. To cut by sweeping strokes; gash. — v.i. To strike violently and at random, esp. with or as with an edged instrument. — n. 1. Act of slashing, or a cut so made; gash. 2. A stroke with a whip.

slaugh'ter (slo'ter), n. Act of killing; as: a Carnage. b Act of butchering for market. — v.t. 1. To kill, esp. ruthlessly or in large numbers. 2. To butcher.

slave (slav), n. 1. A person held in bondage. 2. One who has lost control of himself. 3. A drudge. — v.i. To labor as a slave.

slav'er-y (slav'er-i), n. 1. The condition of a slave; bondage. 2. The institution of holding slaves. 3. A condition like that of a slave. 4. Drudgery.

slay (sla), v.t. To destroy.

slea'zy (sle'zi; sla'zi), a. Wanting firmness, as of texture; flimsy.

sled (sled), n. 1. A sledge. 2. A small vehicle with runners for sliding on snow or ice. — v.t. To convey on a sled.

sleep (slep), v.i. 1. To be or pass time in the condition of repose called sleep; slumber. 2. a To lie dormant. b To be dead. — v.t. To get rid of in or by sleep. — n. 1. A natural, temporary and periodical, diminution or virtual cessation of consciousness. 2. Rest or repose.

slen'der (slen'der), a. 1. Small or narrow in proportion to the length or height; slim. 2. Weak. 3. Small.

slice (slis), n. A thin, broad piece, esp. one cut off. — v.t. 1. To cut into slices; cut a slice from. Also fig. 2. To remove as a slice; cut off.

slide (slid), v.i. 1. To move freely along a surface, as on snow or ice, with little friction; glide. 2. To move or go easily, quietly, quickly, or secretly.

— v.t. 1. To cause to slide along a surface. 2. To pass or put quietly or imperceptibly; slip. — n. 1. Act of sliding. 2. That on which anything moves by sliding. 3. Something that operates by sliding.

slim (slim), a. 1. Frail. 2. Slender. 3. Small in numbers.

slip'per (slip'er), n. 1. One that slips. 2. A kind of light shoe, easily slipped on or off.

slip'per-y (-er-i), a. 1. Allowing anything to slip; having a smooth or slimy surface. 2. Untrustworthy, tricky.

slop'py (slop'i), a. 1. Wet so as to spatter easily; wet as if spattered. 2. Slovenly; careless.

sloth (sloth; sloth), n. 1. Laziness; indolence. 2. Any of several slow-moving arboreal mammals of tropical America.

slouch (slouch), n. 1. A hanging of the head; ungainly gait. 2. An awkward fellow.

slow (slo), a. 1. Moving at a low speed. 2. Not happening in a short time; gradual. 3. Not quick; sluggish. — adv. Slowly. — v.t. To render slow; delay. — v.i. To go slower.

slum (slum), n. A foul street of a city, esp. one with a slovenly, often vicious, population.

slum'ber (-ber), v.i. 1. To sleep. 2. To be in a state of negligence or inactivity. — n. Sleep, esp. light sleep; doze.

slump (slump), n. A falling or declining, esp. suddenly and markedly; a falling off; as, a slump in prices. Colloq. — v.i. 1. To fall or sink suddenly, as into a bog, etc. 2. To undergo a slump. Colloq.

slush (slush), n. A mixture of snow and water.

sly (sli), a. 1. Artful; crafty; marked by artful secrecy; subtle. 2. Lightly artful; roguish.

smack, n. 1. Taste or flavor. 2. A smattering. 3. A loud kiss. — v.i. 1. To have a smack, or savor, of anything. 2. To suggest by its quality. 3. To make a noise by separation of the lips. — v.t. 1. To make a smack (of the lips). 2. To strike so as to make a sharp noise.

small (smol), a. 1. Relatively little in size. 2. Little, or not large, in number, duration, value, etc.

smart (smart), v.i. 1. To feel or cause a pungent local pain. 2. To feel sharp pain or grief; suffer. — v.t. To cause to smart. — n. 1. A quick, pungent pain; a prickling local pain. 2. Sharp pain of mind. — a. 1. Stinging. 2. Vigorous. 3. Brisk; fresh.

smell (smel), v.t. 1. To perceive by the olfactory nerves, or organs of smell; get the scent of. 2. To detect, perceive, or investigate. — v.i. 1. To have an odor or scent. 2. To savor or smack. — n. 1. The sense by which certain qualities of sub-stances are perceived by means of the olfactory nerves. 2. A sensation of odor, scent, perfume, etc. 3. An act or instance of smelling.

smile (smil), v.i. 1. To have, produce, or exhibit a smile. 2. To look joyous. 3. To favor. — n. 1. A facial expression marked by an upward curving of the corners of the mouth. 2. Favor. 3. Gay or joyous appear-ance.

smirk (smurk), v.i. To smile in an affected or conceited way. — n. An affected smile.

smoke (smok), n. 1. The gaseous products of burning materials, made visible by carrying small particles of carbon, which settle as soot. 2. Any visible fumes. 3. Something unsubstantial or ephemeral. — v.i. 1. To emit or exhale smoke. 2. To smoke a pipe, cigar, etc. — v.t. 1. To apply smoke to; disinfect, cure, etc., by smoke. 2. To fill or scent with smoke. 3. To subject to the action of smoke, as for driving out, stupefying, etc. 4. To inhale and puff out the smoke of, as tobacco.

smooth (smooth), a. 1. Not rough. 2. Evenly spread or arranged. 3. Without lumps or with perfect blending of the elements. 4. Without hair. 5. Gently flowing. — adv. Smoothly. — v.t. 1. To make smooth or even. 2. To make easy. 3. To free from harshness.

smoth'er (smuth'er), n. 1. That which smothers or stifles, as smoke, fog, etc. 2. A state of smoldering or of suppression. — v.t. 1. To suffocate. 2. To stifle. 3. To suppress. — v.i. 1. To be suffocated or stifled. 2. To be suppressed or deprived of vent, as wrath.

smug'gle (smug'l), v.t. & i. 1. To import or export secretly an contrary to law or without paying duties imposed by law. 2. To convey or introduce secretly.

snake (snak), n. Any of numerous limbless, very slender reptiles.

snap'pish (-ish), a. 1. Apt to snap at persons or things. 2. Apt to speak sharply or testily.

snarl, v.i. To growl; grumble. — v.t. To utter or express with a snarl or by snarling. — n. A growl; a surly or peevish expression.

snatch (snach), v.t. To seize abruptly, or without ceremony. — v.i. To try to seize something suddenly. — n. 1. A hasty catching or seizing; a grab. 2. A short period. 3. A small piece or fragment; scrap.

sneeze (snez), v.i. To make a sudden, violent, spasmodic, and audible expiration of breath, through the nose. — n. Act or fact of sneezing.

snick'er (snik'er), v.i. To laugh in a partly suppressed manner; giggle. — n. A half-suppressed, broken laugh; giggle.

sniff (snif), v.i. To draw air audibly up the nose. — v.t. 1. To draw in through the nose. 2. To smell. — n. Act or sound of sniffing.

snore (snor), v.i. To breathe during sleep with a rough noise.

snow (sno), n. Watery particles congealed into white or transparent crystals or flakes in the air and falling or fallen to the earth. — v.i. To fall in or as snow. —v.t. 1. To shower down like snow. 2. To cover, or shut in, with snow.

snub (snub), v.t. 1. To check or rebuke with a tart, sarcastic remark. 2. To neglect or slight (a person) designedly. — n. A check or rebuke; an intended slight. —a. Short and turned up; — said of the nose.

snug (snug), a. 1. Trim; tidy. 2. Close; concealed. 3. Fitting closely.

snug'gle (-'l), v.i. To move one way and the other to get close. — v.t. To draw close, as for comfort; cuddle.

S
T

soak (sok), v.t. 1. To saturate in a fluid; steep. 2. To drench. 3. To draw in by pores or interstices. 4. To permeate; saturate. —v.i. 1. To become saturated. 2. To enter (into something) by pores or interstices. — n. 1. A soaking; state of being soaked. 2. Liquid in which anything is soaked.

soap (sop), n. A cleansing agent soluble in water, made, usually, by action of alkali on fat. — v.t. To rub or wash over with soap.

so'ber (so'ber), a. 1. Free from the influence of an intoxicant; not drunk; also, temperate in the use of liquor. 2. Temperate or moderate in thought or action; self-controlled. 3. Not proceeding from or attended with passion; clam.

so'cial-ism (-iz'm), n. A political and economic theory of social reorganization, the essential feature of which is governmental control of economic activities.

so-ci'e-ty (so-si'e-ti), n. 1. The relationship of men associated in any way. 2. A number or body of persons associated for mutual or joint usefulness, pleasure, or profit. 3. The more cultivated or fashionable portion of any community.

so'fa (so'fa), n. A kind of long seat, usually upholstered and having a back and arms.

soft (soft), a. 1. Easily impressed. 2. Susceptible. 3. Delicate. 4. Expressing gentleness. — adv. Softly.

soil, n. 1. The loose surface material of the earth in which plants grow. 2. Firm land. — v.t. To enrich with soil or muck.

sol'ace (sol'as), n. Comfort in grief. — v.t. 1. To cheer in grief or calamity; console. 2. To soothe. 3. To cheer.

sol'dier (sol'jer), n. 1. One engaged in military service. 2. An enlisted man. — v.i. 1. To serve as a soldier.

sole'ly (sol'li), adv. Alone.

sol'emn (sol'em), a. 1. Marked with religious rites and pomps. 2. Serious. 3. Inspiring serious thought.

so-lem'ni-ty (so-lem'ni-ti), n. 1. A religious or ritual ceremony; hence, any ceremony, celebration, or

formal festivity. 2. Seriousness; gravity. 3. Awe or reverence.

so-lic'it (so-lis'it), v.t. 1. To ask earnestly; petition. 2. To seek; plead for. - v.i. To make solicitation.

so-lic'i-ta'tion (so-lis'i-ter), n. 1. One who solicits. 2. Law. a In England, one admitted to practice law (but not to plead) in any court. b The law officer of a city, government, etc.

sol'id (sol'id), a. 1. Capable of resisting, up to a certain limit, forces tending to deform; not liquid or gaseous. 2. Not hollow; full of matter; dense. 3. Cubic; as, a solid foot. — n. 1. A solid substance or body. 2. A magnitude having three dimensions.

sol'i-dar'i-ty (sol'i-dar'i-ti), n. An entire union or consolidation of interests and responsibilities.

sol'i-taire' (sol'i-tar'), n. 1. A single diamond or (sometimes) other gem set alone. 2. A game (as cards) which one person can play alone.

sol'i-ta-ry (sol'i-ta-ri), a. 1. Living or being by one's self or by itself; single. 2. Lonely; desolate; deserted. 3. Single; sole.

so'lo (so'lo), n.An air, strain, or a whole piece, played or sung by one person, with or without accompaniment.

solve (solv), v.t. To clear up (what is obscure or difficult); explain; settle.

sol'vent (-vent), a. 1. Able to dissolve. 2. Able to pay all just debts. — n. A liquid capable of, or used in, dissolving something.

some'how' (-hou'), adv. In one way or another.

some'thing (sum'thing), n. 1. A certain indefinite thing. 2. A thing or a person of importance. — adv. In some degree.

some'time' (-tim'), adv. 1. At a past time indefinitely referred to. 2. Once in a while. 3. At one time or other hereafter. — a. Having been formerly.

some'where' (-hwar'), adv. In or to a place unknown or not specified.

song (song), n. 1. That which is sung. 2. A lyrical poem adapted to vocal music. 3. Poetical composition.

son'-in-law', n. The husband of one's daughter.

soon (soon), adv. 1. In a short time. 2. Early. 3. Promptly. 4. Readily.

soothe (sooth), v.t. 1. To quiet; calm. 2. To soften; assuage; allay.

so-phis'ti-cate (-ti-kat), v.t. 1. To refine overmuch; make artificial; make knowing or worldly-wise. 2. To delude.

sor'cer-y (-i), n. The use of magic; witchcraft.

sore (sor), a. 1. Sensitive to pain from pressure; tender. 2. Distressed mentally; pained; irritable; sensitive. 3. Distressing. — n. A place where the skin and flesh are ruptured or bruised so as to be tender or painful. —adv. Sorely.

sor'row (sor'o), n. 1. Distress of mind due to loss or disappointment; unhappiness; sadness; regret. 2. A cause of grief or sadness; trouble; affliction. — v.i. To feel sorrow; grieve.

sor'ry (-i), a. 1. Grieved for loss; feeling sorrow. 2. Melancholy; dismal; mournful. 3. Poor; pitiful.

soul (sol), n. 1. That which is conceived to be the essence of individual, esp. psychical, life. 2. Man's moral and emotional nature; hence, effective expression of emotion. 3. The seat of real life, action, etc., animating or essential part.

sound (sound), a. 1. Free from flaw, defect, or decay. 2. Healthy; not diseased. 3. Firm; strong; safe; trustworthy. 4. Founded in truth or right; right.

soup (soop), n. A liquid food usually made by boiling meat or vegetables, or both, in water; broth.

sour (sour), a. 1. Acid; tart. 2. Distasteful.

sov'er-eign (sov'er-in; sur'-), a. 1. Supreme; paramount. 2. Supreme in position or power. 3. Independent of, and unlimited by, any other. — n. A person, body of men, or state, sovereign in authority.

spa (spa), n. A mineral spring.

space (spas), n. 1. That which is characterized by dimension, boundlessness, and indefinite divisibility. 2. A small portion of space (sense 1). 3. Quantity of time. — v.t. To place at intervals.

spa'cious (spa'shus), a. 1. Vast in extent; roomy. 2. Large in scale; expansive.

spank (spank), v.t. To strike, or to strike the buttocks of, as with the open hand. — n. A slap on the buttocks.

spar, v.i. To box with fists. — n. A contest at sparring.

spare, (spar), v.t. 1. To forbear. 2. To use frugally or stintingly. 3. To do without. 4. To forbear to destroy or punish. — v.i. 1. To be frugal or saving. 2. To refrain from inflicting harm. — a. 1. Scanty. 2. Lean 3. Superfluous.

spar'kle (spar'k'l), n. A little spark. — v.i. & t. 1. To twinkle. 2. To effervesce.

sparse (spars), a. Of few and scattered elements; scanty.

spasm (spaz'm), n. 1. Med. An involuntary and unnatural muscular contraction. 2. A sudden, violent, and temporary effort, emotion, etc.

spat (spat), n. A petty quarrel. — v.t. To slap. — v.i. To quarrel.

spe'cial (spesh'al), a. 1. Of or pert. to or constituting a species or sort. 2. Pertaining or confined to a single thing or class of things; limited. 3. Of an unusual quality; extraordinary.

spe'cial-ist (-ist), n. One devoted to some special branch of learning or art or business.

spe-cif'ic (spe-sif'ik), a. 1. Of, pertaining to, or constituting, a species. 2. Definite. — n. Something that is specific.

spec'i-fy (spes'i-fi), v.t. To mention or name in a specific or explicit manner.

spec'i-men (-men), n. A sample.

speck (spek), n. 1. A small spot. 2. A small piece or object. — v.t. To produce specks on or in.

spec'ta-cle (spek'ta-k'l), n. 1. A noteworthy sight. 2. pl. A device to aid vision, consisting of two lenses supported by a frame with a bridge over the nose and bows passing over the ears.

spec-tac'u-lar (spek'tak-u-lar), a. Of, pertaining to, or of the nature of, a spectacle, or show.

spec'u-late (-u-lat), v.i. 1. To ponder a

S
T

subject in its different aspects and relations. 2. To enter into a business venture in order to profit by a change in market value.

speech (spech), n. 1. Faculty of uttering articulate sounds or words. 2. Act or manner of speaking. 3. That which is spoken, talk.

speech'less, a. 1. Destitute or deprived of speech. 2. Not speaking. 3. Not orally expressed.

spell (spel), n. 1. a The relief of one person by another in any work or duty. b A period of work, duty, etc., a turn; also, a rest from work. 2. Any relatively short period; as, a cold spell.

spell'ing, n. Act of one who spells; orthography.

spend (spend), v.t. 1. To consume by using; expend. 2. To consume wastefully; squander. 3. To pass, as time. — v.i. 1. To expend, consume, use, or waste something. 2. To waste or wear away; lose force or strength.

spice (spis), n. 1. Any of certain aromatic or pungent vegetable condiments, as pepper, cinnamon, nutmeg, etc. 2. That which gives zest or pungency. — v.t. To season with spices.

spic'y (spis'i), a. 1. Flavored with or containing spice or spices. 2. Producing, or abounding with, spices. 3. Piquant.

spi'der (spi'der), n. 1. A crawling insect having four pairs of walking legs and a body with two main parts.

spin'ach (spin'aj; -ech). A green, leafy vegetable of the same family as the beet.

spi'nal (spi'nal), a. Anat. Of, pertaining to, or near, the backbone.

spin'ster (spin'ster), n. 1. A woman who spins. 2. An unmarried woman.

spir'it (spir'it), n. 1. The breadth of life. 2. The soul. — v.t. To convey rapidly away or off.

spir'it-u-al (-it-u-al), a. 1. Of or pert. to the spirit. 2. Of, pert. to, or like, the soul. 3. Of or pert. to sacred things or the church.

spir'it-u-al'i-ty (-it-u-al'i-ti), n. 1. Quality or state of being spiritual. 2. That which belongs to the church,

to an ecclesiastic in his official capacity or to religion.

spit, v.t. 1. To eject from the mouth. 2. To eject. — v.i. To eject saliva. — n. Spittle; saliva.

spite'ful (spit'fool), a. Filled with or showing spite; malicious.

splash (splash), v.t. 1. To strike and dash about (water, mud, etc.). 2. To fall or strike with a splash. — n. 1. Liquid splashed. 2. Noise made in splashing. 3. A blotch.

splen'did (splen'did), a. 1. Possessing or displaying splendor; shining; brilliant; showy; gorgeous. 2. Illustrious; grand; glorious.

splen'dor (-der), n. 1. Brilliancy. 2. Magnificence.

splint (splint), n. 1. Surg. An appliance, as of wood, to hold or protect an injured part. 2. A thin strip of wood interwoven with others to make a basket.

spokes'man (spoks'man), n. A speaker for another or others.

spon'sor (-ser), n. 1. One who binds himself to answer for another's default. 2. A godparent.

spoon (spoon), n. 1. A utensil having a small shallow bowl, with a handle, used esp. in cooking or eating. 2. Something suggestive of a spoon (sense 1). — v.t. To take up in a spoon.

spo-rad'ic (spo-rad'ik), a. Occurring singly or in scattered instances; separate; single.

spouse (spouz), n. Either one of a married couple.

sprain (spran), v.t. To weaken by sudden and excessive exertion or strain. — n. 1. Act of spraining. 2. Condition caused by spraining.

spread (spred), v.t. 1. To scatter; distribute or extend over a surface; strew. 2. To stretch forth; extend. 3. To divulge; disseminate; diffuse. — v.i. To become spread. — n. 1. Expansion. 2. Extent. 3. A cloth to cover a table or bed.

spree (spre), n. 1. A frolic. 2. Drunken debauch. — v.i. To carouse.

sprin'kle (sprin'k'l), v.t. 1. To scatter so as to make fall in drops or particles. 2. To scatter on or over in small drops or particles. — v.i. 1. To sprinkle something. 2. To rain lightly in scattered drops. — n. A sprinkling; esp., a slight rain.

spruce (sproos), n. A kind of evergreen tree of the pine family; or its wood. — a. 1. Neat and dapper; smart; trim. 2. Overnice. — v.t. & i. To dress smartly; give or restore a look of neatness to.

spunk (spunk), n. 1. Punk. 2. Spirit.

spy (spi), v.t. 1. To discover at a distance, or in a state of conceal- ment; espy. 2. To discover by close search. 3. To explore; inspect secretly; — usually with out. — v.i. 1. To scrutinize. 2. To watch secretly; — with on or upon. — n. 1. one who watches, esp. secretly or furtively, the conduct of others. 2. One who, clandestinely or on false pretenses, obtains or seeks information in the zone of opera- tions of a belligerent, with intent to communicate it to the enemy.

squab'ble (skwob'l), v.i. To quarrel noisily; wrangle. — n. A noisy dispute.

squawk (skwork), v.i. To utter a harsh, abrupt scream. — n. To utter or make a squeak.

squeak (skwek), v.i. To utter or make a squeak. — v.t. To cause to squeak. — n. A sharp, shrill, usually short, cry or sound.

squint (skwint), a. 1. Looking obliquely or askance. 2. Cross- eyed. — v.i. 1. To see or look obliquely or askance; also, to look or peer with eyes partly closed. 2. To be cross-eyed. — n. A squinting.

squirm (skwurm), v.i. To twist about with contortions like an eel or a worm; wriggle; writhe.

stab (stab), v.t. To pierce with a pointed weapon; thrust (a pointed weapon, etc.). — v.i. To thrust or give a wound with a pointed weapon. — n. A thrust of, or a wound made by, a pointed weapon.

stab'i-lize (stab'i-liz), v.t. To make stable; esp., Aeronautics, to maintain the equilibrium of (a flying machine, etc.) by means of fixed surfaces. **sta'ble**, a. 1. Firmly established; not easily overthrown. 2. Steady in purpose. 3. Durable; abiding.

sta'di-um (sta'di-um), n. A structure, with its inclosure, for athletic games.

stag (stag), n. The adult male of certain large deers.

stage (staj), n. 1. An elevated platform, esp. one on which an orator may speak, a play may be presented, etc. 2. A scaffold; staging. 3. The theater; the drama; also, theatrical profession. 4. A place of rest on a road; a station. — v.t. To exhibit on or as on a stage.

stag'ger (stag'er), v.i. To reel to one side and the other, as if about to fall; sway; totter. — v.t. 1. To cause to reel or totter. 2. To cause to doubt, waver, or hesitate. — n. 1. A reeling or tottering movement of the body. 2. pl. A disease, as of horses, attended by reeling or falling.

stag'nant (stag'nant), a. 1. Not flowing; foul from want of motion; as a pool. 2. Not active or brisk.

stain (stan), v.t. 1. To discolor with foreign matter; foul; spot. 2. To dye. 3. To spot with guilt or infamy; soil; tarnish. — v.i. To give or receive a stain. — n. 1. A discoloration, esp. by foreign matter; a spot. 2. A dye, etc., used in staining. 3. Taint of guilt; also, cause of reproach; shame.

stair'case' (star'kas'), n. A flight of stairs with the supporting frame- work, casing, balusters, etc.

stale (stal), a. 1. Vapid or tasteless from age. 2. Not fresh. 3. Trite; commonplace. 4. Impaired in vigor or energy by prolonged activity. — v.t. To make stale or common; destroy the charm or freshness of. — v.i. To become or grow stale.

stal'lion (stal'yun), a. A male horse not castrated.

stam'i-na (stam'i-na), n. Staying power; endurance.

stam'mer (-er), v.i. & t. To speak with involuntary stops or hesitations; stutter. — n. Act of stammering; defective utterance.

stand'point' (-point'), n. A position from which objects or principles are viewed and judged.

stan'za (stan'za), n. A group of verses forming a division of a poem.

starch (starch), n. 1. A well-known

white, tasteless carbohydrate. 2. A paste made of starch (def. 1), for stiffening linen. 2. A stiff, formal manner; stiffness. — v.t. To stiffen with starch.

stare (star), v.i. 1. To gaze fixedly, as through wonder, impudence, etc. 2. To be conspicuous. — v.t. To gaze at. — n. Act of staring; a fixed look, as suggesting wonder, impudence, etc.

star'light' (-lit'), n. The light given by the stars. — a. Lighted by the stars, or by the stars only.

star'ry (star'i), a. 1. Of or pert. to the stars. 2. Consisting of, or proceeding from, the stars; stellar. 3. Shining like stars; sparkling.

start (start), v.i. 1. To move suddenly and quickly; dart; spring. 2. To give an involuntary twitch or spring, as in sudden surprise, pain, joy, etc. 3. To set out; begin. — v.t. 1. To cause to start; rouse. 2. To cause to move or act; set going. 3. To displace or loosen; dislocate. — n. 1. Act of starting; sudden involuntary motion, as from surprise, fear, etc. 2. A spasmodic and brief effort or action. 3. A sudden, capricious impulse; a sudden leap or dash.

star'tle (star't'l), v.i. To move suddenly as in surprise, fear, alarm, etc. — v.t. To excite by sudden alarm, surprise, etc.; frighten suddenly.

star-va'tion (star-va'shun), n. Act of starving; state of being starved.

starve (starv), v.i. To suffer extreme hunger. — v.t. To kill with hunger.

state'ment (-ment), n. 1. Act of stating. 2. That which is stated.

sta'tion (sta'shun), n. 1. Place where anything stands; place where a force is assembled, as in readiness for duty. 2. A regular stopping place, as on a railroad. — v.t. To appoint or assign.

sta'tion-a-ry (sta'shun-a-ri), a. 1. Fixed; not moving; stable; as, a stationary engine. 2. Not changing state or condition.

sta-tis'ti-cal (sta-tis'ti-kal), a. Of or pertaining to statistics.

sta-tis'tics (sta-tis'tiks), n. 1. (sing.) compilation of facts or instances for general inferences. 2. (pl.) Classified facts, esp. those facts which can be stated in numbers.

sta'tus (sta'tus), n. 1. The condition of a person in relation to others, as fixed by law. 2. State or rank of a person. 3. Position of affairs.

stat'ute (stat'ut), n. Something laid down or declared as fixed or established, esp., as a rule or law; esp., a law enacted by a legislature; an act.

stead'fast (sted'fast), a. 1. Firmly fixed or established. 2. Constant; unswerving.

stead'y (-i), a. 1. Firm in position; fixed. 2. Constant, not fickle or wavering. 3. Of a vessel, keeping nearly upright in a seaway. 4. Sober. Colloq. — v.t. & i. To make, or become, steady.

steal (stel), v.t. 1. To take feloniously; take without right and with intent to keep wrongfully. 2. To appropriate to one's self furtively. 3. To move stealthily. — v.i. 1. To commit theft. 2. To move furtively. — n. An act of stealing.

stee'ple (ste'p'l), n. A tall structure, usually topped with a spire, surmounting a church roof.

ster'ile (ster'il), a. 1. Producing little or no crop; unfruitful; barren. 2. Incapable of reproduction. 3. Free from germs, esp. pathogenic bacteria.

ste-ril'i-ty (ste-ril'i-ti), n. State of being sterile.

stern (sturn), a. 1. Having a certain hardness or severity of nature or aspect; severe; grim; austere. 2. Proceeding from, or characteristic of, such a nature or aspect. 3. Unyielding.

steth'o-scope (steth'o-skop), n. Med. An instrument applied esp. to the chest, to convey to the ear sounds produced in the body.

stew (stu), v.t. & i. 1. To boil slowly. 2. To worry. — n. 1. A dish prepared by stewing. 2. Worry.

stiff (stif), a. 1. Rigid. 2. Not liquid. 3. Tense.

sti'fle (sti'f'l), v.t. & i. 1. To suffocate. 2. To stop.

stig'ma-tize (stig'ma-tiz), v.t. To set a mark of disgrace on.

stim'u-late (stim'u-lat), v.t. 1. To excite as with a goad; rouse; spur on. 2.

To excite the activity of (a nerve or a muscle), as by electricity. — v.i. To act as a stimulant or stimulus.

stim'u-lus (-lus), n. 1. A goad. 2. Something that rouses the mind or spirits; an incentive. 3. That which excites a temporary increase of vital action, as of a nerve or muscle.

stin'gy (stin'ji), a. 1. Meiserly. 2. Scanty.

sti'pend (sti'pend), n. Settled pay for services.

stip'u-la'tion (-la'shun), n. An agreement.

stock'bro'ker (stok'bro'ker), n. A broker who deals in stocks.

stock'hold'er (stok'hol'der), n. One who is a holder or proprietor of stock or stocks.

stock'ing (stok'ing), n. A close-fitting covering for the foot and leg, usually knit or woven.

stock'yard' (-yard'), n. A yard for live stock; esp., an inclosure with stables, pens, sheds, etc.

stor'age (stor'aj), n. 1. Act of storing; sate of being stored; safe-keeping of goods in a depository. 2. Space for the safe-keeping of goods, or the price charged therefor.

store (stor), n. 1. That which is accumulated; source from which supplies may be drawn; reserve fund. 2. pl. Articles, esp. of food, accumulated for a special object; supplies. 3. An abundance; great amount. 4. A storehouse; ware-house. 5. A place where goods are kept for sale, a shop. — v.t. 1. To furnish; provide; supply. 2. To collect a supply, lay away. 3. To deposit, as in a storehouse.

stork (stork), n. Any of various large wading birds allied to the herons.

storm (storm), n. 1. A disturbance of the atmosphere attended by wind, rain, snow, hail, sleet, or thunder and lightning. 2. Vehement or passionate outbreak. 3. A deter-mined assault on a fortified place. — v.i. 1. To blow with violence; also, to rain, hail, snow, or the like, usually violently; — used imperson-ally; as, it storms. 2. To rage. — v.t. To attack, and attempt to take, by sudden assault.

storm'y (stor'mi), a. 1. Marked by, or

pertaining to, a storm; tempestuous. 2. Turbulent; violent; passionate.

sto'ry (sto'ri), n. A set of rooms on one floor; a floor; space between two floors.

sto'ry, n. 1. A connected narration of past events; history. 2. a An account of some incident. b A report; a statement. c An anecdote. 3. In literature, a narrative in prose or verse; a tale, esp. fictitious. 4. A fib; falsehood. Colloq.

stout (stout), a. 1. Strong and firm of character; brave; bold; resolute. 2. Physically strong; sturdy; tough. 3. Bulky; stocky; corpulent. — n. A strong malt liquor, esp. porter.

stove (stov), n. Any of various apparatus, commonly of iron, for heating and cooking.

straight (strat), a. 1. Having an invariable direction; not curved or crooked. 2. Conforming to justice and rectitude; upright. 3. Direct; unbroken. 4. Properly ordered or arranged. — adv. Directly; rightly; straightway.

strange (stranj), a. 1. Belonging to others. 2. Unfamiliar. 3. Novel; extraordinary

stran'ger (stran'jer), n. One who is strange; as: a A foreigner. b A visitor or intruder. c A person with whom one is unacquainted.

straw (stro), n. 1. A stalk or stem of grain or pulse. 2. Stalks of grain after threshing.

straw'ber-ry (stro'ber-i), n.The edible red fruit of any of various stemless herbs, or the plant that bears it.

street (stret), n. A thoroughfare, esp. in a city or village.

strength (strength), n. 1. Quality or state of being strong; ability to do or to bear; force; power. 2. Power to resist force; solidity or toughness. 3. Power of resisting attacks; impregnability. 4. Intensity; vehemence; vigor.

stren'u-ous (sten'u-us), a. 1. Eagerly pressing or urgent; zealous; ardent. 2. Marked by zealous energy.

stress (stres), v.t. 1. To subject to mechanical stress. 2. To accent or emphasize. — n. 1. Pressure; strain; hence, urgency; importance, significance. 2. Mech. Mutual force

S T

or action between contiguous parts of a body, due to external force. 3. Force of utterance of words, or syllables, increasing their relative loudness; accent.

strict (strikt), a. 1. Drawn close; tight; also, tense. 2. Exact; precise; hence, rigid in interpretation; without exception or deviation. 3. Rigorous.

strik'ing (strik'ing), a. Very noticeable; remarkable.

stroll (strol), v.i. To wander on foot; rove; saunter. — n. A strolling; ramble.

strong (strong), a. 1. Having great power to act; vigorous. 2. Having ability to bear or endure; hale; robust. 3. Having great resources, as of wealth, numbers, etc. 4. Of specified number; as, ten thousand strong.

strong'hold (-hold'), n. A fort; place of security.

strong'ly, adv. In a strong manner.

struc'ture (struk'tur), n. 1. Manner of building; construction. 2. Something built; a building. 3. Arrangement of parts, organs, tissues, etc.

strug'gle (strug'l), v.i. To put forth great efforts; strive; contend. — n. 1. A violent effort or exertion. 2. Contest; strife.

strut (strut), v.i. To walk with a lofty, proud gait or with affected dignity. — n. 1. A strutting. 2. Arch. Any bar or piece for resisting pressure endwise.

stub'born (-ern), a. 1. Resolute in mental attitude; inflexible; esp., obstinate. 2. Performed or practiced persistently or obstinately. 3. Difficult to manage; refractory.

stud (stud), n. 1. A collection of horses for breeding, racing, riding, etc. 2. The place where a stud is kept, esp. for breeding. 3. A studhorse.

stu'dent (stu'dent), n. 1. A person engaged in study; scholar. 2. An attentive and systematic observer.

stu'di-ous (-us), a. 1. Given to study. 2. Diligent in attention.

stum'ble (stum'b'l), v.i. 1. To trip in walking, etc. 2. To walk unsteadily; hence, to act or perform blunderingly. 3. To fall into sin or error. 4. To

come or happen without design. — n. 1. A strip in walking or running. 2. A blunder.

stu-pen'dous (stu-pen'dus), a. Amazing

stu'pid (stu'pid), a. 1. Very dull; stupefied. 2. Foolish. 3. Resulting from or evincing mental dullness; dull.

stut'ter (stut'er), v.i. & t. To hesitate or stumble in uttering words; stammer. — n. Act of stuttering; a stammer.

styl'ish (stil'ish), a. Highly fashionable.

sub-con'scious (sub-kon'shus), a. Of the nature of mental operation, but not present in consciousness.

sub-due' (sub-du), v.t. 1. To bring under; conquer; vanquish. 2. To overcome, as by persuasion. 3. To destroy the force of, as of a fever. 4. To reduce; hence, to soften.

sub-ject' (sub-jekt'), v.t. 1. To bring under control; subdue. 2. To expose; make liable; cause to undergo.

sub-jec'tion (-jek'shun), n. A subjecting; state of being subject; obedient, or submissive.

sub-jec'tive (-tiv), a. 1. Of the nature of, or pertaining to, a subject. 2. Esp., pertaining to, or derived from, one's own consciousness, in distinction from external observation.

sub-lime' (sub-lim'), a. 1. Exalted. 2. Producing a sense of elevated beauty, grandeur, etc. — n. 1. Chem. To cause to sublime; purify. 2. To exalt; refine. — v.i. Chem. To pass from the solid to the gaseous state; and again condense to solid form, without apparently liquefying.

sub-merge' (sub-murj'), v.t. 1. To put under water; plunge. 2. To cover with water; inundate. — v.i. To become submerged.

sub-mis'sion (-mish'un), n. 1. Act of submitting; esp., yielding to power or authority. 2. State of being submissive; obedience; compliance.

sub-mis'sive (-mis'iv), a. Inclined or ready to submit; yielding; humble.

sub-mit' (-mit'), v.t. 1. To yield to power, will, or authority. 2. To commit to the discretion or judgment of another; refer. 3. To offer as an opinion, or affirm. — v.i. 1. To yield; surrender. 2. To be subject or submissive.

sub-or'di-nate (sub-or'di-nat), a. 1. Placed in a lower order, class, or rank. 2. Inferior in order, nature, importance, etc. — n. One that is subordinate. — (-nat), v.t. 1. To place in a lower order or class. 2. To make subject or subservient.

sub-se-quence (sub'se-kwens), n. Act or state of being subsequent.

sub'se-quent (-kwent), a. Succeeding; following; as, subsequent events.

sub-sid'i-a-ry (sub-sid'i-a-ri), a. 1. Furnishing aid; auxiliary; tributary. 2. Of or pert. to subsidy. — n. One that contributes aid or supplies; assistant; auxiliary.

sub'si-dize (sub'si-diz), v.t. To furnish or aid with a subsidy.

sub-sist' (sub-sist'), v.i. 1. To continue; to exist. 2. To be. 3. To be maintained with food and clothing. — v.t. To support with provisions.

sub-sist'ence (-sis'tens), n. 1. Act or condition of subsisting; existence. 2. Means of support; livelihood. 3. Inherency.

sub-stan'tial (sub-stan'shal), a. 1. Of or pert. to substance; material. 2. Not imaginary; real; true. 3. Having good substance; strong; solid. 4. Possessed of goods; moderately wealthy. 5. That is such in the main 6. Considerable; large. — n. That which is substantial.

sub-stan'ti-ate (sub-stan'shi-at), v.t. To establish the existence of truth of; verify, as a charge.

sub'sti-tute (-sti-tut), n. One put in place of another. — v.t. To put in the place of another.

sub'ter-fuge (sub'ter-fuj), n. A device, plan, or the like, for escape or concealment; artifice.

sub'tle (sut'l), a. 1. Thin; tenuous; delicate. 2. Skillfully or cunningly devised; ingenious; crafty; sly. 3. Nicely discriminating; discerning; shrewd; penetrating. 4. Skillful; expert.

sub-tract' (sub-trakt'), v.t. To take away, as a part from the whole or one number from another; deduct.

sub'urb (sub'urb), n. An outlying part of a city or town.

suc-ceed' (suk-sed'), v.t. 1. To come after; follow. 2. To come next after; hence, to take the place of. — v.i. 1. To come after, follow; hence, to come next in possession; — often with to. 2. To ascend the throne after the removal or death of the occupant. 3. To obtain the object desired; be successful.

suc-cess' (-ses'), n. 1. Favorable termination of anything attempted. 2. A thing or person achieving success.

suc-ces'sion (-sesh'un), n. 1. Act of succeeding; sequence. 2. Act or right of succeeding to a throne. 3. A series of persons or things that follow according to some established rule. 5. A series of descendants; lineage; race; descent.

suc'cu-lent (-u-lent), a. Juicy.

suc-cumb' (su-kum'), v.i. To yield; submit.

sud'den (sud'n; -en), a. 1. Happening or coming unexpectedly; rapid and unforeseen. 2. Hastily prepared, made, done, etc.; quick; rapid.

suf'fer-ance (-ans), n. 1. Patient endurance; long-suffering. 2. Toleration; permission; leave.

suf-fice' (su-fis; -fiz'), v.t. To satisfy; content. — v.i. To be enough or adequate.

suf-fi-cient (-ent), a. Enough; equal to the need.

suf'fo-cate (suf'o-kat), v.t. 1. To kill by stopping respiration; stifle. 2. To extinguish by depriving of air, as fire. — v.i. To be suffocated.

sug-gest' (sug-jest'), v.i. To present (a matter, problem, etc.), usually indirectly, to the mind; intimate; hint.

sug-ges'tion (-jes'chun), n. 1. A suggesting; presentation of an idea, esp. indirectly. 2. That which is suggested; intimation.

su'i-cide (su'i-sid), n. Act of taking one's own life voluntarily and intentionally; self-murder. — n. One guilty of self-murder.

suit'or (sut'er), n. One who sues; esp.: a A wooer; lover. b Law. A party in a suit.

sulk (sulk), v.i. To be sulky or sullen. — n. State of being sulky; sulky

S
T

mood or humor; — often in pl.

sul'len (sul'en), a. 1. Disposed to be alone; gloomily silent; morose. 2. Gloomy; dismal; melancholy.

sul'try (sul'tri), a. 1. Oppressively hot. 2. Very hot and moist, or close and oppressive, as air.

sum'ma-rize (sum'a-riz), v.t. To tell in, or reduce to, a summary, present briefly.

sum'ma-ry (-ri), a. 1. Formed into a sum; summed up; compact; concise. 2. Done without delay or formality.

sum'ma-ry, n.; pl. -RIES (-riz). An abstract, abridgment, or compendium.

sump'tu-ous (-us), a. Involving large expense; luxurious.

sun'burn' (-burn'), n. Inflammation of the skin, from exposure to the sun's rays; tan. — v.t. & i. To burn or discolor by the sun; tan.

Sun'day (-da), n. The first day of the week; widely observed as a day of rest and of religious worship; the Christian Sabbath.

sun'flow'er (-flou'er), n. Any of a genus of plants, of the aster family, with large yellow flowers.

sun'ny (sun'i), a. 1. Of or pertaining to, or like, the sun; shining; bright; cheerful; genial. 2. Exposed to the sun.

sun'rise' (sun'riz'), n. 1. The first appearance, or the rising, of the sun above the horizon; the time of such appearance. 2. The east.

sun'set' (sun'set'), n. 1. The descent of the sun below the horizon; the time of such descent; evening. 2. The west.

sun'shine' (-shin'), n. 1. The sun's direct rays, the place where they fall, or the warmth and light which they give. 2. Anything having a warming and cheering influence.

su'per-fine (su'per-fin), a. 1. Very fine; extra fine. 2. Very subtle or delicate; too nice; as, superfine tastes.

su'per-nat'u-ral (su'per-nat'u-ral), a. Beyond or exceeding the powers or laws (i.e., observed sequences) of nature; miraculous.

sup'per (sup'er), n. The evening meal.

sup'ple (sup'l), a. 1. Plaint; flexible. 2. Yielding; compliant; submissive. 3. Bending to the humor of others; obsequious. — v.t. & i. To make or become supple.

sup'ple-ment (sup'le-ment), n. That which completes something already organized, arranged, or set apart; esp., a continuation of a book or paper to make good deficiencies. — (-ment), v.t. To fill or supply by additions; add to.

sup-ply' (su-pli'), v.t. 1. To furnish with what is wanted or needed; replenish. 2. To give or provide; furnish. 3. To make up for, or repair, as a vacancy or loss; to fill temporarily. — n. 1. Act of supplying. 2. That which supplies a want; esp., the daily food, etc., of an army; stores; — chiefly in pl. 3. Quantity of any article offered at a given price.

sup-port' (su-port'), v.t. 1. To bear the weight or stress of; uphold; sustain. 2. To endure; bear; undergo; suffer; tolerate. 3. To encourage; aid; help. 4. To maintain; provide for. — n. 1. Act or operation of supporting. 2. One that supports.

sup-pose (-poz'), v.t. 1. To assume tentatively as proved or true. 2. To receive as true; imagine; believe; think. 3. To imply. — v.i. To conjecture; think; opine.

sup'po-si'tion (sup'o-zish'un), n. 1. Act of supposing or assuming something, as for argument; assumption. 2. Opinion or belief without sufficient evidence; conjecture; hypothesis.

sup-press' ('pres'), v.t. 1. To overpower and crush; subdue; quell. 2. To keep in; restrain from utterance or vent. 3. To conceal; prevent publication or revelation of. 4. To stop; check; restrain.

sure'ly (shoor'li), adv. 1. In a sure or certain manner; certainly. 2. Without danger; securely.

sure'ty (shoor'ti), n. 1. State of being sure; certainty. 2. That which makes sure; esp., security against loss or damage. 3. Law. One liable for the debt, default, or miscarriage of another. 4. A sponsor.

sur-face (sur-fas), n. The exterior of

anything that has length and breadth; a face of a solid, esp. the upper one; outside. — v.t. To give a surface to; esp., to make smooth or plain.

sur'geon (sur'jun), n. One who practice surgery.

sur'ger-y (sur'jer-i), n. Art or practice of healing by manual operation; science which treats of mechanical or operative remedial measures.

sur-mise' (sur-miz'), n. A thought based on scanty evidence; suspicion. — v.t. To imagine or infer on slight grounds; guess.

sur-mount' (-mount'), v.t. 1. To rise above; overtop. 2. To conquer; overcome.

sur'name' (sur-nam), n. A name or appellation added to the baptismal, or Christian name, and become a family name. — v.t. To call by a surname; give a surname to.

sur-prise' (-priz'), v.t. 1. To come upon or attack unexpectedly. 2. to take unawares. 3. To strike with wonder, astonishment, or confusion, by something sudden, unexpected, or remarkable. — n. 1. Act of coming upon or taking, unawares; surprisal. 2. State of being surprised; astonishment. 3. Anything sudden and unexpected, esp. when causing astonishment.

sur-ren'der (su-ren'der), n. A yielding one's person or a thing into the power of another. — v.t. 1. To yield to the power of another; give up on compulsion or demand. 2. To give up possession of; yield; relinquish. 3. To yield to any influence, emotion, etc.; — used reflexively. — v.i. To give emotion, etc.; — used reflexively. — v.i. To give up to the power of another; yield.

sur-round' (su-round'), v.t. 1. To inclose on all sides; encompass. 2. To inclose, as a body of troops, so as to cut off retreat; invest, as a city.

sur-vey' (-va'), v.t. 1. To inspect; look over or about, as from a height. 2. To scrutinize. 3. To examine with reference to condition, situation, value, etc. 4. To make a survey of.

sur-viv'al (-viv'al), n. 1. Act or fact of surviving; an outliving. 2. One that survives or outlasts.

sur-vive' (-viv'), v.t. To live beyond the life or existence of; outlive; outlast. — v.i. To remain alive or existent.

sus-cep'ti-ble (-sep'ti-b'l), a. 1. Capable of being changed or influenced; readily acted on; — with of or to. 2. Capable of mental or emotional impression; sensitive.

sus-pect' (sus-pekt'), v.t. 1. To imagine to be, occur, happen, etc.; surmise. 2. To imagine to be guilty, without proof. 3. To doubt; mistrust; distrust. — v.i. To suspect anything; be suspicious. — n. One suspected; now, a person suspected of crime.

sus-pend' (-pend'), v.t. 1. To attach to something above; hang; hence, to hold as if by hanging. 2. To cause to cease for a time; stay. 3. To hold in an undetermined or undecided state. 4. To debar temporarily (from a privilege, office, etc.). — v.i. To cease temporarily from operation, esp., to stop payment; — of a business concern.

sus-pense' (-pens'), n. 1. State of being suspended. 2. State of uncertainty, usually with anxiety or expectation. 3. Cessation; pause.

sus-pi'cion (-pish'un), n. 1. Act or fact of suspecting; mistrust. 2. Slight degree; suggestion; hint; as, a suspicion of sarcasm in one's remarks. Colloq.

sus-tain' (sus-tan'), v.t. 1. To bear up; uphold; support. 2. To keep from sinking, as in despondency, etc. 3. To maintain or keep up, as a conversation, an effort, etc. 4. To maintain; support.

sus'te-nance (sus'te-nans), n. 1. Support. 2. That which supports life; provisions.

swag'ger (swag'er), v.i. 1. To walk with a conceited strut; walk and act pompously. 2. To brag noisily; bluster. — n. Act or manner of one who swaggers.

swal'low, v.t. 1. To take through the gullet into the stomach. 2. To take in or absorb; ingulf; engross. 3. To retract; recant. 4. To put up with; bear patiently. — v.i. To perform the act of swallowing something. — n. 1. Act of swallowing. 2. As much as is swallowed at once.

S
T

sway (swa), v.t. 1. To wield with the hand; swing. 2. To cause to incline to one side or from side to side; turn aside. 3. To influence or direct; govern; guide. — v.i. 1. To lean; incline. 2. To swing from side to side; oscillate; fluctuate. — n. 1. Act of swaying. 2. Influence, weight, or authority that inclines to one side. 3. Rule; domination; control.

swear (swar), v.t. 1. To utter a solemn declaration, with an appeal to God for its truth. 2. To make a promise, threat, vow, etc., on oath; vow. 3. Law. To give evidence or state on oath. 4. To curse. — v.t. 1. To affirm with a solemn appeal to God for the truth of the declaration. 2. To make (a promise, threat, etc.) on oath; vow. 3. Law. To bind by an oath; administer an oath to.

sweat'y (swet'i), a. 1. Moist with sweat. 2. Consisting of or like sweat. 3. Causing sweat.

sweep'ing, p.a. 1. Moving swiftly and violently; of great range or scope. 2. That sweeps or cleans with or as with a broom.

swell'ing, n. 1. Act of that which swells. 2. A prominence.

swel'ter (swel'ter), v.i. To be faint from heat.

swift (swift), a. 1. Moving with great speed. 2. Happening or accomplished with rapidity. 3. Quick. — adv. Swiftly.

swin'dle (swin'd'l), v.t. & i. To cheat or defraud. — n. Act or process of swindling.

sword (sord), n. 1. A weapon having a long and usually pointed blade with a cutting edge or edges. 2. Dissension; conflict; war.

syl'la-ble (sil'a-b'l), n. 1. An elementary sound, or a combination of such sounds, uttered with a single impulse of the voice, and constituting a word or a part of a word. 2. In writing and printing, a part of a word separated from the rest.

sym'bol (sim'bol), n. 1. A visible sign of an idea or a quality, or of another object; an emblem. 2. A letter, sign, or the like, representing something, as an operation in mathematics, etc.

sym'bol-ize (sim'bol-iz), v.i. To use symbols or symbolism. — v.t. 1. To regard or treat as symbolic. 2. To represent by a symbol or symbols.

sym'me-try (sim'e-tri), n. 1. A harmonious relation of parts. 2. Correspondence of form, dimensions, or parts on opposite sides of an axis, etc.

sym'pa-thet'ic (sim'pa-thet'ik), a. 1. Feeling, or inclined to, sympathy; congenial. 2. Due to, or expressive of, sympathy.

sym'pa-thize (sim'pa-thiz), v.i. 1. To feel or show sympathy; be affected sympathetically. 2. To agree; accord.

sym'pa-thy (-thi), n. 1. Fellow feeling. 2. An agreement of inclinations causing persons to be congenial. 3. A tendency of things to unite or to act on each other.

symp'tom (sim'-tum), n. 1. A perceptible change in the body or its functions, indicating disease, or the kind of disease. 2. A sign.

syn'a-gogue (sin'a-gog), n. A local assembly of Jews organized chiefly for public worship; also, the place primarily used for religious worship.

syn'chro-nize (-niz), v.i. To agree in time; by synchronous. — v.t. 1. To assign to the same date or period. 2. To cause to agree in time, as a clock.

syn'o-nym (sin'o-nim), n. One of two or more words (of the same language) having the same or nearly the same meaning.

syn-on'y-mous (si-non'i-mus), a. Having the character of a synonym.

syn'the-sis (sin'the-sis), n.; pl. -SES (-sez). Composition, or the putting of things together.

sys'tem (sis'tem), n. 1. An assemblage of objects united by regular interaction or interdependence. 2. An assemblage of objects arranged after a method of plan. 3. A scheme for interrelating things. 4. Regular method.

T

tab (tab), n. 1. A small flap, tag, or the like, as to a garment. 2. Account.

ta-bas'co (ta-bas'ko), n. A pungent

sauce of capsicum berries.

tab'by (tab'l), n.; pl. -BIES (-iz). A brindled cat; popularly, any domestic cat. — a. Brindled.

tab'er-na-cle (tab'er-na-k'l), n. 1. A tent. 2. A Jewish temple.

tab'le (ta'b'l), n. 1. A smooth flat surface or thin slab. 2. An article of furniture having a smooth flat top fixed on legs. — v.t. 1. To lay or place on a table, as money. 2. To lay (a motion, etc.) on the table.

ta'ble-spoon (ta'b'l-spoon'), n. The largest spoon in common use at table.

tab'u-late (-lat), v.t. 1. To shape with a flat surface. 2. To form into a table, or synopsis.

tact (takt), n. Nice discernment of the best course of action under given conditions.

tac'tics (tak'tiks), n. 1. Act of handing or using troops or ships in battle or in the presence of the enemy. 2. Method of procedure.

tail, n. 1. The rear end, or a process or prolongation of the rear end, of the body of an animal. 2. An appendage suggestive of the tail of an animal. 3. The back, last, lower, or inferior part; end; rear. — v.t. To furnish with a tail; also, to follow like a tail. — v.i. To form a tail.

taint (tant), v.t. To infect; poison; corrupt. — v.i. To become tainted. — n. 1. A spot or stain; touch of disgrace. 2. An infection.

take, v.i. 1. To lay hold. 2. To resort. 3. To take effect. 4. To charm. — n. 1. Act of taking. 2. That which is taken.

tak'ing (tak'ing), n. 1. Act of one that takes. 2. That which is taken or received. — a. 1. Alluring; attractive. Colloq. 2. Infectious; contagious.

tale (tal), n. 1. That which is told; story. 2. A libelous report or piece of evil gossip.

tal'ent (tal'ent), n. 1. Superior intelligence and ability. 2. Collectively; persons of ability or skill.

talk (tok), v.t. 1. To deliver in speech. 2. To discuss. — v.i. 1. To speak. 2. To communicate by any means. — n. 1. Act of talking; speech. 2. Report, rumor. 3. Empty verbiage.

tall (tol), a. 1. High of nature. 2. Of a given height.

tame (tam), a. 1. Reduced from native wildness; domesticated. 2. Subdued; also, harmless; gentle; as, tame behavior. 3. Deficient in spirit, interest, etc.; dull; insipid. — v.t. 1. To reduce from wild to a domestic state; make gentle, tractable, etc. 2. To deprive of spirit, courage, etc; subdue.

tam'per (tam'per), v.i. 1. To meddle; try trifling or foolish experiments; — commonly with with. 2. To meddle so as to alter a thing; esp., to make changes without right. 3. To deal unfairly; esp. by bribery.

tan'gi-ble (tan'ji-b'l), a. 1. Capable of being touched; palpable. 2. Real; substantial; evident.

tan'gle (tan'g'l), v.t. 1. To intertwine confusedly; entangle. 2. To involve; insnare; as, to be tangled in lies. — v.i. To be or become entangled. — n. 1. A confused knot, as of hair or threads. 2. State of perplexity; muddle.

tan'ning (tan'ing), n. 1. Art or process by which a skin is tanned. 2. A browning; as of the skin, by exposure to the sun or weather.

ta'per (ta'per), n. 1. A small wax candle; a long wick coated with wax. 2. Gradual diminution of thickness in an elongated object. — a. Regularly narrowed toward a point; conical. — v.i. & t. To become or make gradually smaller toward one end; grow gradually less.

ta'-es-try (tap'es-tri), n.; pl. -TRIES (-triz). A fabric worked on a warp of thread, originally by hand, the designs being usually pictorial. — v.t. To furnish or adorn with or as with tapestry.

tar'dy (tar'di), a. 1. Moving slowly; slow. 2. Late; dilatory.

tar'nish (tar'nish), v.t. To dull the luster of; sully; stain. —v.i. To lose luster; become dull. — n. Quality or state of being tarnished.

tart (tart), a. 1. Sharp to the taste; sour. 2. Severe; sharp; as, a tart reply.

task (task), n. Labor, work, or study imposed, often in a definite quantity; undertaking; work. — v.t.

1. To impose a task on. 2. To oppress with labor; burden.

taste (tast), v.t. 1. To ascertain the relish or flavor of by taking a little into the mouth. 2. To eat or drink a little of, as for testing. 3. To partake of; experience. — v.i. 1. To try food or drink with the mouth; eat or drink a little only. 2. To have a certain flavor or particular quality. 3. To have perception, experience, or enjoyment; partake; — often with of. — n. 1. Act of tasting with the mouth. 2. Quality of any substance as perceived by the taste organs; savor; flavor. 3. Physiol. The one of the five senses by which certain properties of bodies (called their taste) are ascertained by contact with certain organs of the mouth. 4. Intellectual relish; liking; fondness. 5. Power of appreciating beauty, order, etc. 6. Manner as to what is pleasing, refined, or good usage. 7. A little piece tasted; a bit.

taste'less, a. 1. Having no taste; insipid. 2. Not manifesting, or not conscious of what is, good taste; not in good taste.

tat'ter (tat'er), n. A rag or a part torn and hanging; — usually in pl. — v.t. & i. To make or become ragged.

tat't!e (-'l), v.i. 1. To chatter. 2. To tell tales or secrets. —v.t. To utter or disclose by tattling. — n. Idle talk.

tat-too', v.t. To mark or color (the skin) indelibly by pricking in coloring matter. — n. A mark or figure formed by tattooing.

taunt (tant; tont), v.t. To reproach severely or insultingly; jeer at. — n. Sarcastic reproach.

tax'i-cab' (tak'si-kab'), n. A cab fitted with a taximeter.

tea (te), n. 1. A shrub cultivated in China, Japan, India, etc., for its leaves. 2. The dried leaves of this plant, from which a beverage is made by infusion; also, the beverage. 3. Any of various plants more or less like tea; also, an infusion of their leaves.

team (tem), n. 1. Two or more horses or other beasts harnessed. 2. A number of persons associated together.

tease (tez), v.t. 1. To disentangle and lay parallel, as fibers; comb or card, as wool or flax. 2. To teasel. 3. To vex or annoy by petty requests, or by jests and raillery; plague; beg. — n. 1. Act of teasing. 2. One that teases. Colloq.

tea'spoon (te'spoon), n. The ordinary spoon used to stir tea, coffee, etc.

tech'ni-cal (-ni-kal), a. Of or pertaining to or appropriate to, the useful or mechanic arts, or any art, science, business, etc.

tech'nics (tek'niks), n. The science or doctrine of an art or of arts in general, esp. the mechanical or industrial arts; also, technic; technique.

tech-nol'o-gy (tek-nol'o-ji), n. 1. Industrial science. 2. Terminology of arts, sciences, etc.

te'di-ous (te'di-us; ted'yus), a. Tiresome; wearisome.

teens (tenz), n. pl. The years of one's age of which the numbers have the termination -teen.

teethe (teth), v.i. To grow teeth.

teeth'ing (teth'ing), n. The cutting of teeth.

tel'e-graph (-graf), n. Any apparatus or process for communication (esp. by means of electrical transmission) at a distance. — v.t. & i. To send or communicate by telegraph; also, to send a telegram to (a person).

tel'e-phone (tel'e-fon), n. An instrument for reproducing sounds, esp. speech, at a distance. — v.t. & i. To send, communicate, or speak to, by telephone.

tel'e-scope (tel'e-skop), n. An optical instrument used to aid the eye or camera in viewing or photographing distant objects, as the heavenly bodies. — v.i. & t. To slide, or force away, one within another, as do sections of a small telescope.

tell (tel), v.t.; pref. & p.p. TOLD (told); p.pr. & vb. n. TELL'ING. 1. To mention one by one. 2. To narrate. 3. To make known. — v.i. 1. To give an account; make report. 2. To take effect; have a marked effect.

tell'er (tel'er), n. 1. One who tells, or relates. 2. a One appointed to count the votes in a legislative body, assembly, etc. b A bank officer who receives and counts money paid in, and pays money out on checks.

tell'tale' (-tal'), n. 1. A talebearer; informer. 2. Any of various things that serve to give information or warning. — a. 1. Talebearing. 2. Disclosing; betraying.

tem'per-a-ment (-a-ment), n. 1. The physical and mental character of an individual; habitual disposition. 2. Act of tempering, or modifying.

tem'pered (-perd), a. Having (such) a temper.

tem-pes'tu-ous (tem-pes'tu-us), a. Stormy; violent.

tem'ple (tem'p'l), n. The flattened space on either side of the forehead.

tem'ple, n. An edifice for worship.

tem'po-ral, a. 1. Of, pertaining to, or limited by, time. 2. Pert. to the present life; secular; transitory. 3. Civil or political.

temp-ta-tion (temp-ta-shun), n. 1. Act of tempting. 2. State of being tempted, or enticed to evil. 3. That which tempts, esp. to evil.

te-na'cious (te-na'shus), a. 1. Holding fast; inclined to hold fast; — chiefly with of. 2. Apt to retain; retentive.

ten'an-cy (ten'an-si), n.; pl. -CIES (-siz). 1. A holding of lands or tenements; tenure, as under a lease. 2. The period of a tenant's possession.

ten'ant (ten'ant), n. 1. One who holds or possesses real estate by any kind of right; also (as correlative to landlord) one in temporary possession of lands or tenements of another. 2. Occupant. — v.t. To hold, occupy, or possess, as a tenant.

tend (tend), v.t. To attend; care for; watch; guard. — v.i. To serve.

tend'en-cy (ten'den-si), n.; pl. -CIES (-siz). Direction or course toward anything; drift.

ten'der, n. 1. An offer, as of money or service to satisfy an obligation. 2. Thing offered; esp. money offered in payment. — v.t. 1. To make a tender of. 2. To offer.

ten'don (-dun), n. Anat. A tough cord or band of dense, inelastic, white fibrous tissue uniting a muscle with some other part; a sinew.

tense, a. Stretched tight; rigid; —

often fig.; as, a tense moment.

tent (tent), n. A portable lodge or shelter of skins or cloth stretched over a pole or poles, or the like. — v.i. & t. To lodge as in a tent; encamp.

ten'ta-tive (-ta-tiv), a. Of or pertaining to a trial or attempt; experimental.

ten'ure (-ur), n. Act, right, or manner, of holding, as real estate, properly of a superior; period for which anything is had and enjoyed.

ter'mi-nate (-nat), v.t. 1. To set a limit to; bound. 2. To put an end to; end. — v.t. To be limited in space or time; end.

ter'mi-na'tion (-na'shun), n. 1. Act of terminating. 2. That which ends, limits, or bounds. 3. Gram. Ending of a word; a final syllable or letter; esp., the part added to a stem in inflection.

ter'mi-nol'o-gy (-nol'o-ji), n. The technical or special terms used in a business, art, science, etc.

ter'race (ter'as), n. A raised level or platform of earth, often one of a series arranged one above the other on a slope. — v.t. To form into, or furnish with, a terrace or terraces.

ter'ra cot'ta (ter'a kot'a). 1. Hard-baked pottery, esp. that of a brownish red or yellowish red color. 2. A color like that of terra cotta (def. 1).

ter-res'tri-al (-res'tri-al), a. 1. Earthly; — opposed to celestial. 2. Representing, or consisting of, the earth. 3. Consisting of land, in distinction from water. 4. Of or inhabiting the land, or ground, in distinction from trees, water, etc.

ter'ri-ble (ter'i-b'l), a. 1. Adapted, or likely, to excite terror; dreadful. 2. Excessive; extreme. Colloq.

ter'ri-er (-er), n. A dog of any of certain breeds differing much in shape, coat, etc., but generally small vivacious, and courageous.

ter'rif-ic (te'rik'ik), a. Exciting, or adapted to excite, great fear or dread; terrible.

ter'ror (-er), n. Extreme fear; violent dread; fright; also, the cause of such fear.

ter'ror-ism (ter'er-iz'm), n. A

S
T

terrorizing; state of being terrorized; a mode of governing, or of opposing government, by intimidation.

tes'ta-ment (tes'ta-ment), n. 1. A solemn covenant. Obs., exc.: [cap.] a Either of the two main divisions of the Bible, called Old Testament and new Testament. b The New Testament. Colloq. 2. Law. A will; — chiefly in the tautological expression last will and testament.

tes'ti-mo-ny (tes'ti-mo-ni), n.; pl. -NIES (-niz). 1. A solemn declaration or affirmative made to establish some fact. 2. Affirmation; declaration.

tet'a-nus (tet'a-nus), n. A specific disease marked by tonic spasms of the voluntary muscles, esp. of the lower jaw.

text (tekst), n. 1. The words and sentences of an author as originally written. 2. A passage of Scripture, esp. one chosen as the subject of a sermon. 3. Topic; theme. 4. The main body of printed or written matter on a page.

text'book' (-book'), n. A manual of instruction.

tex'ture (-tur), n. 1. Characteristic disposition of interwoven threads, filaments, etc. 2. Disposition of the smaller parts; minute structure.

thank (thank), v.t. To express gratitude to.

thank'ful (thank'fool), a. Feeling or expressing thanks.

thank'less, a. 1. Not acknowledging favors; ungrateful. 2. Not obtaining or deserving thanks.

thanks'giv'ing (thanks'giv'ing; thanks'giv'ing). n. 1. Act of rendering thanks. 2. A formula expressing gratitude, esp. for divine mercies.

Thanks'giv'ing Day (thanks'giv'ing). In the United States, a day (usually the last Thursday of November) set apart each year for thanksgiving.

thaw (tho), v.i. 1. To melt, dissolve, or become fluid or semifluid; — said of a frozen substance. Also, to have its frozen contents melted; as, the pipe thawed. 2. To become so warm as to melt ice and snow; — used with it, referring to the

weather. 3. Fig., to be freed from coldness or reserve. — v.t. To cause to thaw. — n. 1. Act or process of thawing. 2. A condition of the weather caused by a rise of temperature above freezing point.

the'a-ter (the'a-ter), n. 1. A construction or edifice for dramatic performances. 2. A place where events, esp. of importance, are enacted; as, the theater of war. 3. The drama.

the'at-ri-cal (the'at-rik-kal), a. Also **the-at'ric** (-rik), a. Of or pert. to a theater or dramatic representations; histrionic; hence, artificial; "stagy."

theft (theft), n. Act of stealing; larceny.

the'ism (the'iz'm), n. Belief in a god or gods.

then (then), adv. 1. At that time. 2. Soon afterward, or immediately; next. 3. At another time; later. — a. Then being. —conj. In that case.

the-oc'ra-cy (the-ok'ra-si), n.; pl. -CIES (-siz). 1. Government by direction of God; rule by priests as representing God. 2. A state so governed.

the'o-lo'gi-an (the'o-lo'ji-an), n. A person well versed in theology, esp. Christian theology.

the'o-ret'i-cal (-i-kal), a. Pertaining to theory; speculative; not practical.

there'a-bout' (thar'a-bout'); **there'a-bouts'** (-bouts'), adv. 1. Near that number, degree, or quantity; nearly.

there-aft'er (thar-af'ter), adv. 1. After that; afterward. 2. According to that; accordingly.

there-at' (thar-at'), adv. 1. At that place; there. 2. At that occurrence; on that account.

there-in' (-in'), adv. 1. In or into that or this place, time, or thing. 2. In that particular.

ther'mal (thur-mal). a. Of or pertaining to heat; warm; hot; as, thermal waters.

ther'mo-stat (thur'mo-stat), n. An automatic device to regulate temperature.

the-sau'rus (the-so'rus), n.; L. pl. -SAURI (-ri). A treasury or storehouse; hence, a repository, esp. of words, as a dictionary.

the'sis (the'sis), n.; pl. THESES (-sez). 1. A proposition; esp., a position or proposition which a person advances and offers to maintain by argument. 2. An essay or dissertation, esp. by a candidate for a diploma or degree.

thick (thik), a. 1. Of relatively great depth or extension from one surface to its opposite. 2. Measuring in the third dimension (length and breadth being the other two), or from one surface to its opposite. 3. Closely set; dense; numerous; abundant. 4. Having, or being of, relatively great density or consistency. 5. Not clear; turbid, muddy, or foggy. 6. Dull; stupid; dense. 7. Indistinct; muffled; dull; as, a thick voice. 8. Intimate; familiar. Colloq. —n. thickest part, or time when anything is thickest. — adv. Thickly.

thief (thef), n.; pl. THIEVES (thevz). One who steals, esp. stealthily; one who commits theft.

thigh (thi), n. The leg from the knee up.

thing (thing), n. 1. Whatever exists, or is conceived to exist, as a separate entity. 2. a An act or occurrence; event; deed. b A creature, an object, or a material. c pl. Personal belongings; esp., apparel. d Law. Whatever may be owned, or be the object of a right; — distinguished from person. 3. A particular; item; bit; whit.

this (this), pron. & a.; pl. THESE (thez). A demonstrative word, referring particularly to what is present or near.

this'tle (this'l), n. Any of various prickly plants of the aster family. Also (with qualifying word), any of numerous other prickly plants.

tho'rax (tho'raks), n. 1. The part of the body between the neck and the abdomen, containing the heart, lungs, etc. 2. In insects, the middle of the three chief divisions of the body.

thor'ough (thur'o), a. Thoroughgoing; fully executed; complete.

though (tho), conj. 1. Granting or supporting that; notwithstanding that. 2. In case that; if; — usually with as. 3. In spite of that; notwithstanding; yet. — adv. However; for all that; — a familiar use.

thought (thot), n. 1. Act or state of thinking; reflection; cogitation. 2. a Consideration; heed; care. b Solicitude; anxious care. Obs. or Dial. c Meditation; as, lost in thought. 3. The understanding; intellect. 4. That which is thought; an idea; a judgment. 5. A little; trifle.

thought'ful (-fool), a. 1. Full of thought; contemplative. 2. Marked by, or concerned with, thought. 3. Attentive; careful; heedful. 4. Mindful of others; kind.

thought'less, a. 1. Destitute of thoughts. 2. Careless; heedless.

thou'sand (thou'zand), n. 1. The number of ten hundred. 2. Indefinitely, a great number. 3. A symbol for one thousand units; as, 1,000 or M. — a. Consisting of ten hundred; indefinitely, great in number.

thrash (thrash), **thresh** (thresh), v.t. 1. To beat; flog. Colloq. 2. To beat out grain from, as wheat stalks; beat off, as oat kernels. — v.i. 1. To thresh grain or the like. 2. To move violently; toss about. Both thrash and thresh are in use in all the meanings, but thresh is now chiefly used of beating out grain, thrash in the other senses.

thread'bare' (-bar'), a. 1. Worn to the thread; having the nap worn off. 2. Worn out; trite; hackneyed. 3. Wearing threadbare clothes; shabby.

threat (thret), n. Menace; threatening.

threat'en (thret'n), v.t. 1. To utter threats against; menace. 2. To give signs of the approach of (evil); portend. — v.i. 1. To use threats. 2. To have a threatening appearance.

thresh'old (thresh'old), n. 1. The plank, stone, or piece of timber which lies under a door; sill of a door; hence, an entrance. 2. Entrance; outset.

thrift (thrift), n. 1. Economical management; frugality. 2. Any of a certain genus of plants, esp. one bearing heads of pink or white flowers.

thrift'y (thrif'ti), a. 1. Given to or evincing thrift; provident. 2. Thriving by industry and frugality; prosperous. 3. Growing vigorously.

S
T

thrive (thriv), v.i.; pref. THROVE (throv) or THRIVED (thrivd); p.p. THRIVED or THRIV'EN (thriv'n); p.pr. & vb. n. THRIV'ING (thriv'ing). 1. To prosper by thrift. 2. To be successful or flourishing. 3. To grow vigorously or luxuriantly; flourish.

throat (throt), n. 1. The part of the neck in front of the vertebral column; the passage through it. 2. An entrance, passageway, or narrowed place.

throb (throb), v.i.; THROBBED (throbd); THROB'BING. To pulsate; vibrate; palpitate. — n. A beat, or pulsation, as of the heart.

throw (thro), v.t.; pref. THREW (throo); p.p. THROWN (thron); p.pr. & vb. n. THROW'ING. 1. To twist filaments of, as silk, so as to form one thread. 2. To fling, cast, or hurl. 3. To cause to fall; cast down. 4. To shed; cast. 5. To bring forth; produce; bear. 6. To cast, as dice; venture at dice. — v.i. To cats, hurl, or fling. — n.

thun'der (thun'der), n. 1. The sound following a flash of lightning. 2. A startling or impressive utterance of threat, denunciation, censure, etc.

thun'der, v.i. 1. To produce thunder. 2. To give forth a sound likened to thunder.— v.i. To emit or utter with a noise of or as of thunder.

thun'der-bolt' (thun'der-bolt'), n. 1. A single discharge of lightning with accompanying thunder. 2. Something like, or suggestive of, thunder in being sudden and awful, destructive, or startling.

Thurs'day (thurz'da), n. Fifth day of the week.

thus (thus), adv. 1. In this or that manner. 2. To this degree or extent; so far. 3. Consequently.

ti-a'ra (ti-a'ra; te-a'ra), n. 1. The Pope's triple crown. 2. A crown-like head ornament; a coronet.

tick, v.i. To make a small, repeated noise, esp. one like that of a watch. — v.t. To mark, note, or check, by a tick, or small mark. — n. 1. A light, esp. repeated, sound of or as of tapping. 2. Any small mark to direct attention.

tick'et (-et), n. 1. A small piece of paper, cardboard, or the like, serving as a notice, certificate, or token, esp. of a right, as of admission, etc. 2. Politics. A list of candidates, esp. of one party, to be voted for; ballot. — v.t. To distinguish or mark by a ticket. 2. To furnish with a ticket.

tick'le (tik'l), v.t. 1. To touch lightly so as to produce a peculiar thrilling sensation. 2. To please; amuse. — v.i. To feel or to excite a sense of being tickled. — n. A tickling; a light touch on a sensitive part.

tick'lish (-lish), a. 1. Sensitive to tickling. 2. Insecure; unstable. 3. Critical or dubious.

tide (tid), n. 1. Time; season. 2. The alternate rise and fall of the surface of the ocean occurring twice in each lunar day (24 h. 51 m.). 3. Stream; flood. 4. Tendency or direction of causes; influences, or events. — v.t. To carry or help along as by a tide.

ti'ger (ti'ger), n. A large Asiatic carnivorous animal of the cat family, of a tawny color transversely striped with black.

tight (tit), a. 1. Firmly held together; compact; firm. 2. Impervious; not leaky. 3. Fitting close, usually too close. 4. Taut; tense. 5. Scarce; dear; as, tight money; stringent.

tights (tits), n. pl. Garments fitting close to the skin, usually for the lower part of the body and the legs, worn esp. by acrobats, gymnasts, etc.

tilt (tilt), v.i. 1. To lean; fall partly over; tip. 2. To ride or charge, and thrust with a lance. — v.t. 1. To slope; incline; tip. 2. To point or exercise on horseback in which the combatants tilt at each other.

tim'ber (tim'ber), n. a Wood suitable for use in building, etc. b A dressed piece of wood, esp. one of comparatively large size. —v.t. To furnish with timber; — chiefly in p.p., timbered.

time, v.t. 1. To bring, perform, etc., at a particular season or time. 2. To regulate as to time. 3. To ascertain or record the time of. 4. To measure, as in music. — v.i. To keep or beat time; move in time.

time'-ta'ble, n. A tabular statement of

the time at which, or within which, things are to take place.

tim'id (tim'id), a. Wanting courage to meet danger; timorous; shy.

tin'gle (tin'g'l), v.i. To feel or cause a thrilling or stinging sensation, as from cold, a slap, a shrill sound, etc. — n. A tingling sensation.

ti'ny (ti'ni), a. Very small or diminutive.

tip'sy (-si), a. Rendered weak or foolish by liquor.

tip'toe' (tip'to'), n.; pl. -TOES (-toz'). The tip, or end, of a toe; also, the ends of the toes, collectively. — a. 1. Being on tiptoe; exalted. 2. Cautious; stealthy. — adv. Expectantly; eagerly. — v.i.; TIP'TOED (-tod); TIPTOEING. To go on tiptoe.

tip'top' (-top'), n. The very top; acme; the best. — (tip'top'), a. Most excellent; first-rate. Colloq.

tire, v.i. To become weary. — v.t. To decease or wear out the strength, patience, or interest of.

tire'some (tir'sum), a. Wearisome; tedious.

ti-tan'ic (ti-tan'ik), a. Enormous; superhuman.

tit'il-late (tit'i-lat), v.t. & i. To tickle; excite pleasurably.

ti'tle (ti't'l), n. 1. The distinctive designation of a book, poem, statute, etc. 2. A descriptive name. 3. A personal appellation of dignity, distinction, or rank. 4. A claim or right. 5. Legal right to the possession of property; also, the instrument which is evidence of such right. —v.t. To call by a title.

toast (tost), v.t. & i. 1. To dry and brown by the heat of a fire. 2. To warm thoroughly. 3. To drink to the health of or in honor of. — n. 1. Sliced bread toasted. 2. a One whose health is drunk, or anything in honor of which persons drink. b Act of proposing, or of drinking in honor of, a toast.

to-bac'co (to-bak'o), n.; pl. -COS (-oz). 1. A certain American plant of the nightshade family. 2. Its leaves as prepared and used for smoking or chewing, or as snuff.

to-geth'er (too-geth'er), adv. 1. In company, conjunction, or concert. 2. With each other; mutually. 3. In or into union, junction, contact, or the like. 4. In uninterrupted succession; consecutively.

toil, v.i. 1. To exert strength with pain and fatigue; labor. 2. To go or travel with toil. — n. 1. Labor with pain and fatigue. 2. A piece of toil; a labor.

tol'er-ance (-ans), n. 1. Quality or state of being tolerant. 2. Act of tolerating.

tol'er-ate (-at), v.t. 1. To bear. 2. To suffer to be, or to be done, without hindrance.

tol'er-a'tion (-a'shun), n. Act of tolerating.

toll, n. 1. A tax paid for some liberty or privilege. 2. A compensation taken for services. — v.t. To collect a toll.

tomb (toom), n. A grave, chamber, vault, or monument, for the dead. — v.t. To place in a tomb.

to-mor'row (too-mor'o), adv. On the morrow. — n. the day after the present.

tongue (tung), n. 1. An organ of the mouth, serving as the chief organ of taste and in man also as an organ of speech. 2. a Utterance; discourse. b Manner or quality of utterance. c A language. 3. A part like, or suggestive of, an animal's tongue; as: a The flap of leather under the lacing of a shoe. b A bell clapper.

to-night' (too-nit'), adv. On this present or coming night. — n. the present or coming night.

tool (tool), n. 1. An instrument of manual operation. 2. A person used as an instrument by another person. — v.t. To shape, form, or finish with a tool.

tooth (tooth), n.; pl. TEETH (teth). 1. In most vertebrates, one of the hard bony appendages of the jaws. 2. A projection like, or suggestive of, the tooth of an animal. 3. Discriminating taste.

top'ic (top'ik), n. The subject of any distinct portion of a discourse, argument, or composition.

to-pog'ra-phy (to-pog'ra-fi), n. 1. Description of place or region. 2. Geog. Configuration of a surface.

tor'ment (tor-ment), n. 1. That which gives pain. 2. Anguish.

S
T

tor-na'do (tor-na'do), n.; pl. -DOES. A funnel-shaped cloud, like a waterspout, sand column, or dust whirl, with violent eddies and whirls of wind, progressing in a narrow path for many miles.

tor'por (tor'por), n. 1. Loss of motion or feeling. 2. Dullness.

tor'rent (tor'ent), n. 1. A violent stream. 2. A violent or rapid flow.

tor'ture (tor'tur), n. 1. Act or process of inflicting severe pain. 2. Extreme pain. — v.t. To put to torture.

tot'al (to'tal), a. 1. Whole. 2. Complete. — n. The whole. — v.t. To add. — v.i. To amount to.

touch (tuch), v.t. 1. To perceive by the sense of feeling. 2. To come in contact with. 3. To be in contact with.

tough (tuf), a. 1. Flexible without brittleness. 2. Strong.

tour (toor), n. 1. A journey in a circuit. 2. A prolonged journey. — v.i. To make a tour. —v.t. To make a tour of or through.

to-ward (to'erd' tord), **to'wards** (to'erds; tordz), prep. 1. In the direction of, literally or figuratively. 2. Approaching to.

tow'el (tou'el), n. A cloth for drying anything wet.

town (toun), n. 1. Any large collection of houses and buildings. 2. Townspeople.

track (trak), n. 1. Mark left by something that has passed. 2. a A road. b A course laid out for racing, etc. c A metal way for wheeled vehicles. —v.t. 1. To follow the tracks of. 2. To traverse. 3. To make tracks upon or with. U.S.

trade, v.i. & t. 1. To buy and sell. 2. To participate in a sale or exchange.

tra'di-tion (tra'dish'un), n. Oral delivery or transmission of information, opinions, practices, customs, etc., esp. from ancestors to posterity; also, that which is so transmitted.

traf'fic (traf'ik), n. 1. Commerce; trade. 2. The business done on a railway, steamboat line, etc., as measured by the number of passengers or the amount of freight carried. — v.i.; -FICKED (-ikt); -FICK'ING. To barter; trade.

trai'tor (tra'ter), n. One who betrays a confidence or trust.

trance (trans), n. A state in which the soul seems to have passed out of the body or to be rapt into visions.

tran'quil (tran'kwil), a. Quiet; calm.

tran-scend' (tran-send'), v.t. 1. To rise above or beyond. 2. To excel; exceed.

tran-scrip'tion (tran-skrip'shun), n. 1. Act or process of transcribing. 2. A copy; transcript. 3. Music. An arrangement of a composition for an instrument or voice other than that for which it was originally written; adaptation.

trans-fer' (trans-fur'), v.t.; -FERRED' (furd); -FER'RING. 1. To convey from one place or person to another. 2. To make over the possession or control, as a title to land.

trans-fig'ure (-fig'ur), v.t. 1. To transform. 2. To change to something exalted and glorious.

trans-form' (-form'), v.t. 1. To change in form. 2. To change into another substance. 3. To convert. — v.i. To be or become transformed.

trans-gress' (trans-gres'), v.t. 1. To overstep (a limit or rule). 2. To break or violate, as a law. — v.i. To sin.

trans-lu'cent (-sent), a. Transmitting light without allowing objects to be distinctly seen.

trans-mis'sion (-mish'un), n. 1. Act of transmitting. 2. The gear for transmitting the power from the engine of an automobile to the live axle.

trans-par'ent (-ent), a. 1. Transmitting light so that bodies can be distinctly seen through. 2. Open in texture so as to admit the passage of light. 3. Perspicuous.

trans-port' (-port'), v.t. 1. To carry from one place to another. 2. To banish. 3. To carry away or overcome with emotion.

trans-pose' (trans-poz'), v.t. 1. To change the relative place or order of. 2. To change the natural order of, as words.

trap, n. 1. A device or contrivance that shuts suddenly, as with a spring, for taking game, etc. 2. A stratagem. —

v.t. To catch in a trap. — v.i. To set traps for game.

trash (trash), n. 1. Rubbish. 2. A worthless person.

trav'el (trav'el), v.i. 1. To move. 2. To journey. — v.t. To journey over or through. — n. 1. Act of traveling.

trea'son (tre'z'n), n. 1. Treachery. 2. The offense of attempting to overthrow the government of the state to which one owes allegiance, or (in monarchies) to kill or to injure the sovereign or any of his family.

treas'ure (trezh'ur), n. 1. Money, jewels, etc. hoarded up. 2. A hoard. 3. A thing of great worth. — v.t. To lay up.

trem'ble (trem'b'l), v.i. 1. To shake involuntarily, as with fear, cold, etc. 2. To be tremulous. — n. An involuntary shaking or quivering.

tri'al (tri'al), n. 1. Act of trying or testing; test. 2. State of being tried, or tested. 3. A misfortune or affliction. 4. Law. The formal judicial examination of the matter in issue in a cause to determine the issue.

tribe (trib), n. 1. A social group comprising a series of families, clans, or generations, descended from the same ancestor, together with slaves, dependents, etc. 2. A division or class composed of individuals having some common characteristic.

trib'u-la'tion (trib'u-la'shun), n. A state of distress or affliction, or its causes.

trib'ute (-ut), n. 1. A stated payment from one ruler or state to another, as an acknowledgment of submission, for peace and protection, or by virtue of a treaty. 2. A tax; duty. 3. Any personal contribution, as of praise, service, etc.

trick (trik), n. 1. An artifice. 2. a A dexterous or ingenious feat fitted to puzzle or amuse. b An illusion or deception. 3. A prank. — v.t. 1. To cheat.

tri'fle (-f'l), n. A thing of little value or importance.— v.i. 1. To act or talk jestingly, or with levity. 2. To amuse one's self lightly. — v.t. To spend in trifling or on trifles.

trin'ket (trin'ket), n. 1. A small ornament, as a jewel. 2. A thing of little value.

tri'umph (tri'umf), n. 1. Joy or exultation for success. 2. Victory. — v.i. 1. To celebrate victory or success. 2. To prevail.

triv'i-al (-i-al), a. Trifling; petty.

troop (troop), n. 1. A collection of people or of things. 2. Soldiers collectively. 3. Mil. A division of a cavalry squadron commanded by a captain. — v.i. 1. To move or gather in crowds or troops. 2. To go forward, off, or away. — v.t. To unite with, or form into, a troop or troops.

tro'phy (tro'fi), n.; pl. -PHIES (-fiz). 1. Anything taken and preserved as a memorial of victory, as arms, flags, etc. 2. Something regarded as evidence of conquest.

trop'i-cal (trop'i-kal), a. Of, pertaining to the tropics.

trou'ble (trub'l), v.t. 1. To disturb. 2. To worry. — v.i. To take trouble or pains. — n. 1. State of being troubled. 2. That which causes annoyance, etc. 3. Exertion.

trou'sers (trou'zerz), n. pl. An outer garment of men or boys, extending from waist to knee of ankle, and covering each leg separately.

tru'ant (-ant), n. One who stays away from business or duty. — a. Idle, and shirking duty.

truce (troos), n. 1. Mil. A suspension of arms by agreement. 2. Respite.

true (troo), a. 1. Loyal. 2. Actual. 3. Correct. 4. Truthful.

trust (trust), n. 1. Confidence; faith. 2. Hope. 3. Person or thing on which confidence is reposed.

truth (trooth) n.; pl. TRUTHS (troothz; trooths). Quality or state of being true; hence: 1. Fidelity. 2. Sincerity. 3. Conformity to fact or reality.

try (tri), v.t. 1. To purify or refine. 2. To test. 3. To settle. — v.i. 1. To endeavor. 2. To prove. — n.; pl. TRIES (triz). An attempt.

tub (tub), n. 1. An open wooden vessel formed with staves, bottom, and hoops. 2. Amount which a tub will hold.

tu-ber'cu-lo'sis (-lo'sis), n. Med. An infectious disease due to a bacillus.

tuck (tuk), n. 1. To draw, turn, or gather up. 2. To put or press into or as into a snug, close place. 3. To

S
T

cover closely or neatly, as with bedclothes. — n. A sewed fold made for decoration or shortening.

Tues'day (tuz'da), n. The third day of the week.

tu-i'tion (tu-ish'un), n. Instruction; fee for instruction.

tu'lip (tu'lip), n. Any of various plants of the lily family, having a large showy flower; also, a flower or bulb of the plant.

tum'ble (tum'b'l), v.i. 1. To roll over, or to and fro. 2. To fall suddenly and violently. 3. To move, go, come, pass, etc., in a hasty, disorderly manner. — v.t. 1. To turn over. 2. To disturb. 3. To throw down or roll over. — n. Act of tumbling.

tu'mor (tu'mer), n. A morbid swelling or growth, not inflammatory, in any part of the body.

tu'mult (-mult), n. 1. Agitation of a multitude, usually with uproar and confusion of voices. 2. Violent agitation, with confusion of sounds. 3. Irregular or confused motion.

tune (tun), n. 1. Music. a A melody; air. b State or capacity of giving tones of proper pitch. 2. Order; harmony. — v.t. 1. To adjust (a voice or instrument) to a given musical pitch or temperament. 2. To attune. 3. To utter musically. — v.i. To sound in harmony.

tur'bu-lence (-bu-lens), n. Quality or state of being turbulent; tumult.

tur'bu-lent (-lent), a. 1. Violently agitated; tumultuous. 2. Disposed to disorder; restless. 3. Producing commotion; seditious.

tur'moil (tur'moil), n. Harassing labor; worrying confusion.

turn (turn), v.t. 1. To rotate. 2. a To ponder. b To perform or execute by revolving.

turn'out' (-out'), n. 1. A coming forth. 2. A gathering of persons.

tu'tor (tu'ter), n. One in charge of the instruction of another. —v.t. To teach; instruct. — v.i. To do the work of a tutor.

tweak (twek), v.t. To pinch and pull with a sudden jerk and twist. — n. A sharp pinch or twist.

twi'light' (twi'lit'), n. The light perceived before the rising, and after the setting, of the sun. — a. 1.

Of or pertaining to the twilight. 2. Imperfectly illuminated.

twin (twin), a. 1. Made up of two distinct, nearly related, and equal members. 2. Being a twin. — n. One of two persons or things closely related by ties of birth, resemblance, etc.

twin'kle (twin'k'l), v.i. 1. To wink or blink rapidly. 2. To sparkle. 3. To appear rapidly at intervals. — n. 1. A wink. 2. A brief flash or gleam. 3. The time of a wink.

type (tip), v.t. 1. To produce a copy of. 2. To typewrite.

type'set'ter (tip'set-ter), n. One that sets type; a compositor; a machine for setting type.

typ'i-cal (tip'i-kal), a. 1. Of the nature of a type or symbol. 2. Characteristic.

U

u-biq'ui-tous (u-bik'wi-tus), a. Existing everywhere at the same time; omnipresent.

ug'ly (ug'li), a. 1. Offensive aesthetically or morally; repulsive. 2. Ill-natured; quarrelsome.

ul'cer (ul'ser), n. Superficial sore discharging pus.

ul'ti-mate (-mat), a. 1. Farthest. 2. Last in progression or sequence; final.

ul'ti-ma'tum (-ma'tum), n.; pl. E. -TUMS (-tumz) L. -TA (-ta). A final proposition, or condition.

ul'tra (-tra), a. Extreme.

um-brel'la (-brel'a), n. A shade, screen, or guard carried in the hand as a shelter from rain, sun, etc.

un-a'ble (un-a'b'l), a. Not able; incapable.

un'ac-count'a-ble (un'a-koun'ta-b'l), a. Not accountable; inexplicable.

un'ac-cus'tomed (-kus'tumd), a. 1. Not habituated. 2. Uncommon.

un'ad-vised' (un'ad-vizd'), a. Not advised; esp., indiscreet or rash; inconsiderate.

un'af-fect'ed (un'a-fek'ted), a. Not affected.

un'as-sum'ing (un'a-sum'ing), a. Modest.

un'a-void'a-ble (-void'a-b'l), Not

avoidable.

un-bal'anced (-bal'anst), a. 1. Not balanced. 2. Out of equilibrium; deranged.

un'be-com'ing (un'be-kum'ing), a. Not becoming; improper.

un'be-lief' (-lef'), n. 1. The withholding of belief. 2. Disbelief.

un'be-liev'er (-lev'er), n. 1. One who does not believe. 2. A disbeliever; infidel.

un-born' (-born'), a. Not born; future.

un-but'ton (-but'n), v.t. To loose the buttons of.

un-called'-for', a. Not called for; gratuitous.

un-can'ny (-kan'i), a. Mysterious; weird.

un-cer'tain-ty (-ti), n.; pl. -TIES (-tiz). Quality or state of being uncertain; something uncertain.

un-char'i-ta-ble (-char'i-ta-b'l), a. Not charitable; censorious.

un-chaste' (un-chast'), a. Not chaste.

un-civ'il (-siv'il), a. Not civil; discourteous; rude. — un-civ'il-ly, adv.

un-clean' (un-klen'), a. 1. Not clean; dirty. 2. Ceremonially or morally impure.

un-com'fort-a-ble (-kum'fer-ta-b'l), a. Feeling or causing discomfort.

un-com'mon (-kom'un), a. Not common; unusual; rare; hence, remarkable; strange.

un-com'pro-mis'ing (un-kom'pro-miz'ing), a. Unyielding; inflexible.

un'con-cerned' (-surnd'), a. Indifferent.

un'con-di'tion-al (-dish'un-al), a. Absolute.

un-con'scion-a-ble (un-kon'shun-a-b'l), a. 1. Uunreasonable. 2. Not guided or controlled by conscience.

un-con'scious (-shus), a. Not conscious.

un-couth' (-kooth'), a. Awkwardly strange; boorish.

un-cov'er (-kuv'er), v.t. & i. 1. To take the cover from. 2. To show openly; disclose.

un-daunt'ed (un-dan'ted; -don'-), a. Not daunted; fearless; intrepid.

un'de-ni'a-ble (un'de-m'a-b'l), a. 1. Indisputable. 2. Unquestionably excellent. Colloq.

un'der (un'der), prep. Below or beneath. — adv. In a lower

position, or in a subordinate condition. — a. Subordinate.

un-der-cur'rent (-kur'ent), 1. A current below the upper currents or surface of water, etc. 2. A tendency of feeling, opinion, etc., more or less hidden.

un'der-done' (un'der-dun'; un'der-dun'), p.a. Cooked for an insufficient time; rare.

un'der-go' (-go'), v.t.; for prin. parts see GO. To be subjected to; bear up against; endure; suffer.

un'der-grad'u-ate (-grad'u-at), n. A member of a university or of a college who has not taken his first degree.

un'der-hand' (-hand'), a. Secret; unfair. — adv. In an underhand manner; unfairly.

un'der-lie' (-li'), v.t.; for prin. parts see LIE. 1. To lie or be situated under. 2. To be at the basis of; form the foundation of, as of a theory or an argument.

un'der-mine' (-min'), v.t. 1. To sap. 2. To weaken or overthrow secretly, underhandedly, or insidiously.

un'der-neath' (-neth'; -neth'), adv. & prep. Beneath; under.

un'der-sized' (un'der-sizd'), a. Of a size less than is common or proper.

un'der-stand' (-stand'), v.t.; for prin. parts see STAND. 1. To comprehend. 2. To learn. — v.i. 1. To have the use of the intellectual faculties. 2. To be informed.

un'der-stand'ing, pa. Knowing; intelligent. — n. 1. Knowledge. 2. Agreement of opinion; adjustment of differences. 3. Power to understand; the intelligence.

un'der-state' (-stat'), v.t. & i. To state less strongly, or as less, than the truth warrants.

un'der-stud'y (un'der-stud'i), v.t. & i. Theater. To study another actor's part, in order to be his substitute in an emergency. — n. One prepared to act another's part.

un'der-take' (-tak'), v.t.; for prin. parts see TAKE. 1. To take upon one's self. 2. To contract. — v.i. To promise; guarantee.

un'der-tak'er (-tak'er), n. 1. One who undertakes something. 2. (pron. un'der-tak'er; un'der-tak'er) One

U
Z

who takes charge of funerals.

un'der-tak'ing (-tak'ing), n. 1. Act of one who undertakes anything; specif., the business of an undertaker (sense 2). 2. Thing undertaken; enterprise. 3. A guarantee.

un'der-tone' (un'der-ton'), n. 1. A low or subdued tone or utterance. 2. A subdued color.

un'der-val'ue (-val'u), v.t. To value below the real worth; esteem lightly.

un'der-world' (un'der-wurld), n. 1. Hades. 2. The antipodes. 3. The lower, debased, or criminal portion of humanity.

un'der-write' (-rit'), v.t.; for prin. parts see WRITE. 1. To write under something else. 2. To write one's name under, or set one's name to (a policy of insurance), and thereby become answerable for a designated loss or damage, esp. on marine property. — v.i. To do the business of an underwriter.

un'der-writ'er (un'der-rit'er), n. One who underwrites a policy of insurance, a loan, etc.

un-do' (un-doo'), v.t.; for prin. parts see DO. 1. To reverse, as something done. 2. To unfasten. 3. To bring to ruin.

un-due' (un-du'; un'du), a. 1. Not due. 2. Not right. 3. Not agreeable to a rule or standard, or to duty.

un-earth' (-urth'), v.t. To drive or draw from the earth.

un-e'qual (un-e'kwal), a. 1. Not equal. 2. Ill-balanced or ill-matched. 3. Not uniform.

un'e-quiv'o-cal (un'e-kwiv'o-kal), a. Not equivocal; clear; sincere; plain.

un'ex-pect'ed (-eks-pek'ted), a. Not expected; sudden.

un-fair' (-far'), a. Not fair; unjust.

un-faith'ful (un-fath'fool), a. 1. Not faithful; not observant of promises, duty, etc. 2. Inaccurate; untrustworthy.

un-fa'vor-a-ble (-fa'ver-a-b'l), a. Not favorable; not propitious; adverse.

un-feel'ing (-fel'ing), a. 1. Destitute of feeling; insensible; insensate. 2. Cruel; hardhearted.

un-fit' (-fit'), v.t.; -FIT'TED; -FIT'TING. To disable.

un-for'tu-nate (-for'tu-nat), a. Not fortunate; unsuccessful. — n. An unfortunate person.

un-found'ed (-foun'ded), a. Not founded or established.

un-friend'ly (-frend'li), a. 1. Hostile. 2. Not favorable. **un-god'ly** (-god'li), a. Not godly; wicked; sinful. — ungod'li-ness, n.

un-gra'cious (-gra'shus), a. 1. Not gracious; uncivil; rude. 2. Offensive; unpleasing.

un-grate'ful (-grat'fool), a. 1. Not grateful. 2. Unpleasing.

un-hap'py (-hap'i), a. 1. Not happy or fortunate; unlucky. 2. Sad; sorrowful. 3. Marked by infelicity; calamitous; inappropriate.

un-ho'ly (-ho'li), a. Not holy; profane; impious.

u'ni-fi-ca'tion (-fi-ka'shun), n. A unifying.

u'ni-form (u'ni-form), a. 1. Having always the same form, manner, or degree. 2. Of the same form with others. — n. A dress of a particular style or fashion worn by persons in the same service, etc. — v.t. To clothe with a uniform.

u'ni-fy (u'ni-fi), v.t. To unite.

u'ni-lat'er-al (u'ni-lat'er-al), a. One-sided.

un'ion (un'yun), n. 1. Act of uniting two or more things into one. 2. That which is united.

u'ni-son (u'ni-sun; -zun), n. Harmony; union.

u-nite' (u-nit'), v.t. 1. To put together so as to make one. 2. To join by a legal or moral bond. — v.i. 1. To become one. 2. To join in an act.

u'ni-ty (u'ni-ti), n.; pl. -TIES (-tiz). 1. State of being one. 2. Harmony.

u'ni-ver'sal (-vur'sal), a. 1. Of or pertaining to the universe; general. 2. Constituting, or considered as, a whole.

u'ni-verse (u'ni-vurs), n. All created things as constituting one system; the world.

u'ni-ver'si-ty (u'ni-vur'si-ti), n.; pl. -TIES (-tiz). An institution for teaching and study in the higher branches of learning.

un-just' (un-just'), a. Contrary to justice; wrongful.

un-kind' (-kind'), a. Wanting in kindness; cruel; harsh.

un-law'ful (-lo'fool), a. 1. Not lawful; contrary to law. 2. Illegitimate.

un-learn'ed (-lur'ned), a. 1. Not learned. 2. (pron. -lurnd') Not gained by study. 3. Not exhibiting learning.

un-less' (-les'), conj. If not.

un-like'ly, a. 1. Not likely; improbable. 2. Not having prospect of success.

un-lim'it-ed (un-lim'i-ted), a. 1. Not limited; unrestricted. 2. Undefined; indefinite.

un-load (-lod'), v.t. 1. To take the load or cargo from. 2. Fig., to relieve from anything onerous. 3. To remove or discharge, as a cargo.

un-lock' (un-lok'), v.t. 1. To unfasten, as what is locked. 2. To open; to disclose.

un-luck'y (-luk'i), a. 1. Not lucky; unfortunate. 2. Bringing bad luck; inauspicious.

un-man'ner-ly (-man'er-li), a. Not mannerly; rude. — adv. Uncivilly.

un-mer'ci-ful (-mur'si-fool), a. Not merciful; cruel.

un'mis-tak'a-ble (un'mis-tak'a-b'l), a. Not mistakable; evident.

un-nat'u-ral (-nat'u-ral), a. Not natural.

un-nec'es-sa-ry (-nes'e-sa-ri), a. Not necessary; needless.

un-pack' (un-pak'), v.t. To separate and remove, as things packed; open and remove the contents of.

un-pleas'ant (-plez'ant), a. Not pleasant; offensive.

un-prec'e-dent-ed (-pres'e-den-ted), a. Having no precedent; new.

un-ques'tion-a-ble (-kwes'chun-a-b'l), a. Not questionable.

un-read'y (un-red'i),a. Not ready or prepared; not prompt; slow.

un-rea'son-a-ble (un-re'z'n-a-b'l), a. Not reasonable.

un-right'eous (-ri'chus), a. 1. Not righteous. 2. Unjust.

un-rul'y (-rool'i), a. Not submissive to rule or restraint; turbulent.

un-scru'pu-lous (-skroo'pu-lus), a. Not scrupulous.

un-sea'son-a-ble (-se'z'n-a-b'l), a. Not seasonable; untimely.

un-seem'ly (-sem'li), a. Not seemly; indecent. — adv. In an unseemly manner.

un-skill'ful (-skil'fool), a. Not skillful; awkward.

un-speak'a-ble (-spek'a-b'l), a. Not speakable; inexpressible; unutterable; also, unspeakably bad.

un-think'ing (-think'ing), a. 1. Thoughtless. 2. Not indicating thought.

un-til' (-til'), prep. To; up to; till.

un-truth (-trooth'), n. 1. Quality of being untrue. 2. That which is untrue.

un-u'su-al (un-u-zhu-al), a. Not usual; unaccustomed; uncommon.

un-veil' (-val'), v.t. To remove a veil from; reveal. — v.i. To remove a veil; reveal one's self.

un-well' (-wel'), a. Not well; indisposed.

un-will'ing (-wil'ing), a. Not willing; loath.

un-wise (-wiz'), a. Not wise; injudicious; foolish.

un-writ'ten (-rit'n), a. 1. Not written; oral; traditional. 2. Containing no writing; blank.

up (up), adv. 1. In or toward a higher position. 2. At, toward, or to, any point thought of as higher. —prep. To a higher place on or along. — a. Upward. — n. State of being up; prosperity.

up-heave' (-hev), v.t. To heave or lift up from beneath; raise. —v.i. To rise.

up-hold' (up-hold'), v.t. 1. To hold up. 2. To keep erect; support. 3. To aid by approval or encouragement.

up'keep (up'kep), n. Act of keeping up, or maintaining; maintenance.

up'per-most (-most), a. Highest in place, position, rank, power, or the like.

up'right' (up'rit'), a. 1. Erect in position; vertical, or nearly so. 2. Having rectitude; honest; just. — n. Something standing upright, as a timber.

up-ris'ing (up-riz'ing), n. 1. Act of rising. 2. An insurrection.

up-stairs' (up-starz'), adv. Up the stairs; in or toward an upper story.

up-ward (up'werd), adv. Also up'wards (-werdz). 1. In a direction from lower to higher. 2. Toward the source or origin. — a. Directed upward.

ur-gent (ur'jent), a. Urging; pressing;

**U
Z**

calling for immediate attention.

us-age (uz'aj; us'aj), n. 1. Act or mode of using. 2. Long-continued practice. 3. Customary use or employment.

use (uz), v.t. 1. To make use of; employ. 2. To practice, esp. customarily. 3. To behave toward; treat. 4. To accustom.

use'less (-les), a. Being of no use.

ush'er (uz'er), n. A doorkeeper; hence, one who escorts persons to seats in a church, theater, etc. — v.t. To announce.

u-ten'sil (u-ten'sil), n. An instrument or vessel.

ut'ter, v.t. 1. To put in circulation, as money, esp. counterfeit notes or coins. 2. To give expression to; speak.

V

va-can'cy (va'kan-si), n.; pl. -CIES (-siz). 1. Quality or state of being vacant. 2. Vacant thing; as: a Empty space. b An unoccupied office or position.

va-cant (kant), a. Empty.

va-ca'tion (va-ka'shun), n. 1. Act of vacating. 2. Holiday.

vac'ci-nate (vak'si-nat), v.t. To inoculate with a vaccine, as that of cowpox, to prevent an attack of smallpox.

va'gran-cy (va'gran-si), n. State or fact of being a vagrant.

va'grant (-grant), a. 1. Moving about without certain object; wandering without settled habitation. 2. Of, pert. to, or characteristic of, a vagrant; vagabond; erratic; as, a vagrant nature. — n. A vagabond.

vague (vag), a. 1. Not clearly defined, grasped; etc.; hazy; as, a vague idea. 2. Unauthenticated; uncertain. 3. Not thinking, seeing, etc., clearly.

vain (van), a. 1. Without value or importance. 2. Without force or efficacy. 3. Conceited.

val'et (val'et; val'a), n. A manservant who attends a man, taking care of his clothes, etc.

val'id (val'id), a. 1. Founded on truth or fact; sound; as, a valid argument. 2. Law. Having legal force or authority.

val'ley (val'i), n.; pl. -LEYS (-iz). A depression, usually with outlet, between hills or mountains.

val'or (val'er), n. Bravery; courage, esp. in fighting.

val'u-a-ble (-u-a-b'l), a. 1. Commanding or worth a good price. 2. Precious. — n. A possession or thing of value.

val'ue (val'u), n. 1. Worth. 2. a Purchasing power. b Proper, or legitimate, price. 3. Precise signification; import.

van'ish (van'ish), v.i. 1. To become invisible; disappear. 2. To be annihilated or lost; pass away; as, hope vanished.

van'tage (van'taj), n. Superior situation or opportunity; advantage; vantage ground.

va'por-ize (va'per-iz), v.t. & i. To convert or change into vapor.

va'ri-a-ble (va'ri-a-b'l), a. 1. Having the capacity or characteristic of varying; changeable. 2. Liable to vary; fickle; unsteady. — n. 1. That which is variable. 2. Math. A quantity that may increase or decrease, or the symbol for it.

va'ried (va'rid), p.a. 1. Changed; altered. 2. Various; diverse. 3. Variegated.

va-ri'e-ty (-ti), n.; pl. -TIES (-tiz). 1. State or quality of being various or varied; diversity. 2. That which is varied; as: a A collection of different things. b Something differing from others of the same general kind; sort. c A group of animals or plants distinguished from similar groups only by characters too slight to constitute it a species.

va'ri-ous (va'ri-us), a. 1. Different; diverse; several; manifold. 2. Changeable; uncertain. 3. Having varied characteristics; many-sided; also, variegated; diversified.

va'ry (va'ri), v.t. 1. To alter in form, appearance, substance, position, etc.; modify. 2. To make different, or change from one another. 3. To diversify; as, to vary one's diet. 4. Music. To embellish with variations. — v.i. 1. To alter or be altered; be modified. 2. To differ; be different, unlike, or diverse. 3. to deviate;

swerve. 4. To alternate.

vase (vas; vaz; or, esp. Brit., vaz), n. A vessel, usually rounded, and of greater depth than width, chiefly ornamental.

vast (vast), a. Of great extent; immense; very great.

Vat'i-can (vat'i-kan), n. 1. The Pope's palace, at Rome, including museums, library, etc. 2. The papal authority or government.

veg'e-ta'ri-an (-ta'ri-an), n. One who holds that plants afford the only proper food for man. — a. Of or pert. to vegetarians; also, consisting wholly of vegetables.

veg'e-tate (vej'e-tat), v.i. 1. To grow after the fashion of plants. 2. To lead a passive existence without exertion of body or mind.

ve'he-ment (-ment), a. 1. Acting with great force; furious; violent. 2. Very ardent, eager, or urgent; passionate.

ve'hi-cle (ve'hi-k'l, ve'i-), n. 1. That in or on which a thing is carried; a carriage. 2. That which is used as the instrument of conveyance or communications; as: a Pharm. A substance in which medicine is taken. b Paint. Liquid medium, as oil, in which a pigment is applied.

vein (van), n. 1. One of the system of tubular vessels which carry the blood to the heart. 2. One of the radiating or branching ribs forming the framework of a plant or of an insect's wing. 3. a A crack in rock filled by mineral matter. b A lode. c A bed; as, a vein of coal. — v.t. To form, fill, or cover, with veins.

vel'vet (vel'vet), n. A silk fabric having a short thick pile of erect threads. — a. Like, or suggestive of, velvet; velvety.

ven'er-a-ble (ven'er-a-b'l), a. 1. Worthy of veneration; —generally implying advanced age. 2. Rendered sacred by associations.

venge'ance (ven'jans), n. Punishment in return for an injury or offense; retribution; also, passionate or unrestrained revenge.

ve'ni-al (ve'ni-al), a. Capable of being forgiven;.

ven'i-son (ven'i-z'n), n. The flesh of an animal of the deer kind.

ven'om (ven'um), n. That which poisons, embitters or blights.

ven'ti-late (ven-ti-lat), v.t. 1. To cause fresh air to circulate through (a room, mine, etc.). 2. To give vent to; utter.

ven-tril'o-quism (ven-tril'o-kwiz'm), n. Act or art of speaking in such a way that the voice appears to come from a source other than the speaker's vocal organs.

ven'ture (ven'tur), n. 1. An undertaking of chance or danger; a hazard; risk; business speculation. 2. The thing put to hazard; stake; risk. — v.t. 1. To expose to hazard; risk. 2. To undertake the risk of; brave; dare. 3. To put or send on a venture, as a business speculation. — v.i. 1. To hazard one's self; dare. 2. To make a venture; run a risk.

ver-ba'tim (ver-ba'tim), adv. Word for word; in the same words; verbally.

ver'dict (vur-dikt), n. 1. Law. The finding or decision of a jury on the matter submitted in trial. 2. Decision; judgment.

verge (vurj), n. 1. A rod or staff carried as an emblem of authority or symbol of office. 2. A border, limit, or boundary; edge or brink. 3. An inclosing or encircling thing, as a ring. —v.i. 1. To be on the verge. 2. To tend; incline.

ver'i-fy (ver'i-fi), v.t. 1. To prove to be true; confirm; substantiate. 2. To authenticate.

ver'min (vur'min), n. sing. & pl.; chiefly as pl. A noxious animal, esp. such animals collectively, when of small size. Flies, lice, bedbugs, fleas, rats, mice, etc., are classed as vermin.

ver'sa-tile (vur'sa-til), a. Turning with ease from one thing to another.

verse (vurs), n. 1. a A poetic line consisting of a certain number and disposition of metrical feet (see FOOT, n., 6). b Metrical arrangement and language; versification; poetry. c A piece of poetry. 2. A short division of any composition.

ver'sion (-shun), n. 1. A translation; esp., a translation or rendering of the Bible or a part of it. 2. An account from a particular point of view.

U
Z

ver'te-brate (-brat), a. Having a backbone, or spinal column. — n. One of a division of animals (Vertebrata) containing those with a backbone.

ver'ti-go (vur'ti-go), n.; pl. E. -GOES (-goz). Dizziness, or swimming of the head.

ves'sel (ves'el), n. 1. A hollow or concave utensil or receptacle, as a barrel, bottle, kettle, cup, bowl, etc. 2. Any craft for navigation of the water; usually, one larger than a rowboat. 3. Anat. A tube or canal in which a fluid is contained and circulated, as an artery, vein, etc.

vest'ed (ves'ted), a. 1. Clothed; robed, esp. in a ceremonial costume. 2. Law. That has become a consummated right; as, vested interests.

ves'ti-bule (ves'ti-bul), n. 1. A passage, hall, or chamber between the outer door and the interior of a building; a porch, or entrance into a house. 2. An inclosed entrance to a passenger car.

vet'er-an (vet'er-an), a. 1. Grown old in experience; long practiced, esp. in military life. 2. Of, pertaining to, or characteristic of, a veteran; as, with veteran skill. — n. One long exercised in any service or art, esp. in war.

vet'er-i-na'ri-an (-i-na'ri-an), n. One who treats diseases and injuries of domestic animals.

vet'er-i-na-ry (vet'er-i-na-ri), a. Of or pert. to the art of treating the injuries and diseases of domestic animals. — n.; pl. -RIES (-riz). A veterinarian.

vi'a-ble (vi'a-b'l), a. Capable of living.

vi'brant (vi'brant). a. Vibrating; sounding as a result of vibrating; resonant; resounding.

vi-ca'ri-ous (vi-ka'ri-us), a. 1. Deputed; delegated. 2. Acting for another. 3. Performed or suffered in place of another.

vice (vis), n. 1. A moral fault or failing. 2. State of being given up to evil conduct or habits.

vi-cin'i-ty (vi-sin'i-ti), n.; pl. -TIES (-tiz). 1. Nearness. 2. A region about, near, or adjacent.

vi'cious (vish'us), a. 1. Addicted to vice. 2. Characterized by vice, or defect. 3. Impure.

vic'tim (vik'tim), n. 1. A living being sacrificed in a religious rite. 2. One injured, destroyed, or sacrificed, in the pursuit of an object, at the hands of another, or from disease, accident, etc.

vic'tim-ize (-iz), v.t. To make a victim of.

vic-to'ri-ous (-us), a. 1. Having gained victory; conquering. 2. Of, pert. to, or symbolic of, victory.

vic'to-ry (vik'to-ri), n.; pl. -RIES (-riz). Triumph.

vig'il (vij'il), n. 1. Abstinence from sleep. 2. A watch.

vig'or (vig'er), n. Active strength or force, as of body or mind; effective energy or power.

vile (vil), a. 1. Of small account; Ibase. 2. Morally base. 3. Unclean; repulsive.

vil'lage (-aj), n. Any small aggregation of houses in the country, less than a town.

vil'lain (-in), n. Scoundrel; knave.

vin'di-cate (vin'di-kat), v.t. To support or maintain as true or correct against denial.

vin-dic'tive (vin-dik'tiv), a. Disposed to revenge.

vine (vin), n. 1. A grapevine. 2. Any climbing, trailing, or creeping plant.

vi'o-late (vi'o-lat), v.t. 1. To abuse. 2. To desecrate.

vi'o-lent (vi'o-lent), a. 1. Moving, acting, or characterized, by extreme and sudden, or improper, force. 2. Passionate.

vir'gin (vur'jin), n. Being a virgin; chaste; maidenly 2. Pure; undefiled.

vir'ile (vir'il; vi'ril), a. 1. Having the nature or qualities of a man. 2. Masterful.

vir'tu-al (vur'tu-al), a. 1. Of or relating to a real force or energy; potential. 2. Being in effect, but not in fact.

vir'tue (vur'tu), n. 1. Active quality or power. 2. Excellence; merit. 3. Moral excellence.

vi'rus (vi'rus), n. 1. Med. The poison or contagion of an infectious disease; also, vaccine virus. 2. Anything that poisons the mind or the soul.

vi'sion-a-ry (-a-ri), a. 1. Of or

pertaining to a vision or visions; characterized by, or favorable for, visions. 2. Dreamy; imaginative. 3. Fanciful; impracticable. — n.; pl. -RIES (-riz). One who sees visions, is not practical.

vi-tal'i-ty (vi-tal'i-ti), n. Power of enduring.

vi'tals (-talz), n. pl. Organs most necessary for life; esp., heart, lungs, and brain.

vi-va'cious (vi-va'shus; vi-), a. Lively in temper or conduct; sprightly.

viv'id (-id), a. 1. Animated; intense. 2. Lively; active.

vix'en (vik's'n), n. 1. A she-fox. 2. A shrewish, ill-tempered woman.

vo-cab'u-la-ry (vo-kab'u-la-ri), n.; pl. - RIES (-riz). 1. A dictionary or lexicon. 2. Stock of words used in a language, or by a class, individual, etc.

vo'cal (vo'kal), a. 1. Of or pertaining to the voice or speech. 2. Oral.

vo-ca'tion (vo-ka'shun), n. Regular or appropriate employment; calling.

vogue (vog), n. The way or fashion of people at any period.

voice (vois), n. 1. Sound uttered by the mouth in speech or song. 2. Faculty or power of speech.

void (void), a. 1. Empty; vacant. 2. Having no incumbent; unoccupied; — of offices, etc. 3. Destitute; wanting; — usually with of. 4. Not producing effect; useless; null. — n. A vacuum.

vol-ca'no (vol-ka'no), n.; pl. -NOES or -NOS (-noz). A vent in the earth's crust from which hot rock, steam, etc., issue; also, a hill or mountain composed wholly or in part of the ejected material.

vo-li'tion (vo-lish'un), n. 1. Act of willing or choosing. 2. Will.

vol'ume (vol'um), n. 1. Any collection of printed sheets bound together. 2. Space occupied. 3. Music. Fullness or quantity of tone.

vol'un-ta-ry (vol'un-ta-ri), a. 1. Proceeding from the will. 2. Unconstrained. 3. Intentional.

vol'un-teer' (-ter'), n. One who voluntarily enters into, or offers himself for, a service. — a. Of or pert. to volunteer; voluntary. - v.t. To offer or bestow voluntarily. — v.i. To

enter into, or offer one's self for, any service voluntarily.

vo-lup'tu-ous (-us), a. Ministering or pertaining to sensuous or sensual gratification.

vo-ra'cious (vo-ra'shus), a. Greedy in eating; ravenous; rapacious.

vote (vot), n. 1. A wish, choice, or judgment, of a person or a body of persons, formally expressed, as by a ballot. 2. That by means of which a vote (sense 1) is expressed, as a ballot, etc. 3. Votes collectively. — v.i. [1] To signify the wish, choice, or will, as by ballot, etc.; cast or give a vote. —v.t. 1. To enact, grant, determine, effect, etc., by formal vote.

vow (vou), n. A solemn promise. —v.t. & i. 1. To bind one's self by a vow. 2. To swear.

vul'gar (-gar), a. 1. Of or pertaining to the common people; ordinary; plebeian; hence, vernacular. 2. Lacking refinement; low; coarse.

vul'ner-a-ble (vul'ner-a-b'l), a. 1. Capable of being wounded. 2. Liable to injury.

W

wage (waj), v.t. To engage in, as a contest; carry on, as a war. —n. That which is paid for services.

wa'ger (wa'jer), n. 1. A stake; bet. 2. Act of wagering, or betting; a bet; as, to make a wager. — v.t. & i. To stake; bet.

wag'on (wag'un), n. A kind of four-wheeled vehicle.

waist (wast), n. 1. The part of the body between the thorax and hips. 2. A garment, or that part of a garment, which covers the body from shoulders to waist. 3. Part of a vessel's deck between the quarter-deck and forecastle.

wait (wat), v.i. 1. To be in expectation. 2. To stay in expectation, as till the arrival of some person or event. 3. To act as attendant or servant; serve. — v.t. To stay for; await. — n. 1. Ambush. Obs., exc. in to lie in wait. 2. Act of waiting; delay; also, interval of waiting.

wait'er (-er), n. 1. One who waits for

U
Z

or awaits something. 2. An attendant; servant in attendance, esp. at tables. **wait'ress** (-res).

wake, v.i.; WAKED (wakt) or WOKE (wok); WAK'ING (wak'ing). 1. To be awake; also, to keep watch or vigil. 2. To be roused from sleep; awake. — v.t. 1. To rouse from sleep; awake. 2. To arouse; excite. — n. 1. State of forbearing sleep, esp. for solemn or festive purposes; a vigil. 2. The sitting up with a dead body, often attended with a degree of festivity, chiefly among the Irish.

walk (wok), v.i. 1. To move along on foot. 2. To behave; conduct one's self. — v.t. 1. To pass through, over, or upon. 2. To cause to walk. — n. 1. Act or manner of walking. 2. Habitual or proper place or sphere of action. 3. Place where one walks, or for walking.

wal'nut (wol'nut), n. The nut of any of a genus of well-known trees of the north temperate zone; also, the tree or its timber.

waltz (woltz), n. A kind of round dance in triple time; also, music for this dance, or its time. — v.i. To dance a waltz.

wan'der (won'der), v.i. 1. To ramble about without any definite course. 2. To stray off. — v.t. To wander over or through. — n. Act of wandering.

war (wor), n. 1. State of using violence against another; a contest by force between states. 2. State of opposition or contest; hostility; contention; as, a war of words. — v.i.; WARRED (word); WAR'RING. To make or wage war.

ward'en (wor'd'n), n. A keeper; guardian; guard; as: a A chief keeper, as of a prison. b A churchwarden.

warm (worm), a. 1. Having heat, or a sensation of heat, esp. in a moderate degree; not cold. 2. Sending out or imparting warmth. 3. Subject to little or no cold weather. 4. Passionate; sprightly; ardent; excitable. — v.t. & i. 1. To render or become warm. 2. To make or become ardent, animated, or interested; — often with up.

warn (worn), v.t. 1. To put on guard; caution. 2. To notify in advance; notify or summon by authority; bid. 3. To admonish; advise. — - **er**, n.

war'rior (wor'yer), n. A man engaged or experienced in war or in military life; soldier.

wa'ry (wa'ri), a. 1. Cautious of danger or deception. 2. Characterized by caution.

wash (wosh), v.t. 1. To cleanse by dipping, rubbing, or scrubbing in water. 2. To cover with water; wet; flow against or over.

wash'er (wosh'er), n. 1. One that washes. 2. A ring or a perforated plate used to distribute pressure (as of a nut), to prevent play, etc. 3. A machine or apparatus for washing.

waste (wast), a. 1. Desolate; desert; dreary. 2. Unproductive; worthless; refuse. — v.t. 1. To lay waste; devastate. 2. To wear away; impair or diminish gradually. 3. To spend unnecessarily; squander. — v.i. To lose bulk, strength, value, etc., gradually. —n. 1. That which is waste, or desolate. 2. A wasting; thing wasted. 3. That which has no value for the main purpose of manufacture; refuse.

watch (woch), v.i. 1. To be awake; keep vigil. 2. To be attentive; be on the lookout. 3. To be expectant; wait. — v.t. 1. To tend; have in keeping. 2. To give heed to; keep in view. — n. 1. A keeping awake to guard, protect, etc.; vigil. 2. Vigilant attention; vigilance.

watch'ful (-fool), a. Full of vigilance; attentive; cautious.

wa'ter (wo'ter), n. A fluid compound consisting of hydrogen and oxygen.

wa'ter-fall' (-fol'), n. A fall, or very steep descent, of the water of a stream.

wa'ter-mark' (-mark'), n. 1. A mark indicating the height of water. 2. A marking produced in paper during manufacture.

wa'ter-proof' (wo'ter-proof'), a. Impervious to water. — n. Something waterproof, as a kind of cloak. — v.t. To make waterproof.

wa'ter-y (-i), a. 1. Of or pertaining to water. 2. Like, or suggestive of, water.

wave (wav), v.i. 1. To undulate; flutter.

2. To be moved to and fro as a signal. 3. To be sinuous like a wave.

weak (wek), a. 1. Lacking in strength, power, or force. 2. Not possessing mental or moral strength; etc.; simple; foolish.

wealth'y (wel'thi), a. Having wealth; rich.

weap'on (wep'un), n. 1. An instrument of combat, as a gun, sword, shield, etc. 2. Any means by which one contends against another.

wear (war), v.t.; pref. WORE (wor); p.p. WORN (worn); p. pr. & vb. n. WEAR'ING. 1. To carry or bear upon the person. 2. To bear; carry; show; as, she wears a smile. 3. To use up by wearing (in sense 1); hence, to consume, waste, or exhaust gradually.

wea'ry (-ri), a. 1. Fatigued; tired. 2. Having one's patience or liking exhausted; — esp. with of. 3. Expressing weariness. — v.i. & t. To become or make weary.

wed (wed), v.t. 1. To marry; espouse. 2. To join in marriage; give in wedlock. 3. To attach firmly. — v.i. To contract matrimony; marry.

wed'lock (wed'lok), n. Matrimony.

Wednes'day (wenz'da), n. Fourth day of the week.

week (wek), n. A period of seven days, usually reckoned as beginning with Sunday.

weep (wep), v.i.; WEPT (wept); WEEP'ING. To show grief or other passion by shedding tears; to cry. — v.t. 1. To shed tears for; hence, to lament; bewail. 2. To shed, as tears.

weight (wat), n. 1. Quality of being heavy; that property by which bodies tend toward the center of the earth. 2. Quantity of heaviness. 3. Pressure; burden; load. 4. Importance; consequence; influence. — v.t. To put a weight or weights upon; make heavy.

weird (werd), a. Unearthly; uncanny.

wel'come (wel'kum), a. 1. Received gladly into one's presence or companionship. 2. Giving pleasure; grateful. 3. Free or willingly permitted. — n. Cordial greeting to, or reception of, a guest or new-comer. — v.t. To receive gladly; make welcome.

wel'fare (wel'far), n. State of faring, or doing; condition of health, happiness, etc.

well (wel), a. 1. Good or desirable; fortunate. 2. Being in health; sound. 3. Being in satisfactory condition or circumstances.

well'-bred', a. 1. Having good breeding; refined. 2. Of good breed, as an animal.

whale, n. Any of numerous cetaceans, esp. those of large size, in distinction from porpoises and dolphins. — v.i. To engage in whale fishing.

what-ev'er (hwot-ev'er), pron. All that; no matter what.

wheat (hwet), n. A well-known cereal grain.

whee'dle (hwe'd'l), v.t. & i. 1. To coax. 2. To get by flattery or coaxing.

wheel'bar'row (hwel'bar'o), n. A small vehicle with handles and (usually) one wheel.

whelp (hwelp), n. The young of a dog or of certain beasts of prey. — v.i. & t. To bear whelps.

when (hwen), adv. 1. At what time. 2. At, during, or after the time that. 3. At which time. 4. While; whereas. 5. Which time; then.

where (hwar), adv. 1. At or in what or which place, situation, or circum-stances. 2. To what or which place. 3. From what place or source. — conj. Whereas.

where'fore (hwar'for), adv. & conj. 1. For which reason. 2. For what reason; why.

where'up-on' (hwar'u-pon'), adv. Upon which; in consequence of, or after, which.

wheth'er (hweth'er), pron. & a. Which (of two); which one (of two). — conj. A particle used to indicate a following alternative.

whiff (hwif), n. A quick puff or slight gust of air, esp. one conveying some odor. — v.t. & i. 1. To expel in a whiff or whiffs. 2. To convey by or as by a whiff.

whim'per (-per), v.i. To cry with a low, whining, broken sound. — n. A low, whining, broken cry.

whim'si-cal (-zi-kal), a. 1. Full of whims. 2. Odd; fantastic.

U
Z

whine (hwin), v.i. & t. To utter with a low plaintive nasal or prolonged sound; also, to complain. — n. Act or sound of whining.

whisk'er (whis'ker), n. 1. [Chiefly in pl.] The beard on the sides of the face, on the chin, or on both. 2. A hair of the beard. 3. A long hair or bristle near the mouth of a cat, rat, etc.

whis'ky; whis'key (hwis'ki), n.; pl. WHISKIES, WHISKEYS. A distilled alcoholic liquor made from grain or from potatoes.

whis'tle (hwis'l), v.i. To make a kind of shrill musical sound by forcing the breath through the teeth or contracted lips. — v.t. 1. To form or utter by whistling. 2. To signal by a whistle. — n. 1. A sound made by or as by whistling. 2. An instrument in which air, steam, etc., produces (usually) shrill sound.

white (hwit'), a. 1. Of the color of pure snow or sunlight. 2. a Having a light-colored skin; of the Caucasian race. b Wanting in color; pale, wan. c Gray or hoary, as the hair. 3. Spotless; pure.

whit'tle (hwit'l), v.t. & i. To pare or cut with or as with a knife.

who-ev'er (hoo-ev'er), pron. Whatever person.

whole'sale' (hol'sal'), n. Sale of goods by the piece or in large quantity; — disting. from retail. — a. 1. Pert. to, or engaged in, trade by wholesale. 2. Extensive and indiscriminate.

whole'some (-sum), a. Characteristic of bodily health.

whol'ly (hol'li; hol'i), adv. In a whole or complete manner.

why (hwi), adv. 1. For what cause, reason, or purpose. 2. For which.

wick'ed (wik'ed), a. 1. Evil. 2. Mischievous; roguish.

wide (wid), a. 1. Of a specified measure in a direction at right angles to that of length. 2. Having considerable extent between the sides; broad. 3. Spacious, extensive. — adv. 1. To a great distance; widely. 2. So as to form a large opening.

wid'ow (wid'o), n. A woman who has lost her husband by death, and has not married again. — v.t. To bereave of a husband. Usually in p.p.

wid'ow-er (wid'o-er), n. A man who has lost his wife by death, and has not married again.

wid'ow-hood (-hood), n. State of being a widow; time during which a woman is a widow.

wild (wild), a. 1. Living in a state of nature; not tamed or domesticated; as, a wild animal. 2. Not cultivated; as wild cherry. 3. Not inhabited or cultivated. 4. Savage; uncivilized; rude. — n. A wilderness; waste.

will (wil), n. 1. Wish or desire. 2. What is wished by another. 3. Power coupled with desire or intention. — v.t.; WILLED (wild); WILL'ING. 1. To determine by an act of choice. 2. To influence by one's will, as through hypnotism. — v.i. To exercise volition.

will'ing, a. 1. Favorably disposed in mind. 2. Ready to act. 3. Voluntary.

wilt (wilt), v.i. To lose freshness and droop. —v.t. To cause to droop or languish.

win (win), v.i.; pref. & p.p. WON (won); p. pr. & vb. n. WIN'NING. 1. To gain the victory. 2. To succeed by effort in reaching a specified place or state. — v.t. 1. To get by labor. 2. To gain in competition or contest. 3. To achieve by effort.

wince (wins), v.i. To shrink, as from a blow, or from pain. — n. Act of wincing.

wind'fall' (wind'fol'), n. An unexpected legacy or other gain.

win'dow (win'do), n. 1. An opening in the wall of a building to admit light and air. 2. Arch. The shutter, casement, sash, or other framework opening. — v.t. To furnish with a window or windows.

wine (win), n. 1. The fermented juice of grapes. 2. The fermented juice of any fruit or plant, used as a beverage.

win'ter (-ter), n. The coldest season. — v.i. To pass the winter. — v.t. To keep, feed, or manage during the winter.

wipe (wip), v.t. 1. To rub lightly, or with something soft, for cleaning. 2. To draw, pass, or the like, for rubbing or cleaning. 3. To obliterate. — n.

Act of rubbing.

wis'dom (wiz'dum), n. 1. Quality of being wise; sagacity. 2. Learning.

wise (wiz), a. 1. Discerning and judging soundly concerning what is true or false, proper or improper; sagacious. 2. Dictated or guided by wisdom. 3. Having knowledge; learned.

wish (wish), v.i. To desire; long; — usually with an infinitive or for. — v.t. 1. To long for; crave; desire. 2. To invoke or desire in favor of, or against, any one. — n. 1. Eager desire; longing. 2. Expression of desire; request. 3. Object of desire.

wit, n. 1. Mind; intellect; sense. 2. A mental faculty, or power; — chiefly in pl. 3. The perception or expression of associations between ideas or words not usually connected, such as to produce an amusing surprise; power of such perception or expression. 4. A witty person.

with-draw' (-dro), v.t. 1. To take back or away; drawback. 2. To recall or retract. — v.i. To retire; recede.

with'er (with'er), v.i. & t. 1. To dry or shrivel up; fade. 2. To decay; decline; languish.

with-hold' (with-hold'), v.t. & i. 1. To hold back or in. 2. To refrain from granting.

with-in' (-in'), adv. 1. Inwardly. 2. Indoors. — prep. 1. Inside of. 2. In the limits or compass of.

with-stand' (-stand'), v.t. & i.; -STOOD'; -STAND'ING. To stand against, esp. successfully; oppose.

wit'ness (-nes), n. 1. Testimony. 2. One who testifies. 3. That which serves as evidence or proof. — v.t. 1. To act as a witness of. 2. To testify to. 3. To give evidence of. — v.i. To testify.

woe (wo), n. Grief; misery.

wom'an (woom'an), n.; pl. WOMEN (wim'en), 1. An adult female person. 2. Womankind.

womb (woom), n. The uterus.

won'der (wun'der), n. 1. A cause of surprise or astonishment. 2. The emotion excited by novelty or by something strange or extraordinary. — v.i. & t. 1. To be affected with surprise. 2. To feel doubt and curiosity.

won'der-ful (-fool), a. Adapted to excite wonder; marvelous. —

wood (wood), n. 1. A forest. 2. The hard fibrous substance of trees or shrubs beneath the bark. 3. Lumber. —v.t. To supply with wood.

wood'peck'er (wood'pek'er), n. A bird having a chisel-like bill used to drill into wood for insects.

word (wurd), n. 1. That which is said. 2. Statement; promise. 3. Tidings. — v.t. To express in words; phrase.

work'house' (wurk'hous'), n. 1. Workshop. 2. In England, a poorhouse. 3. A house of correction in which petty offenders are confined at labor.

world (wurld), n. 1. The universe. 2. The earth; mankind; the public.

wor'ry (wur'i), v.t. 1. To harass with or as with continual snapping or biting; also, to tear or mangle with the teeth. 2. To harass with importunity, or with care and anxiety. — v.i. To feel or express great care and anxiety; fret. — n.; pl. -RIES (-iz). 1. Act of worrying. 2. Undue solicitude; anxiety.

worse (wurs), a., comparative of BAD. Bad, ill, evil, or corrupt, in a greater degree; less good; also, more sick. — adv. In a worse degree or manner. — n. That which is worse.

wor'ship (wur'ship), n. 1. Reverence, adoration, or homage paid to God, a god, or a sacred object. 2. A title of honor. — v.t. To pay divine honors to; adore; idolize. — v.t. To perform acts of homage or adoration; esp., to perform religious service.

worst (wurst), a., superlative of BAD. Bad, evil, or pernicious in the highest degree. See WORSE. — adv. To the extreme degree of badness or inferiority. — n. That which is most bad or evil. — v.t. To get the better of; defeat; discomfit.

worth (wurth), a. 1. Deserving of; meriting. 2. Equal in value to. 3. Having possessions equal to. — n. 1. The quality or qualities of a thing rendering it valuable or useful; value; hence, price. 2. Excellence; virtue; as, a man of worth.

wound (woond; wound), n. 1. An injury by which the skin is divided; a

U Z

stab, cut, or laceration. 2. An injury or hurt to feelings, reputation, etc. — v.t. To pain. — v.i. To inflict a wound.

wrap (rap), v.t.; WRAPPED (rapt) or WRAPT; WRAP'PING. 1. To wind or roll together; fold. 2. To cover by winding or folding; infold; —often with up. 3. To inclose in a package; do up; — usu. with up. — n. An article of dress to be wrapped round the person; — used esp. in pl., for furs, shawls, etc.

wreck (rek), n. 1. That which has been wrecked or is in ruin. 2. Destruction or injury of anything by violence; ruin. — v.t. To shipwreck; to bring wreck or ruin on by violence.

wres'tle (res'l), v.i. 1. To grapple. 2. To struggle; strive earnestly. — n. A wrestling bout; struggle.

wretch'ed, a. 1. Very miserable; unhappy. 2. Despicable. 3. Unsatisfactory.

wrin'kle (rin'k'l), n. A small ridge; crease. — v.t. To make a wrinkle or wrinkles in. — v.i. To be or become wrinkled.

writ'ing (rit'ing), n. Act, art, or production of one who writes.

wrong (rong), a. 1. Out of order; amiss. 2. Not morally right; perverse. 3. Not legal; not just or equitable. 4. Not according to truth or fact; incorrect; false. 5. Not suitable to an end or object; not according to intention or purpose. 6. Designed to be worn or placed inward. — adv. In a wrong manner. — n. That which is wrong; evil; an injury; trespass. — v.t. 1. To do wrong to; harm. 2. To represent erroneously.

wry (ri), a. 1. Turned to one side; contorted; as, a wry mouth. 2. Distorted, as in meaning; perverted.

X

X rays. The Rontgren rays; — so called because of their enigmatical character, X being used in mathematics to indicate an unknown quantity.

xan'thic (zan'thik), a. Pertaining to, or tending toward, a yellow color.

xen'on (zen'on; ze'non), n. A heavy, inert gas.

xy'lo-phone (zi'io-fon), n. Music. An instrument consisting of a series of graduated wooden bars sounded by striking with two small wooden hammers.

Y

yacht (yot), n. Naut. A vessel larger than a rowboat. — v.i. To sail, cruise, or race in a yacht.

yam (yam), n. 1. The edible, starchy tuberous root of a climbing plant of various species, used as a staple food in tropical climates. 2. The sweet potato.

Yan'kee (yan'ke), n. A native of New England or of the Northern States; among foreigners, any inhabitant of the United States. — a. Of or pert. to the Yankees.

yard, n. 1. An inclosure before or about a house, barn, etc. 2. An inclosure where work or business is carried on; as, a brickyard.

yarn (yarn), n. Spun wool; thread.

year (yer), n. 1. The period of the earth's revolution round the sun. 2. A period of 365 days, in leap year, 366 days, beginning January 1.

year'ling (-ling), n. An animal one year old, or in the second year of its age.

year'ly, a. Happening or coming every year. — adv. Annually.

yell (yel), v.i. & t. To cry out or utter with a loud and sharp noise. — n. 1. A sharp and loud hideous outcry.

yellow fever. Med. An acute, infectious, often fatal, febrile disease transmitted by mosquitoes.

yes (yes). An affirmative adverbial particle; denoting: 1. Aye; yea; it is so; — opposed to no. 2. More than this; what is more; —used to mark the addition of something more emphatic.

yes'ter-day (yes'ter-da), n. The day before the present. — adv. On yesterday.

yet (yet), adv. 1. As soon as now; hitherto. 2. Continuing; still. 3. In addition; further; still. 4. Before all is done; eventually. 5. Although such is the case. — conj. 1. Nevertheless; however; but. 2. Although; though.

yield (yeld), v.t. 1. To give in return for labor, or to produce as interest on what is invested; pay. 2. To produce; furnish; give forth. 3. To give; grant; afford. — v.i. 1. To produce; bear. 2. To give way; submit; surrender. 3. To give place, as to a superior; give precedence. —n. Amount yielded; product.

yolk (yok; yolk), n. 1. The yellow spheroidal mass of food material in the egg of a bird or reptile. 2. A greasy substance in sheep's wool.

you (yoo), pron.; poss YOUR (yoor) or YOURS (yoorz); dat. & obj. YOU. A personal pronoun of the second person, indicating the person or persons addressed, and used as a nominative or objective plural, and as a nominative or objective singular.

young (yung), a. 1. Being in the first or early period of life, growth, or existence. 2. Youthfully fresh in body, mind, or feeling. 3. Immature; inexperienced. 4. Of or pert. to youth. — n. The offspring of animals.

your (yoor), pron. & a. Of or belonging to you; — used as the possessive case of you, or as a possessive adjective.

your-self' (yoor-self'), pron.; pl. -SELVES (-selvz'). An emphasized form for you.

youth (yooth), n.; pl. YOUTHS (yooths; yoothz), or, collectively, YOUTH. 1. Quality or state of being young; youthfulness. 2. a A young person; esp., a young man. b Collective pl. Young people.

youth'ful (yooth'fool), a. 1. Young. 2. Of or pertaining to the early part of life. 3. Fresh; vigorous.

Z

zeal (zel), n. Ardor in pursuit of anything; enthusiasm; fervor.

zeal'ot (zel'ut), n. One who is zealous, esp. a fanatical partisan.

zeal'ous (zel'us), a. Filled with,

marked by, or due to, zeal.

ze'bra (ze'bra), n. Any of several African equine mammals with black or blackish stripes on a white or buff ground.

ze'nith (ze'nith), n. 1. That point of the heavens vertically above one. 2. Greatest height; summit.

zeph'yr (zef'er), n. To west wind; any soft, gentle breeze.

ze'ro (ze'ro), n. 1. Arith. A cipher; nothing. 2. The point from which the graduation of a scale, as of a thermometer, begins. 3. Lowest point; nothingness.

zest (zest), n. 1. Something that gives a pleasant taste or relish; also, the relish or taste as imparted; piquancy. 2. Gusto.

zig'zag' (zig'zag'), n. One of a series of short sharp turns or angles in a course. — adv. In or by a zigzag path or course. - v.i. To form or move with zigzags; make or be zigzag.

Zi'on (zi'on), n. 1. A hill in Jerusalem, where the temple was. 2. a The theocracy, or church of God. b The heavenly Jerusalem.

zir'con (zur'kon), n. Min. A silicate of zirconium, usually in square brown or grayish prisms or pyramids.

zo'di-ac (zo'di-ak), n. Astron. An imaginary belt in the heavens including the paths of the moon and the principal planets and, as its middle line, the ecliptic.

zone (zon), n. 1. An encircling band, stripe, or girdle. 2. Any of five great divisions of the earth's surface as to latitude and temperature. 3. An area or region taken as distinct from adjoining parts.

zoo (zoo), n. A zoological garden or collection.

zo-og'ra-phy (zo-or'ra-fi), n. A description of animals, their forms and habits.

zo-ol'o-gist (zo-ol'o-jist), n. One versed in zoology.

zo-ol'o-gy (zo-ol'o-ji), n. Science of animals; biology dealing with animals.

Zwie'back' (tsve'bak'), n. [Often l.c.] Kind of biscuit or rusk baked in a loaf and afterwards cut and toasted.

U
Z

Directory of Computer Terms and Meanings

The computer has become commonplace in most homes and businesses. The following section of computer terms will help in your understanding of this important area of interest.

Adapter: A circuit as an interface board that serves between the system unit, typically a motherboard and the devices that attach to it.

Address: A location where a piece of information is stored within the computer.

Alphanumeric: An association of characters whose group is comprised of both Alphabetic (A-Z) and Numeric (0-9) symbols.

ANSI: American National Standards Institute. An organization that develops standards and guidelines for both the computer and electronics industries.

ASCII: American Standard Code for Information Interchange. A code used by computers to represent characters such as letters, numbers punctuation marks and other symbols.

Asynchronous: A term used typically to describe a method of data transfer. The timing of which is not directly tied to an external clock. but instead dictated by either of the computers involved in the communication.

Backup: A process of copying data from one type of media to another, for the purpose of preventing data loss in the event the original may become unusable.

Baud: A term used to describe the rate at which data is transferred between two computers. As originally used it was equivalent to the number of bits transmitted per second.

Binary: The Base 2 numbering system used by computers comprised of 1's and 0's.

BIOS: Basic Input/Output System. The part of a computer operating system that is responsible for communications with the machines peripheral components such as the monitor, printer, and keyboard.

Bit: The smallest unit of measure used by computers. The electronic equivalent to a switch which can be either on; high or 1 or off; low or 0. Eight associated bits comprise one byte.

Boot: A term to turning on of a computer and the subsequent describe the loading of its operating system.

Buffer: A section allocated to of memory temporarily store data during transfer.

Bug: A glitch or error in the expected operation of a program.

Byte: The equivalent of one character, typically eight bits.

Clock: A time regulated electronic signal used by the computer to coordinate its operation.

CPU: Central Processing Unit. The main computer chip used within a computer where the bulk of the processing of data is done. Can also refer to the chassis or box in which this chip is located.

Cursor: The small flashing mark usually a line or box that appears on your computer screen signifying the location of where typed key will be located.

Directory: A location on a disk where the names, locations and other information related to files located on that disk are kept.

DMA: Direct Memory Access. An electronic path within a computer for high-speed data transfer. The computers CPU is not utilized in this operation that neither the transfer or system is impacted.

Disk: A magnetic storage device used to store computer information.

Encryption: A method of securing data by changing the codes to unrelated characters which can later be deciphered by use of a key, usually algorithm.

File: A collection of related information or instructions that is usually stored on a disk.

Fixed Disk: A non removable magnetic storage device which retains its memory after power to the computer is turned off. Also referred to as a hard disk.

Format: Preparing a magnetic disk or tape so that data may be stored. This process typically deletes any prior information stored while also checking for any defects or flaws in the surface being prepared.

Gigabyte: A quantity of storage approximately equivalent to one billion bytes. Exactly 1,073,741,824 bytes.

Head: The electromagnetic component responsible for reading and writing information on magnetic media.

I/O: Input/Output. A term used to relate to the flow of information to or from a source.

Interface: To attach through a common point of access two disparate systems.

Interrupt: Abbr. IRQ. An electrical signal with a computer used to temporarily suspend a task in process so that another task may be performed.

Kilobyte: Abbr. Kbyte. or KB. A quantity of storage approximately equivalent to one thousand bytes. Exactly 1024 bytes.

Logical Drive: A function of creating through the operating system the appearance of a specific physical device, but instead may represent another disk drive or directory.

Megabyte: Abbr. Mbyte. or MB. A quantity of storage approximately equivalent to one million bytes. Exactly 1,048, 576 bytes.

Memory: The electronic components within a computer used to temporarily hold information as its being processed. Also referred to as RAM.

Modem: Modulator/Demodulator. A device used to interface computers to telephone lines to link them together. A modem must be in use at each computer to translate the digital signals to its telephone line in compatible analog form.

Network: The linking of several computers together so that physical and data resources may be shared.

Output: Data that is sent to a device such as a monitor, printer, speaker or another physical device.

Parallel: The process of transferring data where the electrical signals are sent over multiple wires simultaneously.

Parity: A method of insuring data integrity by adding an extra bit to each byte in a process similar to check summing.

Partition: A section of a hard disk that has been set aside for use by an operating system.

Peripheral: A piece of equipment connected to the computer. Some typical examples are modems, monitors, printers and disk drives.

Port: The connector that allows for the attaching of external peripherals.

Program: A series of instructions which allow a computer to perform a specific task.

Random-Access Memory: Abbr. RAM. The memory accessed by the computer to run a program or temporarily store data. This memory is cleared and the data lost when the computer is turned off.

Read-Only Memory: Abbr. ROM. This type of memory has the information permanently placed into it which cannot be altered. The information contained in ROM is not lost when power is turned off.

Sector: A sub section of a track of a disk. The size of a sector may vary depending on the drive and operating system in use.

Serial: The process of transferring data or executing tasks one after the other in succession.

Terminal: A separate piece of equipment that is used to input and process information to prepare it for its end use. A complete computer processing station.

Terminate and Stay Resident: Abbr. TSR. A program that remains in memory after it has been loaded and exited.

Track: On a disk it represents one of the concentric circles in which data stored. On a tape the concept is similar but data is stored in parallel lines extending the entire tape length.

Virus: A program designed to attach itself to other programs for the purpose of being unknowingly propagated from computer to computer. The affects of a virus may range from a simple annoyance to the loss of data.

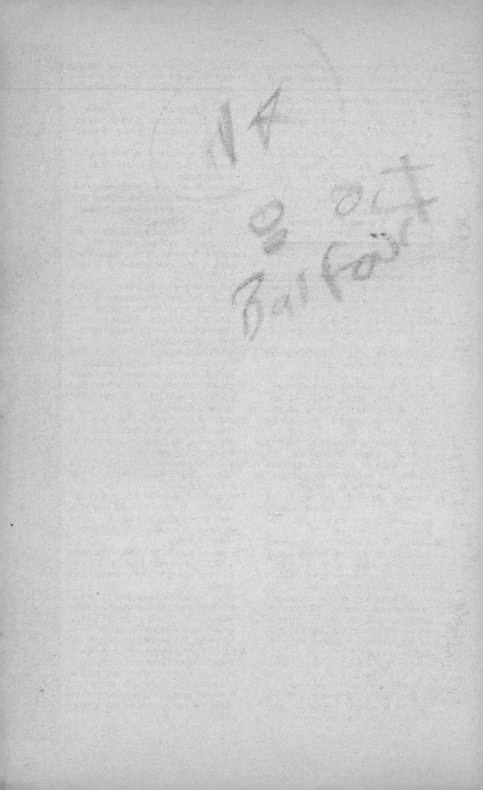